Promoting Competence in Clients

Promoting Competence in Clients

A New/Old Approach to Social Work Practice

Anthony N. Maluccio
Editor

THE FREE PRESS
A Division of Macmillan Publishing Co., Inc.
NEW YORK

Collier Macmillan Publishers
LONDON

THE FREE PRESS
A Division of Macmillan Publishing Co., Inc.
866 Third Avenue, New York, N.Y. 10022

Collier Macmillan Canada, Ltd.

Library of Congress Catalog Card Number: 80-1056

Printed in the United States of America

printing number
1 2 3 4 5 6 7 8 9 10

Library of Congress Cataloging in Publication Data

Main entry under title:

Promoting competence in clients.

  Bibliography: p.
  Includes index.
  1.   Social service—Addresses, essays, lectures.
I.   Maluccio, Anthony N.
HV31.P76   361   80-1056
ISBN 0-02-919830-5

TO CAROL, MICHAEL, and JOHN
*For challenging and nurturing
my sense of competence*

Contents

Preface and Acknowledgments

Social work theory and practice have long been marked by a preoccupation with pathology and with the personal and environmental deficits that hamper the client's capacity to cope. In recent years, however, there has been growing interest in practice approaches that stress the use of resources and strengths in people and their environments. This book reflects and promotes these emerging approaches. It presents a perspective which holds that the promotion of competence in human beings is a significant function of social work intervention. Competence generally refers to the repertoire of skills, knowledge, and qualities that enable people to interact effectively with their environment.

The book focuses on a set of principles, approaches, and strategies designed to promote competence in clients by emphasizing their actual or potential strengths, unique coping and adaptive patterns, and natural helping systems. It stresses use of the environment as a major instrument in the helping process. It reflects the more positive orientation to human beings and problem-solving that has been emerging in humanistic psychology and other fields. In short, the book presents a perspective identified as *competence-oriented social work practice.*

Beginning with some of the early pioneers, social workers have always been interested in changing the interaction between people and their environments in order to improve social functioning and enhance personal growth. Indeed, they have often engaged in the kind of intervention that will be described in this book. They have emphasized the importance of providing services and resources that enrich a client's environment and facilitate his or her natural growth processes and satisfaction.

In various ways, the orientation stressed in the book thus is quite old; at the same time it is new, in that it reflects and builds on knowledge emerging in a variety of disciplines, particularly the sociobehavioral sciences. For instance ego psychology, with its emphasis on coping and adaptation, gives new and expanded meaning to the theme of the *person-environment configuration* that has pervaded social work thinking. Newer bodies of knowledge enrich theory and practice; they provide theoretical support for traditional interventive efforts and suggest ways of refining and improving these efforts.

Competence-oriented social work practice integrates perspectives from such disciplines as psychology, anthropology, ecology, and biology with the progressive themes and best traditions in the field. The combination of old and new in this book represents our effort to contribute to the cumulative building of knowledge so essential in social work.

The volume reflects the thinking and experiences of fifteen social work educators and practitioners whom I invited to prepare original papers discussing selected aspects of competence-oriented social work intervention. It is organized into an introduction and three parts. In Chapter 1, I review diverse definitions of competence and their theoretical foundations in fields such as psychology, sociology, and biology and conclude with a definition of competence in ecological terms as a transactional concept. Building on a range of perspectives, I stress that competence should be viewed as the outcome of the interplay between the capacities, skills, and motivations of a person and the qualities of the impinging environment (e.g., resources, supports, and demands). I then delineate the major features of competence-oriented social work practice: (1) a humanistic perspective on people; (2) redefinition of human problems in transactional terms; (3) reformulation of assessment as competence clarification; (4) redefinition of client and practitioner roles, with clients viewed primarily as resources and workers as enabling agents; (5) redefinition of the client-worker relationship, with emphasis on mutuality and authenticity; (6) focus on life processes and life experiences; (7) emphasis on using the environment; and (8) regular use of client feedback.

Part 1 is concerned with the use of life processes and experiences in social work practice—a major theme in the competence-oriented approach. In Chapter 2, Janet Moore-Kirkland formulates motivation as a transactional concept and derives strategies for mobilizing it to enhance people's coping patterns through procedures such as anxiety reduction, anxiety arousal, enhancement of goal states, and removal of practical barriers. In Chapter 3, Ronald C. Fleming discusses the cognitive processes of attribution and concept attainment, their relation to coping and adaptation, and pertinent practice principles. In Chapter 4, Naomi Golan examines how social work practice can serve to increase competence during transitional and crises situations that human beings experience in the natural course of the life cycle.

Part 2 focuses on the environment and its properties as major instruments of help in competence-oriented intervention. In Chapter 5, Carel B. Germain examines the interplay between the physical environment and human cognition, perception, emotion, and action; she then presents practice implications and illustrations of the use of physical environments to enhance the competence of individuals, families, and groups. The other contributors deal with the role of the social environment in intervention. Carol R. Swenson in Chapter 6 focuses on the use of natural helping networks to promote competence; she delineates a series of practice activities operationalizing the social worker's catalytic role in relation to social networks. In Chapter 7, Richard M. Grinnell, Jr., Nancy S. Kyte, and Gerald J. Bostwick, Jr., expand the traditional notion of environmental modification and present a model for changing the environment to enhance personal and interpersonal competence. In Chapter 8, Ruth R. Middleman concentrates on the role of structured groups such as "life skills" workshops; by analyzing varied practice illustrations, she shows that learning through structured groups leads to increased competence in the participants.

In Part 3, other contributors apply the competence-oriented perspective to practice with selected client groups. These chapters therefore focus on practice principles and guidelines and contain extensive use of "real-life" illustrations. In Chapter 9, Prudence Brown examines the barriers faced by women and presents a framework for organizing social work intervention designed to promote their competence. In Chapter 10, Judith A. B. Lee develops and illustrates various ecologically oriented, ego-supportive approaches to facilitating coping and the acquisition of competence in children and youth. In Chapter 11, Mary Frances Libassi and Nathalie S. Turner concentrate on the aging process; they formulate principles and strategies for providing the prerequisite conditions that support the coping patterns and adaptive strivings of older persons. In Chapter 12, Genevieve B. Oxley examines the special features involved in work with the high proportion of social work clients who are typically described as "involuntary"; she underlines the importance of helping these persons by providing appropriate environmental opportunities which mobilize their own motivation and potential. Finally, in Chapter 13, Eda G. Goldstein focuses on families of psychiatric patients. Arguing that there has been excessive emphasis on family pathology, Goldstein presents a practice model that stresses the family's adaptive capacities, its crucial role in rehabilitative efforts, and the provision of environmental supports enabling family members to cope more effectively.

Preface and Acknowledgments

The contributors to this volume write from different perspectives. However, they share an overriding conviction about competence as a guiding concept and a fundamental feature of social work intervention. Most of them also have in common a conceptual framework that is derived from the ecological perspective and life model of social work practice, as developed in recent years particularly by Carel B. Germain and Alex Gitterman. While writing independently, the contributors thus present a coherent set of ideas on social work theory and practice.

The book is directed to social work students, teachers, and practitioners. It should be useful as a text in a variety of methods courses at both the graduate and undergraduate levels—courses in such areas as integrated practice, clinical social work, casework, and group work. Above all, we hope that it will stimulate our colleagues to think differently about their practice and to find more effective ways of mobilizing human strengths and potentialities.

As Allport has asserted, "we survive through competence, we grow through competence, we become 'self-actualizing' through competence" (Allport, 1961:214). The competence-oriented perspective on social work practice helps us to appreciate the significance of this statement and to act on its implications in the course of our work with individuals, families, and groups. In so doing, it can help us to become even more effective in our efforts to encourage human beings to take advantage of their own natural drive toward effective and satisfying functioning.

Finally, whatever this book may accomplish will truly be the result of the combined efforts and competencies of many persons:

The contributors, who responded with enthusiasm to my invitation to write a chapter. It was a joy to work—and learn—with them.

Carel B. Germain and Mary Frances Libassi, my colleagues at the University of Connecticut School of Social Work, who not only reviewed critically an early version of my introductory chapter but also have shared and nourished my concern with competence and its significance for social work practice.

Susan S. Zegans, a friend and social worker whose keen insights and sharp criticisms contributed greatly to refinement of my ideas.

Gladys Topkis, senior editor at The Free Press, who has been most encouraging since I first mentioned to her the idea for this book.

Margaret Partridge, Lois Pye, and Jeanne Simpson, whose secretarial skills happily interacted with my expectations and with publishing requirements.

To everyone, my heartfelt thanks.

ANTHONY N. MALUCCIO

Notes on Contributors

Gerald J. Bostwick, Jr., is Edith Abbott Teaching Fellow and a doctoral candidate at the University of Chicago School of Social Service Administration.

Prudence Brown is assistant professor at the Columbia University School of Social Work, New York.

Ronald C. Fleming is chief of social work service, Medical Department, Massachusetts Institute of Technology, Cambridge, Massachusetts.

Carel B. Germain is professor at the University of Connecticut School of Social Work, West Hartford, Connecticut.

Naomi Golan is associate professor and director, University of Haifa, School of Social Work, Haifa, Israel.

Eda G. Goldstein is assistant director, Social Service Department, New York Hospital—Cornell Medical Center, Westchester Division, White Plains, New York.

Richard M. Grinnell, Jr., is associate professor, University of Texas at Arlington, Graduate School of Social Work, Arlington, Texas.

Nancy S. Kyte is Edith Abbott Teaching Fellow and a doctoral candidate at the University of Chicago School of Social Service Administration.

Judith A. B. Lee is assistant professor at the New York University School of Social Work.

Mary Frances Libassi is assistant professor-in-residence at the University of Connecticut School of Social Work, West Hartford, Connecticut.

Anthony N. Maluccio is professor at the University of Connecticut School of Social Work, West Hartford, Connecticut.

Ruth R. Middleman is professor at the University of Louisville, Raymond A. Kent School of Social Work, Louisville, Kentucky.

Janet Moore-Kirkland is coordinator of the Governor's Conference on Aging, State of Colorado, Denver, Colorado.

Genevieve B. Oxley is lecturer at the University of California at Berkeley School of Social Welfare.

Carol R. Swenson is assistant professor at the University of Maryland at Baltimore School of Social Work and Community Planning.

Nathalie S. Turner is professor at the University of Connecticut School of Social Work, West Hartford, Connecticut.

CHAPTER 1

Competence-oriented Social Work Practice: An Ecological Approach

Anthony N. Maluccio

Two decades ago Gordon Allport described the drive toward competence as a most significant force in human development and behavior: "We survive through competence, we grow through competence, we become 'self-actualizing' through competence" (Allport, 1961:214). Since then, competence has come to be regarded in various fields as an exciting and promising concept in understanding and working with human beings.

In social work, there has been limited systematic consideration of competence, although ideas pertaining to it historically have been reflected in most perspectives on theory and practice. The notion of competence is implicit in the writings of pioneers such as Mary Richmond (1922) and Bertha Reynolds (1934), who emphasized the caseworker's responsibility to change the environment so as to promote growth in clients. Lucille Austin (1948) stressed the role of positive life experiences in facilitating ego growth and competent functioning. Similarly, in her classic formulation of psychosocial casework, Gordon Hamilton (1951) identified environmental manipulation as an important means of modifying the client's "living experience" and offering opportunities for growth. In the functional perspective on social work, a pervasive theme has been the use of the client–worker relationship to release the person's potentialities for change (cf. Smalley, 1967). Early social group workers in settings such as settlement houses, community centers, and youth service agencies emphasized practice activities designed to enhance individual growth and personality development (cf. Alissi, 1980; Middleman, Chapter 8 in this volume).

There is no doubt that social workers have been influenced by the notion of competence and have engaged in practice activities intended to promote their clients' competence; but much of this has taken place at an intuitive level. Due to the lack of an adequate conceptual framework delineating the applications and implications of the competence perspective, the promise of this approach in social work has not been realized.

In recent years, however, the "life model" of practice has emerged as a useful and relevant framework (Germain and Gitterman, 1979; 1980). This model reflects "a philosophical conception of the human being as active, purposeful, and having the potential for growth, development, and learning throughout life" (Germain and Gitterman, 1979:370). Its practice emphasis is on improving the adaptive fit so that reciprocal processes between people and their environments will be more conducive to the development of human potential and the improvement of environments. Competence is a key concept in the life model, since the thrust of intervention is to promote the person's capacity to interact effectively with the environment (Maluccio, 1979b).

This chapter contributes to the further development of a practice framework focused on competence by providing guidelines and action principles for social workers engaged in work with individuals, families, or groups. I shall begin by reviewing diverse definitions of competence and their theoretical foundations. Next, I shall explain competence and its components in ecological terms as a transactional phenomenon and delineate the major features of competence-oriented social work practice. The overriding theme in this perspective on practice will be reflected in a single, recurring question: What can be done through social work intervention to facilitate natural adaptive processes of clients and promote their competence in interacting with their environment?

Perspectives on Competence

Competence is a promising but vague concept with multiple meanings. Most theorists and investigators from diverse disciplines agree that it "refers to effective functioning within one's environment" (Goldfried and D'Zurilla, 1969:155). However, as the same authors note, "this definition does not represent much advancement beyond Socrates' view of competent individuals," which focused on persons "who manage well the circumstances which they encounter daily, and who possess a judgment which is accurate in meeting occasions as they arise and rarely miss the expedient course of action" (as quoted in Goldfried and D'Zurilla, 1969:155).

Various attempts have been made to define competence and its components more precisely. These include: the *achievement* approach; an approach that emphasizes *internal antecedents* of effective behavior; the *behavior-environment interactions* approach; and the *ecological* approach. Since in social work there has been limited consideration of the concept of competence and related bodies of knowledge, the review that follows is a necessary step in our efforts to develop competence-oriented practice theory.[1]

Achievement Approach

Some theorists define competence as the totality of a human being's specific *achievements* or *accomplishments* in major areas of living. According to Phillips and Cowitz (1953:274), "social competence" means that "an individual has achieved or attained, through his *own efforts,* a successful mastery of certain tasks in life." In their view, competence refers to the composite of socially desirable personal accomplishments.

As indicated by Goldfried and D'Zurilla (1969:156), the achievement approach contributes little toward an understanding of competence. Such a conceptualization focuses on the outcome of effective behavior rather than the behavior itself or the means of achieving it; furthermore, it does not take into account extraneous factors—such as wealth or social supports—that influence one's ability to function or to interact effectively with the environment.

Internal Antecedents Approach

Another approach to competence focuses on the role of *internal antecedents* of effective behavior, such as motives, personality traits, or cognitive skills (cf. McClelland, 1973).

Embodying the symbolic-interactionist tradition in sociology and social psychology, Foote and Cottrell (1955) conceive of competence in interpersonal rather than sociocultural or biopsychological terms. They define interpersonal competence as the skill or ability to perform certain tasks and control the outcome of interaction with others. They argue that competence consists of the following capacities found to some degree in everyone: health, intelligence, empathy, autonomy, judgment, and creativity. In their view, these attributes and social skills govern interpersonal relations (Foote and Cottrell, 1955:51–57).

From the perspective of ego psychology, various theorists highlight the role of competence in personality development and human behavior. Notable among these are Heinz Hartmann (1958), with his dynamic view of human adaptation; Erik Erikson (1959), with his psychosocial, epigenetic formulation of ego development; and Robert White (1959; 1963), with his theory of competence motivation.

White in particular has made important contributions that should be considered in detail. To begin with, he defines competence in bio-psychological terms as the person's achieved capacity to interact effectively with the environment (White, 1959; 1963). In his view, the key manifestations of competence are self-confidence, trusting one's own judgment, and the ability to make decisions. While recognizing the importance of environmental factors, White emphasizes the role of motivation and other internal antecedents of effective behavior. He questions the validity of motivational theories rooted entirely in instinctual drives and tension reduction and postulates that an autonomous drive ("independent ego energies") motivates the human organism to seek competence in dealing with the environment.

In support of his view, White (1963:24–43) cites extensive evidence from research on animal behavior and early childhood development showing that a human being's efforts to reach out to the environment through such processes as manipulation and exploration cannot be adequately explained on the basis of traditional motivational theories. Much activity and learning occur even when the basic drives of the organism are satisfied.

The major concepts in White's formulation are:

1. *Effectance*—the inherent energies of the ego apparatus, which motivate the individual to keep trying out the effectiveness of his ripening capacities for action through manipulation, play, exploration, etc. The person engages in these actions for their intrinsic value and gratification rather than merely for the reduction of drive-determined tensions.
2. *Competence*—the person's capacity to interact effectively with the environment, which is derived from cumulative experiences of effectiveness.
3. *Sense of competence*—the individual's subjective view of his accumulated abilities and effects, particularly in later states of ego development.
4. *Feeling of efficacy*—the experience or satisfaction accompanying each specific transaction with the environment; the feeling of doing something, of being active, of having some influence or effect on the environment.

Harter (1978) has refined and extended White's formulation by casting it within a developmental framework. She elaborates and examines components of effectance as they emerge in the developmental process over the life cycle. In addition to introducing a developmental perspective, Harter expands White's model of competence motivation by focusing on the role of socializing agents, the functions of rewards, and the relative strength of intrinsic versus extrinsic motivation.

The "internal-antecedents" approach is quite valuable. The work of thinkers such as White is richly theoretical and has stimulated important research. But the approach does not describe adequately what constitutes competent behavior or how to facilitate it.

Behavior–Environment Interactions Approach

A third formulation focuses on those *behavior–environment interactions* that are associated with competent functioning.

Inkeles (1966) and Gladwin (1967) offer similar conceptualizations of social competence that stress societal rather than psychological referents. Representing the structural–functional tradition in sociology, Inkeles is concerned primarily with role performance and societal requirements; consequently, he defines competence as "the ability effectively to attain and perform in three sets of statuses: those which one's society will normally assign one, those . . . which one may reasonably aspire to, and those which one may reasonably invent or elaborate for one's self" (Inkeles, 1966:265).

Gladwin (1967:32) states that competence develops along three major interrelated axes: (1) "the ability to learn or to use a variety of alternative pathways or behavioral responses in order to reach a given goal"; (2) the ability to comprehend a variety of social systems within society and in particular to utilize the resources that they offer; and (3) effective reality testing involving not only "lack of psychopathological impairment but also a positive, broad, and sophisticated understanding of the world." Like Inkeles, Gladwin emphasizes the importance of social processes and interactions in the development of competence.

Smith (1968), a social psychologist, proposes an integrative conception of competence that also rests on the interaction between behavior and environment. In his formulation, competence involves intrinsic as well as extrinsic motivation, social skills as well as personal abilities, and effective performance for *self* as well as *society* in one's social roles. In essence, Smith believes that both intrinsic motivation of the organism and social reinforcement are necessary in socialization and personality development. He notes that "it makes no sense to conceive of the individual as unfolding autonomously under the guidance of pure effectance" (Smith, 1968:304). He emphasizes that competent functioning in childhood and adulthood is affected by key factors in the personal system of the organism as well as by strategic components in the social structure. The key factors in the personal system are: the sense of *efficacy* or *potency* in controlling one's destiny; the attitude of *hope;* and a favorable level of *self-respect* or *self-acceptance.* Corresponding key features in the social system are: *opportunity* (e.g., of supports or resources), which stimulates and reinforces the sense of hope; *respect by others,* which provides the social ground for respect of self; and *power,* which guarantees access to opportunity (Smith, 1968:312–13).

These formulations by Gladwin, Inkeles, and Smith are useful not only because they are somewhat more operational than White's conceptualization but also because they add the essential factor of social feedback or social reinforcement to White's notion of the intrinsically rewarding and motivating aspects of the person's actions.

Goldfried and D'Zurilla (1969:158–59) propose a modification of the behavior–environment approach that includes an even more specific, operational view of competence. In their formulation, competent or effective behavior is viewed in terms of its impact on the person's environment; the basic unit in conceptualizing competence is "the *effective response* of the individual to specific life situations" (p. 158). The same authors define effective behavior as "a response or pattern of responses to a problem-specific situation which alters the situation so that it is no longer problematical, and at the same time produces a maximum of other positive consequences and a minimum of negative ones" (Goldfried and D'Zurilla, 1969:158). They further explain that "the ever-changing nature of our environment is such that *life in general* may be viewed as a continuous process of meeting new problematic situations and finding ways of coping with them" (Goldfried and D'Zurilla, 1969:159).

The formulation by Goldfried and D'Zurilla highlights the importance of measuring the effect of a person's interaction with the environment in operational, behavioral terms. This approach, however, needs to be integrated with other aspects, in particular cognitive processes (Sundberg, Snowden, and Reynolds, 1978:207). As demonstrated by theorists such as Piaget (1952), cognition plays a prominent role in the growth and functioning of human beings.[2]

Ecological Competence

Each of the preceding definitions contributes to our understanding of competence by emphasizing a particular aspect of it.[3] But there is a need for a comprehensive formulation that takes into account the multiple dimensions of competence and their dynamic interplay.

Such a conceptualization is suggested by Sundberg, Snowden, and Reynolds, who propose the notion of *ecological competence*. These authors indicate that an adequate consideration of competence should take into account all relevant personal dimensions, such as someone's skills, qualities, and expectations, *and* their interaction with environmental stimuli and situational expectations (Sundberg, Snowden, and Reynolds, 1978:207).

This view of competence is consistent with the approach to social work practice presented in this book, since it reflects the person–environment configuration that is paramount in our efforts to understand and help client systems. In traditional formulations, competence is generally considered a property or trait of the person; the burden of competence is placed primarily on the person. In contrast, in the ecological approach competence becomes a transactional concept; it is defined as an attribute of the *transaction* between the person and the environment. This conceptualization is difficult to translate into action principles or practice approaches. For instance, when we are engaged in assessing the situation of a client coming to our attention, we automatically think in terms of the effectiveness of the person's behavior as a measure of his or her personal or social competence. While we may pay attention to the impact of the environment, we do not generally think about assessing the quality of person–environment transactions as a way of forming judgments concerning competence.

The perspective of ecological competence can sensitize us to the importance of what is happening between people and their environments and the interplay between (1) the person's needs, qualities, and coping patterns and (2) the properties of the impinging environment. As discussed later in the chapter, this view can help us to pay explicit attention to the situational context and transactional nature of people's adaptive behaviors. As we develop practice theory further, we might eventually discover a grammar of person–environment transactions to use as reference points in social work intervention.

Components of Ecological Competence

As shown in Figure 1–1, the major components of ecological competence are *capacities and skills, motivational aspects,* and *environmental qualities.*

Capacities and Skills.   This dimension includes capacities of the person in diverse spheres such as cognition, perception, intelligence,

FIGURE 1-1.   Components of ecological competence.

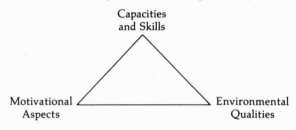

language, and physical health. It also encompasses a person's qualities
in such areas as flexibility, tolerance for diversity, initiative or self-
direction, reality testing, judgment, and tolerance for anxiety. In addition, it refers to specific proficiencies of an individual in such areas as
athletics, interpersonal skills (e.g., knowing how to act in interpersonal
situations), and emotional skills (e.g., self-confidence).

Motivational Aspects.   This category comprises the person's interests, hopes, aspirations—in short, the set of drives or energies variously described as effectance or competence motivation (White, 1959),
intrinsic motivation (Deci, 1975), the search for meaning (Maddi, 1970),
or self-actualization (Maslow, 1954).

While the terms and their underlying assumptions vary, the formulations of these theorists in essence refer to the human being's motivation to deal with the environment, to seek stimulation, to cope with
challenges, to accomplish, to master, to feel competent and self-determining. In short, human beings have a need "to be engaged in the
general process of seeking and conquering challenges which are optimal for them" (Deci, 1975:62).

Environmental Qualities.   As already indicated, a major component
in our definition of competence consists of significant environmental
qualities impinging on a person's functioning at any given point. Examples include environmental resources and supports such as social
networks, environmental demands, and institutional pressures and
supports.

Effective behavior requires a "goodness of fit" between personal
abilities and environmental demands and supports. As Mechanic
(1974:33) has underlined, "the ability of persons to maintain psychological comfort will depend not only on their intrapsychic resources, but
also—and perhaps more importantly—on the social supports available
or absent in the community." The complementarity, or goodness of fit,

between people's needs and qualities and environmental demands and characteristics strongly influences adaptation and competence.

Diversity in Coping Patterns

The above list of components of ecological competence is not meant to be exhaustive but to suggest the kinds of personal capacities, motivation, and environmental qualities that need to be considered in competence-oriented social work practice. These abilities, skills, or motivational features do not apply universally; there is wide diversity in coping patterns and adaptive behaviors of human beings:

> We can consider the possibility that the competencies required for optimal functioning are not the same for all eras and societies and, within specific societies, for all situations. Although the ability to gather and use information can be thought of as a general capacity required in all life situations, effective strategies change as problems change. The problems of the hunter are not the same as those of the farmer; successful strategies for the baker might not work for the plumber. Problems change with changes in tools and materials, with changes in the organizational structure of society (e.g., raising food for a family is not equivalent to feeding a city), and with changes in task requirements (listening to a story is not the same as writing one). [Fein and Clarke-Stewart, 1973:147]

Consequently, it is useful to think in terms of *general* capacities or qualities that are universally required (such as the ability to gather and use information) and *particular* capacities or qualities that are needed in specific contexts (such as certain skills required in industralized societies). Heath's cross-cultural research on maturity supports the assumption that there is a transculturally universal group of traits that define competent persons. Examples include clarity of thought and the ability to anticipate consequences (Heath, 1977:214–15).[4]

Utility of Ecological Perspective on Competence

Questions may be raised about the utility of the ecological conception of competence for practice. Some may argue that it is too all-encompassing. Others will note the overlap with notions such as self-concept, ego strength, coping and adaptation, etc. There is some validity to these criticisms. However, this conception has advantages that make it uniquely useful in social work.

There is, for instance, its heuristic value: By emphasizing the dynamic transaction between people and their environments, the ecological approach helps to sensitize practitioners to the impact that environmental demands and properties have on the personal, interpersonal, or social competence of human beings. Moreover, the ecological emphasis on competence as a transactional concept rather than as a fixed property or trait of the individual can help practitioners to appreciate more deeply the significance of the *context* of human behavior and guide them in identifying, understanding, and manipulating environmental obstacles and supports affecting a client's competence.

In ecology, human beings are seen as engaged in dynamic transactions with their environment, and specifically in a continuing struggle to maintain a "moving equilibrium" while faced with a complex and changing array of environmental challenges. Similarly, in biology there is emphasis on the interplay between the person and the environment—a process of mutual adaptation in which each humam being responds in a personal and creative manner. From general systems theory comes the notion of the human organism as an open system constituting one part in an interconnected, interdependent, and complementary set of parts. As with any other living organism, the human being is constantly influenced by—and in turn exerts influence upon —other systems of varying levels, such as family, school, community, work, or culture.

The integration of insights from general systems theory, ecology, and biology with the ecological perspective on competence suggests several interrelated themes that can guide competence-oriented social work practice:

- The view of human organisms as engaged in ongoing, dynamic transactions with their environment and in a continuous process of growth and adaptation.
- The conception of people as "open systems" that are spontaneously active and essentially motivated to achieve competence in their coping with life demands and environmental challenges.
- The premise that varied environmental opportunities and social supports are necessary to sustain and promote a human being's efforts to grow, to achieve self-fulfillment, and to contribute to others.
- The conviction that appropriate supports should be matched to the human being's changing qualities and needs in order to maximize the development of his or her competence, identity, autonomy, and self-fulfillment.

Features of Competence-oriented Practice

As suggested earlier in this chapter, in the life model of practice the focus of social work intervention is on identifying, supporting, and mobilizing natural adaptive processes through the purposive use of meaningful life experiences and provision of opportunities that can enhance the mutual fit between person and environment. In conjunction with the life model, the concept of ecological competence leads to an approach that views the promotion of competence in human beings as a significant function of social work intervention. The approach reflects themes that are common to other perspectives on practice, but it is characterized by special emphasis on the following features:

1. A *humanistic* perspective on people.
2. Redefinition of human problems in *transactional* terms.
3. Reformulation of assessment as *competence clarification*.
4. Redefinition of client and practitioner roles, with clients viewed primarily as *resources* and workers as *enabling agents*.
5. Redefinition of the client-worker relationship, particularly in terms of *mutuality* and *authenticity*.
6. Focus on *life processes* and *life experiences*.
7. Emphasis on *using the environment*.
8. Regular use of *client feedback*.

In the following discussion of these features, we will see that the essence of competence-oriented social work practice consists of changing the person–environment transaction so as to support and/or enhance the competence of individuals, families, and groups to deal effectively with the environment. A basic premise is that "competence is most effectively achieved when intervention is directed toward an ecological unit, consisting of a person and his immediate social environment, rather than toward the person alone" (Gladwin, 1967:37).

Humanistic Perspective

In this approach, human beings are viewed as striving, active organisms capable of organizing their lives and developing their potentialities as long as they have appropriate environmental supports. This view reflects the ideas of various humanistic thinkers, especially Angyal (1941), with his concepts of autonomy, self-determination, and human striving toward active mastery of the environment, and Maslow (1954), with his emphasis on positive personality growth and human motivation toward self-actualization.

Through its positive emphasis on growth and adaptation, the humanistic perspective leads naturally to de-emphasis of pathology, particularly psychopathology, and recognition of each person's multipotentialities—that is, actual as well as latent resources, strengths, and creativity. Another significant consequence is that the overall purpose of intervention is seen as improvement of the person–environment transaction rather than treatment of the person.

As research has shown, the application of a humanistic perspective requires a shift in the attitudes of practitioners toward their clients. For instance, in an intensive study of perceptions of treatment in a family service agency, striking differences were found in the perspectives of clients and social workers.

> In general, clients presented themselves as *proactive*, autonomous human beings who were able to enhance their functioning and their competence through the use of the service and of resources in themselves and their social networks. Workers, on the other hand, tended to view clients as *reactive* organisms with continuing problems, underlying weaknesses, and limited potentialities. [Maluccio, 1979a:102]

Redefinition of Human Problems in Transactional Terms

Emphasis on coping and adaptation as transactional phenomena results in viewing human difficulties as "problems in living" or as manifestations of the poor fit or lack of mutuality between people and their environments. Problems are placed at the interface between people and the environment; they are conceptualized in terms of the outcomes of transactional processes which create stress and place demand on the person's coping capacities (Germain and Gitterman, 1979:370–71).[5]

Major categories of "problems in living" include: *developmental crises*, such as the impact of a child's birth on the family system; *situational crises*, such as the pressures and challenges resulting from the experience of retirement; and *discrepancies between a person's needs and environmental resources*, such as the situation of a single mother who is finding it hard to care for her children due to the lack of day-care services in her neighborhood.

In contrast to the traditional perspective on pathology, problems or needs thus are not seen as specific weaknesses or properties of the person. "Behavior is not viewed as sick or well but is defined as transactional—an outcome of reciprocal interactions between specific social situations and the individual" (Kelly, 1973:538).

On the basis of this orientation, human problems, needs, and conflicts are redefined in transactional terms so as to suggest ways of intervening into the person–environment transaction. For example, problems or needs are translated into adaptive tasks providing the client with opportunities for competence development (Maluccio, 1979b). Several of the contributors to the final section of this book illustrate how typical life challenges can be redefined as specific adaptive tasks; intervention can then be used to support the person's coping efforts, learning of interpersonal skills, and capacity to have an impact on the environment. Ultimately, this enhances the person's competence.

Reformulation of Assessment as Competence Clarification

In most practice approaches, interventive plans are based on careful understanding of the client system, that is, the special needs, qualities, problems, goals, and behaviors of the person, family, or group. This understanding is typically delineated as assessment, diagnosis, or diagnostic evaluation. These terms connote such aspects as making judgments concerning a person's functioning, adopting a normative stance on human behavior and personality development, and being guided by a disease or medical metaphor that stresses the person's deficits or dysfunctioning.

In competence-oriented social work, assessment is reformulated as *competence clarification*. This concept refers to the process of identifying and understanding the person's or persons' competence in dealing with the environment at a particular point in time. Clarification encompasses, to the extent that is possible, the totality of person and environment. The overall aim is to understand the complexity of the person–environment transaction, since this interface is *the* unit of attention and intervention. Specific purposes are:

1. Clarifying the competence of the client system. Key questions include: What are the unique capacities, skills, attitudes, motivations, and potentialities of the client(s)? What are the particular areas of coping strengths? Which areas of competence need to be reinforced or supported?

2. Clarifying the characteristics of the impinging environment that influence or could influence the client(s)' coping and adaptive patterns positively or negatively. Here one would address such questions as: What are the critical environmental demands and challenges currently confronting the client system? What are the actual or potential supports available in the environment in such areas as social networks? Who are the key people or environmental units that could be mobilized as resources? What are the blocks, obstacles, and deficits in the environment that interfere with the person's life processes and adaptive strivings?

3. Clarifying the goodness of fit between the client system and its impinging environment. Some relevant questions are: How *nutritive* is the environment in relation to the person's needs and qualities? That is, does it contain the ingredients necessary to support, nourish, and challenge the person? What should be added or removed to render it more nutritive? What is interfering with the person's efforts to use existing resources? What are the key points of friction or manifestations

of poor fit at the interface between the clients and their environment? What needs to be changed so as to make the transaction more mutually rewarding, achieve a better adaptive fit, and enhance the human being's competence?

To facilitate the process of competence clarification, in addition to traditional assessment procedures the social worker should become involved in the client's own life space through such means as naturalistic methods of observation. Typical examples are observing a child in the school setting or observing the family interaction at critical points such as meal times. The approach involves seeing and understanding through direct experience what is going on with the person in relevant ecological contexts.

To achieve the purposes of competence clarification, we need to develop or emphasize observation and assessment methods that complement traditional, clinically based procedures. The methods of anthropological research can be very useful in this regard, with their emphasis on such approaches as observation, interviewing, and participation.

Beyond the development of more relevant techniques, competence clarification requires a basic reorientation on the part of the practitioner —a reorientation involving an interrelated set of specific attitudes that flow from a humanistic perspective and the redefinition of human problems and needs. These attitudes are concisely described by Sundberg, Snowden, and Reynolds (1978):

> (a) . . . conscious efforts to avoid the problems characterizing some usage of old labels arising from measurement of intelligence or psychopathology; (b) attitudes toward clients which recognize their multipotentialities based on their current coping repertoire and their learning skills; (c) recognition of the pluralism of cultural backgrounds and values and development of appropriate assessment of culture-relative contexts; (d) recognition of the dangers of normative judgments . . . ; (e) acceptance of the dictum, "No assessment of the person without assessment of present and potential environments." . . . [Sundberg, Snowden, and Reynolds, 1978:207]

Above all, "emphasis is placed on progressive rather than regressive forces, on health rather than on 'sickness,' and on the potential for growth" (Germain, 1979:18).

Redefinition of Client and Practitioner Roles

Another feature of a competence-oriented perspective is the redefinition of the roles to be played by clients and social workers. Clients are viewed as partners in the helping process and redefined primarily as *resources* rather than as carriers of pathology.

In their analysis of "resource exchange networks," Sarason and Lorentz (1979) explain that network participants need to redefine themselves as resources in order to be able to contribute to others as well as to use the resources of other people; they must revise their customary ways of viewing themselves and their capabilities. Sarason and Lorentz further point out that the growing self-help movement can be understood as

> a reaction to the perception that the customary, institutionalized ways by which helping services of almost all kinds are rendered have two characteristics: They make people unduly dependent on these services, and they are constantly and unsuccessfully coping with limited resources. [Sarason and Lorentz, 1979:22]

There is a need for social work practitioners to view their clients more explicitly as resources, as human beings with assets and potentialities that can be mobilized on their own behalf, and also to help *clients* to see themselves as resources.

Such a perspective suggests that clients should play active roles in the helping process and participate meaningfully in such areas as assessment, goal formulation, and selection of interventive strategies. By being fully involved in deciding important issues that arise in the helping process, clients can exercise their own decision-making powers and enhance their autonomy and competence.

Viewing clients as resources does not mean, however, that the burden of change or problem-solving is placed on their shoulders. It would be simplistic to equate this formulation with the popular American notion of "pulling oneself up by one's bootstraps." On the contrary, an essential corollary is that appropriate environmental supports must be provided to enable people to develop their potentialities and to function as resources on their behalf and/or in the interest of others. There must be adequate "stimulus-nutriments" providing opportunities to use and develop ego skills (Holt, 1967:492–500).

For this reason, the roles of social workers also need to be redefined. As was emphasized even more forcefully in an earlier era in the history of social work, practitioners should be viewed primarily as *enabling agents* or change agents who play diverse roles and use varying approaches in order to provide the conditions necessary for clients to achieve their purposes, meet life challenges, engage in their natural life developmental processes, and carry out their tasks.[6] Workers may be called upon to play such roles as clinician, educator, broker, advocate, catalyst, strategy guide, etc.

The ecological orientation emphasizes the creative use of multiple practice modalities and the formulation of interventive plans suited to the client's needs and circumstances. The worker's activities and roles are defined primarily by the "logic and authority of the client's life situation" rather than by methodological predilections (Siporin, 1972:198).

Redefinition of Client–Worker Relationship

The redefined roles that have been suggested for clients and practitioners also lead to changes in their relationship. As explained by Hartman in her discussion of ecologically oriented family treatment,

> the relationship is redefined as one in which two people are working on a shared project. Each brings a special expertise to the task. [For example] the helper has a certain expertise on the way family systems operate and how they might change. The client is the expert on himself and his own family. [Hartman, 1979b:264]

To be effective in promoting client competence, the relationship should be characterized by encouragement of client autonomy, reduction of the authority and power invested in the worker, and elimination of hidden agenda (Hartman, 1979b:264).

As much as possible, workers should reduce social distance and nurture "a relationship that manifests openness, authenticity, honesty, and human caring" (Germain, 1979:18). In this respect, it is noteworthy that, in studies of client perception of treatment, the worker's human qualities seem to be valued by clients more than technical skills. In one such study, it was found that, from the perspective of clients, the "composite picture of the good or ideal worker is that of someone who is warm, accepting, understanding, involved, natural, genuine, competent, objective, and able to share of himself or herself with the client" (Maluccio, 1979a:125).

In work with individuals, families, or groups, practitioners should seek to build mutuality and reciprocity into the relationship, so as to promote the clients' identity, autonomy, sense of relatedness, and competence (Germain, 1979:18).[7] For instance, procedures such as eliciting client feedback or engaging in contract negotiation can help to reduce the power differentials between clients and workers, to enhance the sense of mutuality between them, and to contribute to the client's decision-making and autonomy.

There is a need to demystify the phenomenon of "treatment" in general, and the client–worker relationship in particular. As traditionally conceived in social work, the professional relationship with a client system continues to be a major vehicle of help. In many instances, it is one of the fundamental tools through which the practitioner seeks to promote competence in clients. But it is a tool rather than an end in itself. Moreover, in some situations the relationship with the immediate client(s) may be of limited importance or relevance. For example, in practice with so-called involuntary or unmotivated persons, the client–worker relationship may not be as important as the provision of needed tangible services and the restructuring of the environment. It may be that "in these cases the worker's efforts should be directed not toward engaging the 'client' in the helping process but toward engaging some other system or resource in the environment on his or her behalf" (Maluccio, 1979a:195).

Focus on Life Processes and Experiences

Another distinctive feature of competence-oriented social work practice is the explicit use of the client's own life processes and life experiences in intervention. By *life processes* I mean basic human functions such as motivation, cognition, emotion, and perception—as well as life tasks such as developmental crises and challenges. By *life experiences* I mean experiences, activities, and events that unfold in the natural course of a person's life. Among these are significant life events such as the birth of a child or the death of a parent, beginning a new job or getting a promotion, or a young adult's moving into his or her own home. They also include activities in areas such as work and recreation and relationships with other significant persons in one's social networks.

In short, "life itself is viewed as the arena of change: life experiences, events, and processes can be exploited for their 'therapeutic value' . . . and used to generate opportunities for the productive use of coping, striving, and goal-directed action" (Maluccio, 1979b:289). In formulating and planning interventive activities with their clients, workers should therefore be guided by the conviction that life tasks, life transitions, and social roles can provide opportunities for personal growth, learning of new social skills, and competence development.

Specific principles and guidelines for translating the focus on life processes and experiences into practice have been considered elsewhere.[8] In addition, they are examined in this book particularly in the chapters on cognition (Fleming, Chapter 3), motivation (Moore-Kirkland, Chapter 2), and transitional and crisis situations (Golan, Chapter 4). Rather than repeat this material here, I would like to highlight two themes that have been neglected in social work: (1) the use of cognition in intervention and (2) the role of creativity in human endeavors.

Use of Cognition.   The role of the intellect in coping and adaptation has not been fully exploited in social work practice. Greater emphasis on cognition is necessary in order to arrive at a more effective use of the environment and of life experiences. In particular, there is a need to pay more systematic attention to clients' cognitive functions, to use their cognitive powers in intervention, and to provide cognitive stimulation leading to expanded learning.

There are various ways through which cognition can play an important role in practice. The concept of the contract has already been mentioned; involvement in the deliberative process leading to the contract can stimulate the person's cognitive growth and mastery, broaden his knowledge of different alternatives and their consequences, and mobilize his decision-making function. Client–worker interaction may become more meaningful and productive as both parties go through the process of formulating the contract and reaching agreement on specific goals, tasks, and approaches. Mutual expectations and obligations can thus be clarified, and the problem of double agenda or hidden contract can be minimized.[9]

It is important to engage clients' cognitive resources in efforts to help them to make critical decisions. Furthermore, in an increasingly mass-oriented society, human beings desperately need to be able to make important decisions affecting their lives on the basis of adequate knowledge. The worker has a responsibility to assist the person in seeking and processing the knowledge needed to reach decisions about increasingly complex matters. In a real sense, the availability of adequate information about—and understanding of—the environment is an essential condition for effective adaptation. Problem-solving and the acquisition of competence are in large measure dependent on the extent to which the person can secure, process, and use adequate and relevant information in daily transactions with the environment (Connolly and Bruner, 1974; White, 1974).

The development of social skills that promote competence and adaptation frequently requires learning new information and new concepts. People need to learn how to deal effectively with bureaucratic organizations and how to negotiate their transaction with complex and varied social systems. For example, basic knowledge of the operation of a hospital emergency room would help in alleviating the fears and concerns of people seeking emergency medical care. Similarly, prior knowledge about a residential treatment center can be of help to a child being placed in it as well as to the parents.

Social work intervention is in many ways an instructive process: The worker often has to provide information, impart knowledge, and stimulate new ideas and concepts. The worker consequently plays an educational role—a role that could be further exploited in practice.[10]

In the course of client–worker interaction, it is also important to offer clients regular feedback in relation to their situation, to encourage them to assess the potential risks and benefits inherent in alternative courses of action or choice of different environments, and to help them monitor and measure change (cf. Fleming, Chapter 3 in this volume). All of this cognitive activity contributes to further development of the client's perception, reality testing, and ultimately competence.

Role of Creativity. Additional practice implications may be derived from writings on creativity—an area largely unexplored in social work.[11] Bruner (1970:18) defines a "creative enterprise" as "an act that produces effective surprise." By effective surprise he means "the unexpected that strikes one with wonder or excitement." The surprise may express itself in different forms, such as in interaction with one's children, in painting a picture, or in a business activity. Furthermore, creativity or the ability to produce an effective surprise exists in all human beings, regardless of their intellectual or other capacities (Bruner, 1970:29).

What can workers do to bring out and stimulate people's creative strivings and potentialities, the qualities that are inherent in their quest for competence and adaptation? One answer lies in the provision of diverse opportunities for action—opportunities that may facilitate rather than impede the person's selection of the type of activity most suited to his or her unique characteristics and particular adaptive processes. The diversity of opportunities for action may be instrumental in tapping the individual's potential to look at the world in divergent and novel ways, in stimulating his improvisation of alternative lines of action, and ultimately in his experiencing a sense of effective surprise, with its attendant growth-producing sense of exhilaration.

In his fascinating discussion of human evolution, Dubos (1968) asserts that "man makes himself" through the continuous and creative interplay between his qualities and aspirations and environmental conditions and challenges. In this ongoing life process, the experience of satisfaction or efficacy contributes not only to the development of the person's current sense of competence but also to the enhancement of adaptability, versatility, and coping strategies in future life situations.

Emphasis on Using the Environment

The theoretical perspectives discussed earlier stress that competence flourishes through a nutritive environment that is suited to the person's needs and qualities and that supports his or her natural life processes. Consequently, in competence-oriented intervention there is emphasis on understanding the environment with all its complexities and on restructuring it in a purposive and systematic fashion. Practice activities may be directed to the physical environment, the social milieu, or both. Often, the person's environment needs to be modified or restructured so as to facilitate or support his or her coping efforts and

adaptive strivings. In this regard, social networks are especially important. A key quality of competent persons in fact seems to be that they
are able to identify and use natural helping networks to their advantage. Some people, however, need help so as to be able to make more
effective use of resources existing within their own networks (cf. Swenson, Chapter 6 in this volume).

Emphasis on the client's milieu of course is not new in social work.
Usually we have focused on modifying or manipulating the environment as a means of influencing the helping process. However, we need
to view environmental features such as resources in one's social networks as *instruments of help* rather than simply as *influences on help*
(Gitterman and Germain, 1976). We have to appreciate the environment's potential to release or inhibit human potentialities for growth,
adaptation, and competence.

Much can be accomplished by identifying and using "environmental instruments" (Cumming and Cumming, 1962), that is, people, resources, and facilities that exist in the client's life space or that can be
added to it. For instance, in the area of child abuse, homemakers or
parent aides are found to be effective instruments of help in work with
parents. As Libassi and Turner explain in their chapter on the elderly
(Chapter 11 in this volume), it is helpful to think in terms of "compensatory intervention," that is, the provision of tangible supports or stimulus-nutriments that compensate for significant losses or deprivations.

In short, the competence perspective suggests that in social work
practice there should be more emphasis on changing the environment
than on changing people. Specific practice principles for restructuring
and using the environment are discussed in other chapters of this book.
Germain (Chapter 5) explores the significance of the physical environment in social work practice. Swenson (Chapter 6) examines the role of
social networks and natural helping systems. Grinnell, Kyte, and Bostwick (Chapter 7) focus on environmental modification. And Middleman (Chapter 8) delineates principles and procedures for using
structured groups to promote competence.

As implied in each of the above chapters, workers should be directly exposed to the client's ecological context in order to evaluate its
impact on the person's functioning. As the client's life and environment
become more accessible to them, practitioners can become more effective in aiding the person to identify, seek, or create significant environmental opportunities.

Regular Use of Client Feedback

Throughout this chapter I have stressed the importance of the
client's active involvement in the helping process. This emphasis leads

to the final feature of competence-oriented practice: the use of client feedback. By this phrase I refer to a simple notion: having practitioners obtain, on a regular basis, the views of clients concerning their helping efforts. Various methods of obtaining client feedback have been discussed elsewhere (Maluccio, 1979a).

Client feedback can serve various purposes. At the agency level, it can be a means of monitoring services, carrying out program evaluation, and improving service delivery. At the worker's level, it can be an effective device for monitoring one's practice and improving one's skills:

> By being tuned into the clients' perspectives, workers might be better able to determine for themselves which methods or techniques are effective, what they need to modify in their approach in order to make it more relevant to client needs and qualities, and what questions they need to ask about their underlying assumptions regarding human behavior and interpersonal helping. [Maluccio, 1979a:202]

Client feedback in each case situation can help to ensure that the practitioner is attuned as much as possible to the person's own feelings, needs, views, and qualities. Above all, it can be another valuable means of enhancing the person's competence. In work with individuals, families, or groups, eliciting the view of the client(s) can have a variety of positive consequences, such as providing the individual with opportunities for decision-making, reducing the social distance between client and practitioner, and increasing the client's sense of power and control over his or her life. All of this can promote competence by enhancing each person's self-esteem and autonomy.

Studies of client perception of services show that people are pleased and become involved when a researcher asks them for their opinions, impressions, and suggestions (cf. Maluccio, 1979a; Mayer and Timms, 1970). Clients not only are eager to participate in the research process meaningfully but also express their pleasure in being involved and the feelings of satisfaction and competence that they derive from the research experience.

In short, more explicit emphasis on client feedback as an integral feature of practice can serve to engage the client even more actively in the helping process. At the same time, it can help workers to examine and revise their approach. Client feedback can thus contribute to a mutually rewarding process of interaction and growth between practitioners and their clients.

Conclusion

Our practice experiences as well as the insights of ego psychologists, biologists, and others show that human beings develop through the enduring sequence of specific transactions with the environment and the cumulative experience of doing, of being active, of significantly affecting their surroundings (cf. White, 1963). As Beavers (1977:377) concludes in his presentation of a growth-oriented approach to family treatment, the "development of a competent self is an interpersonal process which requires a rather special kind of growth-promoting milieu." In particular, competence results from the constructive interaction of a person's qualities and potentialities with a nurturing and challenging environment—an environment providing both support and stimulation.

Social workers can help their clients to achieve, maintain, or enhance their competence by paying systematic attention to people's active engagement with their impinging environment and by helping to provide a milieu with appropriate levels and kinds of nurture and challenge. In the chapters that follow, the contributors show how this can be accomplished by following the guidelines and principles suggested by an explicit focus on competence.

Through its emphasis on the interface between people and their environments, on life processes and experiences, and on the purposive use of the environment in the helping process, competence-oriented social work practice can play an essential *triggering function:* It can serve to set in motion or mobilize the client's coping capacities, natural life processes, and strivings toward growth. I learned to appreciate the significance of the triggering effect of social work intervention in a recent in-depth study of client perception of the helping process at a family service agency (Maluccio, 1979a). As clients related their experiences at the agency, I was struck by how some workers appeared to be especially effective as enabling agents or catalysts in the change process. Some clients indicated that they were able to seek new friends or reestablish ties with old friends through encouragement from the worker. Others showed that they developed more satisfying relationships with family members as they worked through some of their conflicts during the course of "treatment." Still others learned to function more effectively as there was some significant restructuring of their environment or as they became involved in meaningful activities.

As these examples suggest, clients in the above study were helped, frequently as a result of client–worker interaction, to make better use of natural resources in their environment; to seek a new environment (such as a job change) that was more suited to their needs; to become freer to reach out to others and act positively on their needs; to interact with significant others in ways that elicited more positive feedback; and to enhance their sense of hope and motivation for change. As these clients spoke, there was "the suggestion of an almost regenerative quality to their functioning: as they had the experience of coping more effectively and gaining some mastery over their environment, they went on to rekindle dormant capabilities and develop new coping patterns" (Maluccio, 1979a:189).

As social workers, we can build on the notion of competence as a significant force in human behavior. In our practice activities, we can become more effective in redirecting the trajectory of coping and adaptation in clients from despair and frustration to satisfaction and competence. In addition, it may well be that this perspective on practice can lead to further rewards for ourselves and help us to enhance our own competence as social workers and as human beings. With social workers as with clients, in the right environment competence feeds upon competence.[12]

Notes

1. This review draws from Goldfried and D'Zurilla (1969); Harter (1978); and Sundberg, Snowden, and Reynolds (1978).
2. Fleming (Chapter 3 in this volume) considers the role of cognition in competence development and social work practice.
3. For further analysis of various approaches to the conceptualization of competence, see reviews by Goldfried and D'Zurilla (1969); Harter (1978); and Sundberg, Snowden, and Reynolds (1978).
4. Heath (1977:202–21) also proposes a transcultural model of maturing in which he substitutes the concept of "mature personality organization" for the traditional notion of the "competent self."
5. For further discussion of human problems in transactional terms, see Gitterman and Germain (1976) and Germain and Gitterman (1979; 1980).
6. The notion of practitioners as *enabling agents* was stimulated by Studt (1968) through her incisive formulation of client and worker tasks. It is similar to the concept of "change agent system" that is a basic component of Pincus and Minahan's (1973) social work practice model.
7. For elaboration of these ideas on the client–worker relationship, see Germain and Gitterman (1979).
8. See Germain and Gitterman (1979a; 1979b) and Maluccio (1974; 1979b).
9. For discussion of practice principles in using the client–worker contract, see Estes and Henry (1976), Maluccio and Marlow (1974), and Seabury (1976).
10. Guerney's (1977) "relationship enhancement" approach is a good example of an educationally oriented practice model.

11. Among the few who have considered the role of creativity in social work is Lydia Rapoport (1968).
12. Promotion of the *practitioner's* competence is another critical—and vast— topic that is beyond the scope of this book. See Clark, Arkava, and Associates (1979) for extensive and stimulating consideration of this aspect.

PART 1

Using Life Processes and Experiences

CHAPTER 2

Mobilizing Motivation: From Theory to Practice

Janet Moore-Kirkland

Clarence has received counseling from school social workers from time to time over the past three years yet continues to disrupt his fifth-grade classroom with his antics and fighting. His parents have refused a referral for family counseling or play therapy.

Barbara Reeves is seeing the social worker in a family medical clinic voluntarily. She fills every session, which she attends without fail, with a recital of marital problems and frustrations with her children, yet she steadfastly resists inclusion of the family in the session, changes the subject at each attempt to explore these problems, and finally states that she really does not want her situation to change. However, as the worker observes her with the children in the clinic, Barbara maintains a constant barrage of verbal abuse and, by her own description, she and her husband are sometimes physically abusive in punishing the children. The family is known to the public child welfare agency.

The Morris family chose family counseling as an alternative to placement of their 15-year-old daughter in a juvenile correctional facility after several shoplifting incidents, but the father informed the intake worker when setting up their first appointment by phone that they considered counseling unnecessary, coercive, and disruptive to the family's work and extracurricular schedule. A wall of hostility meets the worker as she greets the parents and the three adolescent children, and Mr. Morris wastes no time informing her that the other teenagers involved in these police incidents got off with none of "this counseling nonsense." Furthermore, he states, they can afford neither the time nor the money for counseling.

For the potential client like Clarence who seems entangled in a resistive system, the voluntary client such as Ms. Reeves who appears to want help desperately yet resists change, or the blatantly hostile involuntary client system such as the Morris family, a central issue in engaging in any successful treatment effort is motivation. The clients[1] described above are not atypical of the clientele encountered by social workers in virtually any agency setting. Probably equally typical would be the assessment of such clients as "unmotivated" or "highly resistant" to change. By typically defining motivation and resistance as characteristics of the client, social workers in situations such as these limit their choice of interventive strategies: They may work with available motivation through the often frustrating repetition of approaches and techniques that may actually exacerbate resistance. Or they may wait until a major crisis occurs which "mobilizes" the resistant client or provides justification for aggressive intervention, such as the removal of children from abusive parents or the institutionalization of the juvenile offender. Most commonly, they may simply accept the client's eventual discontinuance and attribute the failure to the client's lack of motivation.

The thesis of this chapter, however, is that motivation is not an attribute of the client but a product of the interaction of client, worker, and environment. Motivation is not a characteristic of the client's personality structure or psychological functioning. By approaching it as a transactional concept and a process rather than a trait, as social workers we are able to mobilize motivation in such a way as to build on and enhance the competencies of clients in their life experiences. The objective of this chapter, therefore, is to develop motivation as a transactional concept and to discuss principles and techniques for mobilizing motivation in social work intervention.

Historical Perspectives on Motivation in Theory and Practice

Psychological Theories of Motivation

Attempts to conceptualize and explain what motivates an organism to act dominated the field of psychology for many years, though this preoccupation with motivational theories has been replaced to some extent by greater interest in cognition (Harter, 1978).

Some of the deepest roots of social work treatment are in psychoanalytic theory, in which motivation is determined by the individual's need for tension reduction from sexual and aggressive drives, and resistance is defined as "the expression of defense, unconsciously instituted, against anxiety arising out of conflict" (Blanck and Blanck, 1974:194). Like psychoanalytic theory, behaviorism is considered a mechanistic psychological theory, and although there are substantial differences among behaviorists, their approach focuses on associations which are built up between stimuli and responses and which "drive" the organism. Some behaviorists, like Skinner, contend that one's behavior at any given time is fully determined by one's reinforcement history and that thoughts and choices do not cause behavior. Consequently, some behaviorists reject the construct "motivation," focusing exclusively on observable stimulus–response bonds. On the other hand, Hull, also a behaviorist, provided the first elaborate conception of motivation and has probably had the greatest impact on the field of motivation (Deci, 1975). According to Hull, drives, which are basically tissue needs, activate stimulus–response associations (habits), and drive reduction strengthens stimulus–response associations. Drives are thus the motivational aspect of physiological needs, and reinforcement involves returning one of the organism's tissue needs to equilibrium.

Increasingly motivational theory has moved to try to explain categories of behavior for which no tissue or tension-reduction need can be identified. From Maslow (1943) comes the concept of a motivational hierarchy which includes social and self-actualization motives. Later, in a provocative and now classic paper, White (1959) argued that the traditional drive theories of Hull and Freud were incomplete motivational models of human behavior, and he posited a basic "urge toward competence" as reflected in such behaviors as exploration, curiosity, mastery, play, and one's general attempts to deal competently with one's environment. White contended that competence motivation causes behaviors that allow a person to have feelings of efficacy—to engage in behaviors that allow him to feel competent. Furthermore, he asserted that competence motivation is an intrinsic, on-going process that is periodically interrupted by tissue needs and that is always available to occupy the "spare waking time between episodes of homeostatic crisis" (White, 1959:321). This formulation directs attention to a broader, more pervasive source of motivation that does not exclude drives or tissue needs but goes beyond them. DeCharms (1968) has elaborated on this theory, contending that although general competence motivation differentiates into specific motives as a result of experience with one's environment, "the desire to be in control of one's fate is a contributing factor in all motives" (deCharms, 1968:56).

Deci (1975) has sketched a general framework for the understanding of human motivation incorporating several categories of motivated behavior and motivational theory into one system. He asserts that people choose behaviors they believe will lead them to desired goals. These behaviors are energized by "an awareness of potential satisfaction" that develops out of stimuli from the environment, memory, or internal states. When a person achieves his or her goal, the resulting rewards provide satisfaction. If that satisfaction does not match the anticipated satisfaction, new goals will be established to provide the satisfaction.

Deci (1975) recognizes three sources of motivated behavior: intrinsic, extrinsic, and affective motives. Intrinsically motivated behaviors are those a person engages in to feel competent and self-determining, and this need motivates two different kinds of behavior: (1) behavior that "seeks out" optimal challenges that one can handle, and (2) behavior that conquers challenge, reducing uncertainty or dissonance. Extrinsically motivated behaviors are related to basic drives, and affectively motivated behavior is initiated when a person is aware that he/she could have a more positive or less negative feeling than he/she has at that time.

Motivation in Social Work Literature

The practical implications of these and other theories and research findings on motivation have become the domain of business, communications, and education: Advertising and the mass media have applied motivational theory to influence the eating, drinking, political, and even sexual behavior of consumers; management has used it to increase the productivity of employees; and educators to improve the performance of students.

By contrast with the prominence of motivation in its theoretical forms in psychology and in its applied forms in several other fields, this subject has been treated in the social work literature from time to time under such topics as relationship and diagnosis but seldom as a distinct phenomenon of the social work process. A review of *Abstracts for Social Workers* from 1965 to 1978 reveals five journal entries dealing with client motivation, all of these between 1965 and 1969; only one of these appeared in a social work publication. More often the social work literature has focused on the characteristics of—and techniques for dealing with—certain categories of client that have become almost synonymous with the "unmotivated client"—the alcoholic, the child abuser, the poor, the multiproblem family.

Ripple, Alexander, and Polemis's (1964) motivation–capacity–op-

portunity formulation virtually stands alone as an attempt to conceptualize the role of motivation in social work intervention. "Usable
motivation," they contend, consists of a balance of discomfort and
hope, with discomfort providing sufficient pressure to do something
about the problem and sufficient hope to channel that pressure constructively (Ripple, Alexander, and Polemis, 1964:61). They advise directing attention to this balance as the "most fruitful approach for
economy of diagnosis and for initial treatment planning" and speculate
about the possible effects of treatment factors on changes observed in
the discomfort–hope balance over the limited time span covered by the
study (five sessions). In sum, Ripple, Alexander, and Polemis define
motivation as an individual client attribute, emphasize its importance
as a diagnostic concept, but do not deal with how to enhance usable
motivation in the treatment process.

Generally social workers regard motivation as a characteristic
which the client possesses or fails to possess, and an assessment of its
absence or presence is a component of most standard diagnoses, as the
above writers advocate. The means by which a client engages the services of the social agency is often the basis for our initial assumptions
regarding the motivation of the client, since the involuntary client is
usually assumed to be unmotivated. Blanck and Blanck note, moreover,
that professionals tend to challenge the prospective client's motivation
as part of the initial consultation, in which "the unmotivated patient
pays a severe penalty for any manifest reluctance . . . for therapists
tend to have far more tolerance for resistance in its unconscious forms
than for resistance which has found conscious rationalization and is
displaced upon beginning therapy" (Blanck and Blanck, 1974:197). Not
only is such a diagnostic determination regarding motivation used for
treatment planning, but another practical implication is that it tends to
serve as a screening device to help determine where the individual
social worker and the agency should invest their resources, perhaps as
the functional equivalent of early social work's "deserving" and "un-
deserving" clientele.

Motivation receives further attention at still another phase of the
client's career with the agency in the evaluation-of-treatment outcomes.
Simply put, if clients respond to our services they are considered motivated; if not, they are obviously unmotivated. Thus it is not surprising that one of the reasons most frequently given by social workers
for case closings when termination is unplanned is "client not
motivated."

Many social workers feel that "real" social work can only be accomplished with motivated clients. Briar and Miller (1971:93) describe the
"typical client" in the view of most casework literature as the individual
who brings himself to the agency for help with a psychological prob-

lem, continues voluntarily in treatment for an extended period, and in general exhibits the patterned, focused behavior which suggests motivation for change. Over the past decade increasing emphasis on the social worker–client contract has perhaps inadvertently reinforced a preoccupation with the client who is willing and able to articulate a commitment to change. Indeed the profession's growing interest in private practice may reflect our preoccupation with—and collective aspirations toward—dealing with this ideal client. From this evidence we suggest that social workers either consciously or unconsciously tend to make value judgments about motivation, and, by implication, the "motivated" versus the "unmotivated" client.

This dichotomous, post factum view of motivation poses several problems for the profession and the professional. First, while social workers may feel most comfortable when the client comes with both the problem and the motivation to work on it, much—if not most—of our practice involves those who do not initially ask for help but are identified as being in trouble by a third party—another individual, group, institution, or the community. When such persons present problems which are perceived as having serious consequences for the larger community or society, social agencies are delegated the responsibility of dealing with those who are most often described as unmotivated to change. Greater professional and public interest in such problems as child abuse and alcoholism has forced us to deal with the categories of clients which, as we have noted, have become virtually synonymous with the "unmotivated client."

Thus we are often confronted with clients who appear hard to reach, who deny the need for change, and who may greet our offers of help with hostility or indifference. Yet the worker usually has a contract with the agency to intervene, and one's professional sense of empathy and social responsibility may make the need for intervention particularly compelling. For example, abusive parents are generally regarded as resistant to change; they are not likely to approach a social agency and request help, not prepared for long involvement in intensive, goal-directed treatment, yet the worker must intervene, both because child abuse is a crime with which the social agency has a mandate to deal and because of our recognition of society's responsibility toward the abused child and the abusive parents. By training and often by preference, the worker is prepared to deal with the "ideal client," but the real client frequently appears to be the antithesis of this ideal.

The second problem with the traditional view of motivation is that we often ignore motivational issues facing the ostensibly motivated client or devote exclusive attention to unconscious sources of resistance. Resistance is ubiquitous, and we agree with Blanck and Blanck (1974:197) that it is "theoretically inconceivable that there are more and less preferable kinds of resistance," for approach and avoidance behavior always coexist in the client in the process of change.

The third problem with a static, dichotomous view of motivation in which responsive clients are considered motivated, and unresponsive ones unmotivated, is that it results in feats of circular logic which keep us from diagnosing our outcomes and improving services to those about whom we make our assumptions. In this view, resistant clients become scapegoats for our failure. Rather than adjusting services to deal more effectively with our professional expectations, we frequently stand by and wait until a major crisis occurs, when acute discomfort or even tragedy renders the client "workable," or we may resort to punitive or coercive approaches which further decrease motivation toward a collaborative change effort and undermine the client's sense of competence.

A Transactional Model of Motivation

By contrast with the traditional view of motivation as a client trait, we propose a transactional model dealing with motivation as a process that takes into account the interactions among client, worker, and the environment. We will look at three components of the transactions between these systems in order, first, to analyze the available motivation of participants in a social-change effort, and, furthermore, to attempt to alter the level of motivation to facilitate the desired change. While there is no unitary theory of motivation, we find several features of this construct about which there seems to be agreement among most theories, and we suggest that a dynamic model of motivation will enable us to assess the following factors in relation to the change effort: (1) *affective arousal*—the level of emotional arousal related to the change; (2) *directionality*—the goals or direction of change/movement; and (3) the *environment* as each person in the change effort perceives it.

None of these factors individually can explain or predict the level of motivation available for accomplishing a given task or for initiating change. An aroused organism moves randomly if it has no sense of direction in relation to its own environment. Similarly, if a client is emotionally aroused and wants to change his/her situation, we cannot assess the motivation available to the task without knowing what he/she wants instead (the direction of the desired change) and what practical factors (environment) may impede or enhance the attainment of that goal. Conversely, one may have goals very appropriate to the environment, but may lack the energy or drive to change if he or she is comfortable with the status quo and not emotionally aroused.

Thus all components of motivation—affective arousal, directionality and environment—are interacting, interdependent forces affecting and being affected by the others. All components must be considered in assessing the motivation of a system, and each is necessary but not sufficient to explain motivation or to predict if change will occur. Furthermore, to mobilize or enhance motivation we will look at how to effect change in one or more of these components, recognizing that change in one part of a system affects the entire system.

In doing so we also recognize that resistance—"the unwillingness to act in an expected, desired way or to engage oneself, or to change" (Siporin, 1975:198)—is motivated behavior. Though we usually construe resistance as the antithesis of motivation, the two, counterposed, can be viewed on a continuum in relation to a general or particular goal or direction. If a client is emotionally aroused and wanting to move toward a positive goal, we usually describe him/her as motivated toward that goal. If, however, that person is aroused to move away from or to avoid that goal, this too is motivated behavior, though usually perceived as "resistant" from the worker's perspective. Thus "motivating" the client to work collaboratively with the worker requires recognizing what is already motivating the "resistant" behavior and fashioning the change effort to complement rather than compete with or ignore these motives.

Since resistance is motivated behavior, we can use our transactional model of motivation to analyze it. For example, in analyzing the behavior of parents who repeatedly fail to follow through with treatment plans for their "emotionally disturbed" child and are considered "resistant" (or worse, "disinterested" in the child), we may find these parents highly motivated to be good parents and equally motivated to avoid any threat to their perhaps shaky self-image. Using our transactional model, we can recognize them as: (1) *affectively aroused,* fearful of appearing helpless, dependent, or incompetent; (2) *directed* toward the goal of avoiding persons or situations that further undermine their faltering sense of competence; and (3) in the *environmental context* of critical in-laws and a worker who is also perceived as nonsupportive and critical of their parenting efforts. Once we have recognized the motives behind the parents' resistant behavior, the worker should be better able to select strategies and modes of intervention that will capitalize on these motives, and even regard them as competencies and use them to enhance the change effort by reinforcing rather than undermining the parents' motivation to be competent.

Looking at the interactional context of the social work relationship we shall also examine in this chapter each factor in our model of motivation and potential sources of resistance that each contains. We shall identify these and describe four major strategies of intervention available to the worker—anxiety reduction, anxiety arousal, enhancing goal states, and removing practical barriers. These strategies are designed around the dual objectives of reducing the level of resistance and optimizing the potential for a mutual change effort between worker and client—one which does not assume that the client *is* the problem or is the inevitable or sole target for change.

In discussing each strategy we shall detail and illustrate specific techniques and skills which can be used to enhance client motivation tools that are already within the repertoires of most social workers. Our emphasis will be on the sensitive assessment of the source(s), the differential selection of strategies, and the application of specific skills which may make change relevant, rewarding and desirable for a broad spectrum of clients—voluntary and involuntary, eager and reluctant, the well-functioning individual and the crisis-ridden family. The cases which we will use illustratively deal with individuals, families, and groups, but the transactional model of motivation and the strategies for enhancing motivations can also be applied to others in social systems and to larger systems, including communities and organizations.[2]

Anxiety Reduction

Looking first at affect as a component of motivation, there is ample evidence that excessive anxiety can inhibit behavior. Some of the classic studies of approach–avoidance conflict point out that even a highly desirable goal may be abandoned in the presence of strong fear (McGuire, 1969)—fear that may arise from factors within the immediate environment, such as the threat of pain or physical injury, or from emotional states that may be elicited by the reappearance of certain cues associated with an earlier emotional experience, which may in turn elicit avoidance behavior. This view of affective arousal associated with motivation (McClelland et al., 1953) bears much similarity to the way in which ego psychology has traditionally viewed resistance, i.e., as a means of avoiding or defending against painful or conflictual areas which were not satisfactorily resolved during growth.

In treatment excessive fear may immobilize a person who may deeply desire help, for overwhelming fear disorganizes and renders one unable to focus by tending to "cause older, dominant responses to surface, to interfere with the learning of new ones, and to draw attention away from new cues or behaviors," as Fleming discusses in Chapter 3 in this volume. As a result the client may totally avoid the person or situations associated with this anxiety. Thus the initial questions we may ask when motivation appears to be lacking or when resistance is encountered include: (a) Is the client's anxiety excessive?—and if so,

(b) what is the source of the anxiety?—for anxiety may stem from any of several sources, or from several simultaneously.

Traditionally one of the most closely examined sources of resistance to intervention has been the fear of entering into a relationship with the professional, which prompts the client to attempt to reject before being rejected to protect oneself from intimacy and dependency. When the need for basic trust has never been satisfied, when the client's previous attempts to trust and be cared for have been thwarted, he or she may become extremely anxious when exposed to a situation which requires investing trust in another person. Anxious for approval yet conditioned to expect disapproval, the client may erect barriers to protect him/herself from the anticipated pain of further disapproval and disappointment. A client in a children's protection agency expressed it this way in retrospect:

There was a worker who said she would help, but I'd heard that before. My father always wanted to help—but he took off and left my mother. She wanted to help—but there was always a new baby to take care of. My teachers wanted to help, but when I couldn't do the work they thought I was dumb. When I got married and was about to have my first baby, my husband said he'd be there to help, but he was messing around with my best friend before I even got out of the hospital. The doctors and nurses said they'd help—but they weren't there when I needed them. How could I have known it would be any different with this social worker?

While people are intrinsically motivated to feel competent and self-determining, the process of accepting help may threaten their sense of personal competence, self-confidence, ability to make decisions, and trust in one's own judgment, resulting in anxiety. Maluccio (1979b) indicates that the ego is strengthened through the cumulative experience of producing desired effects upon one's surroundings, but the converse may be true for some who may regard accepting help as an admission of inadequacy and inability to affect one's life and environment. This self-judgment is usually compounded by fear of censure or punishment, real as well as projected. For example, when parents of a juvenile offender are approached regarding their child's delinquent behavior, they cannot escape the awareness that the law—and by inference, the social agency involved—considers them culpable to some degree for that behavior. Thus the emotional vulnerability of a relationship which the client may perceive as a dependent one, and the fear, in turn, of being seen as less than fully competent may result in immobilizing anxiety.

Anxiety tends to be most prominent and recognizable during the initial stages of client contact but may be even more bewildering and difficult for the worker to deal with when it occurs later in the process of change. The anxious client's attempts to keep the worker at arm's length and to test the worker's intentions—whether through overtly hostile behavior, such as angry tirades, or more passive means, such as broken appointments and failure to follow through with agreed to and ostensibly desired changes—may trigger the worker's frustration and anger and eventually may provoke the professional to give the client up as "unmotivated."

If we recognize that fear or anxiety can inhibit motivation—or approach behavior—in the change process, the worker's first task with the anxious client is to bring anxiety within workable limits. Dealing with the fear of the worker and of possible negative outcomes must be primary steps in the process of change before the anxious client can engage with the worker. The latter's empathy and sensitivity to the client's feelings should enable him or her to identify and tolerate these anxieties, help the client verbalize them, and accept them while providing realistic assurance and clarification of the worker's purpose and expectations. Writing of work with resistant alcoholic clients, Chafetz (1965) refers to these activities as establishing "emotionally meaningful communication" and he deems it of paramount importance: "Anything less is wasted, for the therapist who does not recognize the unverbalized needs of the client is speaking a foreign emotional language to him and understanding can never be attained" (Chafetz, 1965:325–26).

The reduction of anxiety is not as massive a task as it may appear, for the objective of dealing with excessive anxiety to enhance motivation is not to eliminate emotional arousal but to reduce and maintain it at a manageable level. Any exploration of anxiety should include discussion of the client's previous experiences with helping persons: If positive, they may provide reinforcement for the process being undertaken; if negative, the worker may deal more effectively with this in the process of discussing and sharing expectations.

With many clients the expression of fear will take the form of testing the worker's interest and commitment, and when the professional's behavior is congruent with verbal expressions of acceptance and willingness to persist with the client, anxiety may decline as the client's fears are disconfirmed. The worker attempting to deal with parents around child neglect may meet with vociferous denial of problems on one visit, conforming behavior the next, and an angry tirade the following time, but as the worker makes an appearance each week and expresses consistent interest in the parents, he or she should verbally acknowledge the family's fears and facilitate discussion of them.

As anxiety is gradually diminishing, the worker should concentrate on establishing credibility in the eyes of the client, pursuing goals that are somewhat rewarding for the client. Focusing on what is most troublesome and least threatening as the client perceives his/her situation, demonstrating an active, consistent interest in the client, responding empathically to the client's verbal and nonverbal messages are all essential in developing motivation around a mutual purpose, as illustrated in the following case:

Barbara Reeves was a veteran of two family agencies and a private psychiatrist's treatment when she requested counseling at the family medical clinic in the community to which she had recently moved. Her initial session with the new worker consisted of a litany of complaints about her husband, his infidelities, their frequent arguments, and his financial mismanagement of the family's resources. She resisted efforts to engage him in marital counseling, thwarted any efforts at problem-solving about the marriage, yet continued to ventilate her distress—the same pattern reported by the previous social workers and psychiatrist.

Exploration of the marital history revealed John's importance in Barbara's life. The couple's previous separations had all been short-lived, each seeking the other out for reconciliation, and each quickly taking up the marital gauntlet once they reunited. Despite invectives against John and threats to leave again, Barbara eventually admitted she probably could not tolerate change in him if he became the loving, faithful husband of whom she dreamed.

In a similar manner came the frustrations with the children, and a home visit revealed that her modus operandi with them was yelling and shaming. Repeatedly Barbara and the worker inventoried the client's concerns over John and the children and translated her desire for change into goals, yet the moment the focus turned to problem-solving in either area, Barbara injected more pressing problems. She was apparently resistant to change in her relationships within the family, and her anxiety about change began to reveal itself more overtly. She was fearful of censure for being such a "bad mother"; she was convinced that the worker, like previous counselors, would "help me give up John"; and she feared accomplishing anything on her own for fear of confirming that she could indeed get along independently of John.

Beneath a gruff, angry, sometimes defiant exterior, Barbara was fearful of losing her husband, her children, her troubled yet predictable abilities to cope with her environment and the relationships within it. As the worker acknowledged these fears, helped to clarify them with Barbara, and accepted the client's immediate goals for herself—improved relationships with friends, a better job—the practitioner delayed work on more critical issues, particularly the relationship with the children, whose welfare Barbara was still too anxious to discuss.

It was at the end of a session in which the subject of the children had not surfaced that Barbara ended with a proud announcement: "I'm not yelling at the children anymore." The following session she greeted the worker with the request to come home with her to meet her husband, who was off work and baby-sitting. When the worker agreed, Barbara ushered her into the house, announcing to John, "You can trust her. This social worker's different; she hasn't prejudged you"—which on examination meant that Barbara realized the worker had resisted her ambivalent attempts to form an alliance with her against her husband.

This case illustrates how the recognition of overwhelming, immobilizing anxiety can enable the worker to employ techniques selectively to reduce the anxiety and mobilize motivation for client-defined change efforts. Providing consistent acceptance, including acceptance of Barbara's resistance—that is, her attempts to protect herself—the worker empathically responded to the client's verbal and nonverbal expression of her fears about the relationship and about the consequences of change, helping her verbalize the fearful aspects and clarifying and giving realistic reassurance as needed. Rather than confronting Barbara with the problems of which she was already very painfully aware yet reluctant to deal with, the worker aligned with the client's motivation to demonstrate competency with less threatening goals, enabling her to exercise autonomy not only in the choice of both explicit and implicit goals for change but in the timing of them.

In a project with hard-to-reach families, Charlotte Henry (1958) has reported that parents frequently brush aside the discussion of a reported complaint or a "problem child" to talk about themselves or other family problems. This may provide an entry point in involving clients in change that is desirable and important to them, as can the performance of a concrete practical task. Locating resources of food, clothing, or shelter, or being available during a crisis may not only resolve immediate problems but may be a potent demonstration of the worker's expertise, effectiveness, and potential usefulness to the client. Too often, however, the worker stops here after an initial flurry of activity, and the often cited adage that "unmotivated" clients are amenable to help only in times of crisis tends to become a self-fulfilling prophecy if the worker withdraws once the immediate problem is resolved. A crisis resolved represents a time of lowered anxiety and may also provide the worker and family with an opportunity to build on success and an enhanced sense of competence. The form and frequency of contacts may diminish after the crisis is dealt with, but the persistent, continuous interest of the worker is essential to dispel excessive anxiety and mobilize motivation for further change.[3]

The need for establishing clear mutual expectations and goals between client and worker becomes particularly important when anxiety is a source of resistive behavior, since ambiguity and uncertainty may heighten anxiety to the point where attempts at intervention may not only be ineffective but the anxiety may spill into the general functioning of the client and may make it more difficult for him or her to cope. Thus unclear goals and agendas may exacerbate the problem to the point where the client becomes immobilized and may decrease rather than mobilize motivation. The case for a clear contract between worker and client regarding the goals and methods of intervention, so firmly established now in the social work literature (cf. Maluccio and Marlow, 1974; Seabury, 1976), is nowhere more vivid than in dealing with the fearful, resistant client.

In summary, dealing with resistance rising from excessive anxiety first requires that the worker recognize the client's motivation to protect himself/herself from real or perceived threats to emotional safety and autonomy. Once these specific threats are identified, the worker can purposively pursue the strategy of reducing the anxiety to a level that provides the "push of discomfort" without the immobilizing effects of overwhelming anxiety. The techniques for implementing this strategy include empathic, explicit identification of specific and diffuse fears, demonstration of active, consistent interest in the client, and focusing on what is most troublesome as the client perceives his/her situation, including clearly articulated mutual goals between client and worker.

Anxiety Arousal

While reduction of anxiety is the strategy of choice in enhancing motivation when anxiety is excessive, some anxiety over the status quo provides a powerful stimulus to action. Hebb (1955:250) postulated the need for an optimal level of arousal for motivation, observing that "up to a certain point, threat and puzzle have positive motivating value, beyond that point, negative value." Thus if there is little or no emotional arousal around a situation that poses significant problems for the client or others, the strategy for mobilizing motivation will entail rousing sufficient anxiety to provide the "push of discomfort" (Ripple, Alexander, and Polemis, 1964:27) and to stimulate interest in change.

When clients do not perceive the same problem as the worker there may be insufficient emotional arousal to motivate action toward a solution. For example, the worker may perceive the client's problem as alcoholism and the resulting family and work-related dysfunction. However, the very nature of the problem is such that the alcoholic perceives neither the problem nor his/her need for help.

Other clients may appear unperturbed by a difficult or chaotic situation, perceiving that it is beyond their control. In his discussion of attribution theory, Fleming[4] indicates that when individuals feel an event is externally controlled, not contingent upon their own behavior, or outside their influence, they tend to feel helpless and are unlikely to seek or benefit from therapy. Although he notes that anxiety is usually attached to these feelings of helplessness, we often encounter it in a form that suggests apathy, passivity, or indifference about the situation itself.

Still other clients may simply be unable to conceive of any other ways of behaving, due to lack of exposure to alternative models—as may occur with the abusive parent who may know only punitive means of child discipline—or the existence of family or cultural norms which may be much more powerful than any alternative. The following case illustrates this:

In a behavioral group of adolescent girls in a family service agency, Mary selected as her goal the termination of the shop-lifting activity in which she had engaged for several years, since she was approaching her eighteenth birthday and feared her luck in avoiding arrest might run out once she achieved adult status. The friends with whom she had participated in the stealing were also in the group and supported her goal, and since Mary was the instigator and leader of shop-lifting incidents the group felt the changes in Mary would effectively end the activity among the group members.

The first week after the establishment of the contract Mary proudly reported to the group that she had stolen nothing, for which she received much reinforcement from the members. The second week, however, Mary was not present, and her friends attributed it to a conflicting activity. When Mary did not appear for the third meeting the leaders questioned the group about her absence, particularly in view of her initial enthusiasm and apparent motivation. Reluctantly the girls explained that Mary, though still fearful of the legal consequences, was continuing to shop-lift with the active encouragement of her mother, who relied on the girl's "take" to clothe the family. Shop-lifting was not only endorsed and reinforced by the mother but was the norm of behavior in the family.

The consequences of the client's behavior—even when that behavior appears illogical and self-defeating to the worker—may be more reinforcing than aversive for the client, and the client may perceive no need for change.

In order to arouse some anxiety as a stimulus for change the client may need to be exposed to a credible source concerning the problem at issue. The following example illustrates how this can be used:

A 7-year-old Native American girl was referred to the school social worker because she did not speak in class, was withdrawn, and was having academic problems as the result. Since her parents knew she could speak well at home, their perception was that the school difficulty was not a problem but represented the imposition of the white values of the school and the worker. They responded by frequently keeping the child out of school so that she would not be exposed to this pressure, and the absenteeism further exacerbated the problem.

The worker consulted with a Native American social worker of the same tribe as the family who was able to gain the parents' confidence and interpret to them the school's interest in the child as well as give them a sensitive description of the child's social and academic difficulties in such a way that the parents were willing to work collaboratively with school personnel to deal with the problem.

The importance of the outsider here was that he was someone who had the respect of the Indian community and shared the parents' values, yet could present information to them in a manner that was non-threatening and credible; moreover, his role was such that the information aroused enough anxiety in the parents to persuade them that some help was necessary without overwhelming them and provoking them to withdraw completely.

Another approach to affective arousal is to actively involve the client's imagination to enable him/her to envision alternatives to the status quo. The device may be as simple as asking, "How would you like things to be?" Working with a family, for example, as the worker asks each member to describe how each would like things to be in the family, the various alternatives described can stimulate some recognition of mutual dissatisfaction and the need for change. By verbally "trying on" new behaviors a client may be able to anticipate the consequences of change. In addition, the accurate perception of alternatives is a powerful stimulus to discontent with current behavior, particularly with clients whose life experiences may have exposed them to much defeat and frustration.

Still another approach when lack of anxiety seems to be thwarting the change effort is the gentle confrontation of dissonance when, for example, the clients' behavior appears to be in conflict with their expressed values. Frequently abusive parents will verbalize that they love their children and have no need for help. Here the worker may validate the parents' love for the child, accept their inevitable anger as parents, yet recognize with the clients how this anger results in consequences no loving parent desires. This accredits the parents' positive intentions and their competencies while acknowledging their negative feelings and behavior; the parents may then be able to face the possibility that without help they may again abuse the child.

When rationalization, denial, projection, or well-intentioned attempts of others to protect the client from the consequences of his/her destructive behavior have enabled the person to fend off any anxiety that would mobilize change, confrontation may have to be more direct —less gentle but equally supportive—to challenge these defenses and thus arouse anxiety. The most dramatic and compelling examples come from alcoholism treatment, where for many years the prevailing treatment philosophy assumed that the alcoholic had to "reach the bottom" with personal crises before he/she could respond to treatment. Like any problem characterized by strong defense against anxiety, alcoholism blunts the victim to the impact of the crises he/she creates, as does the intervention of family and other professionals. Furthermore, when family and professionals are forced to wait out the "natural" progression of the problem, the physical, emotional, and social damage may be irreparable. The essence of confrontation, then, requires that the client experience the full consequences of his/her behavior and the consequences of the crises he/she creates. The social worker may need to help family and friends give up their "helping" or "buffer" role with the alcoholic. The alcoholic's wife may refuse to call her husband's employer to request sick leave when he is hung over, and thus the need to deal directly with the aftermath of a binge may raise the alcoholic's anxiety about his drinking. Direct treatment may also include those closest, most significant, and most interested in the alcoholic—persons who will confront him or her with specific concrete facts about the problem. This must be done in such a way that his or her acts are attacked but the human being's dignity and sense of support are enhanced.

Mr. Lane had been attending Alanon and seeing a social worker for six months to help him deal with his wife's alcoholism. Although he felt that he had made significant changes, Ms. Lane continued to drink heavily, was verbally abusive, and subject to frequent outbursts of rage alternating with depression. Frequently absent from work for "stomach problems," Ms. Lane's job performance as a CPA was suffering, though she reassured herself of her competence and devotion to the job with long hours and boasts of new accounts. Mr. Lane finally admitted to the social worker that while he feared for his wife's emotional and physical health he and the children could not continue to live under such conditions.

The social worker met with Mr. Lane, 14-year-old Jody, 16-year-old Todd, and Ms. Lane's employer and helped them construct a list of things that had happened to each of them as the result of Ms. Lane's drinking, confining the list to her actions while drunk. After two preparatory sessions, the five of them met with Ms. Lane and, assuring her of their concern for her, each of them in turn confronted her with examples of her behavior. Jody described a slumber party at their home at which her mother went into a rage, insulting and berating the girls for leaving their snack dishes un-washed. Todd recalled his scholastic awards banquet when his mother was too drunk to attend the long-awaited event. Her employer confronted her with several errors which had cost the company several accounts. Initially angry, defensive, and threatening to leave, Ms. Lane finally broke into sobs as family members assured her of their love and urged her to get help. She agreed to enter the hospital, whose program also included help for the family.

As Ms. Lane was forced into a position in which she was starkly but supportively confronted with the reality of the problem and the need for change, her anxiety overwhelmed the strong defenses she had erected—defenses which without direct confrontation might otherwise have been breeched only by a dramatic and perhaps tragic crisis.

At times it may be difficult to distinguish between the manifesta-tions of excessive anxiety and insufficient emotional arousal. With abu-sive parents passive resistance may indicate immobilizing guilt, remorse, or fear, in which case the instrumental goal for enhancing motivation would be to reduce the anxiety; on the other hand, this behavior may indicate lack of concern, for which the motivational strat-egy would be arousing anxiety. Since excessive anxiety is observed with much greater frequency among our clientele, we suggest that anx-iety reduction may be the strategy of first choice, although we would note that the techniques for anxiety arousal presented here can be ex-pected to stimulate mild rather than overwhelming anxiety and thus may be used effectively when the assessment of anxiety level is ambig-uous.

Enhancing Goal States

While an optimal level of anxiety is necessary to provide the "push" toward change, discomfort must be balanced with hope. Stot-land (as quoted in Maluccio, 1979a:64) has defined hope as "the per-ceived possibility of attaining a goal," and it is this goal-directedness of motivation that we shall focus on in examining the role of goals in client motivation.

In addition to energizing behavior, motives have directional prop-erties and guide a person toward particular end states or goals. Moti-vation is thus by definition goal-directed, even if there exist several different or competing goals. For Kagan, "a goal is a cognitive represen-tation of future events which will make one feel better, and a motive is the cognitive representation of the end state" (Kagan, 1972:51). Thus the statement "he is motivated" is an incomplete concept until the statement is amended to include an indication of directionality: The concept must therefore state, "He is motivated toward x (y, and/or z)."

White (1959) opened a new chapter in motivation theory when he recognized that among the goals that make people "feel better" is the process of seeking and conquering challenges that are optimal for them —challenges they can handle, the end state of which is feelings of competence in dealing effectively with the environment. Determining the optimal level of challenge for each client is a critical judgment the worker must make in concert with the client in the process of establishing goals that will enhance motivation.

For the worker and client to engage in a collaborative change effort there must be congruity of goals and direction. It is possible that sufficient anxiety may exist to motivate the client toward change; however, if effective goal-setting is not achieved between client and worker, movement may take the direction of a goal that the worker sees as nonconstructive or one that may compound the problem. It is thus necessary not only to mobilize an optimal level of anxiety but also to assure that the goals are desirable to the client as future events "which will make one feel better."

Thus another element of the transactions between client and worker that must be examined when resistance is encountered is the direction of the change effort. Lack of motivation may be attributable to the client's belief that change may create more problems than it would relieve. Change always entails some risk and expenditure of energy, and the risks to the status quo may be regarded as requiring more effort than the potential outcomes merit. In short, the goals may not be desirable, or they may be incompatible with other goals in the client's life.

Apparent resistance may also reflect confusion regarding the direction of the change effort if goals are ambiguous and ill-defined, or if client and worker do not perceive the same goals of change. Maluccio (1979a) reiterates a theme that pervades the literature on outcome studies of treatment: In his research he also found that clients' goals tended to be couched in terms of solutions to specific "problems in living," while social workers were concerned with overall "cures" or comprehensive changes in the individual's situation or personality structure. Diffuse, global goals are not likely to provide an "optimal challenge" that can satisfy the client's need for feelings of competence, nor can they provide an "awareness of potential satisfaction" that energizes behavior (Deci, 1975:106).

To overcome this source of resistance it is essential that the goals of change be mutually defined between client and worker, clear to each, achievable, and, above all, desirable to the client. The starting point must be a problem the client perceives as distressing (even if this does not appear to the worker to be the primary difficulty). Furthermore, the worker cannot assume that the client is the problem or the target for change. A juvenile client, for example, may feel that his major problem is "getting people off my back," regardless of the behavior that led to his referral and regardless of the fact that his own behavior may be perceived by others as provocative. Using the client's perspective as the basis for establishing a contract for the change effort, the worker may help the adolescent select a person with whom he wants to avoid trouble and formulate a reasonable short-term goal, such as avoiding confrontation with a specific teacher for a specified period—a day or a week—a contract that can be amended, extended, and shaped to accommodate not only the changing needs but the changing perceptions of the youthful client.

Two important aspects of this strategy enable the worker to mobilize competence motivation in the service of change. First, the process of shared decision-making regarding the goal meets the client's need for a sense of self-determination. By being involved in the setting of the goals, the client sees them coming largely from himself and more easily incorporates them. As a result his chances for success are enhanced since the problem is one he has helped to define rather than one that has been thrust upon him. Equally important is the feeling of competence resulting from success; the achievement of goals that provide immediate satisfaction demonstrates to the client that change is possible and rewarding, and it lays the groundwork for subsequent success, thus instilling hope. It is not enough for the client to achieve the goal, however; the resulting rewards must be perceived by the client as satisfying.

Using the client's needs for a sense of competency in the change effort requires that the worker be aware not only of how the client responds to him/her but what motivates the client outside the worker–client relationship. Identifying what the client persistently and recurrently is engaging in will help the worker understand what motivations are important in the client's life. Kilguss (1974) describes the use of a passive client's preoccupation with soap operas as a means of becoming involved in a relationship with the client and relating the client's interests to more satisfying means of achieving what she was seeking through television. Observing abusive parents, the worker may discover that they are strongly motivated to achieve companionship and emotional gratification from the abused child but retaliate physically when these needs are frustrated. The worker must not bypass the parent to rescue the child but instead must work with these needs, helping the parent to achieve them in legitimate ways.

The following case illustrates the effective use of existing motives and competencies in the client's repertoire:

Nine-year-old Clarence's resistance to change in his school behavior was legendary by the time the third social worker in as many years was brought in on the case. The pattern had been set—fighting on the playground, clowning in the classroom—and the consequences were equally predictable: His classmates observed with a mixture of mild annoyance and awe, and the teacher, after repeated reprimands and threats, marched Clarence to the principal's office, where the latter earnestly lectured the young recalcitrant on his responsibilities and meanwhile sought to lend an understanding ear to the "disturbed" child. Clarence's academic work was none the worse for these forays to the office, but teacher and classmates were left harried and distracted, with Clarence daily receiving the preponderance of his teacher's energy and attention.

Efforts to change the boy's behavior through individual counseling had failed, as had repeated conferences with parents, provoking demands for intensive therapy for the boy and his parents—a costly alternative, and one that was unpalatable to the parents.

Analysis of the available rewards for Clarence revealed that the only reaction more desirable to him than the approbation of his peers was the undivided attention of the principal, which was assured him at least once daily by virtue of his disruptive behavior. The daily trip to the office appeared indeed to be "motivating" Clarence to maintain the behavior it had been devised to eliminate. The source of Clarence's resistance to change thus became a motivating factor when the trip to the office became contingent on the boy's avoidance of playground fighting and classroom antics, as Clarence began to earn the right to the principal's attentions and subsequently became an office aide after his disruptive behavior virtually disappeared.

The challenge of using goals effectively is that client and worker must assure that they promise a payoff that will exceed the costs of change. If the client is to be willing to expend effort in the process of change, the worker must have an understanding of the costs that this entails for the client—what he or she will be giving up when change occurs.

A technique that may be effective when the client is conflicted over the potential costs of change makes use of paradoxical intention to diminish the threat. The client may be requested *not* to change but to consider what changes might be desirable if one decided to change. Validating the client's right to remain the same may activate the client's motivation toward self-determination in seeking a reasonable challenge, allowing the client to begin shaping goals without external pressure to change—and, indeed, with affirmation of one's competency. Paradoxically, by creating the expectation that no change will occur, the client may in fact initiate change.

Referred to the social worker in a family clinic for behavior problems of recent origin with her 8-year-old son, Juan, Ms. Chavez quickly moved to the stress she was personally experiencing, reciting a year-long series of major and minor crises: her hospitalization after a car accident; the birth of her fourth child; her mother's serious illness; the death of her father; and the marital problems of her numerous friends and relatives in which she had become emotionally involved due ot her inability to say "no" to their demands on her time. She felt herself at the mercy of the telephone, constantly reacting to the needs of others and unable to express the anger and resentment that was building as she increasingly felt out of control of her own life. It appeared to the worker that the entire family was suffering and that much of the turmoil revolved around Ms. Chavez but that it would be difficult for her to relinquish any of the responsibilities that she had assumed without considerable guilt and conflict.

Since Ms. Chavez had ostensibly come regarding concerns with her child and indeed had already begun to recognize the interplay of the family stress with Juan's problem, the worker felt it was important to determine the direction in which Ms. Chavez wanted to go in treatment. He thus asked her to change nothing over the next week but to consider what she would change in her life if she should decide to change.

The following week Ms. Chavez grinned sheepishly as she announced she had begun making some changes over the past few days, having decided that if she were going to take care of her family, she was going to have to take care of herself first. She began by reviewing the baby's sleeping habits as well as other family members' needs for her time—and when they could do without her. Within two days she had found an hour a day for herself by reducing the amount of time she was available to her extended family and giving up some duties she discovered other family members could do; she had also rearranged some household duties to give her more time with the older children, whose company she had enjoyed before.

As she related the excitement of exerting some control over her life and the enjoyment of the activities in which she had indulged herself that week, Ms. Chavez recognized some of the feelings and events that might make it difficult to maintain the changes. It was these issues that the worker and client dealt with in several subsequent sessions; but the feelings of competence achieved by her successful and self-directed efforts toward the goals she had set for herself served as the impetus for other changes.

It is not enough for the client to achieve success; it must be recognized as such by the client, the worker, and others in the client's environment to satisfy the client's need to feel effective and competent. As the worker finds strengths in the client and engineers opportunities to use and build on them, we focus attention "not on exploring pathology, but on finding, enhancing and rewarding competence," as Minuchin (1970:129) suggests in writing of work with "hard-to-reach" families.

Removal of Practical Barriers

We have considered affective and directional factors involved in the process of client motivation, and now we turn to environmental or field factors that must be taken into consideration in analyzing resistance and/or attempting to enhance motivation. Even when the worker has skillfully worked to assure that the client's anxiety is at an optimal level and that the goals are highly desirable to the client, the change effort may fail. The reasons may be very mundane, yet often practical barriers to change are interpreted by social workers in terms of psychological resistance.

Kogan (1957) found that workers tended to attribute client discontinuance in a large majority of cases to lack of interest or resistance, yet about half of the former clients attributed their discontinuance to reality-based factors—inability to maintain contact due to distance, childcare responsibilities, work, or even the improvement of the problem. Kogan (1957:236) consequently concluded that "granting the possibility of rationalization or reluctance on the part of many clients to express negative attitudes, workers tended to underestimate the importance of reality-based factors on discontinuance."

During the heyday of client participation and input in social services in the 1960s, social workers and helping professionals turned their attentions to many of the practical barriers to the involvement of the poor and disadvantaged in service delivery. Although we now tend to relegate such issues to administrators and social planners, the individual practitioner should be aware of the very real practical barriers posed by work conficts, transportation problems, and the financial costs of service. We have long identified clients' needs for services designed to meet their life-styles, schedules, and geographical availability, yet most agencies continue with nine-to-five business-as-usual and continue to interpret client dropout or complaints about service delivery arrangements as resistance to therapeutic involvement.

Failure of the change effort may also result when a client lacks the resources or when his/her repertoire of behavior does not include the skills required for change. The social worker may fail to analyze the skills required to effect the change. Clients may agree to provide more nutritious meals for their children but lack the knowledge to discriminate between a well-balanced meal and a poor one, the experience to know how to prepare unfamiliar foods, or the persuasiveness and patience to interest reluctant children in something different from their usual fare.

Another practical source of resistance may be perceptual distortion of the worker's communication, which can occur in a number of ways. All communication between human beings is fraught with difficulty and uncertainty, as Luigi Pirandello has said:

> And how can we understand each other if in the words that I say I put the meaning and value of things the way they are inside me, while who listens to them will inevitably perceive them with the meaning they have for him, in terms of the world as he has it inside himself. [Pirandello, as quoted in Smaldino, 1975:333]

The uncertainty that afflicts all communication can be aggravated by particular problems as well. Pathological distortion by the client is a commonly cited difficulty, but cultural differences, ethnic and class cleavages, or the worker's use of an unfamiliar language system may make it difficult or impossible for worker and client to reach a common understanding of the problem at hand or the means of dealing with it. Even within the same cultural or ethnic group the client—out of deference to the worker who may be perceived as socially superior or an authority figure—may superficially conform to the worker's expectations despite disagreement or even lack of understanding of what is entailed.

Several techniques for dealing with practical barriers to motivated behavior have been described in connection with other strategies, such as setting specific, immediate goals. Here we reiterate their importance in removing some of the most immediate barriers to change. Providing needed food, clothing, or shelter may not only imbue hope and enhance the credibility of the worker but also make it possible to focus on other problems. Parents may evince more concern for an acting-out child once they are assured that the family will not be evicted from their home and that the children will have clothing for school.

Often it is possible to use the strengths of a client and supports within the environment to provide immediate help with practical problems.

A social worker in a neglect case who had made no gains in engaging an apathetic mother discovered among the rubble and filth of an otherwise bare home a pile of rags and sat down with the client to begin hooking a rug. With each visit the rug became a means of mobilizing the depressed mother into action and fashioning a floor cover on which the children could play. Perhaps more important, neighbors who frequently wandered into the home became involved in the project. While working on the rug, the worker, the mother, and whoever happened to be on hand talked of things that concerned them, often their children; as improvements began to occur in the family, they were supported and encouraged by the neighbors.

In general, the importance of meeting clients where they are, understanding their motivations and perceptions, and working with them and with available support systems toward mutually determined goals cannot be emphasized too strongly. Here again, clear communication is essential, for not only may it reduce anxiety but it is vital to establishing trust and as a basis for any contract for change between worker and client.

To transcend communication barriers, the traditional verbal interview format may have to be abandoned or augmented, as in the above case. Levine (1965) has demonstrated how playing games with a family may be used for communicating in terms that are more effective and comprehensible to the clients. Role play and behavioral rehearsal, too, provide a chance to check out verbal communication, to uncover problems the client may not be able to articulate, and to identify and deal with practical impediments to change while providing a chance to try out unfamiliar behaviors he/she might otherwise resist. Above all, constant clarification, restatement, empathic listening and rechecking perceptions with the client throughout the change process help to diminish the practical barriers that often produce resistance to change. As suggested by Oxley,[5] these techniques are especially useful in work with involuntary clients, but they are often appropriate and necessary with voluntary clients as well.

Conclusion

In approaching motivation as a transactional process we have indicated that in the assessment of existing motivation and resistance the worker should answer the following questions regarding the client in relation to both his/her life situation and the helping process:

1. What is the *level of anxiety* regarding the problem(s), the services, or the relationship with the worker, and what are the specific *sources* of anxiety or lack of anxiety?
2. How does the client perceive the *consequences* of achieving the goals of the change effort?
3. What are the *effective motivators* in the client's life at this time?
4. What *practical factors* might impede change?

These questions are appropriate, even essential, not only at the inception of the change effort but throughout the change process, particularly when the worker encounters apparent disinterest, failed appointments, hostility on the part of the client *or* worker, or failure to follow through with agreed-upon actions. Neither the sources of resistance nor the strategies for dealing with them are mutually exclusive, for resistance may result from several sources simultaneously and may require strategies that deal with each. Conversely, a single technique may mobilize motivation in more than one way; for example, setting immediate, achievable goals according to the client's perception of the problem and its solution may not only reduce anxiety by enhancing one's sense of competence and control but may enhance the attractiveness of the goal itself.

Approaching motivation as a process in which the worker engages with the client suggests a more aggressive, proactive role for the social worker than previous conceptualizations based on accepting the available motivation the client brings to treatment as a predictor of outcomes. However, by viewing the worker's ability to motivate as more important than the client's preexisting level of motivation, we may find that rather than scapegoating the "unmotivated" or "resistant" client we may be tempted to attribute every treatment failure to the worker's inability to motivate the client. Not only would this be simplistic, but it would also ignore several salient practical and ethical issues.

The worker must confront these issues in determining how far to go in efforts to enhance, redirect, or mobilize motivation and in deciding when he/she has the right and even the responsibility to impose himself/herself on the potential client. In many cases, the worker may have the option of mobilizing the motivation of others who can make changes in the environment or provide a needed service on behalf of the client (cf. Maluccio, 1979a:194–95).

The ethical principle of self-determination has great philosophical appeal, bolstered by competence motivation theory that, as we have noted, recognizes the intrinsic strivings of persons for a sense of self-determination. The failure of clients to respond to change efforts or to treatment is often construed as evidence that they have exercised self-determination. Miller (1968) has even argued that social workers should get out of the business of dealing with involuntary clients, contending that persons have the right to "make a shambles out of their lives."

Yet from both an ethical and a theoretical perspective we regard this position as untenable—ethically, in that we are committed to the mutual welfare of individuals and society, and theoretically, in that the interdependence of persons makes it difficult for an individual or group to act destructively, even self-destructively, without injury to others in their social networks. Furthermore, "making a shambles" of one's life is not likely to satisfy the individual's intrinsic need to feel competent and effective in his/her transactions with the environment.

Thus an ethical dilemma confronts the social worker, who must determine what degree of persistence and effort are justified in attempting to motivate the client. In addition to the questions posed above for assessing available motivation and resistance, we must add a fifth question: What are the consequences of no change? Although current theories of human behavior are limited in their predictive value, social workers must make the best judgment possible regarding the risks of no change. Obviously most professionals would deal tenaciously, even aggressively, with clients who present an imminent suicidal or homicidal threat. Less clearcut, but perhaps equally compelling to the responsible social worker, are situations that represent a potential threat of irreparable physical or emotional harm to the client or to others in his/her environment. Here we contend that the practitioner has both the right and the responsibility not to change the client or to demand or coerce change but to pursue attempts to motivate the client to change by assessing the sources of resistance and shaping intervention efforts to enhance motivation.

The worker must have the ethical astuteness and professional judgment to know when one must reach out to the client and the confidence that one has the right to provide help or to offer assistance assertively. One must also be confident enough to question oneself, to recognize that the worker does not have the answers for the client but must struggle with him/her to find a direction that, at minimum, does not threaten the well-being of others. This means recognizing that even the most "unmotivated" client has a logic and coherence to his/her behavior, and the worker must strive to find that logic. This is not easy work, nor does it yield quick results. Virginia Satir has indicated that the worker must be "actively patient and patiently active." [6] Following this slogan requires not only that the worker have confidence, patience, and empathy, but also strong collegial and organizational support.

Social work more than any other profession is faced with the delicate task of reconciling the needs of the individual with the demands of the larger society. To paraphrase Gartner's (1970) conclusion regarding services to the poor, perhaps it is time to stop asserting that it is the unmotivated who fail to use our services and to recognize that it is we as professionals, quick to categorize and stereotype, who must change. By adapting our services to the needs and qualities of people coming to our attention, we can be more effective in mobilizing motivation toward competence development.

Notes

1. While we concur with Pincus and Minahan (1973) that a "client system" does not exist until the person or system has accepted help, we will use the term "client" in the broad sense to refer to potential as well as actual clients.
2. The interventive model is suggested in part by Ripple, Alexander, and Polemis (1964), who have associated motivation with the achievement of a "discomfort–hope balance": sufficient discomfort to exert pressure for action and sufficient hope to channel the pressure into action. The challenge for the practitioner is to make the discomfort–hope balance function in day-to-day practice.
3. See Golan (Chapter 4 in this volume) for further discussion of intervention in crisis situations.
4. Chapter 3 in this volume.
5. Chapter 12 in this volume.
6. Workshop by Virginia Satir, Dallas, Texas (1975).

CHAPTER 3

Cognition and Social Work Practice: Some Implications of Attribution and Concept Attainment Theories

Ronald C. Fleming

Emphasis on the role of cognition in human behavior is a prominent feature of the life model and competence-oriented social work practice (Maluccio, Chapter 1). By "comprehending the role of the intellect in adaptation and in coping, the social worker . . . is free to engage the cognitive functions in mutual learning–teaching activities with clients as appropriate" (Germain, 1975:18).

In this chapter we will discuss the cognitive processes of attribution and concept attainment and their relation to coping and adaptation. Attribution refers to the process by which the individual perceives and ascribes cause and effect relationships (Storms and McCaul, 1976). Concept attainment involves the process by which an individual acquires new information about—and understanding of—the relationships and interplay among persons, events, and objects. Concept attainment also includes understanding the forces that serve to maintain old concepts (Bruner, 1973).

The process of coping and adapting suggests that every individual will experience a variety of crises or problems-in-living, especially at key transition points in development. Each such crisis or problem presents both a potential threat and an opportunity to enhance one's self-esteem and sense of competence (cf. Golan, Chapter 4). The individual's ability to respond creatively to such demands is crucial to the adaptational process.

While many complex forces interact to determine the outcome of the adaptational process, cognitive functions are among the most important. In particular, functions related to the reception, storage, organization, and manipulation of information about the environment play an integral role in adaptive behavior. Whether it be a crisis situation or not, the ability to collect and process relevant information in large measure determines the individual's ability to generate successful responses. Attribution theory and concept attainment theory shed considerable light on how individuals gather, select, and process information. They also clarify how this information becomes transformed into sets of ideas and tendencies to respond.

As this chapter will suggest, these theories enable the social worker to appreciate more deeply the cognitive processes involved in coping and adaptation. After briefly discussing the relationship of cognition to adaptation, we will present the main features of attribution and concept attainment and then consider specific practice implications.

Cognition and Adaptation

The role of cognition in adaptation has been observed for some time. For instance, ever since Freudian psychology postulated the relationship between the perception of danger and anxiety, there has been considerable inquiry into the relevance of cognitive processes to emotional and adaptive behavior. Many current theorists have taken the position that cognitive processes have instrumental value in determining both the quality of the emotional reactions to problems-in-living and the effectiveness of coping responses (Lazarus, 1974; Kovacs and Beck, 1978). Also, treatment modalities such as Rational Emotive Therapy (Ellis, 1962) and Rational Stage Directed Therapy (Lantz, 1978) rely heavily upon cognitive processes.

Adaptation has been described by White (1976) as a striving for an acceptable compromise in interaction with the environment. In White's view, a successful transaction involves the strategic utilization of information, internal organization, and autonomy. Information includes the immediate cognitive field as well as remote sources of data. People are not necessarily limited to immediately available information; they may have access to additional resources such as family, friends, experts, and reading material. The ability to secure and process information is largely a cognitive process and is necessary for adaptive behavior. Internal organization includes maintaining both physical and emotional balance and freedom from serious impairment. Self-esteem is a vital part of the internal organization of the individual in that its disruption can seriously hamper adaptive efforts. Autonomy involves the freedom to act and make decisions.

The ability to cope with the demands of significant life crises underscores the importance of information gathering and processing. Crisis theorists point out that, in general, people "operate in consistent patterns and in equilibrium with their environment, solving problems with minimal delay by habitual mechanisms and reactions" (Moos and Tsu, 1976:13). In a life transition or crisis, however, such customary means may fail to be effective, creating some degree of personal tension and disorganization (Golan, Chapter 4 in this volume). Among the many factors that influence the effectiveness of adaptive behavior in such situations are two predominantly cognitive processes: (1) the quest for and review of pertinent information and learning the nature of existing constraints, and (2) reducing problems into workable pieces and resolving them sequentially (Moos, 1976).

Cognition, then, affects adaptation in several ways. First, the perception of a situation or series of events influences the degree and nature of the emotional and adaptational response. Second, through the securing, storaging, and processing of information, cognitive functions enhance the person's adaptive strivings. Finally, cognitive functions also influence the individual's ability to respond to the special demands of a crisis situation by reducing problems into manageable proportions and generating sets of ideas and tendencies to respond.

Attribution Theory

The underlying premise of attribution theory is that the perception of causality influences behavior (Mahoney, 1974). Among the important features of this theory are: (1) locus of control; (2) misattribution; (3) self-attribution; and (4) labeling. We will first consider these features separately in order to highlight their unique qualities, and then discuss the interplay among them.

Locus of Control

In the perception of cause and effect, human beings believe that events are either contingent upon or influenced by their own behavior (i.e., internal control), or not contingent upon their own behavior or outside their influence (i.e., external control). Persons who perceive a problem as externally controlled will tend to: (1) experience more anxiety; (2) have more difficulty in responding effectively; (3) develop a sense of helplessness; and (4) be less likely to seek or benefit from therapy (Mahoney, 1974).

Mrs. Gray was a 55-year-old married, employed, woman with two daughters and a son. She came to a mental health clinic after a protracted period of "suffering," feeling that, although "it probably would not help, I had to talk to someone." Living with her were an alcoholic husband; an unemployed, inactive son; an employed daughter; and an acting-out daughter in high school. Mrs. Gray felt depressed, helpless, and unable to do anything about her husband's drinking, her daughter's acting-out, or her son's inactivity.

After the initial assessment, the caseworker focused on helping Mrs. Gray to identify areas of her home life over which she did, in fact, have some control or influence. He then helped her to begin changing what she could in each of these areas. The first one involved her husband. Rather than merely tolerating his drinking, Mrs. Gray established clear limits with him as to the conditions under which they could continue to live together. Next, she required the employed daughter to contribute financially to the family if she wished to continue living there. The high school age daughter was pushed to get a job in order to pay for her clothes and extra items that she might want.

As might be expected from a systemic viewpoint, change in one family member precipitated changes in other members. Mrs. Gray began to take an active role in her family life. Her husband entered counseling with her and also went to Alcoholics Anonymous. The employed daughter began to contribute to the family financially as well as personally. The high school age daughter started to work parttime and her acting-out behaviors diminished. And the inactive son moved out of the house.

This example suggests that as long as Mrs. Gray perceived these interwoven events as beyond her control or influence (i.e., externally controlled) she was unable to mobilize her own resources; consequently, she experienced considerable distress and a sense of helplessness, which reduced her motivation to change (cf. Moore-Kirkland, Chapter 2 in this volume). Feeling there was little use in discussing matters she did not control, she put off seeking help for nearly a year. As she began to understand her impact upon events that concerned her, she became more active, setting and enforcing limits in her relationships with family members. As her self-reliance and sense of competence grew, Mrs. Gray increasingly attempted new behaviors on her own without the social worker's knowledge or input. Eventually, although some problems remained, she terminated counseling, emphasizing that "I can handle it now."

Misattribution

Misattribution refers to the attribution process gone awry: An observed effect is ascribed to a source that, in reality, did not cause it. While this process probably occurs untold numbers of times in a person's's life, misattribution takes on special significance if the misperceived cause has emotional relevance to the individual. For instance, two persons begin to experience identical symptoms of dizziness, headache, nausea, and flushing. One of them believes this is due to his having been exposed to some mildly noxious fumes and expects the feelings to pass. The other one assumes that his sensations are evidence of a degenerative psychiatric condition. Clearly the latter person will be more likely to experience pronounced distress that in itself may serve to further the original symptoms (Mahoney, 1974).

As this example illustrates, it is crucial to understand how the client perceives his own situation, especially with reference to the cause/effect process. The expected subsequent actions of the person who thought that he had inhaled some mildly noxious fumes would be quite different from those of the one who assumed that he was experiencing the early symptoms of a degenerative psychiatric condition. Although the cause may have been misattributed, the resulting conclusion will still have a pronounced effect on the individual's behavior.

Self-attribution

A person's self-view has long been known to affect the range and quality of his behavior. One's self-image has many components, one of the most important being the so-called self-statements or self-attributions. An individual who makes certain self-attributions and experiences negative (ie., unpleasant) emotional states as a result will exacerbate existing subjective distress (anxiety). Kovacs and Beck (1978) have shown that depressed people are especially prone to such cycles of thinking and behavior; that is, anticipating the worst, they usually experience it.

Susan Morse was a 24-year-old single woman who sought counseling at a university health service because she was not "doing well in life." She had a stable responsible job, which she had held for six years. She felt that she was not successful in anything and was experiencing a fair amount of guilt and anxiety. Her self-descriptions were filled with statements that began with "I should . . ." or "I'm not . . ." She would complete the sentences with some activity or personal quality.

When pressed for detail as to her concerns, it became evident that Miss

Morse's self-statements were comments she had internalized from various "significant others." For instance, as she had taken similar statements made by her parents and made them self-statements, her anxiety increased. The incongruity between the self-statements and her actual goals caused her considerable guilt and led to her depressed mood. The intervention process emphasized exploration of the dissonance between the self-statements and her actual goals. As Miss Morse began to understand what *she* felt was important for herself, she was able to surrender some of the negative self-attributions (e.g., "I'm not ambitious"; "I should want a different job") and substitute others that were more congruent with her interests and drives.

Labeling

For some clients the self-attribution process may overlap the labeling process (Merton, 1959). For instance, the juvenile who perceives himself as different and ascribes socially undesirable feelings or attitudes to himself may eventually encounter confirming feedback from those around him. Teachers and administrators may act toward him as if he were different, thus exacerbating the original problem. In time the youth may become labeled delinquent, predelinquent, or emotionally disturbed, touching off yet another cycle of self-defeating behavior.

As another example, the alcoholic person typically has an intense internal awareness and self-consciousness about his behavior prior to the inception of the recovery process. Such persons, however, are plagued by numerous self-attributions that interfere with their ability to seek or benefit from therapy. They may view themselves as worthless, despicable "drunks" unable to control their own behavior. Often they encounter the further damage of the labeling process, which historically has stigmatized alcoholics as people who cannot and will not help themselves. As Jones concludes in his discussion of the interplay between self-attributions and the labeling process:

> The important point for our purposes is that persons who communicate a given situational and/or self-definition for themselves have, in effect, delineated both what we can expect from them in the situation and what they expect from those with whom they are interacting. [Jones, 1977:117]

Overview on Attribution

The main features of the attribution process thus far have been considered as discrete entities. However, there is considerable interplay among them, as reflected in situations involving the often-encountered "helpless" client. Such a person usually has had numerous encounters with agencies or treatment centers, but seems unable to learn from them. Often he describes these previous contacts as a source of frustration and dissatisfaction with bureaucratic services, but he also blames himself and stresses some failure on his part.

The "helpless" individual exemplifies features of the attribution process in several ways. First, such a client perceives most events as outside his locus of control, thus seeing little usefulness in attempting to involve himself in interactions that he apparently cannot control. Second, he attributes to an internal source the undesirable consequences encountered, such as anxiety and social criticism, typically feeling that he is at fault. Third, the person tends to misattribute events. He feels that he did not get the job because of some undesirable quality in himself rather than because it was already filled. Finally, the "helpless" person (should this posture become protracted or take on social significance) invariably is labeled in some way by others. This process is often cyclical and repetitive (Kovacs and Beck, 1978; Storms and McCaul, 1974).

Concept Maintenance and Attainment Theory

In attempting to help the client modify dysfunctional beliefs and consequent behavior, the social worker should be aware of the relative strength of the beliefs or tendencies and ways of facilitating more adaptive responses. The work of Jerome Bruner (1973) has special significance in this regard; his formulations in the area of concept maintenance and attainment theory provide insight into the dynamic process by which beliefs are maintained and developed and can help the social worker to engage the client more effectively in a directed problem-solving effort.

Concept attainment theory is concerned with the cognitive processes by which an individual develops sets of ideas or hypotheses about the relationships and interplay among persons, events, and objects as well as the forces that support these ideas. For the purposes of our discussion "sets of ideas" or "hypotheses" may be defined as a highly generalized state of readiness to respond selectively to classes of events in the environment. A hypothesis is inferred . . . from the presence of certain antecedent and consequent events" (Bruner, 1973:43).

The development of these ideas is closely related to attribution. The perception of causality will greatly influence how an individual comes to understand a sequence of events or interactions. While attributional processes affect the manner in which causality is perceived, concept maintenance and attainment processes affect the way such perceptions become transformed into "hypotheses" or a readiness to respond.

We will now discuss the theory of concept maintenance, which delineates those forces that support the maintenance of tendencies to respond in selective ways to interactions with the environment. We will then elaborate on the related theory of concept attainment, which describes the factors that encourage the acquisition of new ideas or tendencies to respond.

Concept Maintenance

As explained by Bruner (1973), the maintenance of a concept and its related behavioral response is associated with the following variables: (1) frequency of past confirmation; (2) number of available alternatives; (3) cognitive consequences of change; (4) motivational consequences of change; and (5) social consequences of change.

Frequency of Past Confirmation.   The past experiences of a person (e.g., someone who was abused as a child) are essentially beyond modification or alteration by any therapeutic process. If an individual has had repeated experiential confirmation of a belief or behavior, modification becomes that much more difficult. He may have habitually misperceived his experience or it may have been misrepresented to him.

Number of Available Alternatives.   A common activity of social workers involves working with clients to increase the number of alternative behaviors available to them. Frequently clients feel trapped and without acceptable choices. The helping process serves to encourage the recognition and development of additional responses. When few alternatives appear to be available, people tend to cling more tenaciously to them, even though they may not be effective. Sometimes an individual who believes that few options are open to him will feel helpless and frustrated in dealing with his environment.

Cognitive Consequences of Change.   Dysfunctional beliefs which are substantially interrelated with other beliefs or behaviors are particularly difficult to change. When the attributional process proves faulty, it is rare that the misconception occurs in isolation. For example, persons who perceive certain events as externally controlled tend to generalize this perception to numerous other events or observations. The degree to which blurring or generalization occurs will affect the relative difficulty that the social worker will encounter in attempting to encourage change in certain dysfunctional beliefs and the development of adaptive responses.

Motivational Consequences of Change. Many times the dysfunctional belief or behavior will directly or indirectly serve to meet certain emotional needs; that is, provide "secondary gain." In such cases, change becomes very difficult, especially if the client sees few other means to meet those emotional needs. The social worker needs to realize to what extent the given problem behavior has instrumental value in meeting specific emotional needs and try to establish more functional means of meeting them; otherwise the client will be likely to resist change.

Social Consequences of Change. The final variable related to the strength of an hypothesis or belief has to do with the social context. An idea or belief actively supported by significant others or by those perceived as knowledgeable will be more resistant to change than a relatively unsupported belief (Berger and Luckman, 1967). In situations where feedback is unclear and information limited, individuals are especially sensitive to social pressure. The social worker therefore needs to understand the context in which the belief was developed and is currently maintained. For this reason, as well as others, assessing the person within the context of his environment is central to the life model of practice (Maluccio, 1975).

Overview on Concept Maintenance. The relative strength of an hypothesis or tendency to respond that develops as a consequence of an individual's interaction with his environment is proportional to the five variables that have just been described. Regardless of the accuracy of the perceptions and impressions gained through the attributional process, these variables will interact with and determine the strength of the resultant hypothesis or behavioral tendency. The social worker, when engaging the client in a problem-solving process, should therefore understand as clearly as possible the factors that support the dysfunctional beliefs or behaviors and how they arose through the process of attribution.

Concept Attainment

As delineated by Bruner (1973), concept attainment theory recognizes at least five forces that affect the person's ability to attain new concepts or behavioral tendencies: (1) definition of the task; (2) nature of the validation; (3) nature of the instances encountered; (4) consequences of a specific decision; and (5) nature of the imposed restrictions.

These variables interact and influence the relative ease with which the individual is able to adapt to the demands of new situations through new or modified skills. All five have particular relevance to the process of social work intervention, regardless of the workers's preferred treatment modality.

Definition of the Task.   Specific definition of the task is crucial since the client's as well as the practitioner's ability to focus energy and effort will vary with the perceived clarity of the objective. To facilitate the adaptive strivings of the client, the worker should begin by establishing a clear understanding of the task at hand, i.e., the goal of the intervention.

While the process of clarifying the objectives of intervention may seem deceptively simple, the worker and the client often find it difficult to define the problem and the goal of treatment. For this reason, many authors have recognized the value of the contract in social work practice and especially the importance of clarity of purpose (cf. Maluccio and Marlow, 1974; Reid and Epstein, 1972). Involving the client in the process of developing a contract not only facilitates task definition but also helps to clarify the respective roles of worker and client. It also serves to increase the client's sense of autonomy and competence.[1]

Nature of the Validation.   This variable refers to the manner in which new hypotheses or concepts may be tested or confirmed. It includes the ease with which they may be tested as well as the timing; that is, can they be tested immediately, after delay, or only after a series of repetitions? To some extent the clarity of the task will affect the ease with which new behaviors or ideas may be validated. For example, intrapsychic change may be very difficult to measure or validate, whereas a behaviorally oriented measure (e.g., the number of times in a week a couple argues) will be simpler. The validation process will have increased impact if it allows the client to self-monitor rather than have the worker monitor the results. Self-monitoring tends to be more immediate and to have more impact upon the client.

The timing of the validation is quite important. As much as possible, a complex task should be broken down into component sequential parts, so as to provide for increased feedback. Rather than requiring a client to go through a prolonged series of changes with feedback only at the end of the task, the worker should divide the task into parts that ideally may be mastered in their own right, thus providing for more immediate feedback.

Nature of the Instances Encountered.   This factor also has a significant bearing on the outcome of the problem-solving process. The instances or situations may vary with respect to their order, frequency, complexity, number, and familiarity. These variables are often beyond the control of either the social worker or the client.

New approaches or ideas may best be acquired when: (1) the client has fairly frequent encounters with situations in which the new behavior will be affirmed; (2) the encounters come in an orderly fashion so as to allow the client to assess each result individually; (3) the encounters are not too complex, so that the person may be sure that the observed result is the consequence of the new behavior; and (4) the instances encountered are at least partially familiar to the client. The following example illustrates these points.

A middle-aged couple went to a family service agency complaining that their four children were unmanageable; they did not believe that they could exert any influence over their behavior. Among other things, the intervention process provided for specific suggestions about new approaches that the parents might take. The social worker selected a few behaviors which were frequent and likely to respond to new parental input. For instance, one task involved limiting the severity of arguments between brother and sister when the children were playing a game; the parents were asked not to intervene unless they both agreed that it was necessary to do so to avoid violence.

The task was one which would occur with some frequency in this family, providing regular opportunity to test the new behaviors. Also, it was relatively simple and orderly, allowing the parents to judge the result easily and without the likelihood of misattributing it. Finally, none of the suggested behaviors or situations were unfamiliar to the family. This style allowed the parents to learn a new method of response. Their success with this task was generalized to other areas of parenting.

Consequences of a Specific Decision.   The acquisition of a new belief or concept involves two related choices: the decision to surrender the previously held dysfunctional belief and the decision to accept the new, apparently more functional, belief. In the process of making such choices, the person is significantly influenced by what he sees as their possible consequences. The social worker should therefore be sensitive to what the client perceives as the potential risk or cost of a given decision.

The degree of risk perceived by the client will be tempered by the extent to which he has confidence in the social worker and feels some sense of safety in making the decision. For example, a social worker working with the mother in a single-parent family may actively model certain parenting behaviors with the children. This enables the mother to witness the actual consequences of a given decision and encourages her to attempt change. The social worker can be supportive of these efforts, thus increasing the mother's sense of safety, both through verbal support and through his presence. As the mother attempts these new behaviors, her own sense of competence and autonomy is enhanced, often leading to an increased willingness to attempt other new behaviors on her own.

Paralleling the concern that the client has as to the possible consequences of a particular decision are the potential consequences of error. Human beings typically concern themselves not only with the viability of a specific choice but also with the possibility of committing a mistake and making matters worse. For example, the following case situation is typical of those encountered by social workers.

Mrs. Sumner went to an alcoholism counseling service because she was concerned about the excessive, habitual consumption of alcohol by her husband. At the time of the initial interview, there was a history of frequent marital arguments, erratic employment of the husband, and inconsistent care of the children. After considerable discussion of her options, Mrs. Sumner began to feel that she needed to confront her husband directly with her concerns. It was therefore decided that she would invite him to the next session with the worker.

Mr. Sumner was not present at the next scheduled appointment. Mrs. Sumner indicated that she had intended to invite him but decided not to do so. Her reason was that she felt he would not agree and that he would become more unreasonable. Having made this assumption, she decided against raising her concerns with her husband. Only after a period of some weeks (and some escalation of the presenting problems) did she decide that she could confront her husband.

As long as the client felt that the consequences of potential error would be more serious than her present situation, she postponed effective action. Only when she felt that the situation was so serious as to justify what she saw as considerable risk did she take direct action.

Nature of the Imposed Restrictions.   This refers to variables that limit the client in his attempts to acquire new concepts or approaches to problems. These restrictions are primarily the result of insufficient access to knowlege or resources. A client may not be able to count on the support or availability of friends, neighbors, or family.[2] Often clients are unaware of community resources that might facilitate their problem-solving efforts. In such instances, the social worker may act as a broker or advocate, helping the client to secure and utilize necessary resources.

Occasionally, the restrictions are the consequence of limitations imposed by the physical and intellectual capacity of the client. Depending on the nature of the presenting problem, the physical handicaps may have a decisive impact on the attempted resolution of a problem. The intellectual capacity of the client will, to a large measure, influence the degree and type of cognitive action undertaken; for example, intellectually limited persons will be less able to deal with abstractions and more complicated tasks. The social work principle of "starting where the client is" should therefore include assessment of the client's physical and intellectual capacity for different strategies of intervention.

A restriction sometimes imposed unnecessarily by the social worker is the nearly exclusive reliance upon verbal and abstract approaches to problem-solving, especially in the analytically oriented treatment models. But many social workers creatively use various concrete and action-oriented methods with their clients. For instance, Perlman (1975) highlights the utility of action-oriented methods in her description of behavioral rehearsal. These methods tend to encourage clients to take a direct, active role in resolving their problems, thereby enhancing their sense of autonomy and competence (Maluccio, 1974).

Overview on Concept Attainment.   The five factors that have been outlined represent forces that influence the ease with which a client will acquire new ideas and behaviors. Each of them needs to be understood as it applies to a particular client in a given situation. The worker can then selectively utilize these forces in the intervention process in order to enhance the person's adaptive strivings.

Implications for Practice

The significance of the cognitive processes of attribution and concept attainment in social work can best be seen in relation to assessment and intervention. Assessment basically involves determining the nature of the problem in its environmental context, along with clarification of the client's capacities and resources. Intervention comprises the actions carried out by client and worker to facilitate the person's coping efforts.

Assessment

One of the goals of assessment is to develop a sense of the problem as the client sees it, especially with reference to its origins and present consequences. Through the cognitive process of attribution, people perceive and ascribe cause and effect relationships. Attribution theory suggests a variety of questions that a practitioner should ask in each case situation:

1. *Locus of control:*   Does the client see the present problem as within or beyond his influence or control?
2. *Misattribution:*   Has the client inaccurately perceived a sequence of events, ascribing an effect to the wrong cause?
3. *Self-attribution:*   Does the client see himself as able to respond effectively to the problem, or has he defined himself as unable to cope?
4. *Labeling:*   Has the client endured his problems long enough and are they of sufficient social concern so that he now suffers from the consequences of labeling (e.g., is described as neurotic or delinquent)?

Concept maintenance and attainment theory helps the worker to understand the forces that support a dysfunctional cognitive set or belief system (which has arisen through the attributional process previously described). Five factors need to be assessed when evaluating the strength of the dysfunctional belief:

1. *Frequency of past confirmation:*   This is essentially beyond modification but may require clarification as to its appropriateness vis-à-vis the developmental stage of the client.
2. *Number of alternatives available:*   Does the client see any alternative ways to conceptualize his situation or problem?
3. *Cognitive consequences of change:*   Is the dysfunctional belief system closely tied to other more functional beliefs? Can they be separated?
4. *Motivational consequences of change:*   Does the dysfunctional belief system have some desirable secondary gain for the client? What emotional needs are met by maintaining it?
5. *Social consequences of change:*   How will alteration of the dysfunctional belief affect the client's interaction with his significant others or peer group?

As can be seen from this list, assessment of the apparently dysfunctional cognitive set or belief system requires attention to the individual in his environmental context. Care must be taken to appreciate the emotional, social, and cognitive consequences of change. A sense of the past experience of the client, with respect to the confirmatory experiences he has had with the dysfunctional belief, may be helpful in understanding the client in his present situation but may not allow for any significant intervention. Clients who are found to be limited in their awareness of—or inability to—generate alternative approaches to or ideas on their problem often can be easily helped by the social worker because the suggestion of alternative approaches is such a common social work activity.

Intervention

Attribution and concept attainment are also useful in the process of intervention. Just as the client may misperceive the experiences that led him to seek help in the first place, he may also misperceive treatment. Several of the attributional subprocesses may therefore be of particular concern to the worker.

1. *Locus of control.*   Individuals who perceive events as beyond their influence or control may generalize that perception to treatment. Whatever change occurs in the interventive process may be ascribed to the social worker, the agency, or some outside force. This may lead to a change in the individual's present circumstances but will probably not generate change which has the power to generalize and enhance coping skills.

2. *Misattribution.*   Persons who misperceive events often do so in a systematic way (e.g., the depressed person who sees all events as negative or undesirable). In treatment this tendency may be repeated, leading the client to perceive inaccurately the motives or behavior of the social worker or agency and the outcome of the service.

3. *Self-attribution.*   Depending upon the nature of the self-attribution, the individual may limit his responsiveness to treatment at the outset. He may see himself as "helpless," thus needing to be cared for rather than becoming an instrumental partner with the social worker in a process of change.[3]

The process of concept attainment is important in that it enables the client to generate new, more adaptive ways to respond to a problem-in-living. These new ideas or approaches to problems will help the client to develop the consequent behaviors that will be necessary to cope with the problem situation. As already discussed, the process of acquiring new concepts or beliefs is enhanced in five ways, which have specific meaning for intervention.

1. *Defining the task.*   In social work this would be better understood as developing a contract or agreement as to the purpose of treatment and the respective responsibilities of client and social worker.

2. *Nature of the validation.*   This refers to the feedback/reinforcement cycle. The validations should encourage the acquisition of the more functional beliefs and behaviors. This process is enhanced when the tasks allow for self-validation or at least prompt feedback from the outside. The timing of the validation is also important: How many tasks must be completed, or how often, before receiving confirmatory feedback?

3. *Nature of the instances encountered.*   In intervention this refers to the order, frequency, number, complexity, and familiarity of the

tasks which the client needs to undertake in order to acquire the new belief and related behaviors. In general, tasks need to be orderly; of sufficient frequency to allow for reinforcement; not overly complex, so as to minimize possible confusion or failure; and somewhat familiar to the client so as to allow for the use of existing coping skills.

4. *Anticipated consequences of a specific choice.* The social worker would already have some awareness of the possible consequences of change from the assessment process. During the interventive phase, however, the client may directly or indirectly let the social worker know that he fears a particular consequence should he adopt the new belief or behavior. In many cases, it is the worker who is obligated to inform the client of the potential consequences of a given type of change.

5. *Nature of the imposed restrictions.* This area, in some respects, overlaps the assessment process, since the social worker needs to understand the physical and intellectual limitations of the client so as to propose appropriate interventions and tasks. In addition, the social worker should avoid unnecessary restrictions such as total reliance on verbal interchange and intrapsychic processes and use such methods as behavioral rehearsal and environmental modification.[4]

We have emphasized that the cognitive processes of attribution and concept attainment have instrumental relevance to the social worker in that they affect assessment and intervention strategies. Attribution influences problem identification, the intervention process, and the benefits realized from treatment. Concept attainment theory can be used to evaluate the relative strength of a dysfunctional cognitive set or belief system and to help the client acquire more effective approaches.

Case Illustration

The following comprehensive case example illustrates how these ideas can be applied in practice.

John Stanton was a single, unemployed, 23-year-old man who went to an outpatient mental health center because he was concerned about a threatened loss of welfare benefits. At that time he was receiving state disability income and vocational rehabilitation services. His history revealed that he came from a troubled, conflict-ridden family in which he had been led to believe that he was the cause of many family problems. Although only 23 years old, he had a long series of psychiatric treatment and hospitalizations. He had been treated variously for suicide attempts, depression, alcohol and medication abuse. He appeared well dressed, anxious, and self-conscious. In describing himself or his experiences he frequently alluded to what he had been told by his family, counselors, or psychiatrists.

The assessment revealed many significant factors. He felt that his family, his doctor, the welfare agency, or someone similar controlled his choices and destiny. At the same time, whenever he had an unhappy or undesirable experience such as an unproductive job interview, he invariably felt that it was "my fault." Over the years he had begun to incorporate many self-statements which suggested that he was often labeled by those who had contact with him. For example, he would say that he was neurotic or disabled. Mr. Stanton's experiences with his family (as the scapegoat) and with agencies had been going on for at least ten years. Previous efforts at change had been met with profound resistance by his family and fear by him, as he had become quite dependent upon the treatment agencies for his support and nurturance.

The interventive process began with defining the key task. All-encompassing change was avoided (e.g., to be less neurotic) and instead the initial goal was to seek and secure a job. This task was broken into a sequence of behaviors. First, the idea was explored verbally in interviews. Next, job interviews were role-played and videotaped for feedback from the worker. After this, Mr. Stanton was encouraged to try rehearsing some interviews at companies where he would not want to work even if accepted. Finally, he was encouraged to seek a job that he desired.

Simultaneously, Mr. Stanton was encouraged to diminish contacts with his family and increase contacts with age-level peers. Eventually, he was also helped to become involved in college courses, which enhanced his social network, reward system, and employment prospects. Soon after, on his own initiative, he entered a self-help group for his alcohol abuse.

As the treatment objectives were accomplished, Mr. Stanton was encouraged to incorporate the gains he had made and diminish his reliance on counseling.

The above case highlights the use of the key features of attribution and concept attainment theories. Several themes became evident in assessment of the client's situation. He tended to perceive events as externally controlled and beyond his own influence. By virtue of a long history of unpleasant family experiences, he misattributed cause and effect in many social interactions, always feeling that he was at fault. The combined impact of his feeling helpless to change the course of events in his life and blaming himself created a variety of negative self-attributions or self-statements. These eventually became rigidified as a consequence of his repeated treatment contacts, which labeled him as disabled, neurotic, and depressed.

The assessment process further revealed that change in Mr. Stanton's functioning would be especially difficult. He had experienced repeated confirmation of his negative self-attributions and saw few alternative courses of action other than contact with treatment agencies.

He had developed numerous interrelated beliefs that hinged upon his distorted world view. His family exerted considerable pressure against change. Furthermore, he had become dependent on maintaining his "sick" image to meet many of his emotional needs.

The process of change began with clear definition of the main task. The task and its components were selected in accordance with criteria flowing from concept attainment theory. Thus they were behaviorally oriented and allowed Mr. Stanton frequent opportunity for experimentation, with clear feedback and reasonable provision for his sense of "safety." The attempt to modify his social network from family to peer group was intended to diminish the consequences of change; receiving satisfaction from his peer contacts was expected to offset the anticipated loss of support from his family. The final consideration was not to impose unnecessary restrictions on the process of change. Therefore, several methods of intervention were utilized, including desensitization, self-help groups, behavioral rehearsal, video tape, verbal discussion, and written material.

Conclusion

Cases such as the preceding one underscore the importance of understanding the cognitive processes by which individuals perceive cause and effect and develop and maintain sets of ideas or behaviors. Attribution theory enables the social worker to appreciate the manner in which an individual processes informational input from immediate as well as remote sources. Concept attainment and maintenance theory clarifies the mechanisms by which these inputs become transformed into sets of ideas or behavioral tendencies. Most importantly, however, concept attainment and maintenance theory can heighten the worker's appreciation of the power of cognition in human functioning and suggest numerous practice implications and strategies. As a result, the worker is better able to use the client's cognitive processes to enhance his or her adaptive responses and competence.

Notes

1. Moore-Kirkland (Chapter 2 in this volume) also stresses the value of specifying goals as a means of mobilizing a client's motivation toward competence.
2. See Swenson (Chapter 6 in this volume) for discussion of the role of social networks and natural helping systems in social work practice.
3. Focusing on situations of crisis and life transition, Golan (Chapter 4 in this

volume) also considers self-attributions and the process of change in one's *assumptive* world, that is, the total set of assumptions and interpretations developed by the person on the basis of previous experiences.

4. For a comprehensive discussion of environmental modification, see Grinnell, Kyte, and Bostwick (Chapter 7 in this volume).

CHAPTER 4

Building Competence in Transitional and Crisis Situations

Naomi Golan

As individuals pass through their life span, they develop skills and competencies in dealing with the tasks and challenges posed by their own developmental processes and by their interactions with their social situations. Usually, as part of this unfolding, they learn to take new demands in their stride and to adapt earlier patterns of effective coping to encompass the new conditions, whether they be anticipated or unexpected. At times of acute crisis or during periods of major transition, when role shifts are sudden and force unaccustomed modes of action, the pressure to effect change takes on new urgency.

In a perceptive essay on the nature of personal change, Perlman (1968:16–17)) notes that it is in the nature of living for crises to occur that may shake the foundations of habit and long-entrenched behavior patterns. Since living is a process of adapting to changing age, circumstances, and relationships, phases in adult life occur that are particularly stressful or feel so to the person because they involve decisions that may determine a whole sequence of consequences. At such times of crisis or crucial periods, when love, socially valued relationships, or physical well-being are threatened, the adult may be forced to change his attitudes, habitual behaviors, feelings, and/or conceptions.

According to crisis theory (Golan, 1974:421–22), when some haz-

74

ardous event occurs, whether it be a sudden cataclysmic blow or a minor incident which comes as the culmination of a series of debilitating assaults, the individual usually responds first in accordance with his characteristic defense patterns and attempts to deal with the consequences by making use of his customary repertoire of problem-solving mechanisms.

If these maneuvers are not successful in handling the stressful situation and in lowering the accompanying rise in tension, the person may mobilize new emergency methods to cope with the situation. However, if the problem continues and cannot be resolved, avoided, or redefined, tension continues to rise until a peak is reached during which self-righting devices no longer operate, and the individual enters a period of disequilibrium and disorganization, a state of active crisis. During this time-bounded interval, when usual coping patterns have proved inadequate or nonfunctional, and when the person and his family are suffering pain and discomfort, he often is found to be more amenable to outside influence and change. Thus, crisis theorists maintain that a minimal effort at such time can produce a maximal effect; a small amount of help, appropriately focused, can prove more effective than more extensive intervention during periods of less emotional accessibility.

If these propositions are true—and abundant case examples have accumulated to attest to the validity of this approach—intervention that concentrates on improving individual competence to deal with the problematic aspects of a high-stress situation and to enable the person to act more effectively within his new social context becomes a significant area of professional service.

This chapter will look more closely at this segment of practice. First, we shall examine how change is brought about and how a client's competence can be increased, both during the sudden, dramatic instances precipitated by acute situational crises and over the longer intervals when he is passing through some significant transitional phase. Then we shall consider both the client's and the practitioner's roles in developing the "conscious, volitional coping" that Perlman (1975) maintains is central to the helping process.

Areas for Change

C. Murray Parkes (1971), the English social psychiatrist, contends that whenever a major change in an individual's life situation takes place, the need arises for him to restructure his ways of looking at the world and his plans for living in it. Effort must be put forth to give up old patterns of thought and activity and to develop new ones. Whether the final outcome is perceived as a gain or a loss, the crucial factor may be the way in which he copes with the process of change.

According to Parkes, the area in which change occurs lies first of all in that part of the external world that impinges upon the self, the person's *life space*, which he defines as "those parts of the environment with which the self interacts and in relation to which [the person's] behavior is organized: other persons, material possessions, the familiar world of home and place of work, and even the individual's own body and mind, insofar as he can view them as separate from his self" (Parkes, 1971:103).

The second area in which change can occur is in his internal *assumptive* world, that is, the total set of assumptions and interpretations the individual builds up on the basis of past experiences in dealing with the outside world.

The life space, serving as the link between the inner self and the external world, is continuously changing as novel stimuli, fresh combinations of events, and unique communications from others are received and assimilated:

> Some of these changes fulfill expectations and require little or no change in the assumptive world; others necessitate a major restructuring of that world, the abandonment of one set of assumptions and the development of a fresh set to enable the individual to cope with the new, altered life space. If the change takes place gradually and the individual has time to prepare, little by little, for the restructuring, the chances that this will follow a satisfactory course are greater than if the change was sudden and unexpected. Thus the transitions of maturation—growing in size, changing in appearance, becoming gradually older and more frail—are barely recognized as changes at all, whereas the unexpected loss of a job or a wife is more likely to be recognized as a major transition. [Parkes, 1971:103]

In order to cope with the changes in his new, altered life space, the person is impelled to set up a cycle of internal and external changes aimed at improving the "fit" between himself and his environment. At the same time, since he is tied to his assumptive world by affectional bonds (e.g., his view of "his" job or "his" home), he tends to resist change whenever it requires giving up part of his accustomed life space, regardless of whether the net result is advantageous or not.

Since the person's assumptive world contains models both of the actual world as he perceives it and of the ideal world as he thinks (or hopes or dreads) it might be, he becomes aware of the discrepancies between the two. If the gap is anticipated and he has time to rehearse in his mind how he would or should act in the face of change, the transition tends to take place smoothly. If, on the other hand, the change is unexpected or unforeseen, it may open up gaps and deficits in his ability to cope with the new situation.

Finally, Parkes notes, the individual is not merely a passive recipient of impressions from his life space. He creates his own assumptive world by reaching out into his environment and sampling it; he reacts to his life space by moving within it to keep it the same or to change it. To do so, he needs knowledge and skills, negotiable possessions (such as money) to obtain the services of others, and the status and role conferred on him by society to make use of its potentialities. Some changes in the life space tend to affect the person's assumptive world more than others. These include the psychosocial transitions leading to changes in personal relationships, familiar environment, possessions, physical and mental capacities, and roles and statuses.[1]

How Change Can Be Effected

Effecting change through intervention in the person's life space has, of course, been a central theme in social work theory since Mary Richmond's day. Recent interest has been spurred by the trenchant observations of Gordon (1969) that the distinctive area of social work activity lies at the interface between the person and his environment, that the professional's social purpose is the realization of human potential, that its knowledge base is related to the coping capacities of people and the qualities of the impinging environment, and that interventions should be directed to either strengthening and enhancing people's coping capacities or ameliorating the external environment or both.[2]

This line of thinking has probably been developed most clearly by the advocates of a life model or ecological approach to social work intervention. Oxley (1971), for example, feels workers can become more effective by basing their treatment activities on the normal growth processes, with their implications for health development.

Germain's life model (1973) stresses the importance of the ecosystems, which would include other people, things, places, organizations, ideas, information, and values. It is patterned upon the behavior of well-adapted, socially competent individuals with varying life-styles in solving problems, in dealing with discomfort and stress, and in managing symptomatology without marked regression or decompensation. It recognizes that the ego has many kinds of skills, not only for coping with difficulties but for enjoying the world, achieving goals, and modifying the environment to meet its own needs. Positive environmental changes can bring about changes in personal functioning through a spiraling feedback effect leading to increased competence in coping with further demands and challenges. One of the chief areas for professional concerns is seen as the transitional problems and needs faced by individuals, families, and groups, including the difficulties in carrying out developmental tasks, the changes in status and role over the life span, and the threats and losses that occur during crisis events (Gitterman and Germain, 1976).

Maluccio (1974) emphasizes the importance of the use of action—both the "artificial" activities that occur during the client–worker interview and the "natural" activities that arise out of the person's own life situation—as a powerful tool in intervention. He feels that natural activities such as work, play, and social interaction tend to be most effective since they are more closely related to the individual's processes of growth and adaptation and promote increased competence motivation. Success in carrying out meaningful life activities leads to improved coping skills, enhances personal well-being, and encourages further attempts to cope.

It should be inserted here, however, that action is not necessarily restricted to behavior. In considering the dimensions of the coping process, Perlman (1975) points out that cognitive and affective ego functions—thought and feeling—affect the executive function of the ego—action. Conversely, action affects thought and feeling. Thinking, which has been termed by Freud "experimental action" and by Piaget "interiorized action," is as much a part of the conscious decision to cope as the external action observable through the person's verbal or motor abilities. This point becomes important in discussing intervention strategies, when we consider both *action-oriented* tasks and *thinking-oriented* tasks.

In discussing how individuals adapt to new situations, White (1974:66) stresses the importance of concentrating more carefully on what clients do, or what they can be encouraged to do by advice or by a suitable arrangement of circumstances. He feels that there must be new sensitivity to potentialities for action, to what the client might just be capable of doing for himself with a little encouragement and to what he might be able to do if he knew it was important and would help him with his problems.

To return to Maluccio's point about the importance of action, Jacobson (1974:816) observes that helping a person function more effectively during the resolution phase of crisis situations tends to set up a benign cycle: The individual experiences feelings of mastery and increased self-esteem, which he projects outward to others, resulting in positive reactions and feedback, leading to heightened feelings of self-worth, which brings forth greater efforts to cope, and so on.

Setting up this benign cycle of action and reaction is illustrated in the following condensed version of an upset situation perceived by the client as an acute crisis, which occurred during a life transition. Instead of concentrating on the client's inability to manage her life stresses—with all of its potential whys and wherefores—the worker focuses interventive activity on consideration of alternate ways of dealing with the current difficulties and on negotiating a plan for future activity. Setting up a structured program of clearly designated tasks proves to be the starting point from which considerable changes in the client's thinking, feeling, and behaving stem. A chain of internal and external events is set in motion which leads to improved performance and significant shifts in life roles and interpersonal relationships.

The Penny Rowe Case

Penny Rowe, 21, small, dark, and disheveled, came into the university counseling center on Monday morning extremely upset. She has been unable to concentrate lately and has stopped attending classes. This morning she told her senior thesis adviser that she wanted to drop out of school and he recommended that she talk to us first. Alternately swept by gusts of tears and anger, she told her story.

Her father, a physics professor at the university, had unexpectedly been invited to spend the year at a "think tank" in England, and her mother had gone along with him. She and her brother, Bob, 19, had elected to remain here, she because she was starting her final year and was involved in a serious relationship with her boyfriend, Rick, and Bob because he was "into" basketball this year and hoped to make the team as a sophomore. Her parents had agreed on the condition that they continue to live at home together and that she keep house for the two of them and take responsibility for her brother, who was just a "big, overgrown kid."

In the beginning, Penny had enjoyed her new role as head of household, doing all the cleaning, shopping, and preparation of meals, even though it cut down on her studying and her time with Rick. Two weeks ago, however, Bob, without consulting her, had invited two of his basketball pals, who had been thrown out of their apartment, to move in until they found another place. Since then, said Penny, conditions had gone from bad to worse. The fellows sat around all day, drinking beer, watching TV, or playing the stereo. Shoes, sports equipment, and empty cans littered the living room, hall, and stairs. Instead of the quiet well-ordered home she had tried to keep up along her mother's pattern, the house had become a shambles as Bob and his friends sprawled all over, ignoring her protests.

The climax had come last Saturday night when they invited the rest of the team and their girlfriends over for a "blast." When she had come home with Rick at 3:00 A.M., they found the place in an uproar, with a squad car parked out front, called by an irate neighbor. The police had turned everyone out and warned them sternly that if they received one more complaint, they would turn the whole mess over to university authorities.

Sunday morning, after Bob and she had had a bitter argument, he left the house in a huff and didn't return until midnight. She worked the entire day trying to clean up the chaos, instead of driving out with Rick to visit his family. She then spent a sleepless night, debating whether or not to call her parents. She knew how much her mother had counted on this "second honeymoon" year. Things had grown pretty tense between her parents lately; she guessed they were going through some sort of middle-age crisis. So how could she add to their worries by breaking it up? Her father would be furious; her mother would insist on returning home; and all their trust would be wiped out. The only other alternative she could see was to stop school until they returned, take over the house management in earnest, and try to make Bob shape up better. She'd probably lose Rick in the process since he was already annoyed with her for letting her home situation take up so much of her time and attention. And she'd have to give up her place in the group thesis project, in which she had become really interested, since it involved going on extensive field trips.

As Penny huddled in her chair, weeping exhaustedly, the worker wondered aloud whether this drastic solution was the only course of action. Were there any other options? Could they try to restructure the situation so that she and Bob could continue to live at home and yet permit her to maintain her own interests without disrupting the family's plans? Dubiously, Penny replied that she didn't know what else could be done, now that things had grown so bad. But she'd be willing to try. As a first step, she agreed to return in the late afternoon with Bob to consider together what could be remedied.

In her notes at this point, the worker observed that she consciously decided *not* to enter into the areas of Penny's overidentification with her mother and excessive fear of her father's anger, although she felt they were central issues. Instead, she chose to concentrate on helping Penny—and possibly her brother—learn to cope with the threats and challenges posed by the current situation.

When Penny came in with a subdued Bob, she appeared far less tense and upset. She said they had already started to cope with the situation: Bob, who had been sternly reprimanded by the basketball coach when he was told about the Saturday night fracas, had informed his pals this noon they would have to leave and they were now out looking for a place. She had returned to her thesis adviser after leaving here this morning and he suggested she take on the slot of "anchorman" in the project, which would involve collating and examining the data brought in by the rest of the group rather than spending so much time herself in the field.

With this head start, the three began to weigh possible options. Penny and Bob agreed that asking their parents to break up their trip abroad was out, except as a last resort. The alternative, the worker reminded them, was learning to deal with their home situation more effectively. In a detail-packed hour, marked by some mutual blaming and bargaining, they worked out a series of house rules and tasks. Bob agreed (1) to clean up his own room and bathroom in order to cut down on Penny's cleaning chores, and to straighten out any messes he and his friends made in the living areas; (2) not to invite in anyone unless he notified Penny in advance; (3) to take on responsibility for keeping the yard and lawn neat and the family car in running order and filled with gas (a sore point between them).

For her part, Penny would (1) prepare meals which would be ready at a specified time; (2) do the household shopping and laundry as well as clean her room and bath and the "common" areas downstairs; (3) pay the household bills and be in charge of weekly correspondence with their parents. She also agreed to let Bob know in advance if she went on trips for the school or with Rick so that he could work out alternate plans.

The next two weeks were busy ones. Penny talked over the home situation with their elderly neighbor, Mrs. Bascom (the one who had called the police), who had become interested in helping them and offered her cleaning woman's services one day a week to cut down on Penny's housework. In addition, they received a standing invitation to dinner on Wednesday's, Penny's late day at school. In return, Bob promised to mow the Bascoms' lawn, along with their own, since it "kept his muscles in shape." Penny had become intrigued with the household management process and had enrolled in an evening course in family budgeting at the "Y" with Rick ("Just in case," she added self-consciously).

By the end of this period, regular sessions with the counselor ended by mutual agreement; instead, Penny would call occasionally for advice on specific issues and to report on the state of affairs. In time, this too tapered off and the last the counselor heard was through a newspaper announcement in February that Penny Rowe and Richard King had become engaged and planned to marry in June, upon the return of Miss Rowe's parents from England and following her graduation from the university.

The choice of areas for action and of appropriate means to implement the agreed-upon plan, as illustrated in the above case, appears to be the nub of bringing about meaningful change. While they probably would vary widely, depending on the strengths, inclinations, and degree of discomfort of both client and worker, some criteria for the selection of goals and tasks during high-stress situations and for their implementation have already been offered.

Choice of Goals and Tasks

Several years ago, while participating in a field test of the Reid-Epstein model of task-centered practice, I worked out a triad for planning treatment strategies with clients:

A. The *target problem*, the "felt difficulty," in specific behaviors or circumstances, for which the client asks for help and on which he expresses his willingness to work.
B. The *target goal*, the projected situation in which the client would feel he no longer needs help, the stage at which he might continue on his own—that is, when he feels competent to manage his life.
C. The *task*, the means of going from Point A to Point B. General tasks become paths of action and operational tasks and subtasks the specific stepping stones along the path. [Golan, 1977:274]

In acute crisis situations, treatment goals tend to be relatively modest and related to amelioration of the immediate disturbed situation and the strengthening of the client's ability to cope and integrate the changes brought about by the hazardous event. Depending on the degree of disorientation and the extent to which the disequilibrium can be reversed, the final lever of readjustment may be lower than, equal to, or higher than the precrisis state.

Rapoport (1970), however, has noted that while minimal goals aim at a return to the precrisis level of functioning and identification of remedial measures that the client can take or that are available through community resources, an additional goal, if the individual and situation are favorable and the opportunity presents itself, would be to initiate new modes of perceiving, thinking, and feeling and to develop new adaptive and coping responses that can be useful *beyond* the immediate situation. This last appears to be the most powerful and challenging aspect of treatment in crisis situations, as indicated earlier.

Thus the deceptively simple description of tasks as "the means of going from Point A to Point B" becomes the crux of intervention during periods of high stress. By taking full advantage of what Robert Havighurst once called "the teachable moment," practitioner and client map out together the specific tasks which the client will carry out, which the worker will do on his behalf, and which they can work on together. The significant factor is that the *client* becomes the prime mover, the one who acts to improve his coping competence by performing a series of planned moves to draw closer to becoming autonomous. Even in the acute phase of a crisis situation, when the person has become numbed by severe shock or exhausted by the batterings of a series of debilitating events and the situation forces the worker to become extremely active, the latter aims as quickly as possible to decrease his own level of activity and to increase the client's by encouraging him to carry out a series of specific problem-solving tasks.[3]

The following case illustrates both the setting up of short-term goals and their implementation through specific client-oriented tasks. Mrs. Brown, immobilized by a self-induced crisis during a significant transitional stage in her life cycle, is helped to reevaluate her priorities and decide upon a series of thinking and action-oriented tasks for herself and for her immediate family. These lead to significant changes in her life space which have long-range implications for both her own and her family's future. As in the Penny Rowe case, we also see how the worker's tempo changes: At the start of the case she is very active and, due to the client's inability to function, becomes quite directive. Soon, however, as Mrs. Brown begins to reactivate her coping capacities, the worker becomes correspondingly less active and, by the close of the case, serves primarily as a "reporting station" and acknowledger and reifier of client competence.

The Sarah Brown Case

Sarah Brown, a neatly dressed, agitated black woman, called for an immediate appointment at the outpatient psychiatry clinic of a large metropolitan health center. She began to talk almost before she sat down about the fierce argument she had had that morning with her oldest daughter who had asked her yesterday to buy a pair of shoes for her and then had gone out to spend seventy dollars on a new permanent. Mrs. Brown became so incensed when she heard about this that she rushed out to her car, drove to work, wrote a resignation notice and put it in her supervisor's box, and returned home immediately without giving further explanation. Appalled when she realized what she had done, she panicked and called the clinic.

Mrs. Brown gave brief background information. She was divorced seventeen years ago and had worked all these years to support her family as an eligibility aide at the county welfare department. Her three children, Janice, 24, Luann, 20, and Percy, 14, live with her. The two girls work but contribute virtually nothing to the upkeep of the home, which she had scrimped and saved to buy and maintain. The argument this morning with Janice had been the last straw in a long series of stressful events that started last April when Luann moved back home unexpectedly when her short, stormy marriage broke up. Two months later, Janice walked in without warning, announcing that she had decided to return to school full time and didn't want to pay rent on her own apartment. Mrs. Brown felt both shocked and imposed upon by her daughters' return yet did not see how she could refuse them shelter or deny them the clothes and small loans they kept asking her for.

Shortly after this, she passed her fortieth birthday, a difficult milestone for her. She had been awaiting the event with considerable trepidation and had planned to make it a starting point to embark upon a whole series of changes in her personal life, including going back to school to get her high school diploma and joining the choir at church. Now she felt forced to put aside her own plans in order to keep up with her daughters' demands. She had grown increasingly depressed, although she tried to deal with the situation by taking on a second job evenings and going straight to her bedroom when she came home to take several tranquilizers and wait until she felt calm enough to emerge. After this last argument, however, she felt herself "falling apart."

The worker first attempted to help Mrs. Brown gain cognitive mastery of the crisis situation by reviewing with her in detail what had happened over the past five months. They agreed that the most immediate problems were the loss of her job and her daughters' refusal to share the support of the household. A third area proposed by the worker, although Mrs. Brown was reluctant to admit it, was her own lack of personal gratification.

They then set up a set of short-term goals: (1) to help Mrs. Brown regain her job and clarify the behavior that led to her impulsive resignation; (2) to get the girls to take on some of the financial burden and to help her cope more realistically with their demands; and (3) to find ways for her to gain more satisfaction in her own life.

With Mrs. Brown's permission, since she felt too embarrassed to do so herself, the worker phoned Mrs. Brown's supervisor to explain the circumstances leading up to the submission of her resignation. The supervisor, who had been dumbfounded on reading Mrs. Brown's note, readily agreed to rescind the resignation since he valued her steadiness over the years and the quality of her work. He suggested that she take two weeks vacation time from her accumulated overtime to "rest and relax." Mrs. Brown was so relieved to hear this that she began to cry; this was the first time she could recall anyone telling *her* to take things easy. She had always prided herself on being self-sufficient; every since Percy's father left her ten years ago, she was determined to support her family herself. She felt ashamed at having lost control this morning but agreed that it was really a cry for help: She had reached the end of her rope.

Once her immediate anxiety was reduced, Mrs. Brown began to express her anger at her daughters for not realizing the pressures they placed on her and how their demands drained her until now she felt "used up." Somewhat doubtfully, she agreed to invite them in for a family session. But when she called that afternoon to set a time, she said she was already feeling less depressed and more hopeful.

The next day, the worker, with Mrs. Brown sitting next to her, told

Janice and Luann, both well-groomed, attractive young women, what had happened the day before. They were shocked; their mother had said nothing to them about the incident. They also had not realized the tensions caused by their returning home and were unaware that they had broken up her personal plans. The situation at home was rehashed in considerable detail. They brought up her long-standing pattern of encouraging her children to remain dependent on her and trying to keep everything "perfect" at home. Mrs. Brown began to talk freely to them for the first time about how she involved herself totally in her children because they were all she had. Raising them properly was her duty, drilled into her as a child by her strict parents. But for her it was her way of showing them love, though she admitted it also protected her from becoming involved with a man (and being hurt again). As the session progressed, the daughters realized for the first time that their mother was a woman who needed male companionship as much as they did.

Mrs. Brown and her daughters proceeded to work on the psychosocial tasks of bringing out the difficulties involved in the girls' presence at home and the mother's inability to assert herself. This opened the way to closer understanding and a bridging of the gaps between them, enabling the Brown family to turn to practical planning. The girls decided that they didn't have to stay at home; since they were both working, they would rent an apartment together and Janice could continue at school on a part-time basis. Mrs. Brown agreed that it would be better for all of them to have Janice and Luann leave the nest and struggle to make it on their own. (Although they had moved away before, the girls admitted they had never felt they had left home.)

For the third session, Percy, a tall, gangling adolescent, joined the rest of the family. The girls reported that they had already lined up a place to live and their mother was helping them sew new curtains and bedspreads to brighten it up. Last evening Janice had helped Mrs. Brown experiment with new hairstyles and this coming weekend Luann planned to take her to a shopping center to help her choose a new fall outfit. Even Percy volunteered shyly that he had lined up an after-school delivery job with the neighborhood florist "to put money [of his] own in [his] jeans." By this time, the worker felt her role reduced to being a "participant observer" on the sidelines.

In a final individual session, Mrs. Brown reported that she had given up her evening job and joined a bowling league with her coworkers at the welfare department—her first social activity, outside of attending church, in the last ten years. She also started looking into adult education courses at the nearby community center "just for the fun of it" and noted that maybe next year she would start to study seriously for her diploma. As she rose to leave, she said with a half smile that maybe her life really *was* beginning at 40—like the radio said.

The cases of Penny Rowe and Mrs. Brown represent situations in which clients experience acute situational crises while passing through significant maturational transitions.[4] The worker's intervention in both instances is directed toward helping clients to effect goal-and-task-oriented changes in their life space by improving their ability to cope competently with the changes in their life course. It might be appropriate at this time for us to examine more closely these underlying transitional processes and the adaptation called for at such time.

Changes during Transitional Periods

As noted earlier, the individual passes through a series of developmental and maturational changes during his life span, sometimes imperceptibly and with advance notice, and sometimes abruptly and unexpectedly. Levinson (1978) has elaborated upon and changed the focus of Erikson's epigenetic table of the life cycle (1959) by plotting out a series of alternating periods of stability and transition in adult life. He points out that the person's life course in punctuated by *marker events*. Among these he includes the birth or death of loved ones, unexpected trauma or good fortune, advancement or failure in work, retirement, war, flourishing times, and "rock bottom" times:

> [These] have a notable impact upon a person's life. Marker events are usually considered in terms of the *adaptation* they require. They change a man's life situation and he must cope with them in some way. The further changes in his relationships, roles, and personality are then understood as part of his adaptation to the new situation. . . . The significance of a marker event for an individual depends partly upon its place in the sequence of developmental periods. [Levinson, 1978:54–55]

These marker events would appear analogous to the hazardous events mentioned earlier. Weiss (1976) points out that crises can end in two ways: by a return to the preexistent situation or by a persisting disruption of that situation. Should the crisis end in change, as during transitions, then both the individual's emotional organization (Parkes's assumptive world) and his relational arrangements (life space) must also undergo change. This could end either in the establishment of a new stable life organization accompanied by a new stable identity, or in entry into a long-term "deficit" situation, in which the person becomes vulnerable to the long-term loneliness and anxieties associated with loss.

What are the changes that must be made during transitional states that can lead to either a new life pattern of stability or deficiency? For some years we have been trying to tease these out in terms of *client tasks* which would have to be carried out in order to pass through stressful periods successfully (Golan, 1978:74–76). It was postulated that for each of the potential problem areas that might be involved (such as income management, health, housing, education, leisure-time activities, and citizenship) or significant role networks that could be affected (marital, familial, occupational, social, and institutional) the individual or family would have to carry out a series of tasks, along two separate but interacting continua, *material–arrangemental* and *psychosocial.*

Along the material–arrangemental axis, he would have to carry this series of action-oriented tasks:

1. Explore available solutions, resources, and possible roles.
2. Decide upon an appropriate solution, resource, and/or role and prepare himself for it.
3. Apply formally for the solution or resource or assume the new role.
4. Begin to use the new solution or resource or function in the new role.
5. Go through an apprenticeship period of adaptation and development of increasing competence until his performance rises to acceptable norms.

At the same time, since individuals, families, and small groups tend to react during periods of heightened stress in complex, nonrational, and often unpredictable ways, the client may have to engage in the following psychosocial tasks which appear to be largely thinking- and feeling-oriented:

1. Cope with the threat to his past security and sense of competence and esteem; deal with his feelings of loss and longing.
2. Grapple with the anxieties and frustrations in making decisions or in choosing the new solution, resource, or role.
3. Handle the stress generated in applying for the selected solution or resource and in taking on the new role.
4. Adjust to the new solution, resource, or role with all that it implies in terms of shift in position and status in the family and community.
5. Develop new standards of well-being, agree to diminished gratification, and be able to delay satisfaction until he can function according to acceptable norms of behavior.

A number of authors have attempted within recent years to enumerate and classify the transitions that are encountered throughout the normal life cycle.[5] Frequently these are grouped in terms of "vertical" transitions in the sense of occurring as part of a particular developmental stage (e.g., transition to marriage or retirement), or as binding two stages together. Others can be termed "horizontal" or "unbounded" in that they can occur independent of a specific age-stage linkage.

Examinations of accounts of how individuals have passed through transitional periods reveal a wide variation in the extent to which they manage to carry out the tasks demanded of the situation in a competent and autonomous way. Many—probably most—persons who have histories of successful coping behind them and who are buttressed by a range of natural and mutual support systems never come to the attention of the professional help-giving community or may need only such minimal assistance as the provision of the names of potential employers or lists of possible apartments for rent. Others, handicapped by a lack of personal support systems or with past histories of unsuccessful or limited coping, may require extensive professional help and may end up, as Weiss (1976) has noted, in a state of permanent deficit requiring extensive support and assistance.

In the following case, adapted from the records of a private migration agency, we see how a normally competent family, passing through two separate but interlocking transitional processes which occur at the same time (bereavement and migration), is helped to adjust to their new life situation by intervention carried out simultaneously at the material–arrangemental and psychosocial levels. The worker helps the family weave back and forth between the thinking- and feeling-oriented tasks involved in their grieving over their lost child and the action-oriented tasks specific to learning to adapt to life in a new country.

The Gross Case

Mr. and Mrs. Gross, Soviet Jewish immigrants from Kiev, arrived in the United States accompanied by their two daughters, 9 and 4. Six weeks earlier, a third daughter had died in Rome, following an emergency hospitalization for gastroenteritis. The parents had experienced difficulty in obtaining the needed medical attention for the baby and were haunted by the feeling that the tragedy might have been averted. When seen by their caseworker in an initial interview, both Mr. and Mrs. Gross were tight-lipped and tense, trying very hard to control their feelings.

Work with the family focused on two vital areas: help with engaging in the mourning process for their dead baby and in carrying out the tasks involved in adapting to their new land. The practitioner helped them work through the powerful emotions which flooded them, threatening their ability to put down new roots. The parents then expressed two wishes that had to do with the "unfinished business" they felt in regard to the loss of their infant. They asked to convey a message of thanks to the worker at the Joint Distribution Committee headquarters in Rome who had been helpful in making burial arrangements. They also wanted information about the exact location of the plot where their child was interred. The caseworker accepted the responsibility for carrying out both of these tasks on their behalf.

During the early part of the contact, the caseworker also met with the receiving family, Mr. Gross's father and stepmother, who had been assisted by the agency a year earlier. Mr. Gross took an apartment close to them and the family settled into their first permanent home in this country. The older couple was a compassionate pair who attempted to help the grieving family. However, they needed the worker's aid in allowing the young parents to express their feelings; initially, the grandparents had advised them not to dwell on their loss, to forget little Anna and to have another baby. The parents' response was to cling to memories of their daughter, giving evidence of their powerful need not to forget her. The caseworker intervened gently when the grandparents questioned the parents' desire to keep a favored toy and a shirt belonging to the dead child. Not only were they helped to understand this as a natural feeling but they were also made aware of their own suppressed need to express their grief over the loss of the grandchild they had never seen. Thus, parents and grandparents drew closer because they could share openly their feelings, which, in turn, enabled them to give needed support to the two surviving children.

The caseworker responded immediately when Mr. and Mrs. Gross wished to have medical examinations for both children, seeing this as a means of allaying their understandable anxiety about the children's health and the availability of medical care. Since they also needed emergency dental care, the entire family was referred to the dental clinic that serves the agency's clientele. During the summer the two children were enrolled in a Jewish day camp at the agency's expense; they also were helped to apply for food stamps and for Medicaid. Since Mrs. Gross expected to work part time, both she and her husband were enrolled in English classes run by the agency's vocational service department.

In time, the caseworker was able to inform the Gross family that the Joint Distribution Committee worker in Rome had been located and duly thanked. A telexed report provided the parents with the exact location of their daughter's burial plot. The medical reports from Rome were translated first into English and then into Russian and given to the parents.

Less than five months after their arrival, Mr. Gross accepted a job in a manufacturing company where his mechanical skill enabled him to start at a reasonable wage. Direct contact with the family gradually diminished. When he telephoned after several months, Mr. Gross told the caseworker in serviceable English that he was getting regular increases in salary. Both children continued to do well in the Jewish day school in which they had been enrolled. Mrs. Gross informed the worker that the stepgrandmother had not been feeling well enough to care for the children after school, so she was staying home for the time being.

Throughout the next year, Mr. and Mrs. Gross continued to telephone the worker occasionally to share with her the family's progress in their adopted country. Despite the trauma of their child's death while undergoing the strain of immigration, it was felt that they had shown remarkable resilience in moving ahead in the adjustment process.

Interaction between Transitions and Crises

Sometimes a normal maturational transition takes on added impetus and its crisis potential increases when it occurs out of sequence in the developmental process or when it does not synchronize with other events taking place in the individual's or family's life course. Pregnancy, for example, can be considered a normal developmental phase (Benedek, 1970), part of the broader anticipated transition of a couple's entering into parenthood. However, when it becomes complicated by being unwanted—or unwanted at this particular time—the biological, psychological, and social pressures which arise as part of the matrix of late adolescence or early adulthood can coalesce into a highly stressful situation. And when the situation becomes further complicated by first the decision to terminate the pregnancy prematurely and then the process of carrying out the decision, the stress factor rises still higher.

Rapoport and Potts (1971) list the key psychosocial tasks which a young pregnant woman faces in such a situation:

1. To accept the fact of pregnancy and to recognize the biological, psychological, and social attendant consequences.
2. To be able to weigh alternative implications to future goals and roles if pregnancy is carried to term or interrupted.
3. To clarify the wish to assume or reject the role of parent at this stage in the life cycle and to continue, at least for a time, the pre-pregnant life-style.
4. To be able to take an active role in decision-making in regard to the pregnancy in contrast to the passive stance that views the self as a victim of circumstances.
5. To be able to sort out contradictory expectations and demands of family members, significant others, and the social reference group and to reconcile them with one's own wishes.
6. To be able to maintain one's self-concept as a socially acceptable

person and to seek out and find new supportive reference groups, if necessary.

7. To be able to manage feelings of ambivalence and loss, both in regard to the fetus and current object relationships.

8. To be future-oriented to the extent of resumption of prepregnancy tasks and roles. [Rapoport and Potts, 1971:260–61]

The practitioner's intervention at such time should thus be directed to helping the woman make the needed decisions and carry out the consequent tasks. Cain (1979) notes that, even in a single interview, an adolescent girl can be helped to understand that the abortion is only one episode in her growth toward adulthood and that she can use the experience to bring about necessary changes in her life.

In their pregnancy counseling program, Russell and Schild (1976) find that their college-level clients are grappling with unresolved adolescence issues or with incomplete mastery of such tasks as formation of identity, development of the capacity for intimacy, and formation of stable affectional bonds. These problems are complicated further by the concurrent maturational tasks of emancipation from parents, vocational selection, and the forging of independent value systems. As students, they may still be struggling to develop competency in the academic area. Russell and Schild (1976) see as the core purpose of counseling to produce growth through increasing the client's competence in coping with her social situation or environment. To do this, the worker must first engage the woman in a helping relationship that will enable her to move forward toward taking control of her situation, then examine with her the various aspects of her problems in living and help her assess her coping skills, identify available support systems, and examine her perceptions of her role. Emphasis in on the *life situation* as the problem rather than on the unwanted pregnancy or on the woman herself. The helping process provides an opportunity for the woman to master earlier developmental tasks so that she can move into independent adult functioning.

This approach is well illustrated in the following case example, in which a young woman views her unexpected pregnancy as the final straw in a series of dilemmas which she is facing in her current life situation. It brings to a head still unresolved developmental issues held over from her late adolescence, such as her inability to break her symbiotic ties with her mother and her struggle to establish her own identity, as well as highlighting her difficulties in building an intimate mutually gratifying relationship with her boyfriend and in taking responsibility for her own future life pattern—the core issues in young adulthood.

The Case of Tina

Tina, a tall, slender woman of 22, with long blond hair and a dramatic manner, spoke in abrupt, short spurts punctuated by tears. She felt shattered, as though she was in a tug-of-war, pulled at from all sides. As a senior, a psychology major, she had to decide within two weeks whether to apply to graduate school or "settle" for a BA. Her parents wanted her to come home after graduation in three months, but her boyfriend, Ron, a graduate student in psychology, wanted her to remain here, move in with him, and continue at the university. Last week, the climax came when she learned she was pregnant. For a few days she thought this would solve everything: They would get married, she'd have the baby and settle down to be a housewife. But when she and Ron talked it over, she realized it just wasn't possible at this time. Since both of them are students, "living on a shoestring," they'd have to work for a while before setting up a household and having children. So they went to a doctor and she is scheduled to have an abortion in three days. Now she's been feeling terribly depressed and weepy and has been having frightening nightmares all week. She wondered if she is doing the right thing; maybe having a baby would make her parents finally realize that she is a grown-up and not a baby herself who has to account to them for every aspect of her life.

When the worker asked, surprised, why this was the key issue rather than how she and Ron felt about becoming parents, she answered impatiently that Ron wouldn't be a problem; if she really wanted to, she could talk him into it, since they were planning on getting married anyway. But her mother never liked Ron and they have been bickering about it all year; now her parents would really hit the roof. Having the abortion would solve that; on the other hand, having a baby might be a way out.

Background Information: Tina is the only child of her parents' second marriage. Both parents are already in their sixties; they come from mid-Europe and lost their first families in the Holocaust. Her father was described as a quiet, reserved person who gives in to her mother as "appeasement." Her mother is very dominant, nervous, obsessed with her own health and fading looks. She is very overprotective and becomes furious when Tina does not share every small detail of her life with her. Tina said, with tears in her eyes, "I get so angry with her; she still calls me 'Baby.' "

Tina had rarely been permitted to go out on her own; although she came to this university to escape from her parents, she still has to return home every weekend. Her mother insists on buying clothes for her and on arranging meetings with "suitable men."

Tina said Ron was the best thing that ever happened to her. Although she had dated since high school, he was the first boyfriend to treat her as a real person. Tina said he has helped her a lot and they are generally "fantastic" together; at times, however, she worries whether she isn't trading one "trap" for another.

Since Tina was so visibly upset, the worker suggested that they meet on a crisis basis to help her arrive at some decisions about the important facets of her life. She was seen for six weeks, initially on a twice-weekly basis. When she went in two days after the abortion, she looked tired and listless but said it wasn't so bad; Ron came and stayed with her the whole time and then took her to his place to recuperate. With a wan smile, she said she promised the doctor to return for a contraceptive device.

The next few interviews were focused on Tina's relations with her parents. Repeatedly she exploded over her mother's "pushing and prying," not leaving her any privacy or independence. Toward her father she felt both pity and anger; she saw him as buying his domestic peace at her expense. Gradually she began to grasp the fear and panic behind her mother's rage. "She was once a famous beauty in Hungary, you know. And now, when I go, she'll have nothing left. I'm all she has." She began to stop yelling back at her mother, and by the end of the month she told her parents that she was cutting down her visits to twice a month.

Gradually the emphasis in treatment shifted to her relationship with Ron, who supported her but demanded that she take responsibility for her own actions. She recalled that once they broke up because he refused to let her manipulate him. For a while she felt wonderfully free and "played the field"; however, she soon realized that his seriousness balanced her own flightiness and felt tremendously relieved when they made up and resumed their relationship. However, she still vacillated between wanting to be free and seeking his support.

Tina took an important step when she decided to postpone registering for graduate school. Instead, she took a part-time job offered by one of her instructors, working with children with learning disabilities. She was told that if she worked out the job could be expanded to full time after graduation. Tina felt this was a tremendous boost to her self-esteem and planned to go on to graduate school the following year to specialize in work with disturbed children. In the meanwhile, it meant that she could move into a decent apartment instead of a student room.

The issue of her lack of confidence came up again and again. Slowly she came to recognize her own ambivalence over taking charge of her own life and her fear of a lasting commitment. A real milestone was passed when her parents offered her a trip to France as a graduation gift—and she turned it down, unless Ron and she could take it together as a honeymoon.

By the time the case was terminated, Tina had made a number of significant "beginnings." She decided she could no longer make up to her parents for the past losses in their lives or act as a buffer between them; she still visited them periodically but felt her mother had lost the power to "get under her skin." She and Ron were planning on probably getting married in June; she felt their relationship was becoming more balanced as she learned to express her own needs and opinions more openly. She saw her job as giving her a new direction that changed her whole attitude about school; instead of its being an escape, she was now getting excited about a possible new career.

The worker's role in this case becomes one of helping the client to make vital life decisions during a period of active transition. The focus is placed on enabling her to overcome developmental obstacles in the current situation and on promoting a more autonomous, competent life-style, rather than concentrating on the pathology apparent in her background.

Use of Support Systems in Transitional Stress

Until now, the emphasis in this chapter has been on how the worker can help the individual or family effect constructive change during periods of transition through his own direct intervention. Actually much of the success of help provided at such times depends on the activation of various kinds of support systems. In Chapter 6 in this volume, Swenson discusses in depth the role of social networks and natural helping systems in developing the competence of human beings; however, their particular usefulness during periods of stress deserves mention here.

Support systems activated at such times are primarily those of the *family, mutual help groups,* and *structured educational programs* aimed at developing client competence during transitional states. Let us examine the use of each of these three forms which can be offered independent of, or supplemental to, direct worker activity.

Families

In looking at the continuum of helping alternatives in a community, Caplan (1976) sees the two- and three-generational family as a fundamental source of help and sustenance in times of stress. It encourages its members to communicate freely about their personal problems and difficulties and actively helps them deal with the cognitive and emotional upsets of a crisis predicament. Family members take concrete steps to carry out the ordinary life tasks, such as child care, which the person may be too hurt and preoccupied to perform. They also give him legitimation for the need to rest and forestall premature closure on his part in carrying out his adaptation to the changed situation. By offering advice and guidance based on their own and other family members' past experiences, they help him engage in his grief and worry work and counteract his feelings of despair and helplessness through their love and sustenance. In the event of irreversible loss through death or disability, they provide him with transitional objects and roles within the family circle until such time as he can resume his own life course once more.

The importance of relatives, neighbors, and natural leaders in providing care in a community during stressful times has been amply described by Collins and Pancoast (1976) and Swenson (Chapter 6 in this volume). The rapid mushrooming of self-help groups and "alternate help services" has become an accepted and widespread phenomenon throughout the world within the last few years (Gartner and Riessman, 1977).

Mutual Help Groups

From some years, Silverman directed a project in which widows helped other widows pass through the transition of their loss of mate (1974). Since then she has broadened her perspective to encompass other transitional groups (1978). She sees such mutual help programs, composed of "people coming together to solve their common problems," as significant enabling services during periods of transition. Help often combines individual counseling with group meetings that usually are led by persons who themselves have either successfully passed through the transition, if it is temporary, or who have learned to accommodate themselves to their changed situation, if it is irreversible. If a professional is involved, it often is as coleader or consultant behind the scene.

From the viewpoint of the person going through the transitional period, Silverman (1978) differentiates three separate spheres of action. During the initial *impact phase,* his major effect is usually numbness and disbelief. If he can be helped to establish a common bond of identity with the helper who has "made it," he gradually begins to give up his use of denial of the marker event (to use Levinson's [1978] term) and to take on his new role. As he starts to recognize part of himself in the helper who is functioning well, he finds concrete evidence and the start of hope that life is still possible and that he can continue.

In the next *recoil phase,* when the numbness lifts and the person must face the reality of his altered situation, his despair, loneliness, and the pain emerge. He must now grasp the reality that he can no longer return to the life that was and concentrate on learning the practical details of how to carry out his new roles and develop new skills.

He also needs to understand that his present feelings and reactions are typical and normal under the circumstances.

In the final *accommodation phase,* he needs help in accepting that both his inner and outer world have changed in the course of the transition and that he is a different person. He practices the new behavior patterns he has learned and, gradually, with group support, begins to integrate the past with the present. If he is successful, says Silverman, his sense of well-being is increased and his ability to deal with future life changes is enhanced. By now, he has moved out of the new member status and has the option of either becoming a helper himself or leaving to continue on his own life course. In groups dealing with permanent loss or disability situations, he may continue on for years as senior member or advocate.

The helper's role in dealing with both transitory and long-term losses runs parallel to that of the newcomer to the group. During the impact phase, he becomes a role model who relives his own experiences vicariously through the others sharing the coping techniques he found useful during his own transitional period. The group itself provides a special climate in which members can offer each other support, direction, and hope.

In the recoil phase, the helper presents specific information on how to deal effectively with the changed situation and/or new role. Group meetings also allow members to make new social contacts and find new friends who give advice about present problems and offer anticipatory guidance about future difficulties which may arise. In the final phase, the gap between old and new members narrows and the veteran helper either starts a new group or yields the role to others.

Baker (1977) has pointed out that the interface between professional and natural support systems has narrowed in recent years as professionals have begun to recognize the importance and usefulness of working conjointly with, and even organizing, support systems of help-givers who can operate outside of, but parallel to, the established professional care-giving system.

Educational Workshops

A promising development in the last few years has been the organization of structured educative workshops and seminars to teach people how to deal with transitions and stressful situations, either before the process begins or just at its inception. In a typical preventive program reported by Kaplan and Glenn (1978), a six-week neighborhood workshop on the stresses faced when moving into a new community was held in the local library of a suburban community. Participants were helped to express their own feelings about the incipient loss of friends, jobs, and familiar home surroundings; to discover and nurture the "basic self" which they would carry with them as part of the process; and to explore what personal growth goals they could set for themselves as part of their putting down roots in the new community.

In discussing the activities of the Transition Center of New Haven, Schwartz (1975) identifies five essential features of what he calls situation/transition (S/T) groups: They are primarily oriented toward helping members cope more effectively with some shared external event; they meet regularly over a period of weeks or months and have the properties of small groups; they are moderated by a trained leader; they offer social support, factual information about the shared life stress, and an opportunity for emotional interaction with others around the group focus; and they do not encourage or require members to espouse a particular moral or behavioral value system.

Two such programs which appear to be unusually well conceptualized and developed deal with different client populations but are geared to the same objective: the improvement of client competence in passing through periods of transition. Weiss (1976) describes a series of Seminars for the Separated developed at the Laboratory of Community Psychiatry at Harvard which have been presented a great number of times. The seminars meet once a week for eight weeks, starting with a formal lecture and then breaking down into discussion groups of five to eight people with a staff member as leader. Topics covered in the eight sessions are: the emotional impact of separation; the ambivalent continuing relationship with the former spouse; the impact of separation on ties with friends, kin, in-laws, and others in the individual's social milieu; the impact on the individual's relationship with his or her children; problems of the development of new relationships; starting over; sources of help; and a final evaluation session.

Participants in these seminars reported that the most immediate benefit appeared to be the reassurance that the emotional distress following separation was a normal and even universal reaction, which resulted in a dramatic reduction in their own anxiety. Membership in the supportive discussion groups was also considered an important aspect of participation in the program. On the basis of his experience with this project, Weiss (1976:225–26) believes that a good transition program should include three kinds of helpers: the *expert* who has studied the problems of a particular type of transition and can speak with authority; the *veteran* who has been through the transition and is able to draw upon his own past experiences; and the *fellow participant* who can offer the immediate understanding that comes from being in the same boat.

A more structured program geared to a different type of transition, entry into couplehood,[6] was developed by the University of Minnesota

Family Study Center in cooperation with five Midwest family service agencies (Beatt, 1976; Miller, Nunnally, and Wackman, 1976). The project was developed as a six-session course of premarital communication training for engaged couples. Using an educative–developmental orientation built around the Foote and Cottrell (1955) concept of interpersonal competence, the program set two primary goals:

1. To increase each couple's ability to reflect on and accurately perceive their own dyadic processes by refining each partner's awareness of his or her contribution to interaction and helping couples explore their own rules of relationship, particularly concerning conflict situations and their patterns of maintaining self-esteem.
2. To increase each couple's capacity for clear, direct, open metacommunication, especially communication about their relationships. [Miller, Nunnally, and Wackman, 1976: 11]

By the time the program was reported on, some hundreds of groups, consisting of five to eight couples each, had undergone the training, which focused specifically on *how* rather than *why* communication between each couple was carried out. Topics covered in the sessions, which were supplemented by a special manual (Miller, Nunnally, and Wackman, 1975), included introduction to the Awareness Wheel, a device for understanding the basic dimensions of self-awareness; learning to exchange accurately information with partners; developing different styles of communication; heightening each partner's ability to build, maintain, or diminish his or her self-esteem and that of the partner; and, finally, integrating what was learned into a common framework (Beatt, 1976:405).

Evaluation of the program has indicated that it offers a meaningful alternative or supplement to traditional methods of preparation for marriage or couplehood. It was also found that the original format could be extended for use with marital partners during later phases of their marriage. Much of its success appeared to lie in its distinctive educational rather than therapeutic emphasis and in the emphasis on the learning of new skills.

Currently, a wide range of similar transition programs are being offered within social agencies, mental health services, religious groups, community centers, and even adult education programs. While the theoretical framework may vary, depending on the particular background and bent of the leaders, the groups share a common emphasis on the improvement of individuals' and families' competence in passing through the developmental and transitional phases of their life span.[7]

Conclusion

This chapter has concentrated on how competence can be enhanced as part of the restitutive phase of acute crises as well as the transitional periods individuals and families experience throughout their life cycle. Certain practice principles have emerged:

1. During periods of acute situational crises and the less bounded but equally stressful periods of transition in the life span, when usual coping patterns no longer suffice and the individual and/ or family suffer pain and anxiety, clients are often particularly amenable to outside influence in order to effect change.
2. These changes should occur in both the person's internal assumptive world and in his life space—the interface between the inner self and the external world.
3. Changes can be effected through the working out of specific goals for action and the development of a sequence of tasks aimed at improving the client's competence in dealing with the immediate stresses in his current life situation and achieving the goals set forth.
4. These tasks can be carried out simultaneously at both the *material–arrangemental* and the *psychosocial* levels and are determined by the specific problem areas or role changes in the client's life situation that have been affected.
5. The worker's role is to help the client identify, spell out, and carry through his specific tasks in both the immediate crisis aspects of the situation and the more fundamental underlying processes initiated by the "vertical" or "horizontal" transitions involved.
6. Strategies for intervention involve not only direct worker–client but also the mobilization of various kinds of natural and formed support systems. These systems both add to and supplement the practitioner's role; they also serve as a bridge to build a supportive network that can become part of the client's life space, once professional activity is terminated, and enable him to function more autonomously and competently in the future.

The application of these practice principles is neither easy nor well articulated in current practice. It demands a considerable shift in the treatment orientation of practitioners as well as development of a new set of practice skills—both in the active intervention into highly stressful areas and in the letting go of such established practice shibboleths as the search for illusive insights and the primacy of client–worker relationships. It demands a reevaluation, in some cases, of agency services and functions to encompass these changes. And, finally, it requires some reorganization of curricula for teaching social work practice, as suggested by Loewenstein (1968), in order to provide an adequate framework of theoretical knowledge and a spectrum of treatment techniques that can provide social workers with a range of alternatives for helping clients to improve their competence during periods of crisis and transition.

Notes

1. For a related perspective on the process of change in one's assumptive world, see Fleming (Chapter 3 in this volume) on attribution and concept attainment theories and their significance for social work practice.
2. For years I have illustrated this point by quoting the homely hymn about the need for help to "strengthen the back or lighten the load."
3. In their compassionate desire to help suffering clients, practitioners in crisis intervention programs tend to lose sight of the point that the primary goal is to increase the clients', not their own, efficacy and competence.
4. Both cases represent anxious, motivated clients who can both *ask* for help and *make use* of it. Work with involuntary clients is discussed by Oxley (Chapter 12 in this volume). In addition, Moore-Kirkland (Chapter 2 in this volume) considers ways of increasing and mobilizing motivation with clients described as unresponsive or unmotivated.
5. Among recent attempts to examine transitions are Feinberg, Feinberg, and Tarrant (1978); Gould (1979); Hoff (1978); Troll (1975); and—probably most widely read—Sheehy (1974). Books and articles dealing with individual bridging periods are too numerous to mention.
6. When I first used the term "entry into marriage," I was informed that not all such relationships culminate in marriage.
7. See Middleman (Chapter 8 in this volume) for further discussion of structured groups to promote competence.

PART 2

Working with the Environment

CHAPTER 5

The Physical Environment and Social Work Practice

Carel B. Germain

This chapter examines the relatively unexplored territory of ideas about the physical environment. Interested social work explorers will need to pick their way through unmapped conceptual thickets and brambles to locate areas that can be cleared as practice sites. While a frontier metaphor can be pushed too far, it does underscore the yet-to-be-discovered practice opportunities (and pitfalls) the physical environment presents to the social worker.

What prompts the exploration is the need to move away from the global concept of "environment" and toward a delineation of the complexities encompassed within the term. Conceptual mapping of the environment is needed if social work practice is to develop differential interventions with environments, and with people–environment transactions, to complement the rich diversity of interventions used with people themselves. Without such environmental and transactional interventions, social work practitioners will be forced to go on acting as if efforts to change people will alone reduce the psychological problems and unmet social needs from which they suffer.

Work on this practice imperative is proceeding productively with respect to the *social* environment. Theoretic concepts, practice principles, and skills have been developed for intervening in organizations (Brager and Holloway, 1978; Germain and Gitterman, 1980); in social networks (Collins and Pancoast, 1976; Lee and Swenson, 1978; Swenson, 1979, and Chapter 6 in this volume); and in such transactional

103

phenomena as stress and coping (Germain and Gitterman, 1979; Golan, Chapter 4 in this volume).[1] But the *physical* environment is still a largely unexplored territory in social work practice and tends to be regarded —when it is regarded at all—as a static setting in which human events and processes occur almost, if not entirely, independently of the qualities of their physical setting. Any possible relation of the physical environment to interface phenomena of adaptation, stress, and coping, and to adaptive achievements such as competence, tends to be overlooked in favor of influences exerted by the social environment.

Hence this chapter will examine some emerging conceptions of the interplay between the physical environment and human cognition, perception, emotion, and action. Modes of human experiencing of the environment and the actual properties of physical environments will be presented in the light of how experiential modes and environmental properties promote or inhibit competence and other adaptive capacities. Practice implications of such conceptions will be considered throughout, with illustrations of the use of physical environments to promote or enhance the competence of individuals, families, and groups.

The Physical Environment

What is meant by "physical environment"? Exploration begins with specifying and describing two layers: the natural world and the built world, and two textures: space and time. Both layers and both textures influence human behavior. The *natural* world comprises animate and inanimate nature. Animate includes the whole ecological web of life forms. Inanimate refers to minerals, land forms such as mountains, plains, and shore, planetary activity such as water, erosion, and earthquake, and cosmic activity such as magnetic fields and background radiation from outer space.[2] The *built* world refers to the almost infinite diversity of structures and objects constructed or fashioned by human beings, including cities and villages, palaces and huts, temples and shrines, objects of art and objects of utility, systems of transportation, and systems of communication. The built world also includes the changes made in the natural world by those constructions and by human activities of clearing forests, tilling land, mining metals, drilling oil wells, and creating wilderness parks, city parks, and village greens. It also includes therapeutic and iatrogenic drugs, alcohol, nuclear and toxic waste, and carcinogens and other pollutants in food, water, and air—all byproducts of human activity in the physical environment. Although increasingly alienated from the rest of nature, human beings are inextricably part of the natural world, so their activity is as "natural" as the nest-building of birds. Nevertheless, the separation of natural and built is a useful heuristic device for delineating environmental complexities, providing its artificiality is kept in mind.

The physical environment is textured by time—by diurnal, seasonal, and annual rhythms of the earth as it travels around the sun and by social cycles of time induced by human activity (Germain, 1976). The physical environment is also textured by open and closed spaces and the arrangements of objects within them (Germain, 1978). All four dimensions of the physical environment, natural and built worlds, and temporal and spatial textures will be explored for their usefulness in microlevel social work practice, with particular reference to enhancing the competence of those who use social work services.

At the outset, note must be taken of the artificiality of separating the physical from the social environment. While this separation, too, is a useful heuristic device, it may lead to oversimplification. Continuous and complex transactions take place between physical settings and social life. Physical settings shape the nature of social interactions which occur in them, and, in turn, are shaped by social patterns, needs, and goals. Not to take this interdependence into account overlooks the complexity.

Oversimplification may also come from overlooking the interdependence of the physical and social environments with the culture. Knowledge and belief systems of a given culture influence the way elements of the natural world are perceived: as a pantheon of gods, totemic ancestors, sources of sustenance, support, and refreshing play or of fear and dread. In the present era, cultural values affect views of the wilderness, for example, and lead to struggles between those who wish to preserve such areas as they are and those who wish to exploit them as economic resources (Graber, 1976; Yi-Fu Tuan, 1976; Krieger, 1973). In the built world, cultural values led western European peoples to devote several centuries to the building of Gothic cathedrals symbolizing man's relationship to God. In the present era, western societies build national monuments to political figures, and top their public buildings with lofty domes, as symbols of national aspirations and power.

Cultural values and norms also affect how people plan and use space and arrange objects within it, and how they respond to the temporal rhythms of earth. The cultural influence on spatial and temporal behaviors is not only intertwined with social patterns and with the physical features of space and time but also with the biological nature of human beings. Some, but not all, scientists believe, for example, that a spatial need such as territory, which appears to be genetically programmed in other forms of life, is also an innate need in human beings. Most biologists do agree, however, that environmental rhythms have been entrained over evolutionary time in human beings as in other organisms, and research has clarified the nature of these biological clocks attuned to planetary time. Cultural orientations to time, including the value placed on past, present, or future times, may or may not mesh with social cycles of time imposed by the organizations and institutions of society. Similarly, cultural or social time may or may not mesh with the inner biological clocks of people.

Environmental Experience

The individual continuously and reciprocally influences and is influenced by the physical and social environments through the life processes of adaptation, stress, and coping and their consequences for growth, health, and social functioning. In attending to people-environment transactions, the practitioner may recognize that people consciously and unconsciously *respond* to the layers and textures of the physical environment, but may be less apt to recognize that people also actively *use* the layers and textures of the physical environment in adaptation. Both responses to and uses of the environment affect the achievement of competence. Both are influenced not only by the symbolic meaning of the environment induced by cultural processes, but also by subjective meanings the physical environment has for the individual, induced by past experience and personal processes of cognition, perception, emotion, and action.

Elements of the physical environment "have some generally shared resonance, but even more of a subjective meaning closely tied to individual or collective experience. The Swiss and the Dutch simply do not apprehend the flatland and the mountain in the same way." (Dansereau, 1975:15). How people experience the environment not only differs because of social, cultural, and geographical influences, but there is variation depending on whether one is male or female, young or old, healthy or ill, newcomer or native, urban or rural dweller, rich or poor. People use different cognitive categories and maps for analyzing their environmental experience depending on their goals, predispositions, expectations, needs, and activities (Ittelson, Franck, and O'Hanlon, 1976). People have differing sensory-perceptual thresholds to understimulating or overstimulating environments and differing psychological capacities for dealing with the stress such environments may arouse. Differences in experiencing the environment may also be generated by anxiety, fear, guilt, shame, rage, despair, or depression, or by the adaptive or maladaptive use of defenses against such affects.

Ittelson, Franck, and O'Hanlon (1976:201–205) suggest there are at least four modes of environmental experience:

1. *Environment As an External Physical Place.*   This mode of experience reflects the long developmental process of differentiating the self from the environment that begins in infancy. Increasingly, the self comes to be viewed as separate and autonomous, and the environment as existing independent of the self. For some people, the environment is experienced predominantly as something external and in terms of its physical properties. They are likely to become "more aware of the consequences of their own actions upon the sequence of changing properties than those who seemed to experience the environment in terms of their own feelings" (p. 202).

2. *Environment As Self.*   People can experience the environment as an important part of themselves rather than as something detachable. "A change in the environment is experienced as a change in the self." Moving from a loved home may bring grief and depression (Fried, 1963). The loss of a treasured object may be experienced as an assault on the self. The enforced relinquishment of personal possessions upon entering a home for the aged, or the environmental rigidity of general hospitals that prevents the patient from impressing his or her own personality on the hospital room, may be experienced as depersonalizing. Such experiences affect the sense of competence.
An important difference exists, however, between adaptive identification with the physical environment, as in the sense of kinship with nature, and the terrifying oceanic loss of self into the environment experienced by the disorganized mental patient. Adaptive reintegration with the environment is characterized by the ability to retain one's sense of humanness and separateness while feeling an identification on evolutionary and physiological grounds with the natural world. It is not oneness; clarity of boundaries is maintained. A disorganized identification with the physical environment comes about through the loss of boundaries between self and environment in which the self seems to melt into the environment, as if lost forever. Searles (1960:3–139) describes how the individual struggles through life to differentiate the self from the social and physical environments. As one succeeds in these differentiations, one is increasingly able to reintegrate the self with the environment and to establish a sense of relatedness to both the physical and the social environment. This adaptive ability enhances competence by supporting exploration of the environment and making decisions about how to change or sustain it as needed.

3. *Environment As Social System.*   Some people experience the environment not as a separate physical place and not as part of the self but rather as a social system or cultural network having a separate existence. The physical setting itself may be entirely out of awareness

so that the environment is experienced solely in terms of the people with whom one is involved. Ittelson, Franck, and O'Hanlon (1976) regard this mode as adaptive in some situations, such as bereavement, or a move to a new area in which one is ultimately concerned with forming new relationships. Even in such situations, however, it would seem that competence is enhanced by awareness and use of the physical setting: finding one's way around a new neighborhood, for example, or receiving comfort from familiar and cherished objects during the loneliness of relocation or of hospitalization. Even the task of mourning is supported by working on the relinquishment of the attachment in the context of shared places, now so stark as one confronts the absence of the loved one.

4. *Environment As Emotional Territory.*   While emotion may be part of all environmental experience, it may sometimes be the dominant mode. The physical environment is then experienced in terms of the emotions attached to memories, associations, or expectations. It becomes an emotional territory. An easterner who returns to his Iowa birthplace every year writes of his "primal connections":

> The farmhouse always looks shabbier and smaller than I expect, our family's possessions in it a little more rundown; but out-of-doors the land flourishes, the trees are higher than I remembered, the fields more luxuriant. This former country life of mine and my current urban existence are joined in an instant, and I feel whole. . . . Coming upon roller skates [in his boyhood closet], high school yearbooks, and a tinfoil badminton trophy for which we keenly contested some summer in the 1930s could produce in me melancholy feelings, but these surprising connections to years long ago also usually elate me. Familiar objects of childhood do not suggest a denial of the passage of time, only disarm the finality of it. . . . I find it nourishing to be in proximity to a still-valid part of me, once a year, even though I don't literally believe ancestors hang about the eaves of the farmhouse or ghosts stalk the bedrooms. Associations thicken the very air, however, inside and out, even in the barns, where I remember long-gone animals—horses, pigs, cows—beings I once knew intimately, whose distinct personalities I sensed. [Harnack, 1977]

Such emotional territories surely account for the power of such practice interventions as the genogram in the metaphorical return to loved places and people, as well as in literal return (Hartman, 1978; 1979a; 1979b).

5. *Environment As Setting for Action.*   This mode of environmental experience is characteristic of architects and planners (and, perhaps, of social workers in the past) who conceive environments only as settings for action. The environment's significance is found only in its provid-

ing an arena in which human events are played out, and no attention is given to the experience people have in playing them out. It is through action that people experience environments, but experience also influences that action. The separation of action from experience overlooks this reciprocal and continuous process. Environmental experience guides the individual's goals and actions, while, reciprocally, environmental action affects the range of future experience in the environment. When action is effective with respect to tasks and goals, the individual experiences a sense of competence.

As a consequence of social, cultural, and personal factors, people's perceived (subjective) physical environment may differ from the actual (objective) environment, or from the subjective environments of others who share the same physical setting. The topological notion of life space attempts to deal with this problem (Lewin, 1951). Since topology refers to the physical configuration of a geographic region, it is an appropriate concept for explorers in a frontier outpost of ideas. For Lewin, the person and his or her perceived environment constitute the life space. In this holistic view, behavior is a function of the life space. Space in this conception is not physical, however, but psychological,

> consisting of the environment not as it exists in the so-called objective world (where, for us, practical matters are usually thought to reside), but in the mind of the person, in his or her *phenomenological field*—including, as especially significant, the world of imagination, of fantasy, and unreality. [Bronfenbrenner, 1977:202]

In Lewin's field theory, it is the perceived phsyical environment that must be explored if we are to understand its influence on behavior. However, the objective environment is also important in understanding such phenomena as delusions and in considering the impact of environmental forces outside the awareness of the person, such as political and economic constraints or the role of cultural values and norms.

Leaving aside epistemological and philosophical problems in the nature of reality, the position taken in this chapter is that the social work practitioner needs to take into account the properties of both the actual and the perceived environment, to the extent possible, in order to understand person–environment transactions and to promote competence.

Properties of the Physical Environment

Steele (1973) provides a useful framework for examining the nutritive properties of physical environments, derived in part from Maslow's (1954) ideas of basic human needs. The framework provides six overlapping and related qualities of nutritive physical environments: security and shelter, social contact, symbolic identification, task instrumentality, pleasure, and growth. Such properties are clearly related to the development and maintenance of competence, relatedness, self-esteem and identity, and autonomy. Examining these environmental properties may yield clues for intervention designed to make physical environments more nutritive for human beings.

Security and Shelter

This is the property of environments to protect people from noxious or unwanted stimuli and from the physical and psychological stress such stimuli create. Physical settings must protect against such excessive stimuli as high noise levels, unwanted intrusion by others, etc. Some hospital emergency rooms, for example, add to the stress of patients and family members by inadequate partitions that expose people to frightening sights, sounds, and smells, thus undermining competence. Newman (1972) suggests that the design of public housing projects gives no opportunity for surveillance by tenants of the semi-public spaces such as lobbies, elevators, hallways, and fire stairs. This factor is thought to contribute to the high rate of crime in housing projects. Physical settings must also protect against inadequate stimuli. Yet bland, stereotyped institutional environments in mental hospitals and geriatric facilities fail to do so. Physical environments must also provide security from noxious stimuli such as toxic substances in work sites and dwellings.

Social Contact

This is the property of physical environments to foster social interaction through spatial arrangements. Osmund (1959) refers to sociofugal space in which furniture arrangement and architectural design discourage social interaction, and sociopetal space in which design and arrangement foster interaction. Sommer (1970) provides an example of a geriatric setting where patients' chairs in the day room were arranged side by side against the walls, making it difficult for the women to converse. Most stared vacantly, becoming less and less involved with others, and presumably more involved with autistic processes. A sociopetal correction was made by introducing small tables around which chairs were placed in conversational groupings. Ultimately, increased interaction among the residents was observed. Seemingly, the physical environment, together with elements of the social environment and personal features of the individual, affects the maintenance of interpersonal skills as a component of competence.

In his framework for understanding how people regulate their social interaction with others, Altman (1975) draws on concepts of privacy, personal space, territory, and crowding in which privacy is the key construct. Privacy is viewed not as a state of solitude as in common parlance but as a boundary-maintaining process between self and others. Distinction is made between desired and achieved states of privacy relating to levels of interaction. In order to realize the desired level, the individual or group uses mechanisms of personal space and territorial behaviors. When the desired level is not realized and there is more interaction than is desired, the individual or group experiences crowding. By definition, crowding is an unpleasant state. Conversely, if there is less interaction achieved than is desired, the individual or group experiences social isolation, also an unpleasant state by definition.

Following the work of Hall (1966), Altman (1975) conceives personal space—an area or zone immediately surrounding the body—as a behavioral mechanism for regulating distance and closeness to others. Hall related zones of distance to their functions: intimate, personal, social, and public. Since people vary in the size of these zones according to culture, age, and psychological states, the possibilities for distortions in communications and relationships are many. Such distortions can create stress. DeLong (1970) suggests, for example, that elderly persons have smaller personal zones than young people. Because of declining sensory acuity, the aged tend to interact more comfortably at the intimate rather than at the personal zone. Young staff in facilities for the aged react to what they perceive as intrusiveness by holding the aged person at arm's length. Such behavior can be dehumanizing and adversely affects the aged person's self-esteem, competence, sense of relatedness, and autonomy.

Disregard for social norms regarding personal and public space creates stress. It has been frequently noted, for example, that city dwellers observe particular norms for maintaining distance in such crowded facilities as elevators and subways by averting the eyes, holding the body rigid, etc. In the following example, another norm was disregarded, creating discomfort:

A woman and little girl get on a rather empty subway car. Girl settles herself with a sandwich, mother reads aloud to the little girl (*The Hobbit*, no less), pausing to ask questions and to discuss every few paragraphs. Her voice rings out in the silence. As the stops go by, the car becomes crowded. She reads on, oblivious. Everyone is astonished, then quietly outraged and somewhat embarrassed. When drunks and psychotics misbehave on the subway, passengers are tolerant; even when people perform (for example, the blind trumpeter), there is some acceptance. But here is an intact middle-class woman turning the subway into her personal living room! The unwritten rules have been violated—public space has been treated like private space.[3]

Territorial behavior, an ethological concept, is considered by Altman (1975) to be another means of interpersonal boundary regulations. Possession, marking, and defense of spaces and objects create boundaries that limit intimacy. Territorial behaviors include verbal and paraverbal communications, and draw on such environmental devices as doors, locks, fences, hedges, partitions, uniforms and badges for boundary maintenance. Territorial behaviors can be observed in individuals, families, groups, and organizations.

Kantor and Lehr (1975) have analyzed the use of spatial and temporal mechanisms in family life by which members regulate their closeness and distance to one another. Each family has to determine means by which members can feel safe in the interior social space of the family and in the exterior space of its environment. With respect to interior space, for example, members must constantly regulate their spatial relations and boundaries to reach a balance between intimacy and separateness appropriate for the life cycle needs of the family members and of the family itself. Moreover, family members have to occupy the same social space, spend time together, and devote energies to the same activities if they are to gain access to love and intimacy, separateness or autonomy, identity, and be able to develop competence. The Smith family of father, mother, and three teenagers who had dropped out of school were beset by many personal, interpersonal, and environmental problems. They were ostracized by their neighbors and had no kin or peer networks. Even the physical appearance of their small apartment reflected a sense of isolation. The curtains were drawn tight, as though the family felt itself under siege:

> Mrs. Smith explained there is no household routine because no one has to be anywhere at any particular time. Family members do not retire or arise at the same time. They do not eat meals together nor share activities except for constant quarreling over TV programs. The TV set is the focal point in the family and is apparently the major contact with the outside world. On the one hand, the family's use of time serves to keep them apart. Yet, on the other, their space is so cramped that when they interact it is almost always in very angry ways, as though to maintain some sense of spatial distance or separateness. [Germain and Gitterman, 1980]

Shapiro and Ryglewicz make an interesting and sharply contrasting observation on the connection between temporal and spatial behaviors:

> People who value neatness are often fond of schedules; the ordering of both space and time enhances their feelings of security. People who are "loose" with space are often "loose" with time. . . . We can feel interrup-

tions of our private time much as we feel invasions of our private space. "Safe space" for the self often means a place, such as home or study room, where one's time is safe from interruption; while "safe time" often means the time spent in a special place or with a special person. [Shapiro and Ryglewicz, 1976:102]

Symbolic Identification

This property of the physical environment refers to the nature of the information it conveys about the individuals or groups connected with it. In many settings in which social workers practice, this property has a negative force. The location, exterior and interior design, and the furnishings communicate society's view of those who use the services of particular agencies and institutions. Public settings such as welfare offices are often dingy, drab, overcrowded, and lack the amenities for comfort, privacy, and relaxed interaction found in some private settings (Seabury, 1971; Maluccio, 1979a). The same contrasts can be found between inner city and suburban schools, public and private mental hospitals, and public housing and private apartment complexes. Such differential messages adversely affect the self-image and professional competence of staff as well:

The district office of a large public child welfare agency occupies the entire ground floor of a dingy building. A previous administrator had removed all partitions on the assumption this would promote more effective surveillance of staff by supervisors. So the floor is one very large office except for the corner space occupied by the district supervisor which is partitioned from floor to ceiling, and unit supervisors' offices along the only windowed side of the room. These are partitioned from the floor to a height of five feet. Social workers sit at desks in the large middle area. The desks face each other, two by two, with one telephone at each pair of desks. The result of "open space" is chaos. There are neither group territories nor personal spaces, and no way to regulate privacy and interaction. The walls, painted institutional green, are dirty and finger-marked; desks are dusty; and the noise level is high. To make matters worse, the front door is permanently locked because of bomb threats in the past. All traffic is through the back door. Each time the door is opened, a loud bell alerts the receptionist to the new entrant who is then checked for the legitimacy of the visit.

This physical setting communicates to those who use its service and those who work there that neither they nor the service is valued by the community. This is an assault on the self-esteem of the citizens dependent on the service, and affects negatively the sense of professional identity and professional competence of the staff. A contrasting example demonstrates the environmental property of symbolic identification in its positive aspect:

The social worker in an inner-city school was concerned about poor relations between parents and the school which compounded the problems children were having in school. She persuaded the principal to turn over an unused room as a parents' drop-in lounge for those mothers bringing their small children to school each morning. She decorated it with plants, had coffee and doughnuts ready. She made each mother feel welcome and valued, and soon had a number of regulars who looked forward to the respite, warmth, and attention given them by the school.

After a bit, the worker was able to engage two groups of mothers in meeting to talk of their shared needs and tasks as single parents living on limited budgets in a harsh environment. In the process, the mothers developed a mutual-aid system, exchanging ideas, resources, and social support. The mothers' competence was enhanced by the increased responsiveness of the school's physical environment induced by a competent social worker. Often a desired change in a social structure can be more easily obtained through a change in the physical structure, as in this instance.

Task Instrumentality

This environmental property refers to how facilities and layouts in dwellings, institutions, and rural and urban communities support the performance of life tasks. Spivack (1973) has developed three concepts applicable to this environmental property: setting deprivation; archetypal places and human life cycle requirements; and critical confluence.

Setting deprivation exists when human habitats do not provide all the behavioral sites necessary for people to carry out species-specific functions and behaviors. The achievement of life tasks and adaptive functioning are impaired, stress becomes unmanageable, and social disorganization, mental and physical illness, and other misery are likely to ensue.

Archetype places (not to be confused with Jung's notion of Archetype) are the basic culturally specific settings in the physical environment which are needed for human beings to "maintain deep, lasting interpersonal relationships . . . their ability to work, provide or eat food, to sleep in deep renewing comfort, play, raise children, explore and protect territory, to meet with their peers, and make decisions which control the shape and quality of life" (Spivack, 1973:35). In short, competence fails to develop to its fullest potential, or is undermined altogether, in the absence of adequate spaces and furnishings which support these basic human needs and behaviors.

Critical confluence refers to the coming together of physiological drive or psychosocial need, the object of that drive or need, the temporal context (life cycle and otherwise), and the specific archetypal place with which the "whole" behavior is associated. If access is blocked to any one of these four elements, the whole behavioral act will be impaired, competence will be diminished, and human relatedness, identity, and autonomy will be undermined.

Spivack (1973) cross-references the thirteen archetypal places with the characteristic life tasks of five stages of the life cycle, and specifies the sixty five functions and their spatial requirements that resonate to the deepest needs of the human being:

> Each phase of the human life cycle has not only a central, drive-related task—such as child rearing—but also an *appropriate* (archetypal) *physical environment* for the proper support and resolution of behaviors related to these tasks. Thus, in the context of the right archetypal surround, we are free to engage in a critical set of actions—such as cradling and nursing an infant. In order to successfully engage in these movement patterns, and to experience the events fully and to the ultimate satisfaction of the drive, particular temporal and physical criteria must be met. [Spivack, 1973:43]

Mrs. May, age 41, and her 5-year-old son, John, are a black family receiving AFDC. Mrs. May has no friends, is depressed and lonely, but also suspicious and untrusting. She keeps John close to her physically and emotionally to "protect" him. And she has not yet sent him to school for fear he will meet the "wrong kind" of children. The boundary problem in differentiation is reflected also in the physical setting. Mother and son occupy a one-room apartment, and share the one bed. There is no physical separation between functional areas in the room:

Interviews were difficult at the beginning, not only because of Mrs. May's suspiciousness, but because John interfered with our talking. Mrs. May's reaction was to hit him with a strap she kept handy. About my third visit, I asked Mrs. May if we might try something new. When she agreed, I explained to John that his mother and I had important business together, and if he played alone while his mother and I talked I would play with him for ten minutes after each visit. Mrs. May and John both liked the idea, and we were able to accomplish more. This seemed to bring about beginning demarcation of mother–son boundaries as well, and we were soon able to talk about Mrs. May's personal need for privacy under the difficult living conditions. An early step involved Mrs. May's purchase of a separate bed for John and room dividers that helped differentiate the functions of eating, sleeping, playing, storage, etc.

As mother and son developed these physical boundaries and achieved some separateness in their life together, the matter of social isolation came to the fore. Mrs. May signaled her readiness for this focus by talking of her loneliness, and I learned about the early sources of her feeling abandoned and unloved. This was followed by trips to the park with mother and son, a gradual relaxing of her reluctance to let him play outside with other children, and her registering him for school. The relationship with me became more trusting (from time to time we had boundary problems there too!); and after about six months Mrs. May initiated exchanges with neighbors and indicated her interest in restoring broken relations with kin.

The structuring of the physical environment was, of course, only one aspect of the long, complex process of building boundaries. Yet it provided a concrete base for psychological differentiation, and for the later step of reintegration to the environment. The spatial unavailability for sleep and privacy, and for education and socialization with peers, threatened to interfere with the life cycle needs of the child to gain age-specific interpersonal, intellectual, motoric, and emotional competence. Similarly, setting deprivation was interfering with the mother's life cycle needs for redefining her identity as a separate person, socializing with peers, and competence in the roles of mother, daughter, sister, and friend.

Pleasure

This property refers to the pure enjoyment places give to those who use them. The pleasure derives from the qualities of the setting itself, one's own history, and one's present mood or inner state. Environmental pleasure in the natural and built worlds arises from pleasing stimuli to all the senses, the distinctive arrangements of space and form, ambiance of landscapes and townscapes, freedom of movement, or the zestful quality of experience within the setting. One's own imagination, especially in childhood, can enrich the pleasurable property of such environments.

Opportunities for such environmental experiences are limited for children, adults, and elderly who are poor. Yet creative social workers, since the days of the settlement houses and fresh-air camps, and including the present, have found ways to provide such opportunities. These include trips to museums, parks, and historic places in the urban environment, exploration and camping experiences in wilderness and rural environments (Cataldo, 1979), and experiences with animals and plants. There is sheer enjoyment in these environmental experiences and actions, yet they have important consequences for competence, identity, relatedness, and autonomy. When one is in a place that transcends everyday life, and that one enjoys, one feels better about one-self. New knowledge, skills, and awareness of self may be acquired, and competence enhanced. Helping people to develop a sense of relatedness to the physical environment may be acquiring a professional legitimacy it has not always had. Its therapeutic potential is being studied and is now more fully understood (Vassil, 1978). Day and resident camps have developed for the aged, blind, diabetic children, developmentally disabled, disturbed children and youth, and, more recently, respite experiences for the "walking worried"[4] and for mothers known to a protective services unit of a welfare department.[5]

Besides the pleasurable experiences and action afforded in these various physical environments, Searles (1960:120) suggests additional fruitful effects of relatedness to the physical environment: "(1) the assuagement of various painful and anxiety-laden states of feeling; (2) the fostering of self-realization; (3) the deepening of one's feeling of reality; and (4) the fostering of one's appreciation, and acceptance, of one's fellow men."

As an environmental instrument possessing the property of pleasure, horticultural therapy is increasingly used in work with the aged, disabled and handicapped, adolescents, and the emotionally disturbed. It is used on farms, in rural villages, suburban towns, and urban ghettos. In any setting, human-plant interaction can help in coping with stress. Lewis (1976) speaks of interaction in this context because the person's activity is guided by the responses and needs of the plants. Feeling needed restores a sense of relatedness to the isolated and a sense of self-esteem to the depressed, and can encourage autonomous behavior in disturbed or acting-out adolescents.

> Mrs. Stanley is a 90-year-old widow. Her husband was a farmer, but like many others during the Depression, the Stanleys lost their land. They moved to a small town. Then Mr. Stanley died. When I arrived, Mrs. Stanley was lying down. Her voice was weak. She was suffering from shingles in her face and she complained of dysentery. She was unhappy, neither the world nor anyone in it seemed to please her. After a while I said, "I hear you have a green thumb." With that a great change came over her. Her expression brightened. Her voice became stronger. She told me of her interest in plants, her rare bulbs, the flowers she had furnished for three weddings, and her hopes for a garden for the coming summer. . . .
>
> I have kept in touch with Mrs. Stanley. . . . I have seen her during the summer pulling weeds and tenderly touching one flower after another. She wrote letters to me telling me when this lily was in bloom and that rose was about to open. Her granddaughter and I took pictures of her garden. In the fall slides of her flowers were shown at a meeting of a newly organized group of older people. Proudly she told about each plant. . . . [Twente, 1965:107–108]

For Mrs. Stanley, contacts with plants fed the eye, employed the hand, and sustained the soul—her pleasure was aesthetic, sensual and psychological (Lewis, 1976:5).

Similarly, animals may be used as environmental instruments of help and as sources of pleasure. Seeing-eye dogs for the blind have been joined by trained dogs for the deaf, pet dogs as therapists for patients in a mental hospital, and farm animals for children to care for in a residential treatment setting. As companions, animal pets of all kinds represent potential for environmental pleasure and for experiences in learning responsibility and competence, and developing relatedness—of loving and being loved. In fact, a recent study reported that "pet owners are statistically more likely to survive a heart attack than are people who have no animal companions."[6]

A final observation about environmental pleasure refers to the deep attachment to place—urban or rural—that many experience. When present, it ranges from a sense of the sacredness of the homeland to the deep and abiding love for places that were intimately associated with activities of one's childhood, youth, or, perhaps, adulthood. Such a place might be a mountain forest, a street corner, a vista, a neighborhood, or a building. The attachment becomes a part of one's sense of identity. Despite the expression "You can't step in the same river twice," treasured places acquire a curious permanence in the memory, their presence evoked by a fleeting sound or scent. This may be what gives significant meaning to snapshots, helping us relive past environmental pleasures with loved persons, places, and times, and helping us regain a sense of continuity with them. And so child welfare services help children develop family albums to take with them into placement or adoption. And snapshots can be helpful in many other cases:

In about our fourth session, Mrs. Peters brought me a box of snapshots, with the comment, "That will keep you busy for a while." Indeed, it kept us both busy over many interviews, as she relived some treasured experiences, and began to see the threads of continuity between her own memories of childhood places and of her parents and some of her hospitalized daughter's experiences with herself and her husband. Her spontaneous associations to pictured places, events, and people lent richness to our efforts to understand their continuation in the present: her love for her dead sister, the early days of marriage and her reawakened pride in her husband's achievements. Pictures of a grandmother, born into slavery, permitted us to deal with deeply felt responses to environmental issues impinging on the well being of Mrs. Peters's daughter.

Snapshots, like genograms, can be important environmental instruments of help when used sensitively by the social worker. They can serve to reaffirm identity, strengthen the sense of competence in past and present, and confirm the continuing threads of relatedness to others and to the physical environment. They can be particularly helpful in work with children (Laird, 1979:198) and in the process of reminiscence with aged persons.

> Seen again, after an interval, snapshots provoke free associations in the form of stories that . . . are myths of origin. If told to children, they people life and fill with meaning the incomprehensible emptiness that existed before they were born. If told to relatives, they resolve every contradiction, confirm or deny every suspicion, and recapitulate every connection to transform existential faith into a dynastic progress. If told to [practitioners] who listen, they reveal the detailed meanings of common life that, until provoked by the snapshot, remained inaccessible even to the most subtle of inquiries. [Lesy, 1978]

Growth

This final property refers to the growth-inducing qualities of the physical environment: its diversity, problem-solving demands, surprise features, social contacts, and provision of feedback to people about the consequences of their action.

Anderson School was located in a middle-class residential area of a medium-size city. Children from the inner city were bused in. The school social worker, with the principal's consent, developed a project she called "Concern for Community," using a team made up of a teacher and several volunteers including a retired social worker. The project involved a series of fifth-grade field trips for firsthand learning about institutions and agencies set up to meet human needs—including hospitals, adolescent group homes, and geriatric facilities. The children studied their city's layout and its implications by locating their own homes on a map in relation to the homes of the other groups members and classmates, and to libraries, parks and other urban amenities. The children also met with the social worker in small groups over the school year to talk about human needs in their community and resources for meeting them.

The project's objectives were to stimulate a greater concern in the children for one another, for human need, and for their shared physical environment, and to increase the children's sense of interdependence, mutual caring and appreciation of one another. The trips, and especially the small group experiences, were evaluated by the school as having met the objectives. One can add that through the purposeful use of and action in their physical environment, the children experienced growth as well as security, social interaction, symbolic identification, task instrumentality, and pleasure. The social worker created a nutritive environment that contributed to competence, relatedness, the sense of identity, and autonomy of all participants.

McBride and Clancy (1976) describe their success in changing some of the negative properties of a residential treatment unit for autistic children, and creating an environment with physical properties that supported the children's growth toward more competent behavior. The children ranged in age from 3 to 12. There were four apartments in the unit, each with two cottage parents and six children. A range of specialists saw the children for various therapies. The children were described as extremely detached or isolated, destructive, and lacking competence in socialization skills including language. The staff had become frustrated and discouraged, and the children were becoming even more isolated and destructive. It was decided to introduce an experimental program with the following objectives:

1. To foster social and socializing interactions between adults and children.
2. To integrate staff skills in order to minimize overlap and energy expenditure, and maximize effectiveness, and to order every part of the children's day.
3. To modify the built environment, initially within a restricted area, the children's living quarters, to complement and reinforce other special programs. [McBride and Clancy, 1976:170-71]

With respect to the third objective, the authors report,

> furniture was positioned to foster and reinforce certain patterns of social interaction, namely child–child vis-à-vis contact; adult contact involving touching, and upper-body contact of a mutually pleasant type. . . . Furniture placement was further used to facilitate learning of a variety of socialization skills. For example, by putting the dining area adjacent to the kitchen the children could now assist in serving food and clearing away. More than that, staff could now remain sitting at the table in face-to-face interaction with the children, altering the type of controls used over their behavior and promoting increased social engagement between adults and children, and the latter with each other. [McBride and Clancy, 1976:172–73]

The experimenters also made use of play equipment to stimulate perceptual and motoric skills. Diversity of color, texture, and sound was provided as well as changeability and manipulability. Visibility of stimuli was extended by making use of floor areas and wall areas, the latter with self-rewarding busy boards. Children thus received some feedback about the consequences of their actions with this equipment.

Within twenty four hours, staff and an independent observer noted changes in the children's behavior. These included more relaxed behavior, more exploratory behavior, increased interaction between child and child, and between children and adults, and a decline in destructive use of the furniture. These and other changes also altered the nature of verbal interchanges between adults and children from angry and restrictive to warmly reinforcing. The improvements remained in place, and by the end of the first month complete elimination of all destructive behavior had been achieved for the first time in the unit's history. By the end of six months, half the children were attending community schools while still living in the unit.

> The difficulty from this point was the lack of a suitable halfway house that would lead back into full integration into family and community, a possibility for a future design project; but we would prefer to see the family fully incorporated from the outset, in treatment of the child's condition, so that a halfway house would be unnecessary. [McBride and Clancy, 1976:176]

Changing the physical environment made an important contribution to the total effort to change the social system. The newly structured physical and social environments were on the way to providing a milieu where children could grow toward greater competence.

Implications for Adaptation and Competence

Adaptation includes processes of changing the self, changing the environment, and moving to new environments. In these processes, human beings grow and develop through responding to and using their environments—that is, through the interaction of experience in the environment and action upon it (Maluccio, 1974). Environmental competence is a combination of awareness of the environment, and its influence on efforts to reach goals and meet needs, and the ability to decide what environmental changes are necessary and to act effectively on such decisions. Competence and autonomy, however, are interdependent. And autonomy requires options for choice and decision-making. In our society, such options depend very much on one's place in the socioeconomic structure, which then determines access to power and opportunities for choice. Poor people without social power, for example, can have little impact on environments created by others, such as housing projects, hospitals, schools, slum housing, work sites, etc. This means that with many issues involving the phsyical environment, the social worker must take mediating, advocacy, and sometimes adversarial roles in helping individuals, families, and groups deal with setting deprivations, and negative properties of physical environments.[7]

From another perspective, people who are extremely dependent on the environment, such as the aged, ill, disabled, and children, have little competence and/or autonomy for influencing their environments. Fortunately, in response to recent federal legislation many changes in the physical environments of communities, institutions, and organizations have been effected for physically handicapped individuals. These changes have increased their mobility, autonomy, and competence. But many mental hospitals, nursing homes, geriatric facilities, and even general hospitals continue to provide stereotyped, understimulating environments for patients/residents. For social workers practicing in these settings, the adequacy of sensory-perceptual, cognitive, and social stimuli is an important area for social work involvement at policy, planning, and programmatic levels. To increase the growth-inducing properties and reduce the negative qualities of such environments, practitioners need an array of "influencing skills" for organizational innovation. These have been covered extensively in the literature and will not be reviewed here.[8] At the practice level, however, providing patients/residents with as many opportunities as possible for decision-making and action regarding their environment (commensurate with physical capacity, interest, and ability) can contribute to the reawakening or maintenance of competence and can restore the sense of autonomy.

Clearly, then, all people, and especially the powerless, need to participate in decisions made about their own physical environments. In Sommer's (1970) example of the chairs and the old women, referred to earlier in this chapter, the patients at first resisted the change, protesting the territorial loss of "their" chairs. Several persisted in pushing the chairs back to the accustomed positions against the wall, even after others began to enjoy the change. Nurses disliked the change because it had been easier to keep track of patients by simply looking down the line of chairs. Maintenance staff disliked the change because their cleaning tasks had been easier when they could push a broom down an empty central area, now cluttered with chairs and small tables. Had patients and staff participated originally in assessing their shared environment—its positive and negative properties with respect to their needs and goals—and in planning for agreed-upon changes, resistance might have been minimized. More importantly, competence would have been enhanced.

In any efforts to influence physical environments, consideration must also be given to outcomes, including unplanned consequences that might be negative in nature. Clients' participation in the evaluation of the environmental change also enhances the sense of identity, relatedness, autonomy, and competence.

People do, of course, get used to arrangements as they are. The known, however unsatisfactory, is often more comfortable than the unknown. The old women moved their chairs back to where they had been; workshop participants at social work conferences put up with uncomfortable or unproductive arrangements of chairs; and families get used to spatial and temporal structures that perpetuate themselves despite the unsatisfactory patterns of intimacy and distance, separateness and togetherness, they may have engendered. Thus the social worker's help may involve: (1) helping individuals, families, and formed and neighborhood groups to become aware of their physical environment and how it influences their efforts to meet needs and reach goals; (2) helping them make decisions about what needs to be changed, how it can be changed, and what resources of energy, information, and material aid will be needed to effect change; and (3) helping them take action and achieve the change (Steele, 1973:8; Altman, 1975:213–20).

Conclusion

A dynamic conception of physical settings adds an important dimension to our understanding of person–environment transactions and expands our repertoire of environmental and transactional interventions. Modes of environmental experience; properties of physical environments associated with competence, relatedness, autonomy, and self-esteem and identity; the significance of archetypal places across the life cycle; and the interplay between all of these and human cognition, perception, emotion, and action suggest many ways to increase practice effectiveness. Experimentation with restructuring space and time, and with using elements of the natural and built worlds as instruments of help, will aid the search for more effective ways to help people improve their physical environments. In achieving a better environmental fit with their needs and aspirations, individuals, families, and groups enhance their competence.

The social worker's unit of attention must be expanded to include the many facets of the physical environment throughout the mutual (worker–client) processes of exploration, problem definition,[9] contracting, assessment and planning, intervention, and evaluation of service outcomes. A central question is: How willing are we to leave our offices and confront the environments of our clients—especially in the face of constraints posed by agency structures, funding and reimbursement issues, and comfort with arrangements as they are? Since the days of the settlement house and the charity organization society, however, the profession's concern has been to meliorate environments. I believe the answer to that central question will lie in the profession's renewed commitment to its historic concern.

Notes

Acknowledgment: I am grateful to Robin Belowsky, MS; Edna Bernstein, MSW; Jean Fields, MSW; and Barbara Loh, MSW, for making their practice experiences in physical environments available to me.

1. Even earlier, work was done on milieu therapy and family therapy.
2. Interesting articles on the relation between these physical forces and human behavior can be found in Moos and Insel (1974).
3. Carol Swenson, personal communication.
4. "Sanctuary for the Walking Worried," *Practice Digest, a Quarterly of the National Association of Social Workers,* vol. 1, no. 4 (March 1979): 17–18.
5. "Mom's Day Out," ibid., vol. 1, no. 1 (June 1978): 15–16.
6. *New York Times,* December 31, 1978, p. E7.
7. An example is provided by Grosser (1979).
8. Two of the most recent presentations are Brager and Holloway (1978) and Germain and Gitterman (1980).
9. An illustration of redefining a problem from psychopathology to an ecological crisis involving a change in the physical environment is provided in Minuchin (1974:11–12).

CHAPTER 6

Using Natural Helping Networks to Promote Competence

Carol R. Swenson

Luisa, 11, was the sole caretaker of her mother, who had an advanced case of multiple sclerosis. Luisa called Inez, their former homemaker, with whom they continued to be friendly, and said: "The food stamps came; could you take me to get groceries?" As they drove, Luisa also told Inez about a neighbor who had gotten milk and oatmeal for them when their money ran out.

Recently a child had to be placed in foster care. The family was fearful of a strange home. However, they did trust the child's day-care mother. She was explored as a resource for the child and was subsequently licensed as a foster home. The family has been able to accept this placement and use it constructively.

What do these two vignettes have in common? Each shows an example of people competently interacting with their social networks as they go about living their lives. In one instance, the events were simply reported; in the other a social worker intervened to facilitate the competence strivings of a family.

As these vignettes illustrate, competence is a fundamentally trans-actional concept;[1] the outcome of each person's efforts at coping depends "not only on his qualities and needs but also on the availability and purposive use of varied environmental resources and social supports" (Maluccio, 1979b:286). Consequently, social workers are increasingly playing interventive roles that are based on the use of natural helping networks and social support systems.

Studies of client feedback confirm the importance of natural helpers for human beings. Leichter and Mitchell (1979) found that the extended family was a valued support for many clients, but that social workers tended to devalue these relationships. Similarly, Maluccio (1979a:142) indicated that "clients . . . pointed to the positive impact of friends, relatives, and informal 'helping' agents in the community"; however, social workers were more negative about these relationships than their clients.

The response of social workers in these studies point to the need to conceptualize more systematically the potential use of natural helping networks to promote competence through social work intervention. This chapter seeks to contribute to this task. It will begin with discussion of selected ideas about natural helping and social networks. Assessment strategies will then be considered, along with the social worker's role as "catalyst." Finally, a series of interventive strategies operationalizing the practitioner's catalytic role in relation to social networks will be described and illustrated.

Natural Helping and Social Networks

Social workers engaged in direct practice have long been aware of the impact of the social environment on people's social functioning, upon self-concept and attitudes, and even upon the survival of the focal unit (cf. Grinnell, Kyte, and Bostwick, Chapter 7 in this volume).

The environment may contain noxious elements that need to be mitigated or removed. However, it also has positive resources that can be identified, mobilized, and, if necessary, strengthened. Even in highly deteriorated, problem-ridden neighborhoods there are individuals or groupings to support and help others. These "natural helpers" can be an invaluable resource to the individuals, families, and groups with whom they are in contact.

There has been much less attention to conceptualizing natural helping than many other areas of prefessional concern. Much of our knowledge is in the form of "practice wisdom," and it needs to be systematically organized or theoretically developed. There is a thread that runs back to the early settlement workers and community organizers, whose programs focused on natural helpers. Such helpers have not generally been considered in casework theory. Bertha Reynolds

(1951) formulated interventive strategies based on concepts of people's interdependence. More recently, Collins and Pancoast (1976) have pursued the concept of natural helping networks. Gerald Caplan (1974; Caplan and Killilea, 1976) has been developing the related concept of "support systems" in community mental health. The President's Commission on Mental Health (1978) has devoted considerable attention to community support systems.

What Is Natural Helping?

In efforts to conceptualize further the use of natural helping in social work, we need to ask first: What is natural helping or social support? While the meaning of these terms is intuitively obvious, formal definitions are in short supply. "Natural helping" appears in the social work literature primarily in contrast to professional helping and is viewed as synonymous with mutual aid (Schwartz, 1961). In the psychological and sociological literature, terms such as social exchange, reciprocity, and altruism are found. Reciprocity implies that each person has certain relatively unspecified rights and responsibilities (Gouldner, 1960; Blau, 1968). There are times when helping takes place without the norm of reciprocity being invoked. This altruistic giving generally involves dependent recipients, like children, the elderly, and the sick (Krebs, 1970). Natural helping, then, has elements of altruism as well as reciprocity. If persons have approximately equal resources, the norm of reciprocity is likely to be invoked; if not, or if they are at very different stages of the life cycle, helping may be altruistic.

A related term is social support, which has been defined by Caplan (1974:5–6) as follows: "(a) the significant others help the individual mobilize his psychological resources and master emotional burdens; (b) they share his tasks; and (c) they provide him with extra supplies of money, materials, tools, skills, and cognitive guidance to improve his handling of his situation." Tolsdorf (1975) indicates that social support can be of instrumental and emotional types. "Natural helping" and "social support" are essentially similar statements about the processes of people helping people.

Natural helping can and does take place, of course, within the traditional units of social work attention—the family and the small group. But it also occurs more broadly in the social environment as well. Therefore, any concepts that increase our understanding of the social environment can help us in identifying and using natural helping.

Social Network Theory

One such conceptual resource is social network theory. John Barnes is credited with introducing the analytic use of the term social network in his study of the social relationships in a small Norwegian fishing village. He stated:

> I find it convenient to talk of a social field of this kind as a network. The image I have in mind is of a set of points some of which are joined by lines. The points of the image are people, or sometimes groups, and the lines indicate which people interact with each other. [Barnes, 1954:43]

Elizabeth Bott (1971) has also done significant research using the concept of social network. In her study of patterns of marital interaction, she found that the degree of closeness between the acquaintances of a couple would influence the quality of interaction within the marital pair.

From the point of view of the applied social scientist, social network ideas are highly evocative; however, they have been used with varying degrees of rigor. In most instances, social network is used to refer to the relationships around an individual, family, or small group. Far less often are the relationships *among* the relationships considered. For instance, in thinking about sources of support for a family, one might not pay much attention to the potential relationships among the natural helpers of that family.

There are two basic ways of looking at a network. In the first, a focal unit is identified and the network consists of the relationships around that focal unit. These are often called egocentric or personal networks, though perhaps focal network would be a better term to communicate that the unit need not be an individual. A network analysis could thus be made around a street-corner gang or an agency, studying their respective environments, as well as around an individual, martial pair, or extended family.

The second approach analyzes the whole network. Here, all the linkages among all the units of a given population are studied. In most instances, somewhat arbitrary decisions must be made about boundaries. For example, in studying a residential school, would families of students be "in" or "out"? What about students' friends at home or the families of staff members?

Various structural and interactional variables have been identified in networks (Mitchell, 1969; Barnes, 1972). Structural variables include range, segmentation, reachability, and density. The interactional variables are frequency, complexity, intensity, and directedness.[2] The example that follows shows how a social worker in a mental health center might apply social network concepts in her assessment of a troubled young woman:

Ms. Keeney was a 21-year-old art student who had been briefly married to another art student. She plunged headlong into new friendships and interests. The *range* of her social network was consequently very large, and she perceived most of her relationships as *intense*. Even her relationship with her parents was intense, though highly conflicted. The largest number of her friends was from the school *sector*. They were not a *dense* cluster, but rather people with whom she interacted on a one-to-one basis.

Other relationships were also diffuse: Her parents refused to have anything to do with her friends at school, as did her fellow waitresses at work. At times, Ms. Keeney could only *reach* her father and brother indirectly through her mother, because of family conflict. Her relationships were highly volatile; although highly *frequent* at one time, they often rapidly dissipated. Most of her relationships were relatively *uniplex,* sharing only a limited area of interest. This added to their transitory quality. Her relationships were often *asymmetrical,* as she sought an intensity the other person did not.

Other approaches to assessment might label Ms. Keeney as a borderline personality and describe her relationships as superficial and immature. Network theory allows for more specific assessment of relationships and may suggest ideas for intervention. For example, Ms. Keeney needs to be helped to narrow the range and increase the complexity and density of her relationships. This will make for deeper and more stable relationship patterns.

Competent People and Their Helping Networks

In spite of the American mythology of self-sufficiency and stalwart independence, the evidence indicates that competent, adaptive people rely substantially upon their social networks (Mechanic, 1974). Indeed, a dense interlocking web of reciprocal help and support seems a requirement for competence in our complex and rapidly changing society, as the following vignettes will show.

The first is about a middle-class, first-generation Polish immigrant:

Mrs. Trecinsky, a divorced working mother of two school-age girls, depended upon several neighbors to keep an eye on her girls after school and a friend to take care of them if they were ill. Mrs. Trecinsky reciprocated in many ways: sharing garden tools, driving extra trips on weekends, cooking a casserole for her friend, and so on. She was so infectious in her helping

that she encouraged a neighborhood "culture" of mutuality and cooperation.

The second vignette involves a young black mother in a midwest-
ern urban ghetto:

Ruby Banks took a cab to visit Virginia Thomas, her baby's aunt, and they
swapped some hot corn bread and greens for diapers and milk. In the cab
going home Ruby said to me, "I don't believe in putting myself on nobody,
but I know I need help every day. . . . You have to have help from everybody
and anybody, so don't turn no one down when they come round for help."
[Stack, 1974:32]

Next is an upper-middle-class Jewish lawyer:

A lawyer called a respected colleague. "Sam, I need some advice; let me
take you to lunch and get your ideas." Later Sam called to ask: "What do
people in your office think of this new regulation?" At one point, the two
men also worked intensively on a professional committee. The relationship
continued over the years, even though at times they did not see each other
for months. Eventually one moved to another city. Now they saw each other
primarily at conferences. One day Sam called long-distance: "There is a
superb opening here for a person with your abilities; I'd like to tell you
about it and submit your name."

These three people live in highly disparate circumstances, yet they
all use their networks to promote their own and each other's competence. Mrs. Trecinsky exchanges services that allow her to negotiate her
two "full-time jobs" and help the busy people in her network as well.
Mrs. Banks, whose issues include more basic survival concerns, exchanges food and clothing. The lawyers swap professional judgment
and technical information. Yet all three interact with their social environments in ways that enhance their own well-being and add to available resources.

More empirical study is needed on the ways competent people lead
their lives. In particular, attention should be given to how competent
people create and sustain helping networks and how helping networks
change over time. We also need to pursue research on those "at risk"
persons who adapt successfully in spite of their special vulnerability
(Pines, 1979).

Use of Natural Helping in Practice

The use of natural helping and social networks concepts in the human services has been reviewed extensively elsewhere (Collins and Pancoast, 1976; Killilea, 1976; Sarason, 1977; Swenson, 1979). A few examples may suggest the range and vitality of these efforts. Dumont (1968) has described a preventive mental health strategy of making contact with "front-line caretakers" such as bartenders and hairdressers. Collins and Pancoast (1976) have elaborated a more detailed strategy for identifying, meeting, and developing a consultative relationship with natural neighbors. Shapiro (1971) has described entering a "bounded" ecological unit, a single-room occupancy hotel, and supporting natural helpers, who can be found even in such impoverished environments.

Others working in crisis intervention programs have engaged network resources for support and problem-solving (Garrison, 1974; Auerswald, 1968). In addition, deinstitutionalization requires mental health professionals to identify potential network resources and find ways to "attach" the previously institutionalized person to the community (Commission on Mental Health, 1978). Self-help groups are formalized natural helping (Katz, 1976).

Catalyzing Natural Helping

In his formulation of competence-oriented social work practice, Maluccio (Chapter 1 in this volume) stresses the *enabling* role of the social worker. Similarly, an appropriate term for a professional role in relation to natural helping is catalyzing. This is an umbrella concept that subsumes a number of strategies and skills in the areas of assessment and intervention. Within this perspective, social workers perceive themselves as energizers of processes they need not control or direct but simply mobilize. These are the processes of natural helping, which have their own legitimacy and internal energy. They are by no means "second best" to professional helping. Workers provide the context in which natural helping can flourish. They recognize that clients and other "nonprofessionals" can be valuable resources for each other and themselves.

Contemporary society is so complex and rapidly changing that individuals get torn from the social fabric of mutual aid, or may never have been woven into it. Catalyzing natural helping can be seen as a special instance of the mediating function described by Schwartz (1961). The social worker mobilizes or creates connections and is available to help relationships overcome obstacles.

In each client system's life space and in each ecological unit there exists the potential of natural helpers. These need to be searched out, engaged, and possibly strengthened. Achieving a mutually satisfactory fit between client and network requires time and skill on the part of the social worker. Some relationships with natural helpers are likely to evolve into ongoing collaboration. The practitioner brings his or her professional knowledge, and the natural helper brings his or her concern and involvement with individuals and the community.

Overall, the thrust of the catalyzing role is to increase the goodness of fit between individuals and natural helping networks. This means that client systems will be able to utilize their network resources more competently as they pursue their lives. It also means that resources in the social environment will be enhanced as people function more competently, support each other, and add to the vitality of the social systems in which they are imbedded.

As discussed in the rest of this chapter, ideas about natural helping and the concept of the worker's catalyzing role have important implications for assessment and intervention.

Assessment

In efforts to utilize natural helping networks to promote competence, there are three areas of assessment that become crucial: (1) assessing existing social networks; (2) assessing clients' competence at utilizing networks; and (3) assessing potential for network development.

Assessing Existing Networks

Practitioners should first focus on locating valued competence in our clients' networks. For this purpose, network mapping can be very useful. It has the advantage of being able to present complex relationships with economy of time and space. Both children and adults enjoy the process. Moreover, it is possible to show changes by mapping the social network at various points in time.

Mapping can be undertaken productively as a collaborative process by client(s) and worker. Clients can be resources on their own behalf in identifying supports and deficits in their social environment. A joint survey by worker and client can simultaneously demonstrate and enhance a client's competence at problem-solving and at negotiating his social environment.

The basic concepts of mapping are very simple. Geometric shapes are chosen, sometimes differentiating males from females and children from adults. Other shapes can be used to refer to groups or organizations. Various qualities of relationship can be shown by the relative locations of the shapes. Lines of various kinds are drawn connecting the points. These can also reflect qualities of the relationship.

An example follows of Will, a child who was seeing a school social worker because of learning difficulties. Together they made a map of all the people who could help Will improve his competence in learning.

"Let's draw a map of all the people who could help you do better in school, Will. We can show people in the family as circles, and people at school as another shape, maybe as triangles, and what for people in the neighborhood?" "Diamonds!" "O.K. And we can make the grown-ups as big shapes, and the children as smaller shapes." "Well, there's mom, she helps me with my reading. And Mike, my friend at school; he's good in math." "Could you ask him to help you with your math?" "Sure; he likes to help kids with math."

"Is there anybody who could help you concentrate a little better at school?" "Well, I don't know . . . maybe I could ask Miss Roberts to change my seat, then Pat wouldn't bother me all the time." "Is there anybody else who could help?" "My sister could quit bothering me when I try to do my homework!" "That *would* help, wouldn't it! Let's see, how could you work that one out?" "Well, I could ask her, and ask mom and dad to help out if she won't stop." "Yes, and I know a boy who lives near you and he'd like someone to play Scrabble with. That would help your spelling and it would help him, too; he has trouble with his legs and can't go to school."

The map they made (Figure 6–1) showed several things very vividly. The dotted line to John indicated a potential new neighborhood

FIGURE 6–1. Example of a map drawn with a child in a school setting.

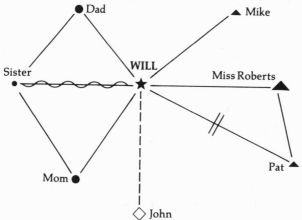

contact. The wavy line to Will's sister indicated their conflict. His ability to "reach" his sister both directly and through his parents was paralleled by his use of Miss Roberts, the teacher, to help him with the troublesome Pat. The breaking of closeness with Pat is indicated by the interrupted line to him. Both Will and the social worker now had some ideas about how to proceed, and Will had gained a bit in his ability to master his life tasks and environment competently. In Gladwin's (1967) terms, Will was learning alternative pathways to his goal of better schoolwork, utilizing a broad variety of social resources in his environment, and deepening his understanding of social relationships.

Maps may be used for the purpose of emphasizing the intensity of the relationships as well as their structural qualities. In this case, a format using concentric circles with the focal unit at the center may be employed. Particular interest in sectors might be indicated by adding wedges on top of the concentric circles. Currently various ways of showing networks are being tried (Attneave, 1975; Hartman, 1978; Pendegast and Sherman, 1978).

Following is an example of the use of mapping in a medical social service:

Mrs. Jordan was overwhelmed by the care of three small children and a bedridden husband. There were financial and legal worries, day-to-day chores, and social and emotional needs of the whole family—all draining Mrs. Jordan dry. The worker helped her to see that she was a very competent woman but that she was burdening herself with more than any one person could—or should—carry. She was also trying to "protect" her husband by doing things that he was perfectly able to do and wanted to handle. Together, the worker and client made a map of the family's network resources. The worker simply asked questions and Mrs. Jordan came up with a rich picture of their world. Then they made a map.

In this vignette, making a network map allowed the client to see more clearly that there were both formal and natural helping resources available to her family. She was able to see how she distanced her husband from needed supports and from the gratification of mastering his own social environment. He was still perfectly capable of competent social functioning, even though he could no longer navigate his physical environment.

In assessment of social networks, it is also useful to consider whether network members have a positive or negative valence for the focal unit; that is, support or nonsupport. It is also important to consider the people who take on supportive and facilitative roles informally as well as the persons and organizations that are formally sanctioned. For instance, there is the AFDC worker, but there is also the woman down the street who brings groceries to the shut-ins. There are biological grandparents, and there are official and unofficial "foster grandparents." A checklist of sectors to consider is a useful memory aide when assessing the social network. Such a list, with formal and informal examples, is available elsewhere (Swenson, 1979).

Assessing Client Competence

Assessment of the focal unit's coping strengths and weaknesses would be carried out at the same time as assessment of the social networks. This will indicate existing competences and deficits and areas where competence needs to be developed. Principles and procedures for assessing competence (or competence clarification) are discussed elsewhere (Maluccio, Chapter 1 in this volume) and need not to be repeated here. What is specifically relevant to this chapter, however, is assessing competence at interacting with helping networks.

Competence at utilizing networks includes many things:

1. A conviction that change is possible and that people can shape that change.
2. The perception of oneself as a person who can legitimately influence other persons and processes.
3. The capacity to identify network resources and deficits.
4. The ability to translate that information into action.
5. The selection of action strategies.
6. The ability to evaluate those actions and the reactions of others.
7. The flexibility to make modifications where indicated.

Each of these processes can be separately assessed, but in some ways each also builds upon the other.

In the example above of Mrs. Jordan, we see a vigorous, capable woman who felt that change was possible and that she could direct it. She could identify resources and translate knowledge into action. She needed help, however, in rethinking her assumption that the competent household functioned without depending on anyone. She also needed a "guide" through the process outlined above, especially when it came time to evaluate outcomes. She found it difficult, in particular, to acknowledge that the evidence showed her in-laws' contributions to be essentially negative.

If Mrs. Jordan had been a more depressed or passive person with doubts about her ability to influence others, intervention would have to begin at a much earlier point in the process. The same would be true if her cultural tradition had included a larger element of fatalistic thinking.

Assessment for Network Development

Many times individuals, families, and groups not only have their own internal weaknesses but also a sparse social network. Often long stays in state hospitals, state schools or prisons rupture whatever meaningful connections a person may once have had. Immigrants and refugees also frequently lose all or important parts of their social network (cf. Golan, Chapter 4 in this volume). Thus there is a particular need to undertake creation of new networks on behalf of these and other at risk persons.

Identifying potentially supportive ecological niches is a time-consuming, personally involving effort of getting to know a community intimately. Formal surveys usually are not highly productive (Collins and Pancoast, 1976). Limitless curiosity, serendipity, and a spirit of adventure seem more useful! Preparation begins with reviewing available data about the demography and resources of an area. Departments of urban planning or comprehensive planning agencies can provide a great deal of information, as can local colleges in their social science departments. However, all this information must be supplemented by browsing in the community.

Browsing means getting to know the people and social fabric of an area on a firsthand, day-to-day basis. One chats with local merchants and residents, goes to area meetings, lingers in local gathering places and coffee shops, reads bulletin boards, neighborhood newsletters, and community newspapers. No bit of information is overlooked as "too trivial," no possible relationship is "too remote."

A small area should be selected to make a detailed study. A census tract or ward is often a suitable size. One's purposes will dictate the size of the area, but depth diminishes with increasing size. One such process was undertaken by a community mental health center. In this example, the interactive processes of assessment and action flow from the disciplined use of network ideas:

The staff became concerned about former state hospital patients who moved into their area and experienced high rates of crisis and rehospitalization. The staff began planning a crisis/support halfway house. As they canvassed the neighborhood for an appropriate site, they found a number of boarding-houses within one area. These were already offering housing to some of the former patients, and some had quite stable residents. Introductions were made by the mental health center staff around their common concern with former patients. The boardinghouse managers welcomed a new, professionally staffed halfway house in their midst. It would clearly be a resource for some of their residents who were having particular difficulty. The owners were able to tell the center staff of some of the bureaucratic complications at the local welfare office.

Intervention

There are a number of distinct strategies in using natural helping networks to promote competence. These include: (1) increasing the client system's competence at utilizing network resources; (2) engaging existing networks to increase competence; and (3) creating new networks. These strategies frequently take place interactively but may also occur separately.

Increasing Competence at Using Networks

This strategy grows out of traditional approaches to individuals, families, and groups. It has four basic parts: (1) establishing the context of taking and giving help; (2) identifying network resources; (3) devising strategies to utilize network resources; and (4) supporting and helping the network. The last two parts are reciprocal processes: As people become more competent at using their networks to obtain help, they are more energized to give help. As they give, they feel more comfortable about taking.

Establishing the Context for Reciprocal Help.   Initially the practitioner must deal with people's attitudes about taking help. The persons involved must be helped to see the necessity of mutual aid in negotiating life competently. Some clients are hesitant to "take," feeling that they do not deserve it. Others, needy and deprived, may have trouble giving. For both, the experience of mutual help can lead to greater interpersonal competence and enhanced self-esteem. The worker actively addresses these issues with the awareness that a fundamental human predicament is involved.

At the same time, the helper will bear in mind network concepts as possible locators of support and aid. Thus the helper will listen to the concerns of the client system: What kind of aid is needed here? Where can it be located? How can it be mobilized?

As an example, a family and children's agency established a group for parents of retarded children, to help them find mutual support and problem-solving help.

The Parents Group repeatedly discussed how lonely and isolated they were, stressing that friends and family avoided them since the birth of their retarded child. As they talked more freely about their own feelings of sorrow, anger, and shame, the worker was able to help them see that in some instances they had pulled back from social relationships because of their own distress. The group discussed how to handle uncomfortable situations with relatives and friends. The parents were then enabled to reach out to their network resources.

Even though reaching out for support seems easy and natural for some people, for others it appears neither safe nor rewarding. For those who have had experiences of deprivation and humiliation, self-protective barriers may feel very necessary. Unfortunately, these may be precisely the people who need the resources offered by social networks. Tolsdorf (1975) has found that psychiatric patients perceive less possibility of support and objectively have less available support than medical patients. Consequently, there may be instances where the process of encouraging a client system to interact with its potential social network is a long-term effort, as seen in the following example of a family at a child welfare agency:

The Broders were a severely isolated family. Mr. Broder worked as a mail sorter and was perceived as a loner. Mrs. Broder had had several psychiatric hospitalizations and was always withdrawn and suspicious. There were three children. Peter, the oldest, was often home from school to help his mother, who could barely manage the two younger children. They were fretful and frequently ill. Aside from trips to the emergency room for the children and Mrs. Broder's psychiatric hospitalizations, the family struggled alone. It was not until the worker, who made home visits, had personally gone through a long period of testing that he was able to begin to link the family to either formal or natural helping resources.

Identifying Resources. It is not enough to believe that there are potential network resources available and to feel comfortable with the principle of using them. Resources must be found, and clients enabled to utilize them. It is not always easy to identify network resources, because their availability may become obscured through conflict, lack of use, or apparent disinterest. As indicated earlier, clients themselves can be resources in identifying network supports. The next step is working with clients to translate knowledge of resources into realistic strategies of engagement.

The following conversation took place in a family agency:

CLIENT. I've had a job offer, which I'd like to take. But I don't know what to do with my daughter.

WORKER. I remember you telling me that Lisa has a neighborhood friend with whom she plays very well. Have you considered asking the mother to be a day-care mother?

CLIENT. Oh, she'd be good! But she isn't approved!

WORKER. Perhaps you could ask her if she'd apply.

CLIENT. Wouldn't she think I'm prying?

Later. . .

CLIENT. You know, I asked my neighbor about the day care and she wasn't offended; she was flattered!

In this instance, the social worker helps the client translate the available information into a possible plan and helps her to evaluate it. The client takes the next step, trying the plan out, on her own. When their conviction is great and the stakes are high, clients may be marvelously resourceful at finding their own network supports.

Mrs. Corey was a middle-aged black woman whose sole income was her husband's SSI benefits. Most of her family and friends were struggling to get by. However, when her son was psychiatrically hospitalized in New York, she canvassed her resources to gather plane fare. She also identified a "friend of a friend" with whom she could stay in New York. After arriving from Chicago, Mrs. Corey made arrangements to take her son home. She cajoled the hospital driver to make an unofficial trip to the airport, and otherwise struggled through the bureaucratic red tape.

In this case a competent woman continued to use good networking skills in spite of stress. The practitioner simply supported her continued adaptive activities.[3]

Developing Strategies to Utilize Networks. Having made the first tentative steps toward a network connection, a client system may still need a good deal of help in developing and sustaining the relationship. A client's overture may be ignored because it is so hesitant or because there are residues of negative feelings. It is during this time, perhaps, that a client system most needs professional support. With its hopes raised, its vulnerability can be very great and anxiety and ambivalence are at a high level.

In the Parents Groups mentioned earlier, the worker began to encourage the parents to reach out again to their networks. Members of the group supported each other as they tried to get reconnected, analyzing encounters the various members had. With failures and successes their confidence grew.

Later the group was criticizing the special nursery for not sharing information with the parents. The worker asked: "What does this remind you of?" One of the parents immediately said: "Hey, isn't this the same as when we were complaining about our families and friends? We can get the help we need! Why don't we ask the teacher to come to our meeting?"

In this group, the worker simply needed to stimulate the good cognitive processing of the members (cf. Fleming, Chapter 3 in this volume). Other clients need a great deal of help in planning, implementing, and modifying action strategies.

The Broders, the isolated couple described earlier, had finally found the courage to talk to their neighbor about how his dog was frightening their children. He had said that he would tie the dog in his yard. But the dog continued to scare their children. The Broders were overwhelmed and their success was totally erased. The social worker encouraged them to ventilate. He engaged them in thinking through what they might do next. Eventually the Broders planned to talk again with the neighbor and thus felt a little better.

The Broders' worker offered an alternative vision to their fear of social interaction. He helped them to perceive at least one point in their rudimentary social network as less noxious.

Supporting and Helping the Network.   As a person or other client system reaches out to a network for help, they often spontaneously become reciprocal helpers.

In the Parents Group the worker initially encouraged sharing around car pooling and the children's needs. After a while, the parents volunteered to help fix up the schoolroom and organized a Clean-up Day, rewarding themselves with a picnic afterward. A year or so later they decided to sponsor a Parents Group in a neighboring town.

As the parents felt supported and more competent, their social network and their capacity to give to others expanded. They began to view themselves as resource persons (cf. Maluccio, Chapter 1 in this volume).

In conclusion, competence at using network resources passes through several stages. As competence matures from an attitude or conviction of the "all rightness" of mutual aid to an operational experience of instrumental and emotional support, it becomes increasingly reciprocal. Individuals then become both better givers and better receivers.

Using Networks to Increase Competence

As mentioned earlier, in addition to helping client systems utilize network resources more fully, practitioners can mobilize networks on behalf of clients. For instance, in the following vignette a social network of both professional and natural helpers aided in dealing with a life task.[4]

When Michael, a resident in a drug-free community, was faced with the unexpected death of his father, staff members feared that this new stress would obliterate his hard-won gains. They organized staff and other residents to take turns being available to Michael while he went through the period of most intense grief.

Networks can also help to increase a person's competence in using varied pathways to goals, understanding and making use of the resources of the social system, and deepening knowledge of the world (Gladwin, 1967).

Mrs. Xavier was upset and frustrated with the school system. Her child was reading far below grade level, but they said she would outgrow it. She contacted her sister, who was a schoolteacher in another state. The sister suggested that Linda sit in on the reading class of a younger grade. The school refused this idea, saying she would not fit in. The sister-teacher came to visit. She helped Mrs. Xavier understand the logic of the school. They made a plan to visit the school jointly and ask for more intensive testing of Linda. When the tests indicated that Linda was mildly retarded, plans were made for her to attend a special program at a nearby school.

In the above vignette, the sister offered a series of alternatives, explained the school system to Mrs. Xavier, and also helped her to come to terms with her child's limitations.

Network resources can help people maintain competence in such ways as avoiding hospitalization, avoiding malnutrition, and preventing self-destructiveness. More positively, network resources can help people to maintain jobs, be better parents, solve problems, develop new skills, enjoy themselves, and increase their self-esteem.[5]

Interventions with social networks are based on the goal of strengthening the competence of the focal unit. Strategies include contacting network resources; consultation with natural helpers; and engaging a whole network.

Contacting Network Resources. Network resources can be contacted indirectly, through a client system, or directly, through a worker's own relationships. Usually the practitioner will suggest that the client invite appropriate others into the work. This is a clinical task comparable to the process of involving a spouse in marital counseling or family members in family therapy. It may require dealing with resistance and unconscious collusion as well as a client's conscious reluctance to ask for aid.[6]

Sometimes the worker will know of natural helping resources through his or her own contacts in the community. The worker will discuss this possibility with the client system and also determine the natural helper's availability. In almost all instances, the linkage will not be made without explicit agreement from the client; occasionally, however, the situation is so critical that an assertive contact into the network may be necessary.

Mrs. Craven called her social worker. "I'm not able to go on any longer. I've just taken a bottle of sleeping pills. I think I may jump from the [tenth floor] window." The social worker knew a friend of Mrs. Craven who lived in the building. She called, and the friend was able to reach Mrs. Craven long before the police or her social worker arrived.

The worker assessed Mrs. Craven's behavior as seriously life-threatening. She felt that the crisis demanded immediate assertive action.

In situations where the helper is widely known in the habitat of a client system, contacts may flow easily and creatively. Knowing the whereabouts of competent people, especially natural helpers, can be extremely productive.

Mr. Ramirez was very upset about the increasing senility of his mother-in-law. The union's social worker was able to provide him with some information about financing a nursing home. She arranged a physical by the union doctor. She was also able to introduce Mr. Ramirez to Mr. Gonzales, who provided emotional support and information about Spanish-speaking nursing homes.

In this case, the practitioner was an established part of the union. It was easy to arrange a contact with a coworker who had recently faced a similar issue and understood the client's cultural context as well.

Consultation with Natural Helpers. Contacting new network resources and making linkages may not always be necessary. Many troubled people are already in touch with natural helpers. These may be beauticians, bartenders, mailmen, or informal day-care mothers who have a special interest in helping people. They may be people whom we often call paraprofessionals, such as foster parents, camp counselors, and paid homemakers. They may be a friend, relative, or colleague of the person in need. In all of these instances a social work practitioner can offer consultation to the natural helpers.

If contacted on behalf of a person about whom they are already concerned, most natural helpers are eager to collaborate. They recognize the practitioner's function and expertise. The difficult process of achieving legitimation and establishing a relationship may therefore move very rapidly. The consultation process will be quite similar to that of traditional mental health consultation (Caplan, 1970). The primary difference is that natural helpers are strongly encouraged to utilize their own ways of problem-solving and interacting. The consultant actively seeks to avoid professionalizing the natural helping process.

In general, natural helpers are highly competent people who have many skills in living. One of the most prevalent issues for consultation is the consultee's proclivity to "do for" clients when they are able to manage for themselves. The important distinction between support and indulgence is the difference between promoting competence and diminishing it. The consultant's special skill may lie in the ability to assess a client system's levels of coping and to communicate this clearly and simply to a natural helper.

Mrs. Ward was an experienced black foster mother with whom the child welfare agency wanted to place Ernest, a much traumatized and very troubled child. Mrs. Ward was hesitant; she had always fostered "normal" children before. The social worker suggested that she attend a self-help group at the agency that was composed of foster mothers with disturbed children. She assured Mrs. Ward that the mothers were extremely competent and were very helpful to each other. Mrs. Ward then accepted the child and joined the group. She veered from expecting too much to indulging Ernest because of the horrors of his past. The group leader and other members were able to help her modulate her demands more appropriately.

The worker and group members offered Mrs. Ward help in gearing her expectations accurately to Ernest's coping abilities.

Engaging a Whole Network. If the practitioner is to have maximal impact on clients and their social networks, the ideal strategy is to engage the whole network. We now appreciate the potential influence of the social network and can begin to conceptualize strategies of intervention more completely. Network theory helps by making it possible to describe highly complex social relationships. Interventions mentioned earlier with client systems and social networks can be combined into an approach involving a whole network. The synergistic effect of such an approach can be seen in this vignette:

A psychiatric ward staff began to redirect its focus from psychopathology and the generation of insight to coping strengths and the promotion of competence. A weekly community dinner was initiated, encouraging patients and staff to interact as "real people." Being present at the dinner made it easier for the doctors to interact with the patients' families, whom they had avoided. Families responded to the increased zest and reality focus of patients on the night of the dinner and were more likely to visit. The social worker met informally with the families on the ward and began a multiple family group. One of the patients suggested a committee be established to clean up the previously messy ward. The hospital administration responded to this evidence of increased concern and activity by expanding the cooking facilities on the ward and donating a secondhand piano.

Illustrated here is an interactive process of change throughout a whole network. Planned interventions produced unexpected change, which could then be clinically exploited.

There have been efforts to relate to whole networks in a variety of settings. Costin (1975) reports interventions in the complex array of systems and subsystems in a school. Weiner (1973) describes a similar process in the work place. A series of other settings are discussed by Schwartz and Zalba (1971), including hospitals, prisons, and foster care. Family network therapy (Speck and Attneave, 1973) and crisis networking (Garrison, 1974) have been mentioned earlier, as has Shaprio's (1971) interventions in welfare hotels. These programs implicitly or explicitly are designed to utilize mutual aid concepts and build competence. They do not use network concepts in their conceptualization.

Neither does Eismann (1974), who reports an approach to a whole network of children and adolescents in the community. These youngsters live in a burned-out section of the South Bronx, a deprived urban minority community with few social resources. Whenever Eismann makes contact with a particular child, he seeks to engage his whole network. He has developed a program based on mutual aid, through which he seeks to enhance competence in survival, bettering one's chances, and particularly in interpersonal relationships. In this way he hopes to increase the community's human resources, particularly in parenting and social support.

A further step in conceptualizing the engagement of a whole social network is taken by Lee and Swenson (1978), who describe a neighborhood agency that identifies and works within the social networks of an inner-city housing project. It was beyond the design or resources of this agency to influence the totality of the network; nonetheless, a substantive beginning was made at identifying and working with natural helping persons and networks.

Sarason et al. (1977) describe a network that crosses professional/

natural helping lines. They view networks as an alternative to the impersonality, ineffectiveness, and rigidity of bureaucracies. Networks offer a solution to the dual problems of limited resources and loss of community. Within networks, exchange on a barter or mutual aid basis takes place.

A university professor was interested in doing research which involved participant observation. She was able to develop an exchange with a community agency. She offered in-service training in the area of her expertise in return for the agency's help in collecting her data.

A professional network thus exchanged needed resources that could not have been obtained through the ordinary budgeting process.

Creating New Networks

As indicated earlier, there are many people who have lost whatever social networks they once had or who have never really had a viable network. People who have traveled great distances or have been dislocated by disaster are one such group. People who have been institutionalized for a long time are another. In fact, people in institutions may have developed networks that tie them to the institution rather than the community (Goffman, 1961; Braginsky and Braginsky, 1973).

There are beginning efforts to systematize the processes of creating new networks. Keskiner (1972) reports a program where many of the residents of a small town were involved in the process of helping former psychiatric patients leave the state hospital. Community meetings were followed by a series of visits between potential foster families and the patients. Discharges were carefully modulated to the readiness of the patients and the foster families.

In a community context, Collins and Pancoast (1976) have developed a strategy for catalyzing natural helping resources for at-risk or underserved populations. It consists of: (1) finding natural helpers; (2) establishing a consultative relationship; and (3) maintaining the relationship. In addition to the processes identified by Collins and Pancoast, practitioners can also (4) link isolated persons to natural helpers, and (5) establish self-help and peer counseling programs.

Finding Natural Helpers   This phase includes highly diverse activites. The practitioner may research the paths of successfully coping members of the target population, attempting to determine what "went right." Other professionals may be canvassed to identify concerned individuals who may be natural helpers. Collins and Pancoast (1976) emphasize the need to get to know potential helpers very well. They suggest approaching a likely candidate as an "expert in the community," and carrying on chatty, wide-ranging conversations, akin to anthropological interviews. One primary focus, of course, would be their mutual interest in the target population. During this period the potential for a rewarding relationship will be tested out on both sides. Establishing the conditions for ongoing work can be a protracted process.

The family agency was concerned about the Vietnamese refugees moving into their city. No one in the mental health community spoke Vietnamese. The agency met Mrs. Nven, who could speak English, when she came with a Vietnamese neighbor to translate. An alert staff member asked if she could visit Mrs. Nven to learn more of her views about problems her compatriots were facing. Mrs. Nven protested that she "was not educated enough to speak." The worker gently persisted and offered to meet with Mrs. Nven wherever she preferred. Mrs. Nven finally agreed, suggesting that they meet at a newly opened Vietnamese restaurant. They were to meet many times over the next few months. Mrs. Nven gradually introduced the worker to many of the staff and customers at the restaurant. She began to describe some of the difficulties that they encountered. Occasionally, she would describe, with great shyness, some ideas or actions of her own in relation to such situations. The worker supported her judgment and encouraged her action.

Establishing a Consultative Relationship. By contrast with the initial period of searching out potential resources, the process of establishing a consultative relationship may occur quite quickly. A first step will be to describe behaviorally how the person is helpful, since natural helpers tend to diminish the importance of what they do. The consultant will also want to describe how his or her professional knowledge could be useful to the natural helper. Finally, a tentative plan of regular meetings will be arranged. These are likely to have a more casual quality than other relationships a professional forms. A natural helper is more likely to reschedule visits, invite friends, or even engage in helping while the consultant is there. The consultant should be prepared for this to occur and feel comfortable with it (Collins and Pancoast, 1976).

In the preceding example the practitioner eventually said to Mrs. Nven, "You know, you've been thinking a great deal about these issues we talk about, and you've asked my opinion a number of times. We could plan to meet regularly for these conversations. We could also talk about some of those times when you're not so sure what to do." Mrs. Nven looked surprised. "What I do is so unimportant!" "Only in your own eyes," the worker replied softly. "And anyway, it's sort of what we were doing already!"

As with any complex interpersonal relationship, there are many issues that must be addressed in consultation. These will require a fairly high degree of clinical skill, though not the clinical mode. The two partners may feel anxious about a variety of issues, including their respective competences and the unknown demands of this new form of relationship. Decreased anxiety, increased relaxation and self-confidence, and liking to be together will signal that an effective working relationship has been formed. There may be an increase in the number of cases a natural helper is involved with at this time.

The next few months with Mrs. Nven were rich ones. Alternately hesitant and self-confident, she described many kinds of troubling situations and her own involvement in them. Most of these the social worker helped Mrs. Nven to handle herself. Occasionally she suggested a community resource to complement Mrs. Nven's efforts. Whenever they encountered a problem that many families shared, they added it to the report they were preparing to present to the community planning agency.

Maintaining the Relationship. It may seem after a while that the natural helper is quite able to go on independently. Collins and Pancoast (1976) advise against terminating with a natural helper, even though the consultant may feel superfluous. It is much preferable to diminish the frequency of the contacts but to remain in regular contact. During this more sophisticated phase of the work, the consultant may be called upon to help the natural helper with obstacles that are related to the helper's own values or prejudices. As with other forms of consultation, the focus should be on the way the helper's attitudes or behavior have become an obstacle to the work, not upon their origins or meaning in the private life of the helper (Caplan, 1970). Endings should be anticipated, as both natural helpers and consultants will make life changes; termination should be handled with full awareness of its significance.

"You know," the worker confided to a colleague, "I'm at the point where I feel like I've learned more from Mrs. Nven than I offer to her. . . . I really feel useless." Shortly the worker went on a brief vacation. When she came back, Mrs. Nven was fuming: "Fine time you chose to go away! All sorts of stuff happened! Just listen to what a lousy job I did." Though Mrs. Nven had done her usual fine job, the worker could see clearly that maintaining the consultation was important.

This extended vignette illustrates the long-term process of establishing and maintaining a consultation with a natural helper. First Mrs. Nven was helped to redefine herself as a valuable, competent helping resource. A warm and supportive relationship was initiated. Later we see an increase in the energy Mrs. Nven directs into helping as a result of her feeling more confident and supported. She eventually emerges as a mature collaborator with the worker. Finally, we see the deep meaning of the consultative relationship for her, and her loss of self-definition as a competent helper when her consultant goes away.

Linking Isolated Persons to Natural Helpers.   Natural helpers may be willing to offer help to isolated clients without network resources. In this instance the first professional task is referral, or, more accurately, linkage. The program for discharged mental patients mentioned earlier (Keskiner, 1972) is one example. Another is a program for Puerto Rican immigrants in New York City where competent families sponsor recent immigrants (Gonzales, 1974). In this program the primary professional role is to arrange the linkages. Making linkages between newcomers and sponsors is also a primary task in self-help groups. A serendipitous example of linkages to a family of natural helpers is illustrated below:

The Romanos called a community mental health center, saying that they would be interested in being unpaid foster parents for an emotionally troubled child. The agency was appreciative, but perplexed: They had never needed such a resource. Then one day Danny Moretti, a troubled child in a very disturbed family, set his bed on fire and narrowly avoided burning himself severely. An emergency was at hand, but all concerned were very reluctant to hospitalize the child, which appeared the only alternative. Then the social worker remembered the Romanos. They were contacted and a rapid assessment was made of the home. A brief stay in the foster home by Danny helped stabilize the Moretti household, partly because the Romanos had become friends of, and potent supports for, his whole family.

In this case, a family of natural helpers was able to offer a kind of service professionals could not. The match with the Romano family served to be a turning point for the Morettis, whose situation had not improved in over two years of intense professional intervention.[7]

Linkages and arranging the right match can require a good deal of professional skill.

Mrs. Devine's depression was of psychotic proportions. She could not manage her own household or care for her four young overactive children. An elderly homemaker was hired who, unfortunately, had many qualities like Mrs. Devine's own mother. Mrs. Devine was locked into a destructive relationship with the homemaker which mirrored her relationship with her mother. Her condition deteriorated. When a professional social worker assessed the situation, it was decided gradually to withdraw the homemaker and replace her with a more benign figure. A vivacious young woman was assigned, who collaborated with Mrs. Devine rather than entrapping her. Mrs. Devine slowly began to improve.

In this example, the assessment was that the first homemaker reinforced Mrs. Devine's pathology. In spite of intensive psychiatric intervention, she could not change while such a destructive relationship continued. Often the personality of a homemaker is of less significance than her homemaking skills, but in this instance it became central. A professional assessment was necessary to locate the obstacle in Mrs. Devine's social environment and to identify its noxious qualities. In the process, qualities necessary for a good match were identified.

Establishing Self-help and Peer Counseling Programs.   A practitioner in almost any setting will find situations where people can be energized to help each other more competently. When people share a common problem and help is perceived to be reciprocal, the term self-help is usually employed. Group meetings are an important part of self-help programs.

Peer counseling is a more diffuse concept. Here the helpers may simply share a common status, such as "student," with the persons they help. This helping is likely to be altruistic, with the benefit to the helper being an increased sense of competence and the gratification of giving. While counselors may meet in groups for training or peer supervision, the form of helping is basically individual rather than in groups.

Self-help groups can be formed around almost any problem. Siblings of handicapped children may be brought together, or alcoholic teenagers, or mastectomy patients, or single fathers. Self-help groups are particularly important for people who have severed ties with earlier networks, or when their networks have many destructive qualities. Examples that come to mind are ex-gamblers, delinquent youth, children who have moved to new schools, and so on. In all of these instances a significant network has been lost or renounced and needs a functional equivalent.[8]

The following vignette is from Overeaters Anonymous:

LAURA called her sponsor. I don't want to dance anymore just as a
    performance. I want to enjoy it, too.
SPONSOR. You do have a choice. You don't have to have it be "just
    a performance."
LAURA. Yes, I know, I think I'll try dancing again and see how that
    affects my weight. But I'm afraid I'll get really compulsive about
    my dancing like I did before.

SPONSOR. But, Laura, you are going to do your food plan one day at a time, and you can dance one day at a time. You don't have to do it any other way.

LAURA. Yes! Oh, it is so good to work on some of these issues!

Laura had been an isolated, perfectionistic young woman who consoled herself for her loneliness with food. Here the sponsor offers a relationship as an alternative to food and helps Laura apply the principles of Overeaters Anonymous to her eating and to other areas of her life. She is encouraged to interrupt the compulsive cycle in relation to her dancing in much the same way as she has begun to control her compulsive eating.

Conclusion: A Partnership with Natural Helpers

Everywhere, as people live their lives, processes of natural help, mutual aid, and social support are going on. Competent people naturally take and give help as an integral and vital part of living. This chapter has begun to develop practice theory based on the use of natural helping networks by competent people. We have identified ways of locating natural helpers and assessing network resources. Interventive strategies have been described that use natural helping networks to promote competence.

Working with natural helping networks is an emerging practice modality. In the past many ideas have been part of practice wisdom or implicitly embodied in program. Relatively little attention has been paid to generating practice theory. Now concepts from social network theory offer new resources for conceptualization.

One of the most exciting aspects of working with natural helping networks is the concept of professionals as catalysts of natural helping. This new view of a partnership between professional and natural helpers, including client systems, emphasizes the complementary nature of their resources. It capitalizes on strengths in clients and their natural environments rather than focusing on deficits and weaknesses (cf. Maluccio, Chapter 1 in this volume). Catalyzing natural helping thus achieves a unique fit with a view of persons based on competence and competence strivings.

Notes

Acknowledgment: I would like to thank Joan Bate, Tom Brinson, Cheryl Bronstein, Norma Chatoff, Jan Douglass, Maggie Seiffert, and Diane Waldgeir, who provided some of the case examples, and Dr. Jane Charnas for editorial assistance.

1. See Maluccio (Chapter 1 in this volume) for further discussion of competence as a transactional concept.
2. For elaboration of these ideas in relation to social work practice, see Swenson (1979).
3. Goldstein (Chapter 13 in this volume) focuses on using the adaptive strengths and processes of families of psychiatric patients.
4. Golan (Chapter 4 in this volume) examines the role of self-help groups in situations of crisis and life transitions.
5. Further empirical studies are needed to indicate how and to what extent each of the various types of natural helping occurs.
6. See Oxley (Chapter 12 in this volume) for analysis of practice with involuntary clients.
7. See Maluccio and Sinanoglu (1981) for discussion of foster parents as resources for biological families of children in foster care.
8. Middleman (Chapter 8 in this volume) discusses the use of purposefully formed, structured groups as a means of promoting competence.

CHAPTER 7

Environmental Modification

Richard M. Grinnell, Jr.
Nancy S. Kyte
Gerald J. Bostwick, Jr.

Environmental modification has long been considered an integral part of social work's helping process. Its importance has been acknowledged not only by theorists and practitioners but by clients as well (Miller, Vaughan and Miller, 1969; Schneiderman, 1971). Paradoxically, its role has been honored more in speech than in action. Typically, it has been regarded as an ancillary intervention requiring less knowledge and skill than "direct treatment" (Hollis, 1972; Perlman, 1972).

Many social workers simplistically view environmental modification as the provision of "concrete services," while others summarily dismiss it as the routine "collateral contact." At the same time, however, most practitioners will readily attest to the many complexities and frustrations involved in effecting environmental change. It is surprising, therefore, that very few attempts have been made to generate systematically the major action principles and techniques that govern what is now rather loosely called "environmental modification" (Grinnell, 1973; Grinnell and Kyte, 1975). Social workers have not yet conceptualized, codified, and articulated the knowledge, roles, and skills necessary for effective environmental modification (Grinnell and Kyte, 1974; Perlman, 1974).

This chapter presents a beginning model for using environmental modification to promote personal and interpersonal competence.[1] It must be emphasized from the outset that this model is clearly in a nascent stage of development. Moreover, the term "model" is being used loosely and not as synonymous with practice model. Rather, it is meant to convey the notion that environmental modification is a type of social work intervention comprised of specific skills and techniques and not tied to any particular practice approach (e.g., task-centered service) or treatment modality (e.g., individual psychotherapy). Instead, environmental modification is viewed as constituting an integral component of social work's overall helping means. Given its limited theoretical development, however, it must be looked at separately at this point in order to facilitate the more precise ferreting out of its unique components and processes. It should also be noted that environmental modification is envisioned as cutting across various levels of social work practice and, therefore, as potentially applicable to individuals, families, small groups, organizations, neighborhoods, and communities. However, a primary focus will be placed here on its use in work with individuals, couples, and families.

The following discussion will begin with a review of the concepts of environment and environmental modification. Subsequent sections will be devoted to description and explanation of the proposed model's major assumptions and underlying conceptual framework. Considerable attention will be given to the major roles and skills of the social work practitioner and the major practice guidelines and techniques of environmental modification.

Environment

Environmental modification cannot be adequately understood without a concomitant exploration of what is meant by environment. Unfortunately, the environment has been conceptualized, for the most part, in highly abstract terms. In addition, social workers have tended to use this word very loosely. For instance, environment has been used to designate (1) social structures (e.g., social class system, ethnicity); (2) social conditions (e.g., unemployment, discrimination); (3) social systems (e.g., economic, health, and educational networks); and (4) specific neighborhood or community resources (e.g., schools, churches, day-care centers, job training programs). The environment has also been classified as primary or secondary, proximal or distal, natural or manmade, internal or external, and physical or social.

Broad perspectives such as these have engendered a rather amorphous view of what is meant by environment. Some theorists have set forth relatively delimited definitions. Richmond (1922), for example, viewed the social environment as the home, workshop, school, hospital, and court; she excluded "all those things which have no real influence upon [the person's] emotional, mental, and spiritual life"

(Richmond, 1922:99). Others have conceptualized the environment more globally, as a continuum of sorts. Stein (1963:70) defined it as "a series of concentric circles of systems of influence, all interacting." At the outer extreme is society as a whole. As we move progressively inward, we encounter regional, urban, and rural variations, followed by the specific influences and conditioning patterns of the neighborhood or community. At the very center of the social environment of the individual we find the family. Siporin (1972) described the social environment as a network of overlapping social systems and social situations (including ecological systems, cultures, and institutions). According to Siporin (1972:98–99), the social situation is "the instrumental life space through which individuals and social systems fulfill their basic needs and actualize themselves as living entities."

Although conceptualizations of the environment have varied considerably in scope and precision, they have generally been undergirded by several common themes. First, a distinction has been made between person and environment and between the physical and social environment.[2] At the same time, their interdependence has been clearly acknowledged. Richmond (1922:99) distinguished between the physical and social environment but noted that "a physical environment frequently has its social aspects; to the extent that it has these it becomes a part of the social environment." Hamilton (1951) pointed to the constant interaction of subjective and objective reality, observing that every case is composed of virtually inseparable internal (emotional) and external (environmental) factors in varying proportions. Hollis (1972) defined the social environment as composed of (1) concrete realities (e.g., food, shelter, medical care); (2) sociopsychological realities (as expressed through interpersonal relationships); and (3) socially determined psychological realities (e.g., ethnicity, social class), which influence one's behavior, values, aspirations, and perceptions of self and others. Hollis also stressed that these external realities constantly interact "with an equally complex set of forces within [the individual's] own personality" (Hollis, 1972:17).

The nature and substance of this interaction was never well conceptualized or operationalized. Thus, we witnessed a fluctuating focus, over the years, on either the person or his environment. By and large, that fluctuation favored the person. The environment, moreover, continued to be seen as essentially static and external to the individual, epitomized in the time-honored phrase "helping the client adjust to his environment" (Stein, 1963). Social workers tended to retreat to a focus on the person, where they felt greater competence and perceived more opportunities for bringing about change.

It has been suggested that social work's past tendency to dichotomize the person and situation and to maintain a rather constricted view of the environment derived in large part from (1) the overwhelming complexities involved in trying to conceptualize the whole person and the whole situation and (2) a concomitant lack of theoretical constructs necessary for bringing them together in a truly meaningful way. Richmond (1922), for example, found the environment to be full of variables to be studied and related, variable by variable, to the client's personal needs and qualities. She struggled in vain with the dilemma of determining which variables to focus on and which to ignore because she lacked access to current systems theory concepts such as reciprocity, salience, and equifinality (Meyer, 1973). More recently, Bartlett (1970) noted that since whole individuals and situations are extremely complex entities, we have had to partialize them in some way for purposes of understanding and analysis. According to Bartlett (1970:102), it was the failure to bring the ideas of people and environment together that blocked integrative thinking in social work for so long. She observed that we can close this gap when we perceive the interaction between people and their environment as an active exchange and when we relate this exchange to open-ended social system, homeostasis, and feedback. These concepts derive largely from systems theory, which did not begin filtering into social work until the mid-1950s.

Today, systems theory plays an important role in social work thinking. It has enhanced our ability to designate more precisely social work's domain as lying at the interface between the individual and his environment, and it has enabled us to conceptualize our traditional unit of attention, the "person-in-situation," in more sophisticated transactional terms. This transactional perspective, moreover, "does not mean a mere addition of components, but rather a reconceptualization of them, so as to be able to view a *system* of interweaving forces, all having reciprocity and feedback with each other" (Meyer, 1976:135).

Systems theory has also given impetus to a burgeoning interest in the relevance of ecology, a science concerned with the adaptive fit between living organisms and their environment and with the means by which they achieve a dynamic equilibrium and mutuality (Germain, 1973; Germain, 1979; Germain and Gitterman, 1980). Through the influence of ecosystems theory, concepts are now being developed that focus not on the individual or his environment but on the continuous transactions that occur between them. As a metaphor for practice, an ecological perspective provides insights into the nature and consequences of such transactions both for people and for the environments in which they function. Accordingly, attention is directed toward (1) releasing, developing, and strengthening man's innate capacity for growth and creative adaptation; (2) removing environmental blocks and obstacles to that growth and adaptation; and (3) increasing the nutritive properties of the environment (Germain, 1979). Although its application to social work is still in an embryonic stage of development, the ecological perspective clearly relates to our need to be concerned with people and their milieus simultaneously. Morever, by clarifying the structure of the environment and the nature of its adaptive and maladaptive influences, it appears to be particularly well suited to the task of developing concepts and action principles for environmental modification (Germain, 1979).

Environmental Modification

Not surprisingly, conceptualizations of environmental modification have reflected many of the same ambiguities, dichotomies, and myths that have characterized our view of the environment. The term "environmental modification" has also been used loosely and as synonymous with indirect treatment, indirect helping, indirect action, social therapy, and social brokerage. Moreover, environmental modification has been classified as a form of treatment, a treatment technique, a therapy, a method of therapy, a technique of supportive treatment, and a process. We are therefore left wondering what it really is.

While definitions of environmental modification have varied greatly, they share at least one feature: Treatment geared toward *psychological* problems has generally been distinguished from treatment geared toward *environmental* problems. Like the person–situation dichotomy, this distinction has resulted in a variety of classification schemes that essentially separate therapy from environmental modification. Richmond (1922), for instance, identified two major casework processes: (1) direct action of mind upon mind (or, direct work with the client) and (2) indirect action through the social environment (or, environmental modification). Similarly, Hamilton (1951) and (Hollis, 1972) differentiated between direct treatment and indirect treatment. Hollis (1972), for example, defined environmental work as consisting of treatment *through* the environment (i.e., using resources that exist or are potentially available) and treatment *of* the environment (i.e., modifying the environment to lessen pressures or increase opportunities and gratifications).

Similar kinds of therapy/environmental modification distinctions were made by others (cf. Austin, 1948; Bibring, 1947; Fischer, 1978; Lowry, 1936; Selby, 1956; and Whittaker, 1974). At the same time, however, many theorists emphasized that the two are not necessarily mutually exclusive. Hollis (1972), for instance, attacked the notion that direct work is psychological and indirect work is nonpsychological, or social. She regarded this as a false assumption since environmental work also takes place with people and functions through psychological means. Some social workers have taken issue with this. As recently as 1964, Scherz chastized Hollis for retaining the myth of "treatment through reducing environmental press." She acknowledged that environmental services fall within the scope of social work and require interviewing skill, but concluded that they do not necessarily constitute treatment:

> Casework treatment, it seems to me, requires primary attention to the psychological processes that are interfering with interpersonal and/or personal operations. Miss Hollis appears to be straddling this issue in an effort to give status to social workers engaged in the work of providing environmental services. [Scherz, 1964:207]

Scherz's comments illustrate another striking paradox concerning environmental modification, namely, its designation as an integral part of social work's helping means and its concomitant subordination to therapy. Paralleling the subordination of the environment to the person, social workers have always reserved a place for environmental modification in their treatment armamentarium but, at the same time, have relegated it to a second-class citizenship.

Several factors appear to have contributed to this neglect of environmental modification. First, because of the difficulties often involved in successfully effecting environmental change, social workers have tended to emphasize interventions in which they are not frustrated by environmental rigidities. As Millar (1939:347) so cogently observed, "From 1922 on, caseworkers were having increased difficulty adjusting the environment to the client, so it was natural that their interest should center not on whether he had a job, but on how he felt about not having a job."

A second factor contributing to the downgrading of environmental modification derives from the prevalent tendency of social workers to conceive of environmental modification as consisting primarily of helping clients with practical problems and tangible services. Consequently, environmental modification has been regarded as requiring considerably less knowledge and skill than direct treatment (Brill, 1973; Grinnell, 1973; Grinnell and Kyte, 1974, 1975; Siporin, 1972; Turner, 1974). Moreover, responsibility for effecting environmental change has frequently been delegated to paraprofessionals or BA-level social workers. It has been commonly assumed that environmental modification is easy, something that untrained workers do because they are not educationally equipped to do "real" casework (Stein, 1971).

In recent years, we have come to understand and appreciate better the many complexities involved in environmental modification. For instance, we have learned that environmental modification is not just a matter of the routine collateral contact, of providing concrete services, of fixing or arranging things. It almost always involves influencing the feelings, attitudes, and behavior of people. Not only is the client involved, but also those others who are to be the instruments or personalizations of the change (Perlman, 1971). Thus, every attempt to modify the environment requires not only that the client be helped to take his part, but also that the social worker engage and favorably influence all those others who will constitute the "living part" of the change. The practitioner must "put to use all his understanding of people and their interrelationships and all the skills by which he tries to set change in motion" (Perlman, 1971:49). Finally, we have learned that the insights and skills necessary for effective environmental modification are equally—if not more—demanding as those required for direct work with the client.

A third major factor contributing to the neglect and low prestige of environmental modification is its inadequate theoretical development. Just as conceptualizations of the person have superseded conceptualizations of the environment, so have psychotherapeutic theories and techniques been developed at the expense of environmental theories and techniques (Briar and Miller, 1971). Ways to influence the thoughts, feelings, and behaviors of the client have been carefully, and at times exquisitely, formulated. However, ways to influence the thoughts, feelings, and behaviors of people who constitute the social environment of the client—and whose actions and attitudes affect the outcome of his problem-solving efforts—have received little or no attention (Perlman, 1972).

The task facing us is clear. We must devote the same intensive analysis to environmental modification that we have devoted to psychotherapeutic theories and techniques—but illuminated now by what we have learned about the person in his situation since Richmond's day (Stein, 1971). This task is a formidable but crucial one if environmental modification is to be truly one of social work's distinguishing, and perhaps distinguished, areas of expertise. In short, we must begin to specify its major assumptions, conceptual frameworks, roles, skills, and techniques.

Environmental Modification: A Proposed Model

For purposes of our discussion, environmental modification will be defined as a goal-directed, problem-solving intervention that is undertaken after a diagnostic evaluation of the environment and the client's unique motivations, capacities, and needs. It involves (1) enriching the environment through the provision of new resources and opportunities, and (2) reducing negative physical, psychological, and social pressures within the person and the environment.

The above definition leaves many questions unanswered. For example, what exactly is involved in making a diagnostic evaluation of the environment? How, more precisely, do we go about enriching the environment and engaging significant others? What knowledge and skills do we need? What roles should we, and the client, assume and under what circumstances? What practice guidelines and techniques should guide our attempts to help the client modify his environment?

A good place to begin, perhaps, is by identifying the major assumptions that underlie the proposed model. These assumptions will help us refine our understanding of the purpose and nature of environmental modification and will lend structure and substance to the ways in which we can successfully effect environmental change.

Basic Assumptions

Our basic assumptions reflect the premises and values of competence-oriented social work practice (Maluccio, Chapter 1 in this volume) and the ecological perspective on social work (Germain and Gitterman, 1979; 1980). First, we view the primary function of environmental modification as the enhancement of transactions between people and their environment. These transactions are conceptualized as dynamic and constantly shifting exchanges of tangible and intangible resources, such as money, food, ideas, values, expectations, skills, knowledge, and relationships. Environmental modification strives to help the client to successfully negotiate his environment and the environment to respond positively to the needs of the client. Second, the practitioner's primary focus is not on the client *or* his environment but on the multiple interactions and exchanges occurring between them. The individual and his environment are viewed as constituting a transactional system in which each influences and is in turn influenced by the other.

Third, problems are conceptualized as breakdowns in the interface between the client and his environment. They are seen as arising from the intricate interplay of life transitions (developmental and social), interpersonal processes, and environmental influences (Germain and Gitterman, 1980). Individual pathology and environmental disorganization are de-emphasized in favor of a focus on transactional dysfunction. This dysfunction is seen as resulting from a disruption in the ecological fit between the individual and his environment. A major objective of environmental modification, therefore, is the provision or restructuring of opportunities and resources that will restore and enhance this mutual adaptation.

Finally, we view every person as continually striving toward competence (Maluccio, 1979b; White, 1963, 1964, 1972). The concept of competence holds several implications for environmental modification. First, it suggests that the worker should help the client acquire the knowledge and develop the skills necessary to restore his competence and to restructure his environment so that it provides opportunities for enhancing his continued growth and self-fulfillment. Second, it suggests that the practitioner emphasize the strengths and positive coping abilities of the client and of significant others wihin the client's milieu. And third, it suggests that the client be actively engaged in the process of bringing about change. Through his active participation, he will acquire not only knowledge and skills he can draw upon in the future but also an increased sense of mastery and effectiveness. The concept of action is central to environmental modification, since active participation in successful transactions with the environment is an important prerequisite to an individual's growth and adaptation (Maluccio, 1974). A necessary precondition for effective action is, of course, the availability of appropriate social systems and supports, of an environment with varied opportunities for success and achievement. Environmental modification plays an important role in helping the practitioner and client to develop, restructure, and humanize environmental conditions so as to maximize opportunities for the client to grow, establish his identity, and achieve an increasingly satisfying level of competence (Maluccio, 1974).

In summary, environmental modification is conceptualized as a multifaceted intervention that operates at the interface between the individual and his environment. Its primary function is the provision and/or restructuring of opportunities and resources that will restore, maintain, or enhance the natural adaptive fit between the individual and his environment, while also promoting the personal and interpersonal competence of the client and of significant others within his milieu (cf. Germain and Gitterman, 1980; Maluccio, Chapter 1 in this volume; Swenson, Chapter 6 in this volume).

Conceptual Framework

An operationalization of these assumptions necessitates a theoretical framework that lends itself to a meaningful consideration and application of concepts such as transaction, reciprocity, exchange, linkage, and the like. To this end, the proposed model draws heavily from systems theory, which is particularly relevant since it enables us to conceptualize reality as systems of interdependent and interrelated entities. Systems theory provides us with constructs that are focused on interface phenomena and that help us to focus simultaneously on people and their environment. It therefore opens the door to and encourages transactional thinking and analysis (Hartman, 1970). Systems theory is not a theory per se but a way of thinking that accommodates knowledge from many diverse sources (Janchill, 1969). It provides us with a conceptual framework for collecting, organizing, and analyzing relevant information about the multiple and complex transactions that occur between the individual and his environment. For purposes of this chapter, the following systems theory concepts have been selected to illustrate their relevance to environmental modification: system, open vs. closed system, energy exchange, and ripple effect.

System. A system may be defined as a set of elements standing in interaction. Each element or component is related to others in a more or less stable way within a particular period of time and space (Bertalanffy, 1956; Buckley, 1967). Of particular relevance to social work is the social system, which is comprised of interacting persons or groups of persons such as a family, a senior citizens' center, or a tenants' advisory board. Most systems can be further subdivided into subsystems. A family, for example, can be conceptualized as a system which is in turn comprised of the marital, parental, and sibling subsystems. It must be remembered, however, that a consideration of subsystems usually entails a new set of relationships. Moreover, the behavior of a subsystem may not be completely analogous with that of the system to which it is related (Hall and Fagen, 1956). A system is also assumed to have a suprasystem (i.e., to be a part of a larger system or systems). The suprasystem of a family may be the neighborhood in which it resides, the ethnic or social class system with which it is affiliated, and so on.

These concepts are applicable to environmental modification which, by definition, requires that the practitioner work not only with the client but also with significant others within his milieu. They suggest the following practice guidelines:

- Identify the relevant systems, their subsystems, and the suprasystems of which they are a part or to which they are related;
- Identify the system interrelationships (e.g., subsystem/subsystem; subsystem/system; system/suprasystem).

To facilitate the above, it might also be suggested that the practitioner

- Draw an eco-map to visually depict these systems and system interrelationships.

The eco-map was originally developed by Hartman (1978) as an assessment tool for use by social workers employed in child welfare agencies. It is a paper-and-pencil simulation that enables the practitioner and client to organize and concurrently present the many variables and systems that together make up the client's total life space. The eco-map pictures the important nurturant or conflictual connections between the client and his surrounding environs: It "highlights the nature of the interfaces and points to conflicts to be mediated, bridges to be built, and resources to be sought and mobilized" (Hartman, 1978:467).

The following case example illustrates the relevance of the preceding practice guidelines to environmental modification:

Mrs. Meyer, a 40-year-old obese woman, was referred to an outpatient clinic for antidepressants and counseling. During the intake interview, she informed the worker that she was concerned about Angie, her 15-year-old moderately retarded daughter. Workers at a public child welfare agency wanted to place Angie in an out-of-town residential trade school because they felt she was not being properly supervised and was spending too much time caring for her mother.

Mrs. Meyer was very upset about the possible removal of her daughter and resented the implication that she was using Angie as a maid. She further revealed that she needed an operation to repair a knee injury she had suffered a year earlier. The operation could not be performed, however, until she lost fifty pounds. The social worker also learned that Mrs. Meyer's sister, Louise, would no longer be able to help her out with various household chores. Louise's husband resented the time she spent at Mrs. Meyer's and had recently demanded that she devote more time to her own family.

Mrs. Meyer was totally overwhelmed by her situation. She felt "caught in the middle' and "buffeted about" by an environment she perceived to be beyond her control and mastery. Mrs. Meyer, intrigued by the social worker's suggestion that they draw an eco-map, decided to give it a try. The outcome of that collaborative effort is seen in Figure 7–1.

As a result of drawing this eco-map, Mrs. Meyer and her worker were able to identify more clearly those systems which were in conflict, those which lacked linkages to one another, and those where more resources were going out than coming in and vice versa. The eco-map also helped them identify resources that were needed and potential strengths that could be drawn upon. Most importantly, this experience helped reduce Mrs. Meyers's feeling of being overwhelmed and immobilized. As a result, she began to feel more confident about her ability to negotiate and have an impact upon her environment.

Open vs. Closed System.   A system can also be classified as open or closed. An open system engages in interchanges with its environment; it receives inputs from and produces outputs to that environment. According to systems theorists, all living organisms are open systems. As

FIGURE 7–1.   Eco-map of Mrs. Meyer's environment.

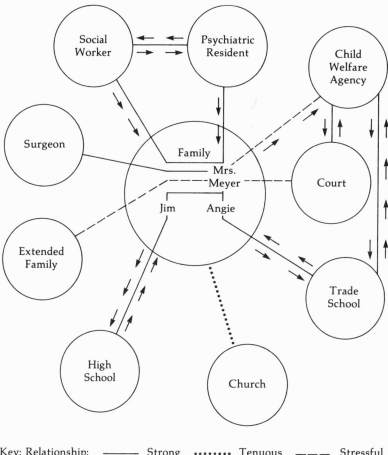

Key: Relationship: ———— Strong ••••••• Tenuous ——— Stressful
Energy Flow: → → →

such, they are continually growing and evolving toward increased order and complexity. This tendency toward increased organization and differentiation is often referred to as synergy. In contrast, a closed system does not interact with its environment; it is isolated from other systems and does not depend upon them for its survival. Closed systems are generally characterized by entropy, or a tendency to move toward a disordered state and a decrease in usable resources and energy. This open vs. closed distinction is never absolute. In actuality, no system is ever completely open, since it would then be indistinguishable from its environment. Conversely, no system is ever completely closed, since it would then cease to exist (Anderson and Carter, 1974).

What is really meant, then, is "relatively more open" or "relatively more closed."

Again, these concepts hold important implications for environmental modification. They reaffirm the importance of restoring, maintaining, and enhancing reciprocally nurturing transactions between an individual and his environment and viewing the health of a system as essentially dependent upon its openness to new sources of energy. They suggest that the practitioner

- Assess the extent to which each relevant system is more or less open or closed;
- Assess how receptive or nonreceptive each system is to influence by the other systems to which it is related or of which it is a part;
- Identify those resources that are currently or potentially available to each system; assess how they are or are not being used; consider the ways in which these, or new, resources may be used to reduce a system's entropic processes and foster its continued growth and development.

Consider, for example, the case of Mr. Powell:

A 65-year-old widower, Mr. Powell was recently retired from his job as an inventory manager for a large manufacturing firm. He had worked for his company for the past thirty two years. After his retirement, he moved from his large suburban home to a small apartment in the city to reduce his expenses and to be closer to his best friend, Jim. Shortly thereafter, however, Jim suffered a severe stroke and was placed in a nursing home.

The social worker at the home observed that whenever he visited Jim, Mr. Powell seemed lonely and depressed. After the visit, he would often sit in the lobby for hours, reading magazines or watching other visitors come and go. One afternoon the worker began talking with Mr. Powell and, in the course of their conversation, mentioned a senior citizens group that had begun meeting at a nearby church. Mr. Powell expressed interest in this group and, at the worker's suggestion, decided to attend the next meeting. The following week, he shared with the worker his feelings of loneliness and isolation. He related that he had few friends, that he had little contact with his children (who lived in another state), and that he found it difficult to meet new people. He indicated that he had enjoyed the meeting but was ambivalent about becoming an active member of the group. He questioned his ability to offer anything of significance.

It was obvious to the social worker that Mr. Powell had suffered many losses and that he needed support and assistance in linking up with resources that would help reduce his isolation (closure, entropy). The worker subsequently helped Mr. Powell hook up with a group of retired businessmen who provided free consultation to various neighborhood organizations. Mr. Powell's expertise in inventory management proved to be a valuable asset and through this experience he gained a renewed sense of competence and self-fulfillment. As his confidence grew, he began attending the senior citizens group on a regular basis, and, through the group, gradually developed new friendships and social outlets (synergy).

Energy Exchange. These classifications of systems as more or less open or closed and synergistic or entropic bring to the fore another central concept, energy exchange. Anderson and Carter (1974) define energy broadly to include both actual and potential resources and information that provide the system with capacity for action, action, and power to effect change. Energy for an individual, therefore, might include such tangible and intangible resources as food, money, clothing, shelter, medical care, relationships, ideas, emotional support from family and peers, cultural sanctions for values and beliefs, expectations of others, creativity, a sense of worth and integrity, physical strength, and a sense of competence.

How, then, is such energy exchanged? For many systems theorists, the concepts of input, throughput, output, and feedback provide handy levers for conceptualizing the exchange of energy. Input refers to the selective importation of energy (resources) from the surrounding environment and from within the system itself (e.g., from its various subsystems). Throughput refers to the process whereby the system acts upon, or transforms and converts, the energy that has been imported. Output is the outcome, or result, of that processing—the products and ways in which the system acts back on itself and on its environment. An input + throughput = output paradigm, however, is overly simplistic and linear and fails to take into account the fact that outcome influences input as well as the manner in which the system processes that input. Thus, a fourth element, feedback, is added. This is the process by which information is fed back into the system as a result of its attempts to affect its environment and its component parts. This information is then used by the system as input to guide its future operations (Whittaker, 1974). Obviously, feedback can lead to positive or negative consequences or a subtle mixture of both.

These concepts are especially relevant to environmental modification and suggest the following practice guidelines:

- Identify the inputs that are currently or potentially available to each relevant system; assess how the system selectively chooses its inputs and what this choice precludes in terms of alternate inputs; identify resources that the system is not aware of;

- Assess what the system does with the inputs it receives; identify any disturbances or deficits in this input processing; assess the consequences of these deficits for the system and for other systems to which it is related;
- Identify the outputs of the system; assess their negative consequences in relation to the system itself and to contiguous systems;
- Identify and assess the system's feedback procedures; identify any blocks to the system's effective use of those feedback mechanisms; help the system increase its diagnostic sensitivity to the effects of its inputs, throughputs, and outputs upon itself and other related systems.

These practice guidelines suggest that the practitioner consider assessing presenting problems partly in terms of their potential manifestation of input, throughput, output, and feedback dysfunctions. They further suggest that the practitioner consider gearing interventions not only to the system's outcome or outputs but also to its inputs, throughputs, and feedback.

Keith Gardner, age 13, was referred by his teacher to a family service agency for counseling around academic problems and disruptive behavior in the classroom. The worker assigned to the case called the parents to request that the whole family be present at the initial interview. Mr. Gardner indicated that this would be impossible, as his wife refused to leave the house. However, he did consent to a home visit.

During this visit, the worker learned that three of the Gardners' four children were in trouble at school and that 15-year-old Justin had been picked up by the police on several occasions for curfew violations. Mr. Gardner was employed as an insurance salesman, and two months earlier had requested additional work assignments requiring extensive travel. As a result, he was rarely at home during the evenings or weekends. Mrs. Gardner was detached, despondent, and withdrawn. She interacted minimally with her family and spent much of her time in her room watching television.

The social worker assessed the Gardner family as being confronted with a number of problems that were draining the family's energy to cope effectively. Using the energy exchange paradigm, she observed that the family was linked to a number of systems, including the church, the school, and the court. A priest visited the family several times a week and the probation officer came by every Friday. In addition, the principals of the two schools where the children were enrolled called weekly. Mr. and Mrs. Gardner interpreted (throughput) these visits and calls (input) as excessive and as evidence that their ability to raise their children properly was being challenged. This was manifested (output) in several ways: (1) mother withdrew and denied that any problems existed; (2) father assumed that devoting more time to his job would better enable him to demonstrate his competence as head of the household; and (3) the children responded by acting-out even more at home and at school. As the family's situation worsened, the school and court began applying increased pressure on the family (feedback, input), suggesting that if something did not change soon, more drastic steps (such as suspension or placement) might have to be taken.

The social worker perceived part of her role as that of interpreter, both for the family and for the various systems to which the family was linked. She helped Mr. and Mrs. Gardner better understand the involvement of the school and court, which in turn served to reduce distorted interpretations of their motives. She also helped the principals and probation officer to appreciate how their efforts had been interpreted by the Gardners as threats to their competence. As a result, the school and court were better able to appreciate the family's struggles and their seeming "unwillingness" to take action. In addition, the school, court, and priest were encouraged to coordinate their involvement with the Gardners through the social worker, thus reducing the felt barrage of inputs on a family already seriously overwhelmed.

Environmental modification was used effectively in this case to enhance the competence of the family members in dealing with each other and in interacting more successfully with their environment. Considerable emphasis was placed on restoring and promoting Mr. and Mrs. Gardner's adaptive strivings toward competence and on restructuring the family's transactions with important systems in its milieu. As a result, the Gardners experienced an increased sense of mastery, a greater understanding of their environment, and a greater appreciation of their ability to have a positive impact on that environment. Concomitantly, the principals and probation officer gained greater respect for not only the Gardners' struggles, but also their many strengths and potentials. This resulted in improved communication and delivery of services, leading in turn to enhanced competence in meeting the family's needs.

When intensive formal intervention was no longer necessary, the social worker explicitly encouraged the continued involvement of the priest, who had long been an important figure in the family's everyday life. The priest maintained close contact with the Gardners, providing ongoing support, facilitating school-family-court linkages, and helping the family make use of other resources available in the community. By enlisting his help, the social worker put into play another important principle of environmental modification, namely the use of central figures in people's *natural* social networks (Swenson, Chapter 6 in this volume). Unfortunately, as a study by Maluccio (1979a) has suggested, practitioners seem reluctant to use informal services and resources in their clients' social networks as an integral part of treatment. Moreover, they tend to attribute much less significance to these social networks than their clients do. This may be due to (1) their tendency to view interventions into a client's life situation as less effective or prestigious than clinical treatment and (2) possible jealousy of the role and influence of significant members of a client's network. Whatever the reasons, greater attention should be devoted to the potential use of social networks and self-help or mutual support programs as instruments *of* help rather than simply as influences *on* help (Germain and Gitterman, 1980; Maluccio, 1979a). It becomes incumbent upon social workers, therefore, to develop formal and informal helping system linkages and to focus more systematically and deliberately on the client's natural life situation.[3]

Ripple Effect.   The many complexities characterizing the Gardner case lead us to another important systems theory concept, the ripple effect. Stemming from the assumption that all systems are interactive and interdependent, the ripple effect principle holds that if change occurs in one part of a system, its effects will be felt in all other parts of the system. Similarly, if change occurs in one system, it is likely to have an effect upon contiguous systems.

Applied to environmental modification, this principle suggests that improvement in one system (or system part) may bring about improvement in another system (or system part). On the other hand, it might instead bring about deterioration, that is, improvement in one system may adversely affect another system. The practitioner, therefore, is well advised to utilize the ripple effect principle to assess all the possible consequences, negative and positive, of any interventions that are under consideration.[4] In planning interventions, the practitioner may also find it helpful to make use of another notion, namely, that every system usually possesses what is referred to as a point of maximum reverberation. This is the spot in the system at which any change will bring about the greatest positive modification of the other parts of the system (Hollis, 1972). The practitioner, therefore, will need to examine carefully the relationships between systems and system parts to determine where the point of greatest potential effectiveness lies.

Closely related to the ripple effect concept is the principle of equifinality, which states that a system can reach the same final state from differing initial conditions and by a variety of paths. Applied to social work practice, this principle suggests that various interventions may lead to the same final effect (Hartman, 1970). Thus, for a child experiencing problems in school, individual therapy is not necessarily the only or even the best choice of intervention. Work with the mother, father, family as a whole, or school may be equally or even more effective. Or the child's school problems may be best approached through such interventions as improved housing, economic supports for the family, or a recreational program for the child (Hartman, 1970).

The equifinality principle also suggests that a system's initial conditions may or may not be relevant to or causally important in the establishment of the final end state (Compton and Galaway, 1975). Thus, practitioners must always guard against allowing a system's initial conditions to color their perspective to the extent that they view the system as so restricted by these initial conditions that it is incapable of growth in the here and now. While the severity and extent of these initial conditions must obviously be taken into account, the central theme should be the potential for continued growth and change, both in the present and in the future. The system, therefore, must be regarded as not only "being" but also continually in the process of "becoming" (Perlman, 1957). In this respect, equifinality is intimately related to the concept of competence; both help us to view the person as active (rather than reactive or passive) and as possessing an innate capacity for growth and change, for affecting as well as being affected by his environment. As Hearn (1969) observed, it is the nature of human beings to be creators. They are not content to merely adjust to their environment; they have an inner drive or compulsion to influence and master it, to shape and change it in ways that create ever more complex relationships between themselves and that environment. Equifinality and competence therefore strongly support the long-standing social work values of respect for the uniqueness of the individual and his right to self-determination. They also reaffirm the role of action in environmental modification and the importance of providing people with a choice of alternatives in their everyday lives:

> The provision of diverse opportunities for action may tap the individual's potential to look at the world in novel ways and facilitate his selection of the activity most suited to his personal method of coping and his particular drive for competence. [Maluccio, 1974:34]

The above concepts lead to the following practice guidelines:

- In planning an intervention, assess all the possible intrasystem and intersystem consequences that might occur as a result of that intervention;
- Remember that since change in one system (or system part) inevitably affects other contiguous systems (or system parts), it may not be necessary to intervene in every system or system part;
- Examine the interrelationships between and within systems to

identify that point where the greatest potential for change may
lie;

- Always consider the multiple possibilities for intervention;
  avoid clinical myopia and preconceived notions about which
  type of cases or clients is best suited to which type of intervention;
- Focus not on a system's weaknesses or deficits but on its actual
  and potential strengths; help the system identify and effectively
  use or further develop those strengths;
- Continually seek ways to promote a system's adaptive strivings
  toward growth and competence, mastery and creativity.

The potential applicability of these practice guidelines is seen in
the following case example:

Tom Mitchell, age 15, refused to attend school, had been stopped by the
police several times for drinking and riding his motorcycle without a license,
and was continually fighting with his mother and 17-year-old sister, Cheryl.
The Mitchell family was receiving public assistance, and their caseworker
referred Tom to a crisis intervention center when she learned that, during a
recent quarrel, Tom had lost control and hit Cheryl in the face with a lamp.
Karen, the oldest daughter, returned home from college when she heard
about the incident and accompanied Tom to the center. There, the social
worker learned that Mr. and Mrs. Mitchell were physically disabled and
unable to effectively set limits on Tom's behavior. Mrs. Mitchell suffered
from muscular dystrophy and was confined to a wheelchair. Her husband
was recuperating from a recent stroke and was having difficulty adjusting to
the attendant paralysis of his left side. Karen had tried to fill in for her
parents, but the distance between college and home made this virtually
impossible.

During a subsequent home visit, the social worker began by helping the Mitchells to identify, partialize, and prioritize the range of
problems currently confronting them. After determining that Tom was
their primary concern, she engaged the family in an identification and
consideration of alternative solutions. Tom's principal, for example,
had suggested that he be placed in a social adjustment school. Tom
vehemently opposed this and indicated that he would run away if this
alternative were put into effect. A worker at a public child welfare
agency had implied that Tom should be declared a ward of the state
and be placed in a residential school for predelinquent teenagers. Mr.
and Mrs. Mitchell, however, were extremely reluctant to relinquish
custody of Tom. They were torn between their felt inability to control
Tom's behavior and their reluctance to have him removed from the

home. For them, the best alternative was for Karen to return home and attend a local college. Karen felt this would be too disruptive of her studies, limit her independence, and place unreasonable demands upon her. She felt the family would best benefit by ongoing counseling. Finally, Tom suggested that he be allowed to transfer to a nearby vocational trade school, which required that its students attend classes in the morning and work in the afternoons. He eagerly pointed out that his uncle needed help in his appliance repair shop and had asked Tom if he would be interested in working for him over the summer. Picking up on this, Mrs. Mitchell observed that Tom had done very well in the electronics course he had taken at school.

After carefully weighing the pros and cons of each of these possible alternatives—in particular the effects they would have on each family member and on the family as a whole—the Mitchells opted for Tom's suggestion. The social worker supported the family's decision to give this alternative a try before initiating any of the others (such as family counseling or Karen's transfer). She subsequently helped the parents to contact the school, the child welfare agency, and the uncle to secure their permission to carry out the proposed plan. Tom was admitted to the trade school and several months later was found to be attending classes and working for his uncle on a regular basis. He was pleased with the opportunity to pursue his long-standing interest in electronics and welcomed the sense of competence and commitment that he was now experiencing. Not surprisingly, these improvements in Tom's behavior, attitude, and feelings about himself reverberated throughout the family. Karen returned to college and tensions at home decreased dramatically. Mrs. Mitchell joined a local self-help group for women with debilitating illnesses and Mr. Mitchell's health improved to the point where he was now taking short walks down to the corner drugstore. The Mitchells, experiencing renewed feelings of mastery and self-worth, were pleased with Tom's progress and felt that no further intervention was needed.

Summary.   Although the preceding discussion provides only a rudimentary introduction to select systems theory concepts, it demonstrates the relevance and applicability of the systems theory framework to environmental modification. Its demand that all phenomena be conceptualized as interrelated and interdependent systems forces practitioners to shift their attention from the individual or his environment to the multiple and complex transactions occurring between them. It therefore enables the practitioner to focus more simultaneously on the individual and on the various formal and informal helping networks in his natural environment. Similarly, the systems theory framework helps expand the actual and perceived boundaries within which social workers employ their knowledge and skills. Thus, it allows us to move toward a broader conceptualization of practice, one where environmental modification is truly an integral component of social work's helping means.

Roles, Skills, and Techniques

At the same time, however, systems theory is highly abstract and does not provide us with a specific model of intervention. It leaves open the question of strategy and technique (Janchill, 1969). One way to conceptualize the strategies and techniques of environmental modification is through the concept of the intervention role; this term refers to the planned activities undertaken by the practitioner and client for the purpose of accomplishing mutually agreed-upon goals and objectives.

Over the years, a variety of roles have been identified as particularly apropos to environmental intervention. These include activist, lobbyist, bargainer, advocate, mediator, aggressive intervenor, broker, ombudsman, enabler, and conferee. The following discussion will focus on three of these roles: broker, mediator and advocate. In our opinion, these roles provide the best rubrics for classifying the various activities associated with environmental modification. Each of these roles is based upon different assumptions and is appropriate for different types of situations. Thus, each demands different kinds of knowledge and skills. If any of these roles is to be optimally effective, however, it must be carried out in a relatively orderly and systematic manner. Problems must be identified, defined, and partialized; goals must be developed; alternative solutions must be identified; the pros and cons of these alternatives must be weighed; a plan of action must be formulated and carried out; and feedback mechanisms to assess the effectiveness of this action plan must be developed.

Like any other social work intervention, brokerage, mediation, and advocacy require skills in effective problem-solving. The problem-solving process has been conceptualized in a variety of ways. Most commonly, however, it is defined as a process involving these phases: (1) problem identification and definition; (2) data collection; (3) assessment and planning; (4) intervention; (5) evaluation; and (6) termination.

The problem-solving paradigm holds considerable relevance to environmental modification and is highly consonant with the systems theory framework. It makes no assumptions as to the nature or location of a problem; it de-emphasizes pathology; and it is not based on any one theoretical orientation (Compton and Galaway, 1975). And, like systems theory, it rests on the premise that each individual is a purposive being whose innate strivings toward competence are strengthened or restored when requisite resources are provided and effectively utilized. The broker, mediator, and advocate roles of environmental modification should therefore be viewed against the backdrop not only of the systems theory framework but also of the problem-solving paradigm.

Broker.   The broker role is a familiar one in such contexts as real estate and the stock market. In social work, it is used to refer to those processes whereby the client is linked or connected with the resources and services he needs (Pincus and Minahan, 1973: Whittaker, 1974). As a broker, the practitioner may provide resources through his own agency, identify and locate resources available in the community, and create needed resources where none exist (Hollis, 1972). In fulfilling this role, he may function variously as a liaison person, referrer, expediter, interpreter, coordinator, and gatekeeper (Siporin, 1975).

Brokerage clearly operates at the interface between the individual and the formal and informal resource system (Briar and Miller, 1971). Moreover, it presupposes a complementarity of interest between the two. It operates at a level of "least contest," for it assumes that "the service providers need populations to receive the services just as the populations need some place to turn for particular goods or services that the broader community has determined to disperse" (Middleman and Goldberg, 1974:65).

The broker role is perhaps the oldest and best known in social work, dating back to the friendly visitors and settlement house workers of the early 1900s:

> The early caseworkers were experts in finding, interpreting and creating resources for the needy. In fact, these activities comprised so much of the work that it hardly seemed necessary to attach a special theoretical significance to them. In large part, this was what any "good" caseworker did. [Middleman and Goldberg, 1974:65]

Unfortunately, today's broker enjoys little status. Brokerage is given limited attention in the literature, receives minimal support in funding, and is often the first role to be given away or sloughed off to others. This may be due in part to a tendency on the part of many social workers to regard brokerage as little more than a matter of routine "collateral contact"—and a time-consuming, frustrating, and irritating matter at that. The broker role, however, is much more complex than it may seem on the surface, partly because of limited, inaccessible, or stigmatized resources.

What knowledge and skills do social workers need to effectively carry out the broker rule? First, they must know what resources and services are available—where they are located, who provides them (and under what auspices), what kinds of help they offer, and to whom they are available. Practitioners would be wise, therefore, to develop, maintain, and continually update an inventory of important resource systems. While such an inventory is essential, it is not, in and of itself, sufficient. The practitioner must also be familiar with the diverse "access routes" to these resource systems. Particularly important is an understanding of the entry requirements and appeal procedures of a resource, as well as its formal and informal policies.

Ideally, the practitioner should have a fairly good idea of what actually transpires from the time a client first contacts a needed resource to his effective utilization of it. Knowledge such as this is rarely obtainable from the standardized directory of services. What is entailed here is firsthand knowledge amassed from actual contact with people in the resource system. This suggests, then, that social workers become personally acquainted with key resource individuals so that they will know exactly what they are talking about when they suggest resources to their clients. Middleman and Goldberg (1974) have further recommended that practitioners "cultivate" their resources in the long-term interests of their clients. This means maintaining contacts with responsive resource systems and working to effect greater sensitivity in unresponsive systems. This should be done at times when no client is in need and no particular crisis demands an immediate response. Thus, when a client is faced with a critical need, the practitioner can more quickly and effectively tap a resource with whom channels of communication have already been established and nurtured.

In fulfilling the broker role, the practitioner will identify with the client the range of resources and services that are available and appropriate to his needs. They will examine together the various alternatives and weigh the pros and cons of each. In the process of selecting a resource, the practitioner will help the client understand what the resource can and cannot offer him, what he is and is not entitled to, what might be expected of him and what he might expect of those he will come in contact with, and what steps will be necessary to make use of the resource. It is important that the client take as active a part as he can in initiating and carrying out the linkage process. By being actively engaged in the doing and deciding, he will acquire important knowledge and skills that he can draw upon in the future as well as an increased sense of mastery and competence. To facilitate this process, the practitioner and client must carefully consider the resources and skills that will be needed to effect the linkage. They must determine together the resources and skills that each possesses as well as the responsibilities that each should undertake. If the client does not possess certain requisite knowledge or skills, he should be helped to develop them; if this is not feasible or the situation demands quick action, the practitioner should pave the way himself. It is very important that the practitioner stay with and support the client throughout the linkage process. If a client is unable to overcome a problem that is preventing his obtaining or using the needed resource, the practitioner may need to shift to a mediator role to explore the blockage, or to an advocacy role to exert pressure on the resource.

In light of the above, various practice guidelines are suggested to facilitate the effective performance of the broker role:

- Develop and continually revise and update an inventory of important formal and natural resource systems;
- Know where these resources are located, who provides them, what kinds of help they do and do not offer, and to whom they are available;
- Know the formal and informal policies, procedures, entry requirements, and appeal mechanisms of these resource systems;
- Become personally acquainted with key individuals in these resource systems; maintain and nurture channels of communication;
- Apply problem-solving procedures to the process of establishing linkages between clients and needed resources;
- Actively involve the client in the linkage process; work with and support him throughout that process;
- Intervene on behalf of the client when he or she does not possess requisite knowledge or skills to carry out an objective, when a crisis situation demands an immediate action, or when the resource is unresponsive to the client's efforts.

The broker role and the above practice guidelines were used in the following case:

Miss Taylor, age 26, was about to be released from the hospital, where she had spent the past two months recuperating from burns and a severe leg injury she suffered when her apartment building burned down. Her physician referred her to the hospital's social service department for help in discharge planning. Miss Taylor's initial plans were to stay with her mother until she could find a place of her own. Because of her injuries, she would also have to relinquish her job as a waitress and seek new employment.

It was evident from the outset that Miss Taylor was reluctant to accept any kind of help. The social worker learned that she was proud of the fact that, unlike many of her friends, she was not receiving public assistance and had, until the accident been "making it on [her] own." She interpreted someone doing things for her as a sign of weakness. The social worker related to and supported her desire to be self-sufficient and suggested that Miss Taylor might think of her as a "resource person," someone who would be able to help her hook up with those resources that she needed to regain and maintain her self-sufficiency. She was quite receptive to this interpretation of the social worker's role.

They then sat down and together made up a list of the various resources that Miss Taylor needed. Initial priorities were obtaining a clinic card, setting up appointments with the physician, getting her prescriptions filled, and enrolling in the hospital's outpatient physical therapy program. The social worker accompanied Miss Taylor to the outpatient clinic, where she completed the necessary application forms for her clinic card and set up weekly appointments with her doctor. They then went to the pharmacy, where her prescriptions were filled. Although Miss Taylor had been approached earlier by a nurse from the physical therapy program, she was unclear about the required registration procedures. Instead of clarifying them for her, the social worker went with Miss Taylor to the physical therapy department and let her find out for herself what those procedures entailed. While registering in the program, Miss Taylor also made arrangements for transportation to and from the hospital. The social worker had overlooked this and supported Miss Taylor's initiative.

Second on the list of priorities was employment. The social worker provided Miss Taylor with a list of several potential employment services, along with the names of key individuals to contact and a description of their general entry requirements and procedures. They discussed the pros and cons of each of these services and Miss Taylor ultimately decided to contact first an association for the physically handicapped. With the help of that association, she was able eventually to secure a job as a telephone operator.

Throughout this process, the social worker encouraged and supported the client's active involvement in initiating and following through with the plan they had developed. She viewed Miss Taylor as having many strengths and potentials for growth and as essentially needing environmental inputs for their effective release and development. Accordingly, her efforts were primarily geared toward helping her to begin reassuming active control over her life. Through her active participation, Miss Taylor's resistance to help decreased markedly and she experienced a renewed sense of mastery, competence, and independence.

Mediator.   A second role relevant to environmental modification is that of the mediator. Like brokerage, mediation presumes a common bond, or complementarity of interest, between the client and the resource system. In brokerage, this common bond is functional. In mediation, however, it has broken down or grown obscure. What results is conflict, a sign that one or both parties have lost sight of their need for one another. The mediator, therefore, positions himself between the conflicting parties. His primary function is to help them rediscover their mutual need, thereby freeing each to contribute again to the other's welfare.

Middleman and Goldberg (1974:60–65) delineate a number of activities and skills that contribute to successful mediation. First, the mediator identifies the common ground—how and where the self-interests of the involved parties overlap. This requires a careful and sensitive use of relationship and interviewing skills to gain a clear understanding of the role each party plays in the other's life (Hollis, 1972). The mediator then looks for that point where the different self-interests seem to converge. He subsequently talks with each of the parties individually, pointing out the stake each has in developing a cooperative relationship with the other. He offers to help each party talk to the other and, if they agree, establishes contracts with each. The mediator then convenes a joint meeting, wherein he identifies the common ground on which the two can meet and establishes a service contract with them as a unit. He sides with neither party, but stands between them, "equally concerned about both, and placing his faith in their engagement" (Middleman and Goldberg, 1974:62).

Once the two parties begin working together, the mediator must be alert to any obstacles that arise and block valid communication (e.g., personal needs, culturally based ethics, authority conflicts). He identifies the obstacle and challenges both parties to confront and resolve it openly and honestly. The common ground is reasserted and each is encouraged to reconsider his need for the other. In addition, the mediator helps the involved parties identify the boundaries beyond which their agreement produces consequences for other systems in their respective social networks. That is, he helps the parties become cognizant of the ramifications that their relationship and decisions may have on other systems to which they are related or of which they are a part. This involves an assessment of the long-term as well as short-term effects of a change, both within and between systems.

The mediator will also play an important role in providing or making available information critical to the decision-making processes in which the two parties are engaged. Since information can be viewed as a resource and since differential possession of—or accessibility to—information can lead to a perceived power imbalance, it is imperative that the mediator establish informational parity. For example, in situations where one party has access to information that the other does not, the mediator will (1) ask that party to share it with the other or (2) provide it himself. And, if the mediator possesses information to which neither party is privy, he will share that information with both. Finally, the mediator should continually project an image of himself as having faith that the outcome of open and honest communication between the conflicting parties will be to their mutual benefit.

The activities and skills necessary for effective mediation suggest these practice guidelines:

- Assess the individual interests and needs of each system in conflict;
- Identify the common ground of the two systems (the point where their individual interests and needs converge);
- Help each system begin working with the other; establish contracts with each system individually and with both systems as a unit;
- Help the systems identify, confront, and resolve openly and honestly any obstacles that are blocking effective communication;
- Help the systems recognize the consequences that will occur (for other systems to which they are related) as a result of their working together;
- Help the system establish and maintain informational parity;
- Assume a position of neutrality, but project hope and confidence in the mutual benefits to be accrued from the systems working together.

The relevance of these practice guidelines and the use of the mediator role are seen in the following example:

Mr. and Mrs. Olson, an elderly black couple, were engaged in counseling at a local family service agency. During their fifth session, Mrs. Olson appeared to be quite upset and angry. Upon exploring this, the social worker learned that she was very frustrated with the resident landlord of an apartment that they were interested in renting. Mrs. Olson felt the landlord was putting them off and inventing excuses (such as plans for extensive remodeling) to avoid renting them the apartment. The Olsons viewed the landlord's behavior as racially motivated and felt they were being given the "runaround." As a result, several intense arguments had ensued, particularly between Mrs. Olson and the landlord.

After contracting to work on the problem, the social worker called the realty office to confirm the availability of the apartment in question. The realtor indicated that the apartment was being painted, but would be available within a week. The social worker then contacted the landlord to arrange a meeting; he consented, but reluctantly. During the meeting, it became apparent that the landlord's ambivalence about renting to the Olsons stemmed not from any racial bias, but from his concerns about Mr. Olson, who was in poor health and unable to get around without the aid of a walker. The landlord was afraid that he would have to install special railings or make other modifications in the apartment. More importantly, he was worried about Mr. Olson's ability to care for himself while his wife was at work. He was afraid that, since he was at home all day, he might have to take on responsibilities he did not want and did not feel capable of assuming. After listening attentively and sensitively to the landlord, the worker suggested a joint meeting with the Olsons. The landlord was hesitant about such a meeting, noting that his previous contacts with Mrs. Olson had always ended in an argument. The social worker also sensed that the landlord was afraid that all three would gang up on him. After reassuring him and stressing that the meeting would be of mutual benefit to him and the Olsons, he finally agreed.

The meeting began with some animosity between Mrs. Olson and the landlord, but by structuring the discussion the worker was able to help them focus on the real issues at hand. It soon became apparent to the landlord and the Olsons that their differing and unclarified interpretations had led to a communication impasse. With the social worker's support, the landlord was able to tell the Olsons that race was not an issue—that his major concern was Mr. Olson's physical health and the added responsibilities he felt this might place on him. After hearing this, the Olsons' anger decreased and they were able to convince the landlord that Mr. Olson did not need special equipment in the apartment and that he could care for himself. This mediational effort proved successful and both parties seemed relieved that the problem had been aired and confronted openly and honestly. The Olsons, moreover, were particularly pleased to have had an opportunity to demonstrate their competence and ability to manage on their own and they welcomed the feelings of satisfaction and self-worth that thus ensued. If the mediation had been unsuccessful, the social worker might have had to turn to a more aggressive approach, namely advocacy.[5]

Advocate.   The advocate role refers to the defending, promoting, or pleading of a cause, to action taken in behalf of an aggrieved individual or group of individuals. The advocate's primary function is to remove obstacles or barriers that prevent people from exercising their rights or receiving the benefits and using the resources they need (McPheeters and Ryan, 1971). In fulfilling this role, the practitioner may function variously as a partisan spokesman, ombudsman, complaint agent, social reformer, norm changer, and aggressive intervenor (Compton and Galaway, 1975; Hollis, 1972; Siporin, 1975). In social work, advocacy is often assumed to entail primarily efforts to make formal service systems more responsive to client needs. However, it can also involve the unresponsive slumlord, the harried schoolteacher, or the dictatorial boss (Briar and Miller, 1971; Middleman and Gold-berg, 1974). It is also frequently assumed that in carrying out the advo-cacy role, the social worker engages the party or parties presumably violating the client's rights and intercedes in his behalf. However, the social work advocate might instead organize those clients whose rights in a given area have been violated and mobilize them to argue on their own behalf.

Whereas the broker role assumes an operational complementarity of interest and the mediator role a nonoperational complementarity, the advocate role presumes a conflict of interest. Thus, unlike the function-alism of the broker and the neutrality of the mediator, the advocate necessarily adopts a partisan stance (Grosser, 1965). As Richan (1969) has observed, advocacy by its very nature calls for the taking of sides. The advocate speaks *for* something or someone; implicitly if not ex-plicitly, he is speaking *against* something or someone else. The advo-cate, therefore, is not nonjudgmental or impartial. He is a champion of a cause or victim. Given its adversary nature and the potentially dele-terious consequences that may ensue (such as retaliation against the client), most social work theorists advise that advocacy be approached cautiously and be undertaken only if other roles (such as broker and mediator) have failed.

If brokerage and mediation have proved unsuccessful and the so-cial worker is considering an advocacy stance, it is imperative that he engage the client in an honest and straightforward discussion of the possible negative repercussions that might occur. As Middleman and Goldberg (1974) have noted, the client of the social work advocate is generally relatively powerless—his resources (e.g., money, political in-fluence) are not equal to those of the withholding party. In addition, he is frequently dependent upon the resources dispensed by that party. Thus, the outcome of opposing that party may be even harder to live with than not receiving the withheld benefit. Since it is the client who must bear the consequences of advocacy, the worker should therefore help him entertain the possibility of defeat and, putting aside his idealism and enthusiasm, respect the client's decision if it should be no.

If the client's decision is yes, the social worker must then consider what the best point of entry into the target system is. The possibility of a favorable outcome is enhanced when the advocate enters that system at the lowest possible hierarchical level and proceeds upward until a concession is obtained. Thus, "the problem should be escalated slowly, with personnel at each succeeding level recognized and afforded ample opportunity to contain the problem at that level by making a positive response" (Middleman and Goldberg, 1974:56). When a concession is made and the client obtains the benefits to which he is entitled, the worker should shift his stance and help the concessioner save face by engaging him as a partner rather than as a defeated adversary.

In short, the advocacy role is as potentially deleterious as it is ameliorative. Therefore, all possible contingencies must be identified and carefully weighed before advocacy is embraced. If advocacy is deemed appropriate, the practitioner would be well advised to take the following steps:

- Engage the client in an honest and straightforward consideration of all the possible positive and negative consequences that might ensue as a result of the advocacy effort;
- Carefully assess the target system's organizational structure and "chain of command";
- Enter that system at the lowest possible level and proceed upward; escalate the problem slowly;
- If the problem is favorably resolved, support the concessioner's decision to help him "save face";
- Carefully consider the potential advantages and disadvantages of actively engaging the client in the advocacy process; since the client's rights are at stake, err on the side of caution.

The following example illustrates the use of the above practice guidelines and the advocate role:

Mrs. Bruce, a public aid recipient, came to her family service worker questioning why the welfare department had not approved her request for an increase in carfare. She told the worker that she was currently enrolled in a job training program that she hoped would lead to her employment as a nurse's aide. The difficulty she was experiencing, and the reason for her request, revolved around transportation. The job training center, which offered the type of training for the job she was interested in, was located quite a distance from her home. Consequently, she needed fifteen dollars more per month to cover her travel expenses.

The family service worker began by helping Mrs. Bruce identify the steps that she had taken and those that would be necessary to effect a change in the department's decision. Mrs. Bruce indicated that she had already contacted her public aid caseworker to determine why her request for an increase had not been granted. This had not been easy for her, as she had experienced considerable difficulty reaching the caseworker by telephone; she finally went to the office in person and, after a three-hour wait, was able to talk with her. The caseworker apparently informed her that she had no alternative but to accept the department's decision. Mrs. Bruce seemed to feel that the caseworker minimized her plight and either did not have the time or was unwilling to consider taking any action on her behalf. She came away with the distinct impression that the caseworker regarded any attempts on the part of a public aid recipient to question the department's rules and regulations as inappropriate.

The family service worker then engaged Mrs. Bruce in exploration of the possible consequences, negative and positive, that might ensue as a result of an advocacy effort. Mrs. Bruce carefully considered the potential risks that might be involved (e.g., hostility, ridicule, direct or indirect retaliation) and decided that she would rather take those risks than face the imminent possibility that she would have to leave the job training program or change to another program (which would in turn mean giving up the job for which she was currently being considered). After further discussion, the social worker and Mrs. Bruce decided that it would be to her benefit if the social worker assumed the major responsibility for initiating the advocacy effort. The decision was based on such factors as the social worker's authority and knowledge of the department's operational structure and procedures and, equally important, her ability to gain access to department officials more quickly and easily than Mrs. Bruce.

The social worker subsequently contacted Mrs. Bruce's caseworker to determine if some sort of compromise could be worked out. The caseworker related to the social worker in the same way she had to Mrs. Bruce, indicating that she was unwilling to take any further steps because a decision had already been made. The social worker then spoke with the caseworker's supervisor. The supervisor was also hesitant to take any direct action herself but agreed to arrange for an informal appeal hearing through the welfare department's grievance committee. This hearing proved successful and Mrs. Bruce's request for a carfare increase was granted. Throughout this process, the social worker related sensitively to the supervisor's fears of possible reprisal for "bucking the system." The social worker supported the supervisor wherever possible, while at the same time encouraging her to intervene in such a way that would minimize her "costs" and maximize the client's "rewards."

Summary. The preceding discussion demonstrates the power of the broker, mediator, and advocate roles and their relevance to environmental modification. Each is based upon different assumptions and requires differing kinds of knowledge and skills. The assumptions underlying these roles provide the practitioner with the criteria necessary for determining which roles are most appropriate for which kinds of situations. By and large, brokerage should precede mediation and mediation should precede advocacy.

It should be emphasized that these roles were presented separately only for purposes of convenience and clarity of discussion. This is not meant to suggest that the roles are discrete or that the practitioner will use only one in any case situation. The realities of practice will frequently demand a blending or combination of brokerage, mediation, and advocacy. This requires, therefore, that the worker develop skills in all three. The practitioner must also be continually alert to the potential ways in which brokerage, mediation, and advocacy on behalf of single individuals or families can be extended to groups of individuals or families experiencing similar kinds of problems.

Conclusion

Environmental modification has long been considered an integral part of social work's helping means. Paradoxically, its importance has been honored more in speech than in action. Despite a recognition of its salience, it has typically been regarded as an ancillary intervention requiring less knowledge and skill than direct treatment. Contributing to the neglect and low prestige of environmental modification has been its inadequate theoretical development.

In this chapter we have attempted to address this theoretical vacuum by setting forth, in an integrated way, some of the underlying assumptions, roles, skills, and techniques that govern the conglomeration of activities that we loosely call environmental modification. The proposed model is in an embryonic stage of development; it makes no claims other than that it represents a beginning conceptualization of environmental modification and its value in promoting competence in clients.

We hope that the model will provide an impetus for social workers to further develop and refine the major concepts and assumptions underlying environmental modification and to test out the proposed practice guidelines. In education for practice, special efforts must be made not only to articulate and transmit the whys and wherefores of these concepts, action principles, and techniques but also to begin giving environmental modification the place and prestige in social work it so justly deserves. And, finally, systematic research on the provision and outcome of environmental modification is sorely needed so that we may gain a better understanding of how, and under what circumstances, environmental services can be most effectively and efficiently delivered. Facing this three-pronged challenge head-on is no easy task. But the potential benefits to the profession—and ultimately to the client in need—more than justify the efforts required.

Notes

1. The notion of developing such a model stemmed largely from a course currently being taught to first-year master's-level students at the University of Chicago's School of Social Service Administration (Mullen, 1978; Mullen, forthcoming). In this course, students are exposed to a broad spectrum of theory and research related to social work practice and are expected to develop a personal model for practice by formulating "summary generalizations" and derivative "practice guidelines" for each major topic covered (e.g., psychodynamic, behavioral, and cognitive theories and interventions; family, small group, organizational, and community theories and interventions).

2. See Germain (Chapter 5 in this volume) for a comprehensive analysis of the physical environment and its significance in social work practice.

3. See Swenson (Chapter 6 in this volume) for extensive discussion of social networks and natural helping systems.

4. In his discussion of cognitive theories, Fleming (Chapter 3 in this volume) also stresses the importance of providing feedback to clients regarding the possible consequences of their interventive actions.

5. Lee (Chapter 10 in this volume) considers the worker's role as mediator in intervention with children and youth.

CHAPTER 8

The Pursuit of Competence through Involvement in Structured Groups

Ruth R. Middleman

If we could distance ourselves from present-day services delivery and look back on them, we would see that a striking feature that surfaced during the past several decades is the enthusiasm for group approaches. Social workers, like the other people-serving professionals and service consumers, have discovered and embraced the group!

Why are groups so popular today? Partly because they are viewed by service providers as time-savers, as a means for reaching larger numbers and as cost effective. In addition, the self-help group approach has political appeal in highlighting "activated consumers," that is, individuals involved in meeting their own needs. But mainly, I believe, adults find groups a more natural and less stigmatizing context for help-seeking than individual counseling sessions. Groups are less continuously demanding minute by minute. Moreover, they contain socializing side effects; as the participants compare themselves to others and get to know them, friendships may develop that transcend the particular group experience.

Two of the most recent group phenomena are the structured group and the self-help group. Both reflect, at least in part, reactions against an earlier, almost messianic fervor about the group. The structured group, not yet widely described in the literature, represents a move away from the less structured therapy, sensitivity, growth, or "potential" groups, with their emphasis upon high emotionality, unprogrammed interactions, intimacy, and global changes. It reflects a move toward more limited, defined and described goals. The self-help group, on the other hand, represents a reaction by persons in trouble and eager paraprofessionals (Reissman, 1979) against a professional establishment of people helpers perceived as expensive, controlling, or removed from "knowing" the problems involved.

In this chapter, I shall describe and illustrate a practice approach that utilizes structured groups as a means of promoting competence in clients. The central thesis will be that learning through structured groups can lead to increased competence.[1]

Structured Groups

A structured group is a time-limited enterprise that utilizes an educational metaphor, *the learning experience* (where participant is learner and practitioner is facilitator, instructor, trainer, or resource provider) in order to help the participants deal with selected shared problems and/or common developmental needs. Emphasis is on experiential or whole-person learning via doing and talking with other participants and the worker, with the aim of affecting some or all of the range of learning domains—thought, wishes, values, feelings, or behavior.

While certain group therapies (for example, Gestalt) also may use experiential approaches and exercises, a key difference is that the practitioner in a structured group is viewed by members as facilitator or trainer rather than as therapist or treater. Structured groups offer piecemeal, partial developmental opportunities in line with a delimited, stated goal; they do not attempt any restructuring of the whole personality or move beyond their agreed upon focus.

Structured groups are closely compatible with a competence promoting goal, chiefly from the view of the client as a learner, as "a normal" who seeks to develop in a particular area. The content deals with selected skills that the learner sees a need to master, or with common problems/situations of living, or with coping with upheavals in living stemming from natural developmental life "passages" or sudden external, environmental shifts.

Service Context and Sponsorship

Structured groups have flourished in settings where the practitioner is free to draw back and consider the needs of whole populations without having to define persons as patients in order to obtain fees for service. Thus, it is not surprising that most of the innovation, experimentation and theoretical development has been achieved apart from the mental health establishment.

In the main, structured groups have been developed as adult services in growth centers, community centers, churches, and other agencies that attract middle class, discontented, "underactualized" individuals. They are also found on college campuses, where young adults seek preparation for future life roles; in public schools, where groups focus on the psychosocial life of students; and in business, government and human service organizations, where structured groups are used for staff and organizational development.

Categories of Structured Groups

Drum and Knott (1977) offer a useful classification for differentiating among various groups: Life Skills, Life Themes, and Life Transitions. There are distinctions among these subtypes as to goal, content, time orientation, and degree of structure and practitioner control.

As Figure 8-1 shows, Skills Groups are here-and-now–oriented; Theme Groups utilize a present/future focus; and Transition Groups may employ all three time perspectives. Practitioner activity and control of the group process, as well as the overall degree of structure, are highest in Skills Groups and lowest in Transition Groups (which at times may even appear much like personal growth, treatment or therapy groups).[2] The goals of each of these groups provide the key distinc-

FIGURE 8-1. Structured groups.

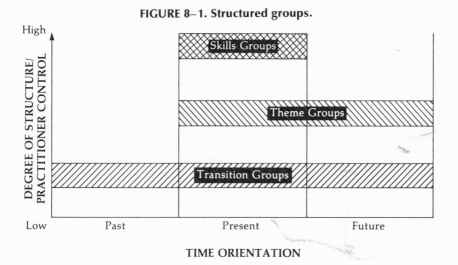

tion among them and determine the content and techniques that would be appropriate for the practitioner to use.

Theme Groups deal with common problems/issues of everyday living (for example, loneliness, intimacy, male/female consciousness) that hold more or less immediate importance to the participants but enough interest to enlist their commitment. Ordinarily these are discussion groups, but they may also involve activities and interactional tasks. When a given theme is cast into a "how to do it" format, then emphasis is placed on behavior and specific skills more than on a general theme.

Skills Groups use the present focus of the group experience to practice and rehearse specified behaviors with the other participants. For example, within the general theme of female consciousness, a "Women Alone" Skill Group might deal with component behaviors that enhance or impede the participants' situations: how to budget; relaxation exercises; how to start a conversation with a new acquaintance; and so forth.

Transition Groups have particular themes that highlight traumatic or sudden changes, anticipated role or life shifts, and unexpected, stressful, fear-laden events, for example, "empty nests," entering a new school or job, and physical injury. Moreover, the group members are experiencing the dilemmas of the event or crisis in the living moment! They are immediately rather than remotely or casually involved and draw on material from the past as well as the present as they try to formulate their futures. A Retirement Group for recent retirees who have just experienced the shock of their new life situation is a Transition Group with its special focus, goal, and process. On the other hand, a Retirement Group may also be organized as a Theme Group for middle-aged persons who want to begin to plan ahead.

Major Features of Structured Groups

The earliest use of structured groups within the social work profession can be traced to the early group workers in the settlements, the Ys, Boys and Girls Clubs, Jewish Centers, camping, and other leisure-time agencies, which stressed a teaching/learning approach to individuals and groups. Workers in these settings emphasized the following elements that are standard features of present-day structured groups: the view of the participant as a learner; the use of activities as a means for whole-person learning; the selection of special interests of the participants as determinants of group membership; the use of role modeling, telling and showing; the class format; the emphasis upon persons' learning from each other; and the focus on the group first and the individual(s) secondarily.[3]

There are, however, certain features of structured groups that are distinctly innovative and were not characteristic of early group work. Foremost is the open identification of emotions, communication, and interpersonal relationships as the targeted interests to be pursued directly rather than indirectly. Other new features are working contractually with participants, specifying goals and procedures for their attainment, and using self/other observation and various process assessment instruments as instructional and evaluative tools.

Another unique characteristic, perhaps the most distinctive advance in method, is the emphasis on an inductive teaching/learning approach through what I shall call the constructed experience: the simulation, game or task which is experienced and then discussed in order to connect experiential and cognitive knowing.[4] I shall return to the constructed experience later in this discussion.

Other innovations in format in current structured groups include direct practice and drill in various skills and activities, marathons and other intensive time frames, coleadership, and "homework" assignments that link, intensify, or generalize the group's themes to other situations.

Structured groups differ from group therapy, treatment, or encounters, which may emphasize transference and interpretation, or relationship and process, or cohesion and trust. Structured groups emphasize goal setting; specificity in arranging with the participants how the goal(s) will be approached; diverse techniques that deal with perceiving, thinking, feeling, behaving and valuing; and the integration of the structural components toward the achievement of competence in a specified realm.

In short, these groups provide an opportunity for group members to meet a limited, identified need or deal with a developmental gap successfully. Their structure and defined conditions reduce the power of the worker. The practitioner is a catalyst and designer of the components of the experience, not of what each participant will learn. Much of the practitioner's special knowledge and skill may be "invisible"— that is, exerted before the group meets, in terms of meticulous construction of the elements and conditions of the overall learning experience. The short-term emphasis and limited goals of a structured group do not promise personality overhaul and thus are consonant with many clients' reluctance to "being helped." Further, their mutually agreed-upon objectives make them congenial to a contractual, client-involving service from the outset, as well as to a research- and evaluation-based format.

Structured groups accent the groupness of the experience. That is, the self-monitored learning experiences hinge equally upon what participants learn from each other and on what the practitioner may say or do. This necessitates special consideration of group-process dynamics and skills in maximizing between-member communications.

Competence and Structured Groups

According to Kipling, the elephant's child got his long trunk because he asked too many questions. He had insatiable curiosity. When he asked the crocodile what crocodiles ate for dinner (at too short range), he had to yank mightily to extricate his nose from the snapping answer! While the trunk part of this story might not seem "just so," it is plausible that elephants are curious and that human beings are even more insatiably curious. Curiosity may have landed the elephant in trouble and may also have "killed the cat"; but curiosity, according to White (1959), is a basic motive in persons—a motive that leads to competence.

Competence may be thought of as an underlying need that impels individuals to explore or search for the challenging, new experience; it may also be viewed as outcome—the mastered act, the learned material, the acceptable performance of some specified task.[5] It may refer to a general potential for achievement or to the particulars that one can display in terms of knowledge, skills, motives, traits, and self-image—subcomponents termed competencies.[6] Since each person's life and learning experiences are unique, each one's competence repertoire is different from all others'—much like one's thumbprint.

In relating competence to structured groups, both aspects of the definition—as motive/need and as outcome achieved—would apply.

In Skills Groups, the focus is on enacted outcomes, on producing specified behaviors upon demand. This requirement calls for the display of both knowledge and skill components for "competence," a vastly different assessment estimate than paper-and-pencil measures of knowledge, which, as McClelland points out (1973), are mainly measures of test-taking ability. In Skills Groups, competence is seen as the ability to do rather than the ability to demonstrate knowledge. Or, as Tyler (1978) indicates, it is composed of the specifics that one knows about *and* can do—the aggregate of diverse competencies (particular skills and strategies) that comprise an individual's behavioral repertoire.

In Theme and Transition Groups, even more than in Skills Groups, there is emphasis on whole-person learning and encounters with others that elicit affective, attitudinal, and values challenges as well as challenges to cognition and behaviors. The more global view of competence would apply—one that sees the person as a striving, achievement-seeking individual eager to encounter the new experience or the new level of stimulation. The new experience or novel challenge has often been routinized away in the workaday world and confined mainly to intellectual stimuli in the schools. Much of the appeal of Theme and Transition Groups thus resides in their experiential/cognitive formats that demand interaction among participants toward unanticipated outcomes and communicative expressiveness of various levels, even playfully.

The essential seriousness of play, for children and adults, is well known, and its separation from work is a dichotomy of little usefulness. In fact, the non-sense involved in "only playing"—that is, testing the possibilities in behavior without receiving real consequences or punishment—leads directly to learning adaptive responsiveness in real life activities. This "playing"—in role-playing, simulations, and other constructed experiences in structured groups—provides the stimulus for learning adaptive responsiveness with other participants that can be transferred to "back home" situations.

At the heart of experiential learning is the worker's intervention through the constructed experience, a not-for-keeps, safe way to try out behavior, see what happens, modify it, and then try again. Through such experiences group members are reinvolved in the way they learned how to do and be as children: Through pursuit of doing-oriented activities and tasks, they learn the rules of the life-game as well as how to innovate, create, risk, and develop their own unique style of living (Middleman, 1968:264–65).

The Learning Experience

Understanding learning is as complex as understanding personality. There is no grand theory to account for how one learns. Rather, there are many competing theories and many types of learnings; for example, intellectual skills, verbal skills, cognitive strategies, motor skills, attitudes, feelings, and values (Gagne and Briggs, 1974). Additionally, there are nonverbal information handling skills and interactional skills.

Learning theorists in psychology have mainly followed either behavioral (stimulus–response) or cognitive orientations. The former view learning as habit acquisition through trial and error, while the latter consider it to be the acquisition of increasingly complex cognitive structures which lead to insight, understanding, and problem-solving.

Learning Defined

In his analysis of public education, Cremin (1976) differentiates the concepts of maturation, learning, development, and education as follows:

Maturation: changes in the individual that are relatively independent of external conditions or experience.

Learning: changes in behavior resulting from experience.

Development: changes resulting from the interaction of maturation and learning.

Education: deliberate efforts to acquire knowledge, attitudes, values, skills and sensibilities and any outcome of those efforts. Education also is used to describe the outcomes of the efforts of others (such as teachers) in these areas.

Education ideally results in learning, but not all learning is a result of education. Education can contribute to development, although not all development is a result of education. Education, which I now connect with structured group experiences for our purposes, differs from development but is close to it. In its secondary sense (the efforts of others), education (or structured group experiences) can be thought of as *augmented* development. That is, the practitioner supports the natural process of development (the interaction of maturation and learning) by providing selected experiences that speed up, intensify, or otherwise heighten these processes.

I have found Hall's (1959) anthropological orientation to learning most useful in conceptualizing the learning experiences of structured groups, especially because it connects the individual with the group and the group with the cultural surroundings. Hall (1959) distinguishes three kinds of learning:

Formal Learning.   Via tradition and cultural norms, one is directly confronted with "the good" and "the bad" way to be. Early in life, one learns through mistakes and corrections (of parents, authorities, the church, etc.) and through precept and admonition: "Do this; do that." It is hard to alter such early learnings about the right and wrong ways to be, think, and feel.

Informal Learning.   Via watching others (or through television), one learns much without necessarily realizing it. Thus, many things are learned through modeling and imitation outside of conscious awareness. There is no knowledge of the rules or patterns or elements involved in the learning process.

Technical Learning.   Via reading or hearing (lectures), the knowledge that is organized by the instructor or textbook is processed by the learner according to his motivation, intelligence, and familiarity with the language or symbols. This is very conscious learning: The knowledge is with the instructor or technical manual and is imparted piece by piece to the learner. This form of learning is the easiest to be assimilated and the easiest to forget.

In Hall's schema, formal learned patterns of behavior are at the core of the individual's learnings, with certain informal adaptations made over time (for example, by watching others in one's peer group) and supported by technical props (learnings acquired through various types of informative experiences). The heart of meaningful learning (change) is to identify the successful *informal* knowings and bring them out of unconscious awareness to consciousness by labeling them, talking about and processing them cognitively, and bringing them under conscious control. This informal-made-conscious learning can then become or affect the formal type.

A Learning Theory for Structured Groups

Using this view of formal, informal, and technical learning, I propose that structured groups operate by helping participants to know and review their *formal* learning (how they "really" act with one another, how others think and act, etc.) and to bring their *informal* knowledge to conscious awareness so that decisions can be made as to what, if anything, should be changed. The practitioner augments this learning/development by presenting *technical* knowledge—for example, definitions of skills, readings, discussions, etc.

In order to bring technical information to bear, the practitioner (and other group participants) utilize various structures—for example, phsyical environment, time, space, numbers of participants, selected role plays and other tasks. Skills-development groups are focused at the technical-learning level. They are didactic, specific, and precise. The practitioner follows the "best" or most efficient method of introducing the learners to a serially ordered set of instructions that, when practiced with trials and feedback as to results, will lead to an accurate performance.

A major means of bringing informal learning to conscious awareness is the deliberate application of selected structural components (in simulations, tasks, and interactional activities) that simultaneously confront the learners with a range of previously out-of-awareness phenomena. Here, each person's learning may be different from that of others, depending on past experiences, mood and interest, perceived importance of the event, and so forth.

This key design element constitutes the constructed experience, through which the group participant is reintroduced by the worker to his childlike mode of learning things informally—that is, learning gestalts through interacting with others, watching, risking, and so forth. As an adult, the learner is thus exposed to demands for spontaneity, expressing feelings, and other half-forgotten learning trials-now-made-safe by the purpose of *this* group experience and the sometimes playful, even frivolous-seeming modalities of interaction (games, drawing, pretending, etc.).

Middleman and Goldberg define the constructed (or structured) learning experience as

> a closed system deliberately constructed and set in motion by the trainer or facilitator. It has a boundary which separates it from the talk about the situation as well. . . . Within this boundary a set of conditions is established which affects the roles and/or rules, and/or the processes of interaction. Finally, the trainer or facilitator introduces a task to be pursued under the structured conditions. This task constitutes the moving dynamics of the learning situation. Participants must function within those particular conditions and experience both the opportunities for and constraints on pursuit of the task and on human behavior in general that are generated by these conditions. [Middleman and Goldberg, 1972b:205]

Major Principles

The structural perspective on learning leads to the following principles that guide the use of constructed experiences in work with structured groups for the purpose of promoting competence.

1. Knowing that derives from direct experience is different from knowing about, which is what the more vicarious, didactic, or discussion methods yield.

2. Social situations may be delimited by imposing particular structures (for example, time limits, rules, roles, tasks) that will highlight certain features of the situation and screen out others. By attending to the emphasized element(s), certain predictable interactions may be expected to occur. While the general interaction pattern may be anticipated, each individual's particular reaction and/or learning is unique and not predictable.

3. All structural elements are interrelated and cannot be understood without reference to total pattern or gestalt of their workings; that is, size of group, available resources, locus of power, time of day, physical setting, etc., all affect each other and the learning environment.

4. Individuals will bring previously learned behavior to meet new

learning challenges within the alternative opportunities that are available.

5. The boundaries that separate the experience from the talk about the experience impart a spirit of exploration, discovery, and intensified self/other scrutiny. The constructed experience ("exercise") which begins and ends thus has a built-in safety factor that permits participants to experiment with new behaviors, evaluate the consequences, and make adjustments or repeat them another time.

6. The acquisition of competence (that is, knowing about and knowing how to do) is facilitated through a format that combines doing with talk about doing, connecting the particular with other learnings, adding knowledge about other related experiences and more general information, and transferring the new learning to other instances.

7. The key emphasis is on the *person* and the *experiencing* rather than on a specific content vehicle or task. Cognitive material is present but is always related to the person's feelings, meanings, perceptions, and values.

Examples of the Constructed Experiences

In order to clarify the concept of the constructed experience, I will cite several examples from work with different groups.

A Citizen Participation Workshop with Eighty Older Adults

After a brief lecture/discussion about such topics as communication, leadership, and getting along with others, the group is divided into ten small groups of eight in order to try out some of the tasks and behaviors previously discussed. Each group is given the following instructions: "Your group has just been left five thousand dollars to use for older adults. You are to come up with a plan that is (1) satisfactory to all members of your group; (2) fair to all; and (3) not previously tried. You will have ten minutes."

One person in each group is the observer and is asked to report to the total group what he or she notices after completion of the group experience —for example, how was leadership attended to; how was the decision made? Then the total group discusses the various elements of the group process and persons' performances in order to come to greater awareness of these elements in action and transfer their learning to other outside situations.

A Leadership Workshop for Community Development Workers

This workshop is for a group of seven community development workers. A topic to discuss is given via a newspaper story (for example: "Three hundred workers in the CETA will be out of work in one month"). Group members are asked to participate in dealing with this problem by assuming that they are a group with power to intervene in the situation. Different roles are described on pieces of paper, with appropriate instructions. Each person randomly picks a role.

Roles include: (1) *Initiator:* help start discussion, organize group, introduce new ideas, raise new questions; (2) *Eager Beaver:* want to take action without thinking; complain to others that they're too cautious, etc.; (3) *Wet Blanket:* find fault with others' ideas; spread doom and gloom atmosphere on the planning. There are other helpful and distracting roles, one for each person in the group.

New topics and new roles are assigned at five-minute intervals.

The learning in this example involves practice in discussion leading under such circumstances plus follow-up discussion of what happened, alternate ways to handle the situation, etc.

Helping Prison Correctional Officers Learn How It Feels to Be Isolated and Excluded[7]

Officers are asked to form groups of six and told they have five minutes to figure out a means of excluding one person from the group. They resist this task but are held to it. Eventually they may pick "the one with glasses," "the one who has red hair," etc. The excluded ones are then re-formed into one group and required to sit with one of the facilitators, while the others are given a coffee break.

Typically, the "free" group taunts and laughs at the seated ones. A discussion follows in which the feelings generated on both sides are explored and then transfer is made to how inmates might feel.

As these examples show, the notion of constructed experiences refers to the within-session designed elements (often termed exercises or simulations) that instruct *inductively* within the thinking, feeling, and doing domains of learning.[8]

From Theory to Practice

Drawing from the structured perspective on learning and from the concept of the constructed experience, we now turn to ways of promoting competence through the use of Skills, Theme, and Transition Groups. Each type of group will be described briefly in terms of key elements, illustrated with practice examples, and linked to the theme of enhancing competence. The purpose of this discussion will be to highlight the distinctiveness of these groups as learning opportunities that emphasize adaptive responsiveness through their focus on action, information getting, achieving comfort vis-à-vis others and the environment, and experiencing options and choices.

The illustrative groups are introduced within a hierarchy of developmental complexity; each in turn deals with the achievement of life tasks from the most primitive to advanced competency demands. Thus, in the examples that follow, the aged residents in the nursing home need to reconnect with the living world; the ex-mental patients are isolated from others by lack of some basic skills for everyday survival; and the retarded persons are working at the most complex developmental level in contemplating roles and rules for a small society. Only the first-time mothers would be considered "normal" in the ordinary sense of the word; their developmental gap (mastery of the tasks of parenting) is a consequence of present societal circumstances that have eliminated the three-generational family as a functional support system. While nursing home residents, ex-mental patients, and retardates are not usually viewed by society (or professional helpers) as "normals," a key element in the illustrations that follow is that they are approached *as if normal*.

Skills Groups

Skills Groups are behaviorally oriented. They focus on the development of specific behaviors and the elimination of self-defeating actions. They aim at certain critical skills, perhaps incompletely learned in the process of socialization into adulthood, that are needed for the diverse roles which human beings must assume. While the emphasis here is mainly on Skills Groups for clients, such groups may also form the core of staff development and in-service training for workers and practitioners. Familiar examples include stress management, assertiveness training, decision-making and problem-solving, and communication.

In these Skills Groups the worker is the expert in a particular content area and plays an active role in preplanning the format and sequenced sessions as well as in offering brief lectures of theoretical and informational content. At the heart of this type of structured group are identification and description of specific behaviors, role-playing, modeling, instructing/coaching, homework, and practice-plus-feedback from the worker and peers.

Skills training groups generally reflect one of two orientations: (1) following Rogers (1951), interpersonal skills are viewed as qualities that will have a constructive impact on the other person (for example, empathic understanding, congruence, and sensitivity); (2) following Fine and Wiley (1971), skills are derived from analysis of tasks that need to be accomplished and the elements of tasks are then specified (for example, listens, persuades, and compares). Once defined, the skills or desired competencies must then be operationalized, sequenced, and serially presented with a technology of instruction that derives from an understanding of skill learning processes.[9]

These learning experiences are precise instructional formats made possible by theory development in behavioral analysis, technology for specifying performance objectives (Mager, 1962), one-way mirrors, and audio-visual technology that provides observational immediacy and minute examination of behavior. As Table 8–1 shows, the skill learning process is comprised of several hierarchical levels of ascending complexity. The learning experiences are activity-based but may use paper-and-pencil drills and tests to encourage conceptual understanding of particulars.

The table summarizes my analysis of the steps involved in mastery of the components of a given skill and some suggested approaches that practitioners may use to enhance the learning experience. Most short-term Skills Groups rarely have time to move beyond level 3 (Imitation) and rely upon continued practice by participants after the group ends to approach more refined enactments of behavior.

Skills Groups are illustrated in the following examples from practice with aged residents in a nursing home and with former psychiatric patients.

"Awareness Skills" Group for Aged Residents.   All five participants had lived in a long-term care nursing home for over six months. Most were confused at times, but not grossly so. For example, with prompting, they could participate in group activities. Three men and two women made up the group.

The goals were: (1) to increase the members' awareness of surroundings by involvement in activities of a sensory nature; (2) to increase their competence in functioning within the group by focusing on six specific skills: participation in the activity, responding to conversation with the worker, initiating conversation with the worker, initiating conversation with one another, recognizing others, and call-

TABLE 8–1. Hierarchy of Processes for Learning Skills

Skills Groups ←——→   *Life-long Learning* ←——————→

Skill Learning Process	Description	Means for Enhancing the Learning
(Informal Preparation)	Emphasizing experimentation and exploration with materials and elements without definite instrumental ends.	Play; work; trial and error learning by pursuit of activities of interest.
1. Observation	Emphasizing seeing and hearing ideal versions of the acts to be performed.	Observe a teacher or practitioner; video tapes; listen to audio tapes.
2. Conceptualization	Emphasizing inspection, dissection of components; identification and analysis.	Charts; lectures; written information plus discussion.
3. Imitation	Emphasizing duplicating and reproducing the components of the act sequentially.	Role playing plus feedback; video-taping self in action; interactional games.
4. Precision	Emphasizing accuracy, exactness, fidelity, and control with reduction of errors.	Paper and pencil activities; group discussions; role play plus feedback; use of mirror; tape recorder.
5. Coordination	Emphasizing production of an articulated, integrated series of acts with concern for accuracy, speed and pacing.	Role playing plus feedback; interactional games; videotape self.
6. Habituation	Emphasizing repetition to make the act routine, consistent, automatic, natural and spontaneous.	Deliberate use in real situations with others.
7. Instruction	Emphasizing designing and presenting to other learners with clarity the means for exploring and experiencing the skill learning processes, levels 1 through 6. *and/or*	Repeated experiences with developing, offering and analyzing the impact of teaching attempts plus written/oral feedback (tests and evaluative measures) from learners. *and/or*
and/or Stylization	Emphasizing adding one's individuality and humanity, elegance, simplicity, flexibility, intuitions, artistry, and warmth to the enactment of the whole.	Repeated performances plus feedback from other(s) and continuous self-reflection and analysis.

ing others by name; and (3) to transfer the skills learned in the group to their life in the nursing home.

The participants met for six weekly sessions of one hour each in a special private meeting room. Stimuli such as musical records, objects, posters, and food were used. Each session focused on one of the following skills or content areas: awareness of sounds; recognition of objects; touching; smell; taste; and music. In each session there was extensive use of selected exercises related to the particular skill, resulting in increased awareness and involvement on the part of most participants. For example, this is how the social worker describes the fifth session, which focused on taste:

Everyone really seemed to enjoy this session. Maybe it was because of all the goodies there were to eat. I had decided to use things that people generally like to eat—potato chips, ice cream, etc. Everyone really participated and more of the participants initiated contact with one another. Three of the five group members initiated conversations. This is something I never thought would happen. In addition, one of the women decided that one of the men was really handsome, told him so, and said she was going to "cabbage him"! He certainly seemed to perk up.

In this group, as well as the ones discussed later, one may think of the goals on two levels: the outcome, or basic goal, and the proximate, or instrumental goals. The basic goal was the regeneration of an interest in living while the proximate goals were the opening up of sensory awareness and increase in social interaction.

The basic goal was approached by the worker's use of a directed small group experience focused upon stimulating interaction between herself and each participant as well as encouraging interaction among the participants. At the instrumental level, an important component was the engagement of the sensory organs so as to receive information. Through the group experience, the aged residents were gently prodded to be people again, to enrich their lives, to care about living, and to use their sensory apparatus. All of this helped to regenerate learning capacities and curiosity.

For effective involvement in structured groups with this client population, the worker needs to have a belief in the possibility that the cloistered older adult can relearn basic skills when given sufficient interest and attention; a willingness to slow down in expectations of rate of accomplishment and tempo of involvement; considerable patience; ability to value tiny gains, often amorphous; and commitment to the nitty-gritty, mundane aspects of living as valuable for learning and resocialization.

"Social Skills" Group for Ex-mental Patients.   The ex-mental hospital patients in our next example were also working on basic survival skills but at a higher level developmentally.

The seven participants ranged from 20 to 60 years of age and included both blacks and whites. There were four males and three females. All had severe emotional problems, were unemployed and came from the city's most dilapidated area. The criteria for group membership were the referring counselor's statement that the client might benefit from the experience and the client's wish to attend.

Specific goals were: (1) to increase social interaction; (2) to stimulate reality orientation; (3) to facilitate independence through information; and (4) to train clients in the use of the telephone for personal and employment purposes. While the instrumental, or proximate, goals concerned how to use the telephone and deal with emergencies, the basic goal was to enhance self-esteem and self-value by providing a learning experience in reaching out to others and in being responded to.

Group members met for six one-hour sessions in a small classroom at a community-based, partial hospitalization unit of a mental health center. Equipment included a chalkboard, colored posters, telephone books, pens, paper, typed handouts, and a teletrainer set (two phones connected to a central switchboard operated by the workers and a sound amplifier).

The sessions convered such topics as voice qualities on the telephone and how they affect the listener; elements of telephone courtesy; using the telephone book; phoning for information, taking information, and making emergency calls; making long-distance calls; and dealing with the telephone company.

Further details about the work of this group are summarized in the following excerpts from Session Four:

The main goal in this session was to practice the skills involved in phoning for information, giving information, and making emergency telephone calls.

As the session began, a handout was distributed which contained a set of attitude questions about the topic, such as "I would feel comfortable in calling for bus schedule information" (agree/disagree). Each question was read aloud to members as they scanned their pages, since literacy was a problem. Questions and answers were then discussed among them.

Cards with typical situations in this learning area were given to the members and these were used for structured role-play situations. Here is an example:

Card A: You are lying in bed at 3:00 A.M. and you smell smoke. The door handle of your room is hot so you want to call the fire department.

Member A then calls fire department (played by Member B).

Card B: You are the fire department dispatcher. Fill in the following information and be able to report it from the conversation: name, address, phone, nature of the emergency, help needed.

This group offered an experience in normalization. Despite limitations in basic developmental tasks such as reading, writing, and number skills, the "classes" and school-type atmosphere with quizzes and tutoring stimulated the participants in an appealing way to experience normal behaviors. Beyond merely dealing with reading the telephone book or using the telephone, the participants were taught how to ask others for help. Asking for help not only reduced their social isolation but also increased their feelings of self-value, autonomy, and control over their lives.

Persons such as these may or may not ever learn reading and writing skills commensurate with their age group, but they can be helped to acquire adult functional competence in the ability to approach others more readily, to imagine themselves in another's situation, and to take care of themselves.

Theme Groups

Theme Groups are organized to attract individuals interested in examining a common topic so as to enhance meaningful living. Typically, these are discussion, problem-solving, or task-centered groups that focus on a key topic. Issues may be intrapersonal ones (clarifying values, black identity, self-esteem), but the group process is used to help the individuals clarify their understanding.

These groups may involve one- or two-day workshops or extend over several weeks. The theme may be connected with age-related tasks —for example, intimacy and sharing for young adults or new couples or community service for adults. The theme may also be gender-related —for example, the working mother, the liberated male—or problem-related—for example, alcoholism or ex-offenders. The problem-related groups are quite familiar to social workers, although they are often conceptualized as therapy rather than as educationally oriented approaches.

Theme Groups attract participants in relation to some common shared concern. The worker needs to determine, first, which of the learning domains are of primary importance within the theme: values? feelings? cognitions? behaviors? some or all of these? Accordingly, she then plans for the kind of format that has the best chance of tapping into the desired learning domain(s). As summarized in Table 8–2 and

TABLE 8–2. An Orientation to Learning and Design of Activities in Theme Groups*

Learning Domains	Activities
Values Exploration of beliefs; comparison to others' beliefs; assigning priorities to own beliefs; rearranging/modifying one's priorities.	Experience-sharing discussions; constructed experiences: simulations involving choices, rank ordering decisions under limited conditions; debates; confrontations.
Feelings Expressing emotion in the here-and-now situation; seeing impact of one's feelings on others/knowing how it feels to receive positive and negative feelings from others; distinguishing feeling from talk about feeling.	Role-play, especially role reversal; constructed experiences: games, tasks; practicing skills of expressing and dealing with emotions; interactional experiences.
Cognitions Getting/internalizing information; generalizing out of experience; applying information and generalizations to other situations; analyzing components of experience and tasks; evaluation of current and other experience (past/future, here/there).	Lecture; TV; debate; dialogue; demonstration; discussion; reading material; paper-and-pencil tasks.
Behaviors Practicing new ways of performing; noting the impact of actions on others; selecting valued old ways/discarding dysfunctional behavior; experimenting with diverse roles; seeing what works/does not work; observing others.	Practicing behaviors; self–other observation; coaching others; rehearsal and self-mental dialogue.

*Lists are suggestive rather than comprehensive.

illustrated in the example that follows, certain types of activities are especially appropriate for each domain of learning.

Theme Group: Planning Group Home Rules with Developmentally Disabled Adults. This group consisted of eight adult workshop clients, four males and four females, whose IQs ranged from 42 to 72 and whose physical and mental impairments were diverse. Three resided with their families and five were in a long-term care private institution. They were recruited from the workshop and expressed interest in a "planning" group, since they were considering moving into a group home setting.

The goals were: (1) to formulate appropriate guidelines for daily living in a group home facility for retarded adults; (2) to enhance socialization and group functioning skills; (3) to increase feelings of self-esteem and self-worth; (4) to increase problem-solving and task skills; and (5) to develop knowledge about competencies needed for independent living and self-management.

Group members met in a private meeting room at a community-based sheltered workshop for four weekly sessions of one hour each. Equipment included notebooks, pens, and tape recorder.

Each session covered rules and issues arising in a group home facility in such areas as house maintenance, visitors, and television. As can be seen in the following summary of the first session, the worker used a variety of techniques to help group members plan group home rules and enhance their competence in functioning in a group living situations.

My first session was an unbelievably good experience. They were so receptive. I emphasized positive reinforcement and they really picked up and ran with it. I explained that it was a task group and I needed their help in writing rules and regulations for a group home for the developmentally disabled. They all described their living situations (private homes and institutions) and we discussed problems in living with others.

Two of the members were also in a therapy group at the workshop and the others expressed good feelings about being in a group. We discussed what being in a group means. They felt that the most important things were sharing and talking. There seemed to be some prestige involved with being in a group at the workshop and they were all very positive about participating in this one.

The task for today was upstairs rules. Group members were perceptive and down to earth in thinking of things that might be problems. They decided that both men and women should live in the Home. I only had to mention twice that we needed to talk about only upstairs rules. After that, the members reminded one another when they were getting off the task. I reinforced any ideas presented and we decided that we would save "fun stuff" (dating, recreation, etc.) for later meetings. One member did, at times, seem to get excited about living in the Home and all the members helped to remind her that "this is pretend."

One participant was somewhat disruptive, that is, he didn't want any staff to live in the Home, he didn't want any restrictive rules, and he thought that many things were "women's work." One important concept was that both men and women had to learn and share in all household tasks. All of the members tried to get the one rather stubborn, disruptive fellow to go their way, and a few times the group became involved in a group shout. I only had to request turn taking and partializing once; they did it effectively the other times.

After about an hour the members seemed to be getting restless. As promised, I rewound the tape and let them listen to themselves. I left them alone in the room to do this for ten minutes. I wanted them to have time as a group to process our session without a leader present. When I returned, I gave them small notebooks and pens to keep and use to draw or write down anything they might think of to report to the group to help with our task. They expressed concern about not being able to write but seemed pleased to have the supplies to draw on. They did so well that we even completed kitchen rules.

In this first meeting the group produced twelve upstairs rules and five kitchen rules. They thought through such matters as men and women living together yet in separate bedrooms; keeping one's room and personal possessions clean and orderly; how and when to visit others; dress code and bathroom use; quiet hours, and so forth. They also planned how cooking, washing dishes, cleaning, and shopping for food would happen and examined arrangements for snacks, lunches, and the exclusion of alcoholic beverages in the group home.

In this example, retarded individuals were involved in the complex social issues of developing a minisociety. At the proximate goal level, they encountered matters of planning and future thinking, distinguishing the projected from the here-and-now reality, engaging in turn-taking and orderly decision-making, focusing and impulse control, and dealing with a wide range of values, attitudes, feelings, and information. At the skills level, they were involved in the requirements for thinking in a group, practice in reflection and thinking back on what was said by rehearing the audiotape, and practice in being on ones' own without a worker in charge.

While the special theme of this group concerned developing rules and roles for an orderly small social unit, the basic goal was to help them join with the rest of the world—that is, to take increased responsibility for themselves and to gain more autonomy in living within boundaries. Despite their limitations, these persons were introduced through this constructed experience to brief slices of adult competence behaviors.

Transition Groups

Transition Groups, which are often thought of only as crisis service, typically deal with regular, expected life developmental shifts or with unexpected, often traumatic "accidents" such as loss of a loved one, new caretaking of an ill or injured spouse, and retirement. The goals in these groups include helping participants to deal with the immediate situation, restoring some of the balance disturbed by the event, and learning to cope with similar situations in the future.

In Transition Groups, participants may gain support from the shared discussion of ways to deal with changes and comparison of their way with others'. There is emphasis on getting and giving information and exchanging strategies and coping skills among the participants. In some situations, society offers ritualized events that demarcate beginnings, endings, and transitions: school graduation, marriage, housewarming, etc. Other equally unsettling events may be overlooked or may be gaps within a person's support systems—for example, moving to a new community, starting back to school, divorce. In such instances a Transition Group may be useful in providing a missing structure and assisting the participants in restructuring the present situation and adapting to an altered life-style. The experiential components are diverse and often "lifelike": for example, dinners, social evenings, trips, and other events planned to fill gaps in one's living situation and develop means for building a future life.

As discussed by Golan (Chapter 4 in this volume), a limited amount of social work intervention with persons going through a transitional state can be very effective in promoting competent functioning. This is shown in the following example of a Transition Group with new mothers. This particular transition is considered a pleasant one, but it is nonetheless traumatic and unsettling to previously established roles, relationships, and patterns of living; most new mothers have to go it alone, perhaps with advice and support from spouse, friends, or family. As this example will show, such a major role shift may become a point of impact for a vital social service.

Transition Group: Growing Child—Growing Parent. The participants were seven first-time mothers who had been recruited through announcements in the Jewish Community Center's newspaper and by word of mouth. They attended with their babies. The social worker was an older student with two children. The goals were many and varied: (1) to gain knowledge about one's self as a parent; (2) to socialize with other new mothers, share thoughts and feelings in the group, value own knowledge and management skills as well as add new ideas and skills; (3) to learn about the psychological, social, and cognitive growth of children; (4) to develop knowledge and skills in stimulating infants; (5) to gain knowledge and skills in self-care—for example, relaxation techniques, work and leisure activities; (6) to examine the impact of the parental role on spouse, family, and friends; and (7) to learn the value of a support system and how to develop continuing supports for oneself following the group's termination.

The group met weekly for six sessions of one and a half hours each. The participants and their children used two rooms: a comfortable lounge for mothers and a nearby supervised room with playpens and toys for babies and toddlers. A fee was charged and participants were asked to bring a familiar blanket or toy for the child and an emergency card with special instructions. Equipment used in the group included notebooks, pens, coffee, handouts, film, checklists, and evaluation instruments.

Each session focused on one of the following topics: getting to know each other—getting to know yourself; psychological and social development of young children; language development and communication; infant stimulation and cognitive and physical development (two sessions); and taking care of yourself.

As shown in the following summary of details from the third session, the participants and the worker employed a range of techniques to achieve the group's goals.

Language Development and Communication

1. Ask if anyone has anything special to share. Suggest that they talk about women and work when they eat lunch together today, or say that we can go back to this the last week if they would prefer (ten minutes).

2. Give out handouts and plans for next week: meeting in the baby-sitting room with the children to share ideas about encouraging physical, cognitive, and socioemotional development. Ask each mother to bring at least one toy or idea to share—something that she really enjoys doing with her baby.

3. Introduce "Qualities I Admire" exercise as explained last week (fifteen minutes).

4. General discussion about communication. Ask, "How does your baby communicate?" Encourage answers that show an understanding of verbal and nonverbal communication—for example, crying, pointing, squealing, raising arms, frowning, smiling, and staying close to mother.

How do you encourage your baby to vocalize? Try to get them to discuss voice quality, direct eye contact, repeating the baby's sounds, using language to describe what you're doing when you're with the baby, especially action words, etc.

Talk about the use of music, books, rhymes, finger plays, puppets, pictures, and sounds in encouraging language development.

Discuss the impact of language development in the young child's life (twenty minutes).

5. *Baby Observation.* A mother with her 9-month-old son (who are not members of the group) has agreed to come in for an observation session. We will all sit on the floor with the guests. I will spread out five or six toys and other objects for the baby to explore (telephone, drum and drumstick, ball, busy box, and car). Each mother in the group will be given a paper and

pencil and asked to record certain behaviors: (a) baby's use of mother—turning to her, etc.; (b) baby's response to the toys—how used—what he does with them; (c) language behavior—verbal; (d) physical reactions of baby—use of hands, etc.; (e) nonverbal language (ten to fifteen minutes).

After observations are recorded, each will report and discuss them in terms of learnings about the baby's stage of development. Discussion themes include: Babies are sensitive to verbal and nonverbal cues even at an early age. How do they react when we are tense? Angry? Happy? Where do they get these cues? Communication is a two-way process (thirty minutes).

6. If time permits: Hold baby on lap facing away from the mother. Let mother try voice variety (whisper, questioning) with others observing. Discuss differences in tone and reactions of baby. Summarize session.

This group was not merely a class, although the worker knew much about instructional methods and learning domains. It was an interesting mixture of considerable information related to the work of parenting and a focus on the self of the mothers in relation to their new role, family situation and larger environment, and their self-concept in relation to each other in the group experience.

Group members focused on their present experiences, on the here-and-now parent–child relationship with worker and others watching and commenting, and on how they could become more comfortable in their new role in days to come. There was an emphasis on helping the participants risk trying out different behaviors within the supportive atmosphere established by the worker and enhanced by the others with their in-the-same-boat mentality. The whole-person learning was prominent here: thinking and understanding, engaging feelings, values, attitudes, and actions.

In this instance the structured group was a reconstructed peer group set in motion by the worker to promote understanding that new mothers in earlier times learned spontaneously. The group may be seen as a response to twentieth-century transient society, where otherwise competent individuals encounter a role shift for which they are not prepared. It aimed at reconstructing modes of advice-giving and support inherent in simpler times within families and community networks and to combat present conditions of isolation.

We may think of the *basic* group goals as (1) filling gaps in self-confidence and awareness acquired more naturally in other times, and (2) providing selected information about being mother and wife. The *instrumental* goals are learning to observe behavior minutely, to talk about own ways of mothering and see those of others.

In this example we see basically competent individuals having an experience that adds new competencies to their repertoire. These are persons who are already by and large self-accepting. They are more likely able to benefit from success experiences and feedback that is directly verifiable and minimally evaluative than "deficiency-oriented" persons with little self-acceptance who may be in greater need of support and dependence (Argyris, 1968). However, as seen in the earlier illustrations, even "incompetent" persons may be treated in the structured group *as if competent* and in this way may be involved in experiencing little moments of competence that can positively influence their lives.

Conclusion

This chapter has focused on some of the unique features of structured groups and their use in promoting competence in clients. The work itself may seem similar to other activities with groups familiar to the reader. What is new is the focus on teaching and learning as a useful format of engagement, along with deliberate attention to the more mundane elements of living.

One final note of caution regarding this approach is that the work should not be mechanistic. The magic is not in the content or the way the content is introduced. If magic there is, it grows primarily from the living relationship developed between practitioner and group participants, as with any form of helping. I am reminded of Bertha Reynolds's concern about "Subject Matter in Its Place" (1942). She described the teaching dilemma of either letting "subject matter blind the teacher to the active responses of living persons" or encouraging student "talk" as more crucial than any content the teacher might bring. Her wise caution still holds true. The structured group, with its emphasis upon particular content areas of concern in living, establishes what the practitioner aims to deal with in the group but remains subordinate to the use that the participants and the practitioner make of it.

Notes

Acknowledgment: My deep appreciation and thanks go to the following students who have contributed illustrative material from their group work: Margery H. New, Martha Wahl, Pamela Schuble, Rose Blanford, and Lynn Silk.

1. See Swenson (Chapter 6 in this volume) for consideration of self-help groups and their role in promoting competence.
2. For detailed examples of structured groups in the social work literature, see *Skills Group*, Rose (1975); *Theme Group*, Lee (1979); and *Transition Group*, Roskin (1979).

3. See Middleman (1968) for a more extensive discussion of the use of activities by group workers, the teaching/learning emphasis, and the gradual shift away from doing-oriented to talking-based groups as group work became more identified with the social work profession.
4. For further exploration of teaching/learning approaches, see Middleman and Goldberg (1972a; 1972b) and Middleman (1977a; 1977b).
5. See Maluccio (Chapter 1 in this volume) for further discussion of various perspectives on competence and their significance for social work practice.
6. For a fuller description of these underlying components that combine to comprise competence, see Klemp (1979).
7. This example is adapted from Goldberg (1975).
8. The more didactic formats of skills development groups are also constructed but are considered "constructed *routines*" herein for conceptual clarity.
9. Various formats exist for identifying specific skills (e.g., Egan, 1976; Middleman and Goldberg, 1974). Reviews of research on skill training approaches are also available (Marshall, Charping, and Bell, 1979; Ruben, 1976).

PART 3

Practice with Selected Client Groups

CHAPTER 9

Women and Competence

Prudence Brown

In a society characterized by rigid sex role socialization and institutional discrimination against women, it is not surprising that women are generally thought to be, appear, and/or perceive themselves as less competent than men. An ecosystems perspective would suggest that it is more useful to view competence as a function of the individual's transaction with environment than as an innate ability (cf. Maluccio, Chapter 1 in this volume). White (1963), for example, defines competence as the ability to interact effectively with the environment. The fact that the environment systematically affords women less opportunity, respect, and power (Smith, 1968) than it does men makes the meaning of sex differences in competence more complicated than the stereotype of the incompetent woman suggests.

The goal of this chapter is to examine the barriers women face in being and perceiving themselves as competent and to present a framework for conceptualizing and organizing social work interventions designed to promote competence in women. First, sex differences in competence are explored to evaluate the empirical evidence for women's competence-related difficulties. Sex role socialization patterns, environmental opportunities and reinforcements, and sociocultural factors are explored as potential sources of barriers to female competence. This is followed by a brief critique of the ways in which the social work profession has often reinforced female incompetence and a discussion of several practice stances or practice principles that can enhance a worker's effectiveness in working with women. Finally, a framework for organizing social work interventions designed to promote competence in women is presented; both individual and environmental strategies are suggested and illustrated in case examples.

Sex Differences in Competence

In order to evaluate the empirical support for the cultural stereotype of the incompetent woman, the concept of competence must first be examined to assess whether there is any sex bias inherent in the way it has been defined. The definition of competence can be seen as problematic for elucidating sex differences for three major reasons. The first has to do with the nature of the different environments men and women confront as children and as adults. The question is, essentially: What constitutes "effective interaction" with a sexist environment? If the environment affords men more opportunities than women to develop and exercise competence, what is the meaning of a sex difference in the ability to interact effectively with the environment? Are there situations in which women may be interacting most effectively with the environment by not being competent? How do women become competent when given limited opportunities to have a major impact on the environment, a crucial means of developing a sense of competence according to White (1959)?

Secondly, the roles women traditionally play and the areas in which women are expected to develop skills tend to be culturally devalued with the result that many women who have impressive skills are perceived or perceive themselves as incompetent. The role of homemaker, for example, while requiring a wide range of management and interpersonal skills, rarely promotes feelings of competence in women. It is an ascribed role whose satisfactory performance is expected, having little prestige or visibility and being relatively isolated from the ongoing, systematic feedback and expectations usually encountered on a job (Gove and Tudor, 1973; Oakley, 1974). Similarly, welfare mothers who manage to negotiate the various service bureaucracies to provide their families with an adequate standard of living may be very skillful and knowledgeable but are rarely seen as competent. What a society defines as competent or effective interaction with the environment necessarily reflects the predominant cultural values. A society which tends to place value on the things men do and the roles they play and to devalue female roles and skills can expect to produce more men than women who are or perceive themselves as competent.

Finally, research on competence has often involved indicators of success, achievement, a sense of efficacy or potency, autonomy, and so forth. While desirable for both sexes, these qualities have tended to characterize the traditional male role. For instance, research on sex differences in self-esteem indicates that women rely more heavily on their ability to maintain good social relationships as a primary means of determining their self-worth, whereas males tend to measure their value in terms of their objective accomplishments (O'Leary, 1977). Possible additional aspects of competence in the interpersonal and affective spheres that are more traditionally female in nature are less likely to have been used in experimental studies of competence. Jean Baker Miller (1976:87) describes affiliation as a characteristically female strength: "One can, and ultimately must, place one's faith in others, in the context of being a social being, related to other human beings, in their hands as well as one's own." A man who has the resources to control the environment to get what he wants may perceive himself or be perceived by others as very competent, in control of his life choices, self-confident and so forth even though it may require other's (often women's) subordination and limited development.[1] Being effective while maintaining close and respectful connections with other people constitutes a redefinition of competence which includes both the traditionally male and female experience and may ultimately reflect a more humanitarian understanding of effective interaction with the environment.

Thus, a review of the literature on sex differences in competence must recognize the biases and limits in the current measurement of the concept and interpret the findings in this light. As expected, recent research does reveal consistent evidence that women perceive themselves to be less competent than men; this perception may be linked to less competent behavior in certain realms such as academic and occupational success. Frieze, Parsons, Johnson, Ruble and Zellman (1978:59) report that studies of achievement-related competence or expectations for success indicate that females have "relatively negative evaluations of their own abilities, performance, and likelihood of future success as compared to males." Women are more likely than men to anchor their self-definition and esteem externally, often in the achievements and expectations of the men in their lives (Klein, 1976). Such other-directedness is considered pathological in men but natural in women unless it reaches "hysterical" proportions (Wolowitz, 1972). While no less achievement-oriented than males, females (particularly adolescents and young adults) are more attuned to the potential costs of success, which for them is often in the form of affiliative loss, and thus can be characterized by less sustained, anxiety-free, goal-directed behavior (Mednick, Tangri and Hoffman, 1975). Sex differences have also been found in the acquisition and development of competence: Males tend to learn effectance through environmental mastery, while females learn to be effective through eliciting the help and reassurance of others (Hoffman, 1972:148).

These empirical differences are consistent with the traditional stereotype of male and female roles in this culture. Men are expected to be competent, independent, dominant and instrumental, while women are viewed as passive, dependent, submissive, and expressive. Despite the fact that many of these stereotypes are not substantiated empirically, they currently operate as powerful cultural prescriptions which men and women incorporate into their self-descriptions and their expectations for others. Support for the pervasive impact of sex role stereotyping comes from a variety of sources including the helping professions. For example, the now classic study of Broverman and colleagues (Broverman, Broverman, Clarkson, Rosenkrantz and Vogel, 1970) asked clinicians to respond to a list of 122 bipolar items with one of three sets of instructions: Describe a healthy, mature, socially competent (1) adult, sex unspecified; (2) man; or (3) woman. Results indicated that respondents ascribed traits describing a healthy, mature, socially competent adult more often to healthy men than to healthy women. This double standard of mental health suggests that women can be feminine or competent but not both within the prevailing norms of the culture (Sherman, 1976).

Barriers to Female Competence

The barriers women face in experiencing and perceiving themselves as competent are a function of the interaction among sex role socialization patterns, opportunity-role structures in the environment, and sociocultural factors. Looking first at socialization factors, Hoffman (1972) reviews the research findings in child development and concludes that girls are trained to engage in less independent exploration of their environment than are boys. Contributing factors include parents offering daughters as compared to sons less encouragement and reinforcement for independence and achievements, less vigorous play and more protectiveness, "less cognitive and social pressure for establishing an identity separate from the mother" and "less mother-child conflict which highlights this separation" (Hoffman, 1972:147). As a result, Hoffman suggests that girls do not develop skills in coping with their environment nor confidence in their ability to do so. She notes that

> such patterns—in which autonomy and independence of this sort are encouraged more in boys than in girls—can be extremely important in the development of sex differences, even though they may originate only in cultural stereotypes. I do not think the daughter is trained in dependency so much as she is deprived of the training in independence that her brother receives. It is the boy who is seen as having to earn a living outside the home among strangers, and as such, he must have encouragement in

independently coping with the environment. The boy's experience in these independent explorations, which girls lack, very likely has considerable importance in the development of independent coping skills, a sense of competence, and even specific skills. [Hoffman, 1977:649]

Although different theories of sex role acquisition place differential emphases on the role of identification, social learning, modeling, and cognitive-developmental factors, it does appear that current socialization patterns are sex differentiated and play an important role in the development of female competence (Block, 1979).

Competence, however, is not solely an internal trait that is stable across situations and over time but is also affected by opportunities and reinforcements in the environment for competent behavior. In addition to a socialization which has been characterized as "helplessness training" (Seligman, 1975), girls and women confront on a daily basis real limitations and constraints on the exercise of competence. Discrimination, both blatant and more subtle, in education and employment restrict the kinds of roles women are allowed or encouraged to play. The economic and political dependence of women in this society create a social context in which competence and self-determination are limited. Traditional female roles in the family emphasize reliance on the male provider for sustenance and status and living through and for others (men and children), both of which can contribute to feelings of powerlessness, lack of autonomy and low self-confidence.

Finally, sociocultural factors such as class and ethnicity also play a role in the development of female competence. Each cultural subgroup has its own stereotypes and conceptions of the female role as well as its particular opportunities for the exercise of competence. Unfortunately, there has been very little research on variations in female competence across class and ethnic groups; what research has been done has yielded somewhat contradictory results. For example, there is some evidence that the "Black woman's social role has been traditionally perceived as more valued in the Black community than that of the White female in the White community" (O'Leary, 1977:137). Lower-class black adolescent females tend to view their mothers and other black female models as independent, self-reliant, and strong, qualities they do not perceive as incompatible with femininity (Ladner, 1972). This may explain, in part, why studies of female achievement report that black women are more likely than white women to perceive competitively based achievement as sex role appropriate (Weston and Mednick, 1973). On the other hand, black women have historically been exposed to an environment which affords them less opportunities and resources than white women due to racial discrimination in employment, education, housing, and so forth. Seifer (1973) and Rubin (1976) both discuss the

white working-class woman's perception of herself as powerless to affect the direction of her life, lacking the skills or opportunities to bring
about change. The interaction among ethnic, class, and sex role values
requires much further study to determine their impact on the development and exercise of competence in women. Despite cultural and class
variations, however, no woman in this society is totally untouched by
the ways in which sexism and the traditional definition of the female
role have operated to restrict the opportunities for women to engage in
competent behavior and have negatively reinforced competence in
women when it becomes too visible or threatening.

Social Work and Female Competence

Recent critiques of sexism in the helping professions have discussed some of the ways in which professionals have reinforced rather
than challenged incompetence—real and perceived—among women
(American Psychological Association, 1975; Maracek and Kravetz,
1977). Despite the principle of client self-determination to which social
workers are universally committed, an effective operationalization of
the principle has been lacking as far as women are concerned. Instead,
social workers unwittingly tend to adopt, overtly and/or covertly, prevalent cultural values regarding women and contribute to the status of
these entrenched societal norms in their practice. Some feminists would
suggest that the helping professions have, in fact, an investment in
maintaining women's incompetence and lack of meaningful control
over their life choices. A more benign interpretation might alternatively
identify the source of the problem as a lack of sufficient professional
understanding of the internal and external barriers women face in developing competence and/or a lack of effective intervention strategies to
promote competence. In either case, the following examples illustrate
some of the ways in which sexism in professional practice has operated
to restrict the development of female competence.

1. Fostering traditional family and work roles and viewing the failure of women to adjust to these roles as an individual problem or sign
of pathology. The literature abounds with cases in which women who
do not seek or successfully secure traditional female roles (e.g., divorced women, nonmothers, single-parent mothers, lesbians, women
in nontraditional jobs, etc.) are explicitly and implicitly labeled as disturbed, emotionally immature, selfish, and so forth. Efforts to promote
a woman's competence are doomed when the worker is simultaneously
giving the client the underlying message that she will only be valued
and deemed healthy if she exercises her competence in a prescribed
and limited range of roles and arenas.

2. Encouraging excessive dependence of the female client on the

worker. By denying a woman's self-actualizing potential, being blind to her areas of strength and untapped skills, and endorsing the cultural image of the passive and helpless female, a worker undermines a woman's perception of her competence and responsibility for developing and using her own resources.

3. Discouraging assertive behavior by labeling it unfeminine, selfish, castrating, and so forth. Competence involves the belief that one can make an effective impact on the environment rather than be a helpless victim of life's events and others' demands. Discouraging a woman from expressing her feelings in a direct and honest manner, making decisions and taking action in her own behalf inevitably decreases her ability to take control of her major life choices and responsibility for her actions.

In addition to these and other ways in which professionals have tended to undermine female competence on an individual case level, sexism has also operated to affect female competence indirectly. For example, what kind of statement does the social work profession make about female competence when women constitute about two-thirds of the membership of NASW, while about two-thirds of the administrative positions in social work are held by men, and the ratio of female to male administrators is actually declining (Chernesky, 1980)? Similarly, male control of the profession exists within schools of social work; salary differentials between men and women in similar types of social work positions have also been documented (Fanshel, 1976; Kravetz, 1976). Other critiques of the profession have been aimed at social work education for reinforcing stereotyped views of women; professional ideology which is still deeply affected by the disease model; and agency services which are often inaccessible to certain groups such as working women or lack relevance for others such as low income women, battered wives, etc. (Berlin, 1976; Schwartz, 1973). The fact that many self-help groups have been developed in the women's community in such areas as health, rape, divorce, and sexuality speaks to the perception among at least some women that traditional services have not responded effectively to women's needs. While the profession has made some gains in becoming more responsive to the needs of women, sexist practices are slow to change. Assuming that part of the resistance to change comes from a lack of knowledge about alternative approaches with women clients and with the conditions which create problems for women, we now turn to an examination of practice interventions which may have particular relevance for promoting competence among women.

Practice Stances to Promote Female Competence

Before discussing specific change strategies for promoting competence among women, two practice stances are presented as practice principles which can organize a worker's understanding of a case and provide an orientation to planning for change. The worker's commitment to view the world through such practice stances may, in fact, be as important as the choice of any one particular intervention strategy.

The first practice stance involves an endorsement of an androgynous as opposed to a sex-typed model of healthy functioning. Previous research on sex role identity was based on the assumption that masculinity and femininity were extremes of a bipolar continuum. More recent research produced evidence (Bem, 1975; Spence, Helmreich, and Stapp, 1974)that masculinity and femininity are independent dimensions: Some individuals can be classified as psychologically androgynous, that is possessing both masculine and feminine characteristics. Research into the correlates of androgyny provides tentative support for the hypothesis that androgynous individuals score higher on measures of self-esteem, mental health, and behavioral flexibility (Bem, 1975; Bem and Lenney, 1976). Maracek (1977) suggests that psychological androgyny may, in fact, become a necessary adaptation to the changing roles women are assuming in this culture.

The general explanation for these findings is that highly sex-typed individuals are motivated to keep their behavior consistent with an internalized sex role standard, thus suppressing any behavior that might be considered inappropriate or undesirable for their sex role identity. This process can restrict the range of behaviors available to an individual as he/she moves from situation to situation and produce feelings of anxiety when cross-sex behaviors are required. An androgynous sex role orientation allows an individual to remain sensitive to the changing constraints of situations and engage in whatever behavior seems most effective at the time, irrespective of its stereotype to one sex or the other.

To be effective as a catalyst for change, a worker must reject practice models which define competence in general or competence in certain traditionally male domains as primarily a masculine characteristic. Because of the pervasiveness of traditional sex role norms which are internalized early in life and reinforced throughout the life cycle, workers need to pay particular attention to the ways in which they or their agencies may be negatively reinforcing strivings toward competence among women. A belief in the potential of women and a commitment to help each client express her unique characteristics and develop herself free from culturally imposed sex role prescriptions are critical practice orientations in working with women.

Another practice stance that can enhance a worker's effectiveness in promoting competence in women involves a sensitivity toward the connections between a woman's perceived lack of competence in relating to the environment and the limited opportunities in the environment for power, respect, and control over basic life choices. Unless the pervasiveness of sexism is acknowledged, the worker may communicate a "blame the victim" stance. Attribution theory suggests that men tend to attribute their failures to outside causes, luck, and so forth, whereas women are more likely to attribute their failures to inner deficiencies (Deaux and Farris, 1977). Therefore, a worker must be particularly careful not to encourage or reinforce a woman's tendency to assume blame for situations over which she has little or no control. Similarly, promoting a stance that places the full blame outside the individual simply reinforces feelings of victimization. The goal is not to attribute blame to either one or the other but rather to acknowledge the real existence of sexism in our society and help a woman see the relationship between her personal problems and the sociopolitical context in which she has been brought up and currently lives. Unlike depression, which results from self-blame or a sense of victimization generated by blaming the environment, acknowledgement of the connections between the personal and the political can help women take responsibility for making the changes they desire in their lives.[2]

Framework for Organizing Social Work Interventions

A sense of competence emerges from the transaction of the individual and the environment. A woman can be or perceive herself as incompetent despite a high level of ability if her environment is very demanding and/or does not provide sufficient opportunity to receive feedback concerning her personal effectiveness. Alternatively, a woman with less developed skills can experience herself as competent within the context of a supportive environment that gives her the message that what she does is valued and taken seriously. Therefore, both internal and external factors must be challenged for women's self-definition and behavior to change in the direction of competence.

It is clear that for women to become and perceive themselves as more competent, they must undergo a complex process of cognitive, emotional, and behavioral change which must be supported simultaneously by commensurate changes in the environment. An ecosystems perspective suggests that all of these arenas for change are highly interdependent: Change in one arena often necessitates shifts in a variety of other areas which then recycle to stimulate further changes at the original point of intervention. However, for the purposes of examining different intervention strategies, individual–environment interaction is partialized into six points of entry. The schema in Figure 9–1 illustrates the framework around which the rest of the chapter is organized.

Individual Points of Entry

The three types of change at the individual level (cognitive, emotional, and behavioral) are intimately related in any one person. One consequence of this interdependence is that a client and worker can be working primarily in one area and still report changes in the other spheres. Acquiring more skills (behavioral change) is likely to affect how a woman feels (emotional change) and defines her life choices (cognitive change). Similarly, new insight into the internal and external forces that have contributed to her view of herself as incompetent often frees a woman emotionally to act in new, more competent ways or to test out her skills in unfamiliar arenas.

Thus, interventions can rarely be classified as purely cognitive, emotional, or behavioral. They are treated separately for the purposes of this discussion to underline the practice *emphasis* at each point of entry. Case examples are described to highlight one particular type of intervention rather than illustrate all the possible individual and environmental strategies that might be appropriate. In reality, case assessments often suggest that multiple interventions at a variety of different levels are desirable.

Cognitive Change.   The goal of cognitive change is to "raise consciousness regarding sex role socialization and to modify belief systems" that prevent women from being or perceiving themselves as competent (Rawlings and Carter, 1977:74). One way to operationalize this goal is to examine, explicate, and redefine the double-binds women in this culture confront in the area of competence.

As mentioned previously, current sex role socialization tends to

FIGURE 9–1.   Individual–environment transaction.

convey to a woman that she must choose between being traditionally feminine (and culturally devalued) or being competent (and "bad" because she has violated her natural role). Miller (1976) notes that men derive self-esteem from taking action in their own behalf whereas women, socialized to gain satisfaction and a sense of identity through serving others, find the notion of acting in their own interests either as inconceivable or as a threat to their sense of worth. Maccoby and Jacklin's findings (1976) that self-esteem is more likely to be defined by competence and achievements for men and by affiliative success and interpersonal feedback for women underline the conflict women face in trying to be competent without violating internalized cultural prescriptions about appropriate female behavior.

When the individual's adaptation to the "no-win" conflict generated by having to opt for either traditional femininity or competence or some combination of the two becomes too painful or dysfunctional, she is likely to seek help (Heriot, 1979). Take the situation of Monica described below.

Monica is a 35-year-old journalist who has an impressive list of credits to her name and has just taken a new supervisory position in a national newspaper where most of her colleagues and staff are men. Despite her acknowledged success as a writer, Monica feels that she has somehow achieved what she has by accident and is terribly anxious that someone will find out she is a fraud.[3] Furthermore, she finds it very difficult to give her staff any negative feedback even when it is obvious to her that such feedback would be useful. But she very much wants the staff to like her. She knows that, as one of the few women in her position, she is being closely watched and is experiencing difficulties writing with the creativity and energy she had before.

Monica came to a counseling agency for help when she was unable to handle the demands of her new supervisory position at work. While she clearly had the skills and talent to do the job, successful performance of her new role was at direct odds with her own definition of herself as a woman. The worker's first intervention was to help her understand the nature of the cultural double-binds she faced by having her describe the messages she received both as a child and in the present that were interfering with her performance and sense of competence. Monica's internalized messages were like those of many other women in the culture: the most important thing is to be liked; don't be too successful (i.e., more successful than your male colleagues) or you won't be liked; a woman who criticizes men is castrating; and so forth. Furthermore, her current supervisor was contributing to the conflict by letting her know that she was a "test case" for the newspaper and (just as he had expected) it was beginning to look as though she was not capable of exercising appropriate authority and leadership as a supervisor. By explicating the double-bind situation she was in, the worker helped shift the definition of the problem from Monica alone to her interface with the environment, thereby decreasing her feelings of personal incompetence.

The next intervention involved helping Monica clarify the positive and negative consequences of the way she was coping with the double-binds she faced. She described the positive consequences as not having to incur the risk of overt rejection or dislike from her male colleagues; being spared some of the anxiety of competition; risk-taking and full responsibility for her professional activities; and retaining some fundamental sense of being a "real" woman. The negative consequences were more obvious to her: decreased job performance and creativity; feelings of anxiety and lack of control; little confidence and almost total dependence on others for her sense of success on the job; underlying anger at the power she gave her staff to evaluate her and make her feel good.

Once Monica understood both the factors contributing to her conflict on the job and the consequences of her particular resolution of that conflict, she was in a much better position to evaluate alternative resolutions and take more control of her life choices. This is not to say that cognitive change was either a prerequisite for other changes or that changes at other levels were not equally important in helping Monica gain control of her situation. For example, she learned skills and techniques for supervising her staff, setting limits and running staff meetings effectively (behavioral change), and felt less conflicted about the exercise of these skills (emotional change). Similarly, by teaching Monica about the dynamics of organizational change and helping her formulate strategies to create a more supportive work setting for herself, the worker was also intervening at the environmental level. But a major piece of the work for Monica had to do with cognitive mastery; that is, an increased understanding of the factors that contributed to her dilemma and a restructuring of her self-definition as a woman to include competence as a desirable aspect of being female. In this case, it was particularly helpful for Monica to have a competent female worker who could serve as a model[4] and to join a consciousness-raising group of women[5] in similar professional roles who could provide mutual support for the right to self-definition and a kind of resocialization process through which to define themselves in new ways.

Emotional Change. Closely connected to change on the cognitive level is emotional change through which emotional barriers to being or perceiving oneself as competent, such as anxiety, guilt, fear, or anger, are modified or removed. While an understanding of the factors that contribute to these feelings may help decrease their intensity, often further work is needed to fully free a woman from their pervasive impact. Consider Jane, a battered wife whose feelings of terror and helplessness have prevented her from taking any action that would significantly modify her current situation.

Jane is a 23-year-old woman with a 2-year-old daughter and another child on the way. Her husband has a history of beating her since their marriage three years ago and has recently escalated his violent outbursts. Jane feels she is a failure because of her husband's abuse: While she tries to be a good wife and mother, something inside her tells her that she deserves the abuse. At the same time, though ashamed of her situation, she knows she must get help if her new baby is to be born without physical damage. She is terrified because she has no one to turn to and feels totally helpless and paralyzed to take any action.

A "victim of oversocialization into the stereotypical feminine role" (Ball and Wyman, 1978:546), Jane has learned to be passive, nonassertive, selfless, and devoted to pleasing, nurturing, and being responsible for others but not herself. Whenever thoughts of leaving her husband cross her mind, Jane becomes tremendously anxious and guilty. The idea of taking action in her own behalf is so threatening to her sense of self (Miller, 1976) that she insists she is incapable of making it on her own. This insistence of her own incompetence is further reinforced by cultural expectations and real limitations in the environment: Where can a pregnant woman with a small child go, how can she support herself, etc.?

In responding to Jane's dilemma, it was important to provide a range of different services such as a support group of women in similar situations to decrease her sense of isolation and shame, housing and concrete help if she decided to leave her spouse, self-defense to combat her feelings of victimization, and so forth. Even though she came to see that she was not responsible for her husband's actions, she still *felt* guilty and responsible. It was critical for the worker to deal with these feelings at every stage of the helping process because they always had the potential to block her effective actions. Use of Gestalt techniques, creative fantasy, continual reassurance that she was not a failure as a wife because her husband was abusive, and help in recognizing and channeling her anger into constructive action are all interventions aimed at change at the emotional level.

The major emphasis of assertiveness training is on the modification of self-defeating behavior patterns and the development of behavioral skills to protect one's basic interpersonal rights (Osborn and Harris, 1975). Jakubowski (1977:178), however, describes one stage of her four phase assertion training program as having a primarily emotional focus to "reduce or remove psychological obstacles which prevent clients from acquiring or using their assertive skills." Examples of specific strategies in this phase include rational–emotive procedures (Ellis, 1974), relaxation training, systematic desensitization, and bioenergetics. For example, after Jane decided it was in her better interests to move into the battered women's shelter rather than risk further physical abuse, she was still faced with considerable anxiety which made it difficult for her to actually make the move. The worker first used relaxation training whereby Jane was taught to reduce her anxiety by relaxing various muscle groups (Wolpe and Lazarus, 1966). Then, while relaxed, she was asked to visualize a series of successively more anxiety-producing situations in which she was acting assertively, e.g., making arrangements for moving into the shelter, packing her clothes, actually leaving her house, etc. This technique, in combination with skill training and environmental support, enabled Jane to take action that was consistent with her desires and thus increase her sense of being in control of her life and able to interact effectively with the world.

Behavioral Change. Hand in hand with perceiving oneself as competent and feeling competent is acting competently, mastering skills that enhance effective interaction with the world.

Rose is a 46-year-old mother of three teenagers who was recently widowed by her husband of twenty-three years. During their marriage, Rose had been primarily responsible for raising the children, taking care of the home, and attending to the family's social and emotional needs. She was very well liked in her suburban community, active in church and school activities, and volunteered three mornings a week at the local hospital. The end of her marriage has left Rose feeling depressed, overwhelmed, and unable to function effectively in her new roles as breadwinner, head of household, and single-parent mother. The decrease of economic resources available to her, the increasing isolation from her couples-oriented social network, the multitude of new tasks and demands (for which she was largely unprepared) confronting her in her new roles, and the difficulties she faces in obtaining a job have undermined her ability to make decisions and feel effective in any sphere.

Rose went to a family services agency because she was feeling totally unprepared for and overwhelmed by her new responsibilities. Like many other women, she had not been raised to anticipate, accept, or even value the function of providing for herself or others (Barnett and Baruch, 1978) and experienced severe role discontinuity when called upon to function competently as a single-parent head of household employed outside the home. Rose's situation is a good example of the situational nature of competence; having perceived herself as a highly competent mother and home-maker during her marriage, it was only when she was confronted with a whole new role set that her competence came into question.

One of the first interventions the worker in this case made was to help Rose clarify for herself what her goals were. Because women do not usually set goals as independent people but rather in relation to others (husbands, lovers, children, etc.), they often find it difficult to specify their own desires and preferences (Cammaert and Larsen, 1979). As a result, it took some time for Rose to get in touch with possible alternatives that were available to her as a woman entering the labor force at her age and to prioritize these alternatives in terms of their desirability. The next step was to locate all the internal and external resources which could be used to help her achieve her goals. Because the sex role socialization process often blinds women to areas in their life where they possess strengths they could use in their own behalf, Rose again needed help to identify her own areas of skills and strength. One useful technique here was a life review in which the worker asked Rose to discuss previous periods of her life (such as high school, a period of working before marriage, her previous community and volunteer activities) to identify forgotten or untapped areas of competence. This is an important task especially in light of the research finding that married women tend to perceive themselves as decreasingly competent over time (Bernard, 1972).

It was only at this point when alternatives had been specified, resources identified, and choices made that it became clear what additional skills Rose would need to carry out her goals. In her case, these consisted of a job training course in computer sciences and a family life education program on the single-parent family with teenagers. The process of decision-making and owning her own choices, the increased awareness of her own strengths and competencies, and the new skills she was learning in her training program all contributed to Rose's increasing sense of effectiveness, trust in her own decision-making and problem-solving skills, and control in responding (rather than reacting) to the new life situation which she faced. Behavioral change, in the form of new skills in the parenting and occupational arenas, clearly affected and was affected by changes in self-perceived competence and feelings of control and mastery.

To be effective in promoting competence in the previously described cases, workers must continually reevaluate their role in the helping process. On the one hand, they need to be attuned to the possibility of having to assume an active role such as an advocate for a woman whose basic rights are being denied or as a mediator in a woman's dealings with a sexist or unresponsive system.[6] Because women have not had access to the economic and political resources controlled largely by men, they may realistically need to "borrow" the power of the worker and the agency he or she represents to accomplish their goals. On the other hand, workers must be careful not to "over-help" women struggling to become and perceive themselves as competent. This means discouraging unnecessary reliance on worker skills and assistance and, instead, identifying a woman's untapped areas of strength and competence and supporting helping modalities designed to increase a sense of her own skills and responsibility for developing these skills. If social work is in the business of empowering people to do things for themselves, it is important that workers be careful to neither fall back on the hierarchical authority model of a worker–client relationship nor mystify the nature of the helping process in their work with women.

Environmental Points of Entry

The importance of feedback from the environment in promoting or impeding a sense of competence is particularly salient for women for two reasons. First, as noted earlier, current sex role socialization tends to encourage women to learn effectance through eliciting the help and reassurance of others rather than through environmental mastery (Hoff-man, 1972). Because they are taught to use feedback from others in that way, women tend to be more reliant on and responsive to such feedback than are men. Secondly, in a society characterized by institutionalized sexism, the environment is a constant source of negative reinforcement for competence among women. Affording women less opportunity, respect, resources, and power than men, the environment becomes a critical and necessary target for social work intervention.

In the examples that follow, interventions to bring about environmental change are discussed both as strategies to be used with individual cases and as interventions designed to affect change at a broader level.[7] For example, a distinction can be made between case advocacy that is directed toward securing certain rights or services for an individual woman and advocacy that attempts to secure those rights and services for all women. Both types of environmental change, as well as change efforts that serve remediative and/or preventive functions, are included here as important social work domains.

At least three different environmental approaches can be taken to promote competence among women. These involve: (1) increasing positive feedback from the environment which gives a woman the message that she is competent in the roles she is already playing; (2) increasing women's access to valued social roles; and (3) creating new roles for women to which visibility, social value, and positive feedback are attached. By changing the social context of existing roles or promoting access to new roles that have new contingencies for success, the barriers women have faced to perceiving themselves as competent are challenged.

Increase Support in Current Roles.   A major question the practitioner must address in working to enhance the adaptive fit between the client and the environment involves the identification of potential supports that could be built into the client's current roles. Let us take the role of mother, for example. Bernard (1974:9) points out that the "way we institutionalize motherhood in our society—assigning sole responsibility for child care to the mother, cutting her off from the easy help of others in an isolated household, requiring round-the-clock tender, loving care, and making such care her exclusive activity"—works directly against the competent fulfillment of the role. Many supports need to be built into the role of mother as currently conceived to make it a viable, satisfying, and productive endeavor. Such supports can be primarily instrumental, such as accessible pre- and post-natal care and adequate day care, or more social or emotional in nature, like support and self-help groups, both of which can increase a mother's role competence, decrease social and physical isolation, enhance problem-solving around common needs and interests, and promote more enjoyment of the role. Clearly, the instrumental and socioemotional functions of environmental supports are closely related and suggest, again, the intimate connection between restructuring the individual's internal and external environments to promote both real and perceived competence.[8]

Although family work is not a major focus of this chapter, it should be noted that mothers have been traditionally given the major responsibility for the happiness and general well-being of other family members. Women often seek help for problems they perceive as their own but which are actually a function of the way family roles have been defined and, therefore, involve the whole family. Consequently, workers need to learn how to help women see beyond their initial complaints, which may represent their acceptance of a narrow view of what is proper for women to complain about (Klein, 1976), to an exploration of contributing factors in the family environment. Such a reframing of the problem is usually most effective when the whole family is involved.

The strategy of increasing support for women's role functioning is particularly critical for women occupying devalued or stigmatized roles such as the divorced mother, the single woman, and the lesbian. Sexist cultural norms and institutions subject these roles to a variety of negative social, economic, and/or psychological sanctions. Since a woman's worth is often evaluated on the basis of her ability to "catch" and "keep" a man, she may experience herself as a failure despite competent functioning in other spheres. Consequently, the practitioner and client need to devise strategies that buffer the negative effects of female role devaluation. Creating a "community" of women in similar roles is particularly effective for decreasing isolation and perceived uniqueness. Self-help groups, social and recreational groups, and political groups that define social action in their own behalf as one of their goals are of major importance.

Increase Access to Valued Social Roles.   One of the consequences of institutionalized sexism in this culture has been the limited access women have had to valued social roles. In combination with traditional sex role socialization patterns, formal and informal discrimination in such areas as education, employment, and politics has prevented large numbers of women from occupying roles characterized by social value, economic rewards, and power. Being denied access to these roles and their commensurate rewards on the basis of sex rather than ability serves to undermine a woman's competence or belief in her ability to control the contingencies affecting her life. In addition, the lack of role models involving women in positions of power and prestige reinforces the cultural stereotype that power and femininity are incompatible and makes these roles seem even less accessible.

One goal of the social worker is to help break down whatever barriers prevent women from occupying desired social roles to which they may have been traditionally denied access. While social workers tend to focus first on internal barriers that prevent change, they are also sanctioned to intervene in the environment to promote women's competence through increasing their access to valued social roles.

Let us take the example of a woman, Kate, who seeks help because she is feeling depressed, unsure of her own competence as a worker, and unable to derive major satisfaction on her job. Initial discussion reveals that she has been recently turned down for a promotion at her job in an insurance company and suspects that the male candidate who did get the position had less seniority and training than she. Embarrassed and afraid to make waves with her employer, Kate has responded to the situation with a combination of thinly veiled anger, self-blame, a questioning of her own abilities, and rationalization that the job was not what she was looking for anyway.

While a social worker confronted with a client like Kate may want to employ individual level strategies such as helping her to clarify her goals and learn to be more assertive with people in positions of authority, it is essential that the worker also deal directly with the issue of potential discrimination. This involves knowing how to file a sex discrimination complaint (e.g., what is the law, who is covered, where and how to file a complaint, what are the potential risks, etc.) and presenting the client with this knowledge and alternative for action. Similar situations in which women are systematically denied access to valued social roles and their commensurate rewards are abundant: discrimination against older women returning to the labor force after a number of years of raising children; dismissal from a job due to pregnancy; unequal pay for similar work; limited access to a field that has been traditionally controlled or dominated by men such as carpentry, trucking or law enforcement, etc. The multitude of barriers women face in gaining equal access to the roles society has deemed valued and financially rewarding combine to reinforce the message that women are not competent enough to perform such roles. Many competent women have not been traditionally successful in the public sphere due to lack of opportunity rather than lack of skills. Social workers committed to promoting competence in women have a responsibility, then, to promote opportunities for the exercise of competence for their female clients.

In addition to formal barriers, women often face informal discrimination in their attempts to assume valued social roles. One example within the profession of social work involves the underrepresentation of women in administrative positions in proportion to their number in the profession. Excluded from the "old-boy" network, women frequently get bypassed for promotions and positions of status and visibility as they have little access to communication networks and information, a more difficult time acquiring mentors or sponsors, and fewer opportunities for mobility from their current positions (Chernesky, 1978). The NASW Women's Issues Committee of New York City is one example of a group that is trying to combat these informal barriers through the creation of an informal, interpersonal support system through which women professionals can share their information and contacts concerning job openings, gain support and advice, and "identify and locate those persons who can directly affect their mobility" (Chernesky, 1980:248). Such a network can help women move into administrative and leadership roles in which they have the opportunity to develop and demonstrate their competence. Similar self-help networks for job advancement have been developed for women in blue-collar positions, clerical jobs, and other areas of the labor market. Social workers can both help their clients get hooked up to these networks and help stimulate and organize the networks themselves.

Thus, the social worker needs a large repertoire of intervention strategies ranging from persuasion to legal action, network building to political action, depending on the nature of the barriers women come up against in their desire to assume valued social roles and the sanctions for change. He or she must also be skilled at a number of roles in employing these strategies: advocate, mediator, organizer, educator, etc.

While the primary emphasis of the environmental strategy of increasing women's access to valued social roles is on "getting a bigger piece of the pie," the focus of the final strategy, creating new social roles for women, is on changing the nature of the roles open to women to eliminate the barriers women currently face to being both female and competent.

Create New Social Roles.   It is clear that in the long run the conflicts women face about being or perceiving themselves as competent must be eliminated if women are to develop their potential to the utmost and feel positively about that development. The final environmental strategy toward that end involves two components. New social roles for women can be created by: (1) revaluing traditional female areas of competence and creating new roles which draw upon these areas, and (2) changing those aspects of the sex role socialization process and social structure which foster helplessness among women and contribute to the definition of competence as primarily a male trait. While these social work goals are primarily indirect in that they may not involve any one client, they are included here both because prevention is an important mandate for the profession and because individual work with clients is better understood and carried out in the context of the whole with a knowledge of and appreciation for all possible levels of intervention.

Regarding the strategy of creating new social roles that draw upon revalued female competencies, it is first critical to acknowledge the many areas of competence associated with the traditional female role. Raising children, for example, requires an extraordinary number of skills of both an interpersonal and a concrete nature. The same is true of such roles as homemaker, single-parent head-of-household, corporate wife, and so forth. One major problem with these competencies, however, is that they have been culturally devalued and not afforded the same respect, worth, or monetary rewards associated with male roles in this culture. A striking example involves couples obtaining a divorce after twenty-five years of marriage: Until recently, a woman's contribution to the marriage in terms of being primarily responsible for the child-rearing and household management had no recognized monetary value in comparison to the husband's role of worker outside the home. Performance in these female roles is generally given attention only when there is some failure to function competently: potential child abuse or neglect, poor housecleaning, and so forth. This suggests an intervention that recognizes the successful performance of traditionally female roles and creates new roles that make use of the competencies developed in these traditional areas.

One such intervention is exemplified in a community-based agency's "grandmother program" in an urban ghetto. Noting that one of the major populations at risk in the community were isolated mothers, the agency set up a program which made creative use of the competencies of older women (ages 45 to 60) who had successfully raised children in the same community. Functioning as part of an interdisciplinary team, the "grandmothers" were paid to work with the multi-problem families in such areas as child growth and development, nutrition, budgeting and household management. This involved mutual problem-solving, emotional support, skill development, modeling appropriate mothering behaviors in interactions with the children, and so forth. The explicit message from the agency to the grandmothers was that they were the experts who had themselves managed to bring up children in a chronically stressful and depriving environment. They had developed a whole array of competencies ranging from shopping and preparing meals on a limited budget to dealing with an unresponsive school system, handling appointments at the welfare office, coping with the problems of drugs and gang involvement with the children. By focusing on these rarely acknowledged or valued areas of competence rather than on the ones society tends to assign more worth, such as educational attainment, economic success or previous job history, the agency was, in essence, revaluing female competencies and creating opportunities for their exercise. In paying the grandmothers (money being one measure of societal worth in this culture) and being sensitive to the fact that it would take some time for the grandmothers to conceptualize their "natural" skills as valuable and perceive themselves as competent (given years of cultural devaluation), the agency further contributed to the positive impact of involvement in the program on the grandmothers.

A second and more far-reaching strategy to create new social roles for women involves changing societal institutions that foster both internal and external barriers to the female experience and exercise of competence. Until competence is perceived as a human trait rather than as belonging primarily to the male domain, women will always face special conflicts in acting and feeling competent. Because social work has a professional commitment to enhance the unique potential of the individual, it must be concerned with the eventual modification of sex role socialization practices, opportunity-role structures and cultural values that impede the development of female competence.

Large-scale institutional change is too complex a process to discuss in any depth here. Changes in the power relations between men and women, in the economic and employment situation of women, in their educational options and family roles, and in the sex role socialization processes that reinforce narrow definitions of sex-typed behavior all must occur for women to be free to interact most effectively with the world. As women are socialized to take more control of their basic life choices (in the areas of work and family roles, health, sexuality, etc.) and as institutions change to afford more opportunity for the exercise of this control, competence will replace a sense of victimization characteristic of many women today. Contributing to this societal change through organizing women to act in their own behalf, lobbying for legislative and policy changes, educating parents and teachers about the negative effects of rigid sex role typing, modeling new roles, and demonstrating new institutional arrangements are just a few examples of legitimate and much needed social work functions to promote competence among women.

Conclusion

As sex role norms change and work and family roles become less sex-typed, competence-related difficulties may decrease for women. Aslin's (1977) recent replication of the Broverman study indicates that there appears to be a shift in attitude since 1970, at least among female therapists who reported valuing competence as a characteristic which was socially desirable for "mentally healthy women" as well as "mentally healthy adults." Hoffman (1977) notes that the increasing number of women in the labor force may contribute to changes in sex role socialization. For example, she reports that daughters of working women tend to view women as more competent than do daughters of women not employed outside the home. Thus, it seems that women may feel less and less pressure due to the cultural double-bind that has traditionally forced them to choose between being feminine and being competent.

This is not to say that there is still not much work to be done in promoting competence among women. Competence implies equal access to environmental resources; women can expect resistance from those who are being asked or forced to give up their exclusive control of such resources and power. Attacks on women who are competent, particularly those in visible leadership positions, may become implied rather than explicit but are not likely to disappear altogether. This chapter has attempted to demonstrate the variety of levels at which social workers can intervene to help promote competence in individual women and to change the conditions which create competence-related difficulties for women in the first place.

Notes

1. Swenson (Chapter 6 in this volume) stresses that competent people are particularly adept at using resources in their social networks.
2. See Fleming (Chapter 3 in this volume) for extensive discussion of attribution theory and its implications for social work practice.
3. The issue of "waiting to be found out" is discussed by Resnick (1979).
4. There has been much recent research on the role of sex of worker in affecting client assessment, choice of intervention and/or client outcome (Billingsley, 1977; Fabricant, 1974; Orlinsky and Howard, 1976). The findings are somewhat contradictory and suggest a complex interaction among sex of worker, worker attitudes and ideology, nature of presenting problem and client–worker similarity. Rawlings and Carter (1977) note, however, that one advantage a female worker can offer a female client is to serve as a role model. Learning through role models may be particularly important in dealing with certain kinds of competence-related problems among women.
5. While not focused solely on issues of competence, women's consciousness-raising groups can play a major role in decreasing a woman's sense of isolation and powerlessness and offering a vehicle through which to generate direct social action (Davis, 1977); enhancing autonomy and overcoming passivity (Eastman, 1973); helping women make the connections between their own problems and the sociocultural context (Kirsh, 1974); and providing problem-solving and support for adopting new roles and behaviors (Brodsky, 1977). Also see Middleman (Chapter 8 in this volume) for discussion of structured groups as a means of promoting competence.
6. Grinnell, Kyte, and Bostwick (Chapter 7 in this volume) examine the worker's roles of advocate and mediator in competence-oriented social work intervention.
7. See Grinnell, Kyte, and Bostwick (Chapter 7 in this volume) for further discussion of environmental modification.
8. Swenson (Chapter 6 in this volume) considers the importance of social networks and natural helpers in competence development.

CHAPTER 10

Promoting Competence in Children and Youth

Judith A. B. Lee

In memory, childhood is a magic time. Once we leave it we hide it way somewhere inside ourselves, sometimes returning to remember. For the child it can be the best of times and the worst of times. It is a time of fantasy, dream, and even nightmare; a time when a new pair of sneakers "can jump you over trees and rivers and houses" and when scary monsters lurk waiting in the darkness (Bradbury, 1957). For it is a time of psychosocial, psychosexual, and intellectual–cognitive foundation laying. It is a time of tremendous change and asynchronous growth that demands constant adjustment and readjustment.

The child is confronted with a proportion of newness that would dazzle the coping capacities of any adult. These constant challenges take place in a social context that may be nutritive or nonnutritive, extending from the first relationship with the mother out to the family and the community which can welcome, overlook, or prey upon the child (Stone and Church, 1957:377–83; Murphy, 1962). While most parents nurture and protect their young, the alarming facts of child suicide, child abuse and neglect impel us to reconsider the ways in which social work can help children and their families (Fontana, 1976; Bronfenbrenner, 1976).

Social work is one of the key societal institutions that exercise a protective function on behalf of the child. But social work also has a unique role in promoting "normal" ego growth and the acquisition of competence in the child. The problems of children grow out of the normal expectable stresses of childhood and out of the less predictable forces of life and the times in which we live (Murphy, 1962). Using an ecological perspective, Bronfenbrenner (1976:8) suggests that children today are living a more alienated existence from families and significant adults. He calls our attention to the "host of factors which conspire to isolate children from the rest of society" and interfere with their growth and development. These range from the fragmentation of the nuclear and extended family to the disappearance of neighborhoods and the supreme importance of television and other technological media.

This chapter will examine various ecologically oriented ego-supportive approaches to promoting coping and the acquisition of competence in "latency" or "middle age" children and youth. There will be emphasis on the life model and the interactionist perspectives on social work practice, which place the social worker at the developmental and transitional points in life and at the juncture where the relationships between people and their institutions break down (Germain and Gitterman, 1976; Lee and Swenson, 1978; Schwartz, 1971). These approaches stress that both the individual and the environment can be bolstered and brought more meaningfully together through social work intervention.

Practice illustrations will focus on meeting the child where she or he is, using the child's life experiences and feelings about them, and mediating in the life space of the child to strengthen coping abilities in the arenas of the friendship group, the school, and the family. These are critical arenas, since the tasks of the child are to play, to learn, and to develop interpersonal relationships within and outside of the family. Play and peer groups provide a child-ordered structuring of experience. Education, when it is at its best, is the more formal way to provide and structure experience for learning and growth. The school is potentially the most important arena of "industry" and interpersonal growth outside the family. The family, while receding in importance somewhat, must remain a nutritive source throughout middle childhood and adolescence.

By placing the social worker in these key arenas of childhood, the way is paved for more competent adult functioning and a happier time of being a child. Competence in dealing with the tasks of childhood promotes ego development, growth, and self-esteem. Difficulty or failure, whether originating in the child or in the environment, creates serious problems later in life. The sense of inferiority and the unmanageability of the world accrued from the lack of competence in childhood follows one long throughout life.

As various practice examples will show, much can be done to support the child's natural life processes. Above all, social work approaches that value and promote competence help to build a sense of worth and adaptability in children and youth.

Conceptual Framework

Ego psychology, the ecological perspective, the life model of practice, and the skills of mediation provide us with a dynamic focus and some action principles for our work with the child. Although some child therapists emphasize that parents and others are interferences in work with the child, the social work perspective is one that takes into account the significance of the child's environment. (Haworth, 1964: 67–90). We need to find the child where she or he is, within the larger society and within the "society of children" (Stone and Church, 1957). This latter, almost anthropological approach, is particularly important for we as adults have joined quite another society and need to tune-in once again to the folkways, norms, and customs of this special society which we have so long forgotten. Artists seem to capture its qualities most vividly. For example, Francois Truffaut dramatizes the social organization of children in a small town so well in his film *Small Change*. Ray Bradbury captures the essence of the interplay of fantasy and reality in *Dandelion Wine* (1957), and Mark Twain, Louisa May Alcott, and others have offered us rare glimpses of what it means for a child to struggle for competence in his/her world, a world very separate from our own, to quote Ray Bradbury's 12-year-old Doug: "The reason why grown-ups and kids fight is because they belong to separate races. Look at them different from us. Look at us different from them . . ." (Bradbury, 1964:20). While this is not quite true, the respect of the child's different and unique struggle is critical to our understanding. Struggling to view the world from the child's perspective, we move into our discussion of promoting competence in children and youth.

Direct work with the child as well as work within the environment are dual means of helping in the middle childhood and early adolescent years. Hollis points out that "with children especially lasting personality change occurs rather readily in response to environmental change, and this is the predominant method of casework treatment with children (Hollis, 1972:22–24, 110–14). Further, strengthening the child's abilities to act effectively and providing growth-producing experiences and opportunities for success and mastery are valid approaches along with changing the environment. As White says: "The concept of competence subsumes the whole realm of learned behavior whereby the child comes to deal effectively with his environment. A child's actual competence is built from his history of efficacies" (White, 1960:70). The ego of the child is fluid and malleable, growing constantly from actual experience. Writing on education of preschool children, Biber et al. note that "competence of all kinds contributes to the development of ego strength. In the last analysis, ego strength depends upon the way in which the individual's competence is tied in with one's sense of competence, with motivational systems that propel behavior, and with modes of interaction that yield productive outcomes" (Biber et al., 1977:7).

Erikson (1963), Murphy (1962), Murphy and Moriarty (1976) and Whittaker (1977) have made landmark contributions toward developing a theory of competence in children and youth. Erikson (1963) directs us to the developmental tasks of industry vs. inferiority which must precede that of identity formation. Successful doing is a prerequisite to a positive sense of self. It sets the stage for competence in work later in life.

> The child's danger, at this stage, lies in a sense of inadequacy and inferiority. . . . Many a child's development is disrupted when family life has failed to prepare him for school life, or when school life fails to sustain the promises of earlier stages. . . . This is socially a most decisive stage: since industry involves doing things beside and with others . . . we have pointed to the danger threatening the individual and society where the schoolchild begins to feel that the color of his skin, the background of his parents, or the fashion of his clothes rather than his wish and will to learn will decide his worth . . . and thus his sense of identity. [Erikson, 1963:260]

Thus we see the role of the social worker as mediator between the child's drive for industry and mastery and the systems that may frustrate and head the child toward a sense of inferiority. Murphy (1962) discusses the importance of mastery and competence in the preschool years as well. She, too, focuses on the interplay of the child's inner resources with the environmental supports.

> Each experience of mastery is not only a momentary conquest but a promise of more to come, a reassurance of the capacity to grow up. . . . All ego functions arise from genetic dispositions which carry their own energy; at the same time their development takes place in an interpersonal context . . . and with the investment in the environment that augments and nourishes or deprives the so-called autonomous ego functions. [Murphy, 1962:373]

Murphy points to coping as the process, adaptation as the result, and competence as the skills achieved in the process (p. 5). So the social worker's role is to enhance the process of coping. Each time the child can say "I can" instead of "I cannot" is a triumph in mastery. In everyday living, learning, and having fun there are opportunities for new coping. Promoting coping leads to competence. Murphy echoes Piaget in the principle that

> sheer functioning modifies structure. In every day parlance we say that success breeds success. . . . That is, triumph or successful results of coping efforts produce motor, affective and cognitive changes which predispose and equip the child for more efforts. [Murphy, 1962:373]

Murphy and Moriarty further raise the question as to what ecological settings stimulate or fail to arouse coping efforts. They propose a notion of optimal stress—that children should not be faced with too little or too much stress from the environment. "Optimal stress contributes to the development of effective coping" (Murphy and Moriarty, 1976:357). Parents who neither overindulged nor overprotected seemed to produce the best copers. "They respected their children's capacities, encouraged and rewarded their efforts, and offered reassurance in times of frustration and failure" (p. 349). All children demonstrated some vulnerability to stress and developed both defense and coping mechanisms to deal with it. Flexibility seemed related to resilience. Most important for the social worker to note is that "ability to evoke help and to respond to help were seen in resilient children along with the capacity to identify with the resilient care given" (p. 346). Further, the notion of proceeding from the child's shoes into his world, customs, norms, and social systems means recognizing that "Adaptation by children is not seen as simple compliance with adult demands, but as coming to them in such a way to get by with the adults while meeting their own needs as children" (p. 346). When a child is able to cope "by some combinations of selection, escape, protest or reconstruction of the situation—tolerance, strength, creativity or triumph, or all of these may be the outcome" (p. 13).

Whittaker, continuing with the ecological developmental perspective, says that:

> Competency acquisition occurs on three levels:
> 1. Intrapersonal, by helping the child to deal effectively and appropriately with impulses and emotions—anger, sadness, fear, elation, and excitement. Children learn through insight to link feelings, thoughts, and actions, and in essence, to gain control over their internal environment.
> 2. Interpersonal, by helping the child to interact effectively with peers and adults. . . .
> 3. Environmental, by helping the child to master the multiple world he inhabits. This involves academic skills and physical skills. . . . The development of a broad range of competencies means that any single area —home, school, peer group—thereby assumes less critical importance. [Whittaker, 1977:187]

In the discussion that follows, practice illustrations will show the social worker mediating in the intrapersonal, interpersonal and environmental spheres delineated by Whittaker.

Use of the Group with Children and Youth

An interpersonal task of the middle age child is to form meaningful and cooperative relationships outside of the family. The peer group seems to be the significant natural helping network of the child (Swenson, 1979, and Chapter 6 in this volume). The familylike potential for intimacy of the small group can be a strong growth-producing factor. In view of this, and since children are struggling to maintain defenses and achieve ego development, the group modality is often found to be an avenue of least resistance and most benefit and enjoyment for its participants (Hajal, 1978; Lee and Park, 1978). Similarly, the sharing of experiences and feelings and the use of play and activity as the medium of the child in the group are also critical (Hajal, 1978; Lee, 1977). Working with children in the natural friendship group or in school groups is especially effective.

Unlike other aspects of social work, group work has traditionally worked with "normal" people in their own life settings. The concept of working with club groups, both formed and natural, has a long and varied history in old-time group work agencies (Hartford, 1978; Middleman, 1968). Yet, as group work merged with the profession in the 1950s, it also moved from the field of recreation and activity groups for "normal" children into other agency settings with more "therapeutically" oriented purposes. However, the profession needs to maintain the connection with that part of our early heritage that sought to promote coping in the "normal" child. This is closely related to the life model of social work practice (Euster, 1978). This early group work approach addressed itself to "industry" or success at *doing* as a critical part of the child's development, along with success in interpersonal relationships and the building of democratic values. It recognized that doing and having fun together promoted more competent people.

Friends are a very important part of the world of the child. Many recent articles, such as Lewis and Weinstein's (1978), show the use of the group to help children form friendships. It is this important developmental area of interpersonal competence and the subsequent intrapersonal competence that the following work with a natural friendship group will illustrate. Also shown in later sections will be individual work with the child as he or she reveals the need for it within the group and mediating in any area of life that needs intervention or restructuring, such as the family and the school.

Formation and Beginnings of the Secret Soul Sisters—
A Friendship Group: Meeting the Girls Where They Are

A settlement house deployed a worker to a nearby public housing facility that served a low-income, predominantly minority group population. This project had no social services but it did have an after-school center for children and youth. The worker employed a "population approach" in order to develop a group service for girls age 10 to 12 (Shapiro, 1971). The worker observed that the center served a large complement of children in a large group and lounge-type approach. There were a few game rooms supervised by older youth, and children of all ages filtered through these rooms usually in small subgroups. There was also a meeting room where a large group of children rehearsed a play. The climate as a whole was chaotic as children bickered, competed, and clamored for attention. With the director's approval, the worker moved among the children for a few weeks, observing them in this life space and forming some relationships. During this time, one subgroup came to the fore. It consisted of six girls, five black and one white. Four of the girls were obviously bright, active, assertive, sometimes to the point of getting in trouble with the staff; but Peanut was neither small nor bright, and Regina, her buddy, was a small 14-year-old white girl who was emotionally and socially immature. These six were a definable and consistent subgroup that traveled together or in twos and threes. Peanut and Regina were the most friendly, almost clinging. Louise and Barbie were the most appealing. In predictable approach–avoidance, they engaged the worker by shooting rubber-bands at her and retreating in giggles (Garland, Kolodny and Jones, 1975). The worker engaged by laughing, chasing them a bit, and returning rubber-band fire. Cathy was more cautious and engaged by making negative comments, while Mary, obviously the brightest, engaged around the sharing of a magazine. The worker then approached the girls with the offer to become a special club group within the center. They were delighted and jumped at the chance for a worker and room of their own. Although this was a natural group, it was formed into a formal group with social work purpose by this process (Hartford, 1971). The girls agreed to vote upon the addition of new members if others indicated their interest, and to meet twice a week.

The contract was offered as a "group where they could have fun, do activities, and talk about being girls who lived here, went to school, had families, and were beginning to approach their teens. They could help each other with this growing up" (Schwartz and Zalba, 1974; Maluccio and Marlow, 1974). They eagerly bought this. But since they had never worked with a social worker before and this center was known to them as "a place to go to have fun," the verbal part of the contract needed time to develop. Initially they called the worker "teacher" and were a bit stilted in their talking and sharing. The worker explained that this could be a special place to share their thoughts and feelings and constantly sought ways to encourage this through activity and by being a sharing and feeling person with them. The girls had been out of school for a month as a result of a teachers' strike and their thoughts and feelings about this were an easy focus of discussion as the group began. In one meeting, disillusionment and anger at the teachers poured forth. Work in the intrapersonal sphere of promoting the expression of feelings and thoughts toward the acquisition of competence is shown. As seen in the worker's recording (the worker records her interventions in the first person):

Mary said, "This is the first time I noticed that I like school. I'm bored." Louise said the teachers are stupid and don't care. I said they were angry at the teachers. Cathy zeroed in on her feeling that "They don't like us anyway because we're black. They wouldn't do this to white kids." Mary said white kids in the city were suffering too. But Louise, cautiously looking at me, said that Cathy was right anyway because everyone in her school was black. Everyone agreed, including Regina! I said white kids were affected by the strike too, but Cathy was right that racism did have something to do with the strike, and it was very hard to be black, and be and feel poorly treated by whites. They were silent and thoughtful. Louise said, "But you're different." I said that everyone including me has a little of the disease of racism, explaining it a bit more, but that I hoped I would be fair and caring. I hoped we would help each other with this. Louise and Barbie said they had white teachers that they liked, and really missed this year. Peanut said Regina wasn't white and neither was I, and everyone laughed.

The culture of sharing thoughts and feelings evolved as part of the mutual aid function of the group. The worker relates with understanding and honesty about racism. She is aware that it can be a mitigating force against the development of a positive, healthy self-image (Clark, 1963; Clark and Clark, 1950). She is also aware of the ego strengths developed by minority children in order to deal with living in a pathological society (Ladner, 1972: 77–108). Her focus is to ally with and build upon these strengths.

The doing was also very important in this group. The first few sessions were spent almost entirely in cutting and pasting and drawing. The worker records:

They were almost absorbed in activity. It seems like an attempt at structuring their own lives without school. I only intervened to help with a task or credit their work. It's almost unnatural—you can hear a pin drop! . . . In the midst of this strange quiet they asked me to leave the room. With some anxiety I did. There was a lot of buzzing inside. Barbie came and got me. They had used the glitter, red felt, and paste to make me a heart that said "I love you." I was so moved. I hugged each one. Cathy told me she didn't help and left the room. Louise said, "Don't pay her no mind," but when I went for her she was gone.

In the above excerpt we see the group engaging in activity, that is, in the stage-appropriate task of industry vs. inferiority. The existence of the school strike merely heightened their need to accomplish and do, and made for the unusual quiet. The use of activity was an ego-building device used throughout the group's life.[1]

We also see the continued approach–avoidance behavior of Cathy. Soon the group entered the power and control stage, and Cathy led in the testing behavior (Garland, Kolodny, and Jones, 1975). Regina was scapegoated in part as "substitute" for the worker, who was also white. The worker's skill in clarifying what was happening and setting appropriate limits aided them through this difficult but normative stage. As the group progressed, Regina continued to be scapegoated from time to time, but now on her own merits, or lack of them. One of the worker's strategies was to help Regina more competently handle herself in the group so as to provoke less scapegoating. Interpersonal competence is a critical theme (Foote and Cottrell, 1965; Whittaker, 1977). On the one hand, the worker clarified the situation for the whole group, and on the other, she helped each side hear the other's thoughts and feelings. For example.

Barbie made fun of Regina's work and Regina sulked. I said, "Barbie, Louise hurt your feelings saying your picture was ugly and now you pick on Regina. But, Regina, if you didn't whine so much over your work, Barbie wouldn't have anyone to pick on." Barbie said, "Yeah!" And Regina agreed. Louise said, "Amen!" I said, "Louise, are you having trouble with your work?" "Yeah," she said. "You never help me." I said, "Never?" Louise smiled and said she was sorry to Barbie, who in turn apologized to Regina.

As the worker individualized each girl in her doing, and worked on the interpersonal area, the tensions eased. The group moved slowly into the intimacy and differentiation stages, though there was always some level of testing. The girls were competitive for the worker's attention and approval. Nevertheless, they grew closer to each other and more able to do the work of the contract.

As intimacy grew, some very pressing concerns were brought to the group. The following excerpt from a group meeting illustrates this level of sharing, and the mutual aid function of the group is also clearly seen:

Louise and Cathy were debating over who got the most homework. Peanut then shared that the work was too hard for her. The others asked to see her homework. They were able to offer her help, which she accepted gladly. I asked the girls if anyone else ever found homework hard. We talked awhile about what each girl found difficult. During this Barbie was remarkably silent. I asked why. She said, "Because I don't go to school." Cathy said, "Shush, don't tell; you'll get in trouble." The others encouraged her to tell. Barbie said, "We trust her" (meaning me) and proceeded to unfold a story of her mother and seven siblings being illegal residents in their grandma's project apartment since last April due to a fire, and her mother being afraid to register her because of this. She added she misses school very much and also hates sleeping on the floor. I said I could certainly understand her feelings in this awful situation. The others agreed. I used this opportunity to say I would like to be of help to them and each of their families and asked the group if that would be O.K. Cathy said to start with Barbie's family. The others agreed. Barbie was delighted as long as I understood her mother was sick and couldn't help the mess they were in. I said I understood. I strategized with Barbie and the others how I could approach Barbie's mother and grandma. Barbie would tell them first that I wanted to help and so forth. Louise then said her family has a big problem too. She proceeded to tell it.

The girls continued to be able to share such real and pressing concerns along with accounts of their everyday struggles and triumphs in living. The preceding excerpts show the worker encouraging mastery through activity and through the expression of feelings and thoughts in both the intrapersonal and interpersonal areas. In the final excerpt, deeply personal material is shared with a sense of urgency. The worker must now move into the third area delineated by Whittaker (1977), the environmental area. Not only does the worker help Barbie to cope with the stressful situation but also she offers help to Barbie's family.

Environmental Restructuring

Minuchin (1970) warns against conceptualizing poverty-stricken families in terms of pathology. He redefines pathology as a product of the transaction between families and other systems. While the extended family has been viewed as pathological, he defines it as a significant support system. This suggests the need for an approach that recognizes and capitalizes on the strengths in families and restructuring of familial roles as well as the environment itself in order to effect a better fit.[2]

> Family services oriented toward the total family within its ecosystem are becoming more and more the treatment of choice for a wide range of families, not just members of the low socioeconomic groups. . . . The emphasis throughout would be not on exploring pathology, but on finding, enhancing, and rewarding competence. People change . . . through the development of competencies. [Minuchin, 1970:129]

The dual focus on using family resources and restructuring the environment is illustrated in work with the friendship group described in the preceding section.

The matter of school registration for Barbie was worked out fairly easily. But relocation and helping her 27-year-old mother, who had severe health problems, plan for herself and the six children was a much longer process. The grandmother, a strong woman who was nevertheless "tired of the burden," was used as an ally and was the only reason that temporary placement was avoidable. Eventually, with much help in negotiating the welfare system and local realty companies, the family was relocated to an apartment in a two-family house.

Both the worker and the grandmother performed the functions of mothering the mother so she could continue to care for herself and her children. The welfare worker was also very helpful. Barbie was able to continue with the group and felt relieved of the role of oldest child and surrogate mother for her mother.[3] The neglect petition earlier drawn up by the welfare worker was happily destroyed.

Family restructuring (Minuchin, 1970; 1974) and relocation were both parts of restructuring Barbie's environment, removing her from the position of parental child, and placing the whole family in a better housing. The worker records:

Barbie's ego strengths were remarkable. She was very bright, able to think clearly, formed very good object relationships, performed well in school despite the loss of school time, and was the best worker at group activities. She defends with intellectualization. It was no wonder that she had been so serious and sad. All of the complex and frustrating work with mother and welfare was worth it to see Barbie have a few moments of freedom from the family burdens. The group is a haven for Barbie, a place where she can enjoy being an 11-year-old child.

The worker was unable to involve herself with each family as fully as she had with Barbie's, nor was such extensive work needed in all families. Mary came from a well-functioning, intact family; Sandy and Alice, new members, had strong working mothers. Cathy came from a tight-knit family of ten siblings, and was the second from the youngest. Louise was living with an aunt while her mother went in and out of mental hospitals. Peanut was the youngest of eight. Regina was the youngest of four but had spent six years in foster homes, from age 5 to 11, due to her mother's mental illness and alcoholism. The family was functioning marginally, but functioning. The worker decided to spend her out-of-group energies on Regina's and Peanut's situations since the need for further work was pressing in each of these. Peanut's situation was far easier. Peanut appeared to be retarded. But a home visit yielded the fact that she actually had extensive hearing loss, her hearing aid didn't work right, and she refused to wear it. Mediation with mother, teacher, and medical center as well as individual and eventually group support to Peanut in this area was very helpful environmental restructuring.

Regina's situation was more difficult. Her needs were greater than the group alone could meet. The worker records:

Regina is bright and outgoing but small for her age, immature and lacking in self-confidence. She is not able to finish anything on her own. She has weak ego boundaries, sometimes mixing up the pronouns "you," "I," and "she." Her object relations are all of a dependent, clinging nature. Her defenses are primitive. She denies, incorporates, and splits. She seems overwhelmed and frightened in this world where vulnerability is sometimes preyed upon. Her history makes this understandable.

The worker's focus was to get Regina into private therapy, but her mother's fears of outsiders made this a long-term goal. The mother herself needed great support and help. The case was referred to another agency that made home visits. Regina did continue with the group, but the worker knew that group dynamics would not permit her to see Regina individually. Regina did relate to her new family social worker, who also had the goal of getting her into therapy. As she continued with the group, she did grow in her ability to complete tasks successfully. As this happened, her whining quality was reduced and she seemed to enjoy more acceptance from her peers. Still very vulnerable and in need of therapy, she did grow in her self-confidence and interpersonal competence. Thus, we see that the group itself as well as outreach to Regina's family became a critical factor in the restructuring of her environment. This restructuring promoted growth despite Regina's tenuous psychosocial functioning. For Regina, and much more for the "healthier" girls, the group itself and the worker's intervention in family and other systems promoted her ability to cope and master.[4] Yet, all of this progress was contingent upon the worker's ability to see the world from the child's viewpoint.

Entering the Society of the Child

The choosing of a name for the friendship group by the members was an interesting phenomenon in glimpsing into their world:

Louise said, "We can't be a group unless we have a name." Everyone agreed. I asked what they would like to call themselves? "The Dragon Ladies," said Peanut, " 'cause if anybody bothers us, we'll breathe fire on them and eat them up." Everyone laughed. Mary said, "No; the Egyptian Queens because we're beautiful." They paraded around the room like fashion models behind Mary. Cathy said, "No; we should be the Jokers because we act stupid," as everyone convulsed in laughter. Sandy said, "I got it; listen everybody . . . the Soul Sisters. "Yeah," said Barbie;" but how about the Secret Soul Sisters, 'cause we don't want everyone to know our business." "Yeah!" said Cathy. Mary said, "It fits 'cause everyone is a girl, a sister, and everyone's got soul—even you and Regina. You don't have to be black to have soul." I said thanks, and Regina said, "I got a soul, don't I?" Mary said everyone did, and soul means being "together" and if you're in this group, you're "together." Regina hooked her fingers in her lapels and strutted about saying, "We are a 'together' group," and everyone followed in a parade. And so the group became the Secret Soul Sisters. . . . We also agreed in this meeting to freeze the membership at nine.

We see the need to be part of a secret society, the need to be identified, to have an in-group, and to exclude others. (Stone and Church, 1957). We also see a beginning search for identity both sexual and racial. These were recurrent themes in the group. The need to exclude was particularly strong. They especially needed to exclude their younger sisters, who frequently tried to tag along. In response, the worker brought in another settlement house social worker to set up a group for the younger girls. This caused momentary calamity in her own group. It also continued the theme of how they feel about their families. One basic method of promoting competence in children is to get across the message that "You are an important person in your own right, your thoughts and feelings count." This meeting also illustrates that strategy:

Sandy said she hated her sister too and asked if I would put her in Ms. K's group to get her out of her hair. I agreed. Cathy, Barbie, and Mary were mad that I put their sisters in the newly formed group. Cathy expressed that "We hate them and don't want them to have a good time. What do you care about them for anyway?" Barbie and Cathy said that they always fight their sisters and brothers about me. I said I got the feeling that they didn't want to share me with anyone. Louise said that was right, and that I shouldn't buy refreshments for the other group. I explained why I did that today, and recognized that they felt happy to have a grown-up all to themselves. I said that I was their social worker, and that part of helping their families was getting someone to work with the little kids so I could devote more of my time just to them. Cathy said that she didn't like me to pay any attention to the brats. I asked if they felt that the little girls stole all the attention from their mothers. Cathy said "Right" and everyone agreed. Barbie added that they steal all of the attention from everyone—except from me. I said that they were my group, and special to me and they knew it. They agreed. I said that it must be hard to have to share everything, and I know it's hard to share me even a little. Cathy said that it would be O.K. if I left Ms. K. on her own now and didn't help her. I said that Ms. K. could take care of herself and her group and I would take care of them. They agreed that that was a deal!

This excerpt illustrates the practice principles of gratifying dependency needs and accepting and acting on the feelings expressed by the girls. As they experience their words and feelings having an impact on a significant adult, they gain a sense of power over something important in what is often a world they cannot control. Yet, the girls are also helped to accept the needs of other people—in this case, younger sisters—thereby also promoting growth in the interpersonal area.

Using Limits and Confrontation

The use of limits and confrontation on their negative interpersonal behavior was another strategy used to promote competence in the interpersonal area as the following excerpt shows. The girls needed help in accepting that the worker and others had limits and feelings.

A recurrent theme was around the giving of food. . . . They complained that I didn't give them food at every meeting or have a party each time as Ms. K's group was now having. I said that I knew food was one way of showing I cared—and although we didn't meet to eat, we could have refreshments when we planned a party together. They said they wanted a Valentine's Day party, which we planned and carried out. . . . There was a great deal of acting-out about the food—hoarding, not sharing, taking from one another, making the other kids jealous, teasing, etc. I confronted them with this behavior and pointed out the consequences of making the others jealous— the other kids hit them, didn't like them. I said that this was mean of them. They felt embarrassed but began to cease some of the acting-out behavior toward nongroup members and were more caring toward each other. I think the confrontation worked because it was reflecting and making connections about something we have worked on in other meetings—they knew they were sometimes selfish and hurtful toward each other. They also knew I understood why they acted this way and was not judging them but rather showing where it was happening and how it might be different. As I pointed out the behavior, I said I knew they had to fight for everything that was theirs, but here maybe we could trust a little—maybe try it differently."

The combination of caring and setting limits on behavior seemed to promote more positive interaction. The worker's choice of program media also provided limits and structures in order to help them feel accomplishment and gratification while inhibiting impulsivity. Activities were chosen that had a progressive end toward building internal controls rather than a regressive effect. Through experience, the worker found that no one could handle clay without wildness, modeling feces and phalluses, and mass group contagion. (Haworth, 1964:339–65; Middleman, 1968). Paints were usually used well, but on a "bad day," when the girls were upset, they were also regressive. Soft materials like felt, material, cotton, etc., were relaxing and calming and brought out a softness in the girls. Hard materials like wood, sticks, beads, jewelry-making implements, etc., were good for helping the girls to "pull themselves together." Games with rules and structure also had this effect. The girls seemed to be able to choose the type of activity that would help them at the moment. The primary strategy was to enable the youngsters to share their thoughts and feelings verbally about themselves and their environment, but the following work shows the helpful interplay of talking and activity.

A particularly charged area was coping with sexuality. In what should be a psychosexual moratorium, sometimes defenses were bombarded. It is important for the worker to help the girls express their feelings in this area while shoring up the defenses, for flooding in from this area is most threatening to stage-appropriate competence and mastery (Freud, 1946).

After much embarrassed hysterical giggling over seeing two teenagers kissing in the hall, Mary got the group into a serious mood by relating how she saw a man exposing himself. The girls agreed they had seen this too. It was disgusting! I said it was very upsetting to see something like that. They then got into a discussion of what happens in the neighborhood . . . how teenagers make love on the roof . . . they go up and watch and laugh. I said I didn't think it helped them to go up and watch. Mary agreed it got her very nervous. Regina wanted to talk about kissing and hugging boys—and said, "Peanut lets them do things to her." When asked what things? Louise, Cathy and Peanut didn't want to talk anymore, held their ears and ran out of the room. But they returned and I helped them to see they felt two ways— wanted to talk, did talk about this among themselves, but somehow it was frightening and made them nervous to talk here. Those who wanted to talk said this was the first time they talked about this to a grown-up; it felt "funny." The others giggled and hooted nervously. I said we didn't have to talk about it if half of the group isn't ready. They asked me to talk with people individually and not in the group. Mary said, "Aw." I said I would talk to whoever wanted to—whenever they were ready—and it is still O.K. to talk about it in the group when they want to. It was "resolved" at this.

The next meeting was like a retreat into activity. First they played Jacks, then they were completely absorbed in orderly painting (as differentiated from their acting-out through paint—smearing it, etc.). They wanted me to teach them to mix colors. I did and they worked hard as if to make life simple and manageable again. Very little other discussion. I did reflect at one point that they seemed happy to be doing, and not talking about sex anymore. This drew serious, relieved, agreement—not the usual laughter the word "sex" would bring. I left words at a minimum and helped them to collect themselves through mastering the activity.

These two meetings so dramatically portray the conflicts of the older middle age child in moving toward adolescence and sexuality, particularly when the environment contains many elements of over-stimulation. They are curious, yet frightened, and defend as best they can against the forces from within and without that threaten the integration they have so far achieved. They court the dangerous stimulation (e.g., going to watch) while literally running from talking about it and retreating into the safety of the childhood things with rules, structures, and controls, e.g., playing Jacks, mixing colors. The group offers them reinforcement in this, allowing for the place to be children, and the opportunity to talk about without acting on their thoughts and feelings in this important developmental area. Thus, defenses are appropriately shored up and coping is promoted. The girls are then free to continue to work at handling their age-appropriate life tasks of learning, relating, and integrating feeling, thought and action with greater competence.

Some of the highlights of the work in promoting competence in this group of children have been illustrated and analyzed. Underlying all of the work, enriching and facilitating the development of competence, was the growth of intimacy and the ability to care for each other. Moments shared between the worker and members as they walked along the seaside gathering seashells together in a spring trip show this aspect: Louise said, "I love the group; it's my family." "Mine too," Barbie, Regina, Peanut, and Cathy agreed, and added: "We are a fine group!" These moments essentially show that the most important work of the group was to promote the development of trusting object relationships, member to member and member to worker, which in turn promotes the self-image of competence. The development of positive relationships was an inherent strategy as well in all of the group's work.

Intervention in the School

We have met the child in his/her informal life experience with the friendship group. We shall now turn to the other critical arena of childhood where the task of industry vs. inferiority gets seriously tested: the school. Education at its best is a growth-producing experience. Success at learning promotes cognitive growth as well as social and emotional growth.

According to Biber, "At school-entering age the child is ready to loose himself from his early bonds and limitations; he needs, for his emotional security, a growing sense that he can relate himself to that part of the world around him that is not family-encompassed. Now he needs to feel his own growing competence, and to give over leaning on the powers of elders, to whom he so recently attributed omnipotence" (Biber, 1967a: 5–6). Meeting the child where she or he is and connecting his/her experiences, thoughts, and feelings to the subject matter at hand are time-honored educational principles that bridge the gap between the child's life experiences and the subject to be mastered. The use of the child's experiences and the structure of learning to spur inquiry is an important component of the role of the teacher (Dewey, 1963). And, as Biber points out, "It is the teacher's choice of techniques and skill in using them that determines the extent to which the child's learning, achievement, and mastery become the framework for positive ego-growth, and contribute to the child's growing feeling as a knowing, doing, confident self in relation to a knowable, manageable world"' (Biber, 1967b: 6). Proper education is of itself, therefore, a prime tool for promoting competence in children and youth. Yet we know that, for many and complex reasons ranging from the sociopolitical structure to teacher training and fiscal situations affecting large city school systems, education is for many children a frustrating and ego-deprecating experience. Whether our attention is directed toward the child who is unable to relate to the educational system or to the system that is unable to relate to the child, someone is needed to stand as mediator in the transaction between the child and school (Gitterman, 1974). The social worker may do this from many standpoints, as a school social worker, or as a social worker from another agency dealing with the child or offering a service in the school setting. The example given earlier of speaking to Peanut's teacher about her problem in wearing her hearing

aid illustrates this latter type of mediation for an individual child. Gitterman (1974) describes how a community social service agency satu-
rated the schools in its area with group services for children whom the
school identified as needing help. He also discusses the role of the
worker as mediator between children and each other, the child and his
learning difficulties, children and the teachers and administrators.

The following recorded excerpt from a seventh-grade girls' group
illustrates this strategy of mediation.[5] It shows the worker preparing
the girls to express their concerns to a teacher who embarrasses them
publicly. Her first strategy was to help the girls gain competence in
handling the matter more positively themselves. The girls had initially
handled their feelings of humiliation and shame by making wisecracks
and further infuriating the teacher.

Then Ruth brought up Ms. P., saying, "That's a crazy teacher." I said I'd like
to know some more about her. The others agreed with Ruth. "You're lucky
you don't know her." I said I guessed she must be pretty bad and I was
wondering if they could show me what she was like. There were choruses
again about her attitude, and Yola said, "And she reads out, 'Yola Lane,
your grade is twenty.' " I asked if she read out grades a lot? Did she read out
everybody's grades? Yes, they agreed. I said, "That's embarrassing." Yola
said she felt like two cents. I said maybe we could role-play the grade
reading. Ruth said, "I'll be Ms. P." She strolled around criticizing each girl
in a threatening voice—"Jane, sit up straight," etc. Then she mimicked,
"Yola Lane, twenty; Jane Garcia, thirty. . . ." Jane said under her breath,
"You're a size thirty," and the girls laughed. I said, "Is this what happens
—do you get her back with jokes?" "Yeah," said Yola, "but then she gets
us." She mimicked, "Since these grades are so high you'll only get ten
additional math problems to do." I said, "Let's think of some other ways to
let Ms. P. know what you feel about the grade reading." Ruth said, "We feel
cheap; our feelings get hurt." Agreement. I said, "Do you feel a little angry
too?" "Sure we do—what do you think?" I said I thought so. But how could
they let Ms. P. know how hurt they felt? I suggested we role-play it. Ruth as
Ms. P. read the grades again; Yola raised her hand and said, "You are
embarrassing us; we feel bad. We can't do better when we feel so bad.
Could you just hand back the papers with the grades on them?" Everyone
clapped.

In order to help restructure this learning situation the worker also
mediated directly with the teacher. A young teacher, who was shocked
and frustrated by the low math level of her seventh-grade students, she
welcomed the worker's understanding and suggestions not only around
the girls' feelings and her handling of grades but around making math
more relevant to the girls' life experiences. The use of role-play is also

an excellent technique with children and youth; it is an extension of playing "make believe" that provides rehearsal for life experiences.

Yet sometimes it is not the schoolwork or the interaction with teachers that impedes better school performance. There are times when even the brightest, most well-functioning children have struggles and life situations which mitigate against learning. One community agency in a "deteriorated" neighborhood decided to offer group services to those youngsters designated as "needing" the service by the school and to the brightest and most well-functioning children as well in order to facilitate their maximum growth. It was not surprising to learn that the best functioning had as many personal concerns which interfered with more optimal functioning as those who were designated as "in trouble." For one "best-functioning" group the brightest boys in the sixth grade were chosen. They scored higher than others on IQ tests, were on or above grade level in reading and math skills, posed no behavior problems, and were seen as positive, eager-to-learn children.

The use of activities that promote the expression of feelings is a technique often used with school groups. In a fifth meeting of this group the worker asked the boys to leaf through several popular magazines and cut out a picture about which they could tell a story that had something to do with what they were thinking or feeling about themselves and their lives. They could write a related story or poem or make a collage if they chose. The worker records:

Tom cut out lots of pretty girls and there was giggling and grabbing at his pictures. Ralph chose pictures of cars, offering a running dialogue on each one. Tito chose pictures of games and toys. Eric chose food, mostly desserts. Juan was unusually quiet and refused to show the others what he was doing. When I asked, he smiled shyly and said I could see it. He had cut out a picture of a young man's face. The man was Hispanic and had a look of anguish and sadness that was very dramatically portrayed. He had pasted it in a folder and written the following poem on the other side:

Loneliness

That's the only shit that bugs me,
like when I have a problem there's
no one to face but me.

Who knows when the world is in danger
everybody is caring for there own life,
nobodys elses but own.

In this world there's only fear
no happiness, no joy, only fear.
You have to care for your own life

*There's no one to face but to care
for your own life.*

I was very moved. The others became quiet, noting my mood while reading it. They asked Juan if they could see it. He said yes quietly. I asked him to read it to the group. The boys became serious. I asked if he wanted to say something about what he wrote. Did he have a particular problem to share? He smiled and said no. I waited. Then I said the poem does speak for itself, but I was wondering if the others felt some of the fear and sadness that the poem expresses. Ralph said once his mother sent him away down South and he felt that way. He knew no one and was alone and scared. Juan said, "Yeah, and you had no one to talk to about it, right?" Ralph agreed. They all did. I asked if they thought they could share problems here. Juan said we already did today! I said they certainly did, and that was part of what the group was for. . . . Ralph said, "Next week let's talk about Tom's pictures." Everyone laughed. I said O.K., I bet girls can be a problem to them. They sure are, the boys agreed.

The poem and the work do speak for themselves. They speak to the need for children to share profound concerns and feel the support and help of peers and a concerned adult who can help. While there were no objective measurements taken, the teachers reported that the boys were doing "better than ever" as the group progressed. It could be said that Juan's "depressiveness" was an individual phenomenon. But that would contradict this author's experience. It seems more appropriate to say that the often pathological and non-nutritive environment of poverty, added to normal developmental struggles, produces some depression in even the strongest of children. These are children who do cope adaptively but whose anger may also turn inward, putting a ceiling on their level of mastery. Further, as Bronfenbrenner (1976:6–9) suggests, this deep sense of loneliness may be a fact of our times in all socioeconomic groups, as meaningful contact between children and adults steadily decreases.

One further example from an eighth-grade girls' group is illustrative of the developmental and environmental struggles that may also interfere with learning. The composition of this group was mixed, with girls who cut classes and did poorly and girls who did well enough but were described by the teachers as being "overly quiet and uncommunicative." The work that follows may seem unusual, though it actually reflects a frequent theme in working with adolescents:

Julie started by saying, "I hate school; it makes me sick." The others joined in with complaints about teachers and studies. Vicky said she wrote a poem about hate. She was encouraged to read it. Laying her head on the table she recited her poem, entitled "Mother." It was full of curse words, anger, and sadness. Sandra said she felt the same way: "My mother treats me like a slave. I have to do everything and my little sister gets away with murder." Julie said, "My mother always curses at me." Ada said, "mine doesn't trust me with the key so I'm always waiting in the cold." They all agreed they'd like to leave home. I said they have it rough, but how are they going to make it with their mothers until they can be on their own? Vicky said, "I tried to kill myself once." I was struck silent but then said, "My God, you must have been very unhappy." Vicky told about her home situation and her mother's relationship with an abusive paramour. Sandra said, "You know what? I took fifteen pills and tried to kill myself too, but they pumped my stomach out." Julie said she thought about it, but she's too afraid. I said I was glad she was afraid of that, I was very concerned about how unhappy they are, and the extreme self-hurting things they are describing. Julie said, "Yeah, I could never hurt myself. But I want to hurt someone." Vicky said, "Life isn't worth it." Sandra said, "No, it is. I scared myself so bad when I took those pills I swore I'd never do it again. I'd like to be a doctor some-day." Julie said, "Or maybe a social worker like you." I said, "You want to be something someday, but feel very discouraged now; someday must seem far away." Ada said, "Yeah, we'll never make it anyway. We'll just get pregnant and have babies." "No," said Sandra, "not me, I'm gonna stay in school and get good grades." Vicky said, "You used to cut a lot last year." "I don't anymore, though," said Sandra. I said it is important to make it in school. It's also important to keep talking about the things that make you unhappy and get in your way.

The work of this group went on to face the painful feelings while promoting competent action, e.g., regular school attendance, studying, and so on, in the school and also in the interpersonal sphere. In a circular way, as competence was attained, depression lessened and vice versa (Lee and Park, 1978). Preventive social work intervention like this is essential, for once again Bronfenbrenner taps the pulse of our times: "Self-destructive behavior among youth has also become a serious problem. The suicide rate for young people aged 15 to 19 has more than tripled in less than twenty years . . . and in recent years there has been an increase in suicides among younger children, some as young as 10" (Bronfenbrenner, 1976:9). Groups such as this, held in the life space of the child, which provide an opportunity to share such common feelings and experiences, are one effective way in which social work can pro-mote a better sense of well-being, connectedness, and competence.

The Family and the Child

The foregoing leads us to the heart of the matter. Children cannot experience success and competence when families are in serious trouble. At times one can focus on the child and help the child to deal with the family situation. This was one strategy employed in the earlier example of Barbie (in the friendship group), although the worker also moved into the family and environmental scene as well. At times the worker must move into the family situation and work from within.

Before introducing another practice example, I want to stress the importance of a family orientation as differentiated from being wedded to a particular family treatment "method." With this orientation, the worker can never think of the child in isolation from his or her family or the family in isolation from its social context (Minuchin, 1970). Many methods are available to the worker with this orientation, for no one method offers a sure-fire mechanical formula for helping in the familial-social-ecological context (Haley, 1971). Yet, it is all too easy to become technique- rather than person-oriented. The danger is that in finding such coherent psychosocial formulations as family treatment theory we "forget" the basic skills in helping people, primarily those of relating to thinking, feeling human beings in thinking, feeling ways. The temptation may be to restructure as if people are objects to be moved about rather than people with feelings. Family therapy theories provide us with a knowledge base of social systems and social interaction; they do not provide us with a map of the territory or a blueprint to follow.

A prime contribution of family theory is the concept that no one member can be the problem. This is particularly relevant, as one of the most frequent presenting requests in family and child guidance agencies is the child as the problem bearer or "identified patient" (Satir, 1964). While the child may indeed have troubles and make his or her own contribution to the interactional problems within a family, in this orientation it is the interaction itself that is "the" problem. The family may be helped as a unit and/or in its various subsystems. Yet, the whole family is constantly kept in mind even if only one family member is currently seen by a worker.

The following case example employs this orientation. The overall strategy was to build competence in the "identified problem bearer," the child, while providing help to the family as a whole, which involved some inevitable family restructuring.

The Allen Family

Mrs. Allen brought 12-year-old Karen to the agency at the request of the school guidance counselor after Karen failed all of her sixth-grade subjects at midterm. Karen had always been a good student, but the counselor felt she was "depressed and withdrawing." Mrs. Allen presented the problem as Karen's laziness, because while she "was never the brightest child, she always passed." She hastened to add that her 9-year-old son, Stan, was "getting all A's." The family consisted of Mrs. Allen, age 32; Mr. Allen, age 43; Karen, 12; Stan, 9; and Lisa, 4. Karen is Mrs. Allen's child by a former marriage that lasted two years. Mr. Allen did adopt Karen. Mr. Allen is a diagnosed "paranoid schizophrenic" who also had serious current medical problems, a possible cancerous blockage. He was receiving psychiatric and medical treatment at a veterans' outpatient facility. The family now lives on his army pension. Before the war he had been a writer and journalist of some success. Mrs. Allen came from a small rural community and had not completed her high school education. Mr. and Mrs. Allen are of different religious faiths. All of the children, including Karen, have taken on the father's religion and most of their neighbors and friends are of this religion. His extended family is supportive of the family. Mr. Allen was not able to participate in help for Karen. According to his therapist, he was in a "regressed period" emotionally due to the current uncertainty of his medical condition. Within a few weeks after beginning with the Allen's, his condition was determined to be noncancerous, but emotionally he continued to be regressed and unapproachable for many months. The work, therefore, takes place with Karen alone, Karen and Mrs. Allen, Mrs. Allen and the three children, and Mrs. Allen alone. Although never present physically, Mr. Allen was considered as a presence in all interviews.

The first helping strategy employed was to help Mrs. Allen and the children get in touch with their feelings and think about the ramifications of Mr. Allen's uncertain medical picture and the corollary increase of his mental symptoms. The problem was thus recast not as Karen's school failure but as the family's response to this uncertainty. This is not to say Karen's school problem was forgotten but that it was placed in a family perspective. As the worker met with the mother and children individually and together on this issue, the unspoken was expressed and energies were released for action in many areas. Mrs. Allen was able to review her social network and enlist the help of Mr. Allen's brother in helping him keep medical appointments. The children were also able to discuss what they were worried about, and free to perform in school. When it was learned that the condition was not cancerous, the worker then focused on helping the family adapt strategies of dealing with Mr. Allen's now psychotic behavior, withdrawal, paranoid yelling at everyone, and so forth. This consisted of helping the family understand what was happening to Mr. Allen and encouraging them to share their feelings and reactions about Mr. Allen and to develop ways of avoiding as much unpleasantness as possible.

As the family worked together on these concerns, the family dynamics also became apparent. It became clear that Karen felt like an outsider in this family, as did Mrs. Allen. In fact, Mrs. Allen had difficulty in seeing Karen as different from herself and projected her feelings of low self-worth and "being stupid" on Karen. Stan was "smart" like Mr. Allen, and Lisa, of course, would be too. But Karen was only a younger version of Mrs. Allen, according to both Mrs. Allen and herself. In Karen's individual sessions she shared that she loved Mr. Allen and wanted to please him and be like him (smart). She took his illness to mean he was displeased with her. She was also in a beginning identity struggle, wondering what her original religion was about, and who her biological father was. She felt very guilty over wondering this, particularly now that Mr. Allen was sick. She was also developing an interest in boys and said that she was distracted in her studies, first because she wasn't very smart and second because she thought about boys a lot. She was able to work on these pressing concerns in her individual sessions with the worker. She developed a realistic understanding of Mr. Allen's illness and a better sense of what he was able to give her. She was able to accept her own good intellectual abilities without distortion. She became freer to perform in school. However, the whole family was still bound to the home as Mrs. Allen was afraid of leaving Mr. Allen alone. There was no play time for the children. Karen frequently watched the two younger children when the mother went to the stores, etc. This additional closeness compounded the structural problems in the family. Mrs. Allen was totally overburdened and had nothing for herself in the family. She in turn turned to Karen for alliance and support. This was worked on individually with both Mrs. Allen and Karen, and with Mrs. Allen and all of the children. In one later family meeting the interaction looked this way:

The family session began before we entered the room. Karen eagerly shared how happy she was that she passed everything and got a good grade in English for this marking period. Stan grabbed my hand and told me he got ninety in math and Karen got only seventy-five. Mrs. Allen told him not to brag. As we settled in, I said I was glad to hear how well they both did. Karen told about her English grade. Stan got up and stood by my side. Lisa said she wanted to go to school too. I told Lisa that was something her mommy and I were going to work on for her. She would go to nursery school soon. She settled into playing with her doll. Mrs. Allen said, "Thank God, I'll have a break." I agreed she needed one!

I then said that I thought now we might try to share Karen's happy moment since she had had such a tough time in school. Karen beamed, told how she studied real hard, did an extra report, and so on. I asked how everyone felt about Karen's success. Stan said she did work harder, but he got nineties. I said I knew Stan did very well too. Mrs. Allen said she was really surprised that Karen had it in her. But she added Karen still isn't doing well in science, she barely passed. Karen's face fell. Stan beamed. Lisa said she wanted to go to the bathroom. I said that it seemed hard for the family to share Karen's success, everyone was saying, "hey, look at me." It was hard to allow Karen her moment. Karen said, "Yeah," quietly. Mrs. Allen said, "I'm just as guilty of this as the kids are." I said whenever we got together as a family group, I could really understand the pressure she felt from three children all competing for her attention. She said it was terrible, she didn't know who to hear first, and Karen as the oldest probably got the least.

Karen said, "Yeah," louder this time. Stan said, "Ma, you don't listen to me so good either; you haven't let me go to the Cub Scouts and I do well in school and everything." I said it's tough for all of them, with Mr. Allen sick, and mommy is having a tough time listening to everyone. Karen said, "I listen to her and help her." I said I knew she did. Mrs. Allen agreed. I said I would like to listen to Mrs. Allen for Karen and then Karen could be freer to study and have fun, and maybe then Mrs. Allen could hear Stan and Lisa's requests better too. Mrs. Allen said she would really like that. . . . Karen said, "And I could go to the community center!"

The worker became Mrs. Allen's ally and gave her a place of her own for support. Mrs. Allen was able to look at how she viewed Karen (like herself) and did over time separate who Karen was from who she is. She also began to work on feeling better about herself and "getting off Karen's back" both in terms of depending on her and "putting her down." She was able to allow Karen to join the youth group she so wanted to join, and to let Stan join the Scouts, and to send Lisa to nursery school. This meant much to each child, and greatly eased family tensions and the intense rivalry that prevailed as each had a special place to shine outside of the family. The family was also encouraged to reach out to the extended family and other parts of their social network for help in staying home with Mr. Allen.

In her individual sessions, Mrs. Allen then moved into serious discussion of her marriage. She had no interest in separation but expected a lot more from Mr. Allen than he could ever give. Work was centered on giving to herself and developing her own talents and interests. She enrolled in a sewing course and was proud of the clothing she made herself and the children. The worker made contact with Mr. Allen's therapist, who agreed to hold several joint sessions with Mr. and Mrs. Allen and to see Mrs. Allen alone for a few sessions, around strategies of coping with Mr. Allen's illness. Mr. Allen had been improving somewhat and was worried about Mrs. Allen and the children. These joint sessions proved fruitful for both Mr. and Mrs. Allen.

Ultimately, the whole family benefited from this family-oriented approach. Karen was now free to enjoy her own growth and not fear it; she applied herself to school and returned to her earlier good functioning with some needed recognition of her abilities and worth by the family. While there was no major change in the family—the father remained quite ill—the family was helped to cope with its predicament in a more adaptive way. The children were freed to be children to a significant extent.

Once again, we see the worker using a holistic approach, relating to and encouraging the expression of feelings in each family member, helping the mother to respond to the children's feelings and requests so they could feel their impact, and at the same time helping the children to see that grown-ups, even mothers, have feelings too, thus promoting interpersonal and intrapersonal coping. The worker also helped family members to find areas of life outside of the family where they could enjoy success and build upon that success (Maluccio, 1979b). Reliance upon other people in the family's social network was encouraged (Swenson, Chapter 6 in this volume). In addition, as Karen was moved from the position of being "the problem" and the crisis of the father's illness was put into perspective, she was able once again to perform well at school. As her good abilities were reflected upon in individual and family sessions, her competence in the academic area and her self-confidence greatly increased. With this approach, a more competent family, not only a more competent child, evolved.[6]

Conclusion

We have looked at theoretical and practice approaches to promoting coping in children and youth, at play, at school, and in the family.[7] Several practice principles were highlighted and applied. We met children in their own life space and on their own terms. We moved into the child's world, appreciating the types of relational systems the child is engaged in and providing help in the one-to-one, family, small group, and larger systems.

As this chapter has shown, in work with children and youth a fundamental approach is to mediate in and between significant systems, helping the child and each relevant system reach out to each other (Schwartz, 1971). Environmental restructuring as well as direct practice skills are used. Opportunities for successful mastery are provided. Activities are chosen with progressive ends in mind. Feelings are considered of prime importance and their expression is encouraged. Structure and limits are also employed to promote interpersonal competence. The ecological perspective provides the overall framework, while interactionism provides the skills and ego psychology the basis for promoting coping and ultimately the acquisition of competence in children and youth.

Yet, a chapter on promoting competence in children and youth should not end without a further word about the societal context in which all our living and practicing take place. The ecological perspective with its competence-promoting thrust is a positive and highly appropriate approach to the child in his or her world. But the overall world context is one in which many children are hungry, unclothed, and unvalued, living on the edge of political-social turmoil. The tensions of the nuclear age, our computerized society, and the "new age of narcissism" form a stark backdrop for the coping efforts of children and families. The level of stress is well above optimal. Classist, racist, and sexist attitudes are still hallmarks of our times. The practice illustrations used reveal this clearly.

The profession of social work has responsibility to move into these larger spheres toward economic, social, and political change that guarantees that basic needs are met in more than the current minimal and begrudging manner. Many children who live on public assistance in our country live on bare subsistence levels. We also need to promote competence in the institutional structures of our society so that its ways of meeting the needs of its newcomers and the shapers of its future— its children—can be on a more adequate level. If we can meet generously our children's physical and psychosocial needs, we lay the foundations for their competent acts to take a positive direction for the future of us all. Competence in itself is important, but the directions that competent people take are equally important to emphasize. One can be competently destructive if that is in tune with the spirit of the times. Social workers have a responsibility to examine and have an impact on the times in which we live. We need to help our children pursue those values which lead to a world where each person's basic needs are well met and stress is at a manageable level.

Notes

1. See Maluccio (1974) for more extensive consideration of the use of action to promote competence.
2. Focusing on psychiatric patients, Goldstein (Chapter 13 in this volume) also stresses the importance of using the resources of families and improving their environments to enhance their competence.

3. See Swenson (Chapter 6 in this volume) for extensive analysis of social networks and natural helping systems in social work practice.
4. For further discussion of environmental modification, refer to Grinnell, Kyte, and Bostwick (Chapter 7 in this volume.)
5. The author wishes to thank Cara Hofer, Susan Siegeltuch, and Catherine T. Bush, who provided examples of working with school groups.
6. For further discussion of the life model as related to helping families see Maluccio (in press).
7. See Oxley (Chapter 12 in this volume) for another perspective on practice with children as "involuntary" clients.

CHAPTER 11

The Aging Process: Old and New Coping Tricks

Mary Frances Libassi
Nathalie S. Turner

Human beings who make up the aging segment of our population have long been neglected. Aging is viewed as a time of decline and the aging client as one who is beginning to fail. Not enough emphasis is placed on aging as a developmental stage with its own unique life tasks requiring new coping strategies. Not enough attention is paid to the often heroic efforts of elderly people to cope with and adapt to situations of multiple losses and environmental deprivation.

Focusing on the possibilities and the problems of aging as a life stage, in this chapter we present and illustrate an ecological approach to social work intervention with older persons that is designed to promote their competence. Our key notion is that aging people are capable of competence when prerequisite conditions are available to them at the personal as well as environmental levels.

Myths and Stereotypes of Aging

Some of the obstacles to competence development in older persons are reflected in the myths and stereotypes about aging which prevail in our society and contribute to our pessimistic notions about old age and the usefulness of social and mental health services for this segment of our population. The elderly are not generally viewed as having potential for change and growth. Consequently, they make up only a small portion of those being seen by social service agencies and mental health facilities. Cohen (1976) reports that less than 4 percent of clients seen in private psychiatric practice or in community mental health centers are over 65 even though 10 percent of our population are in this age bracket and have a higher incidence of mental health problems than any other group. The myths and stereotypes also affect the types of services provided. Some of the stereotypes are held with such firmness among our service providers that symptoms presented by older people are often neglected and untreated: They are assumed to be the inevitable concomitant of old age, a result of the aging process itself.

Let us examine several of these myths, in order to clarify attitudes toward the older population and foster a sounder approach for social work intervention.

The Myth of Senility

On a visit to a long-term care facility, the social work consultant heard the shouts of Mrs. Janus through the halls. When asked what the problem was, the nurses responded, "Don't pay any attention. She's only senile." When the shouts occurred again, the social worker went to Mrs. Janus, took both her hands, leaned over and looked her in the eyes, and began a conversation, fully expecting a lack of orientation to time or place. Instead, Mrs. Janus responded quite coherently with full understanding of who and where she was and considerable ability to engage in conversation with the worker. Her major problem appeared to be loneliness rather than senility.

In this practice example, an elderly woman with problematic behavior was dismissed as senile and therefore did not receive the therapeutic attention she needed. Senility, although not an actual medical term, has come to be used by both practitioners and laymen to cover a variety of conditions and behaviors among old people, such as mild to severe forgetfulness, mental disorientation, depression, and grief. These conditions may be viewed as chronic and untreatable. There are problems of brain disease among the elderly which cause mental disorders, but these disorders vary in intensity and severity and in treatability and untreatability. All must be viewed as discrete conditions that call for proper study, assessment, and a variety of interventive strategies (Butler, 1977).

The Myth of Chronological Age

Discussion of senility leads to a second myth, that one's chronological age is an absolute clue to physical, intellectual, social, and emotional functioning. It is surprising how people of the same age will be viewed and treated as though they are similar, despite the fact that research has shown a greater range of differences among elderly people than any other group. This myth, much like that of senility, causes us to view the aged as a homogeneous group rather than individualizing them in terms of problems as well as capabilities.

The Myth of Resistance to Change

Another myth that directly affects our attitudes toward the viability of mental health intervention with the elderly is the notion that the elderly are rigid and resistant to change. Such attitudes are in direct opposition to our notion of growth and development over the life cycle, as formulated in theories of ego psychology. However, this myth continues to prevail in many sectors, contributing to insufficient concern and commitment on the part of social service and mental health personnel toward serving the elderly.

The Myth of Disengagement

Finally, the myth arising from the theory of disengagement (Cumming and Henry, 1961) has contributed to our inability to view the elderly as capable of and responsive to action within their environment. This theory postulates that psychological well-being for the older person is characterized by withdrawal of both the individual and society from each other. Such mutual withdrawal is seen as a normal part of the aging process (Butler, 1977). The elderly are considered passive and dependent, no longer searching for ways to have an active impact upon their environment. They are viewed as withdrawing from social interaction and social roles in order to prepare themselves for the approach of death. Although these ideas have been somewhat dispelled by gerontological research, they continue to influence service approaches.

In summary, myths and stereotypes contribute to our pessimistic notions about old age, and these, in turn, shape social work practice. Particularly affected are our efforts to work with the elderly in developing new coping skills or in mobilizing old skills in the service of adaptation to the myriad life changes involved in the everyday life experience of aging. Practice with the elderly population is most often in the form of services to and for them. These stereotypic attitudes, combined with our traditional social work preoccupation with pathology and disease, have resulted in a negative orientation to the elderly and little confidence in them as individuals with potential for growth and change. Furthermore, these attitudes may serve as reference points from which the elderly evaluate themselves (Mechanic, 1976).

Competence and the Elderly: A Theoretical Base

In recent years, new theoretical approaches, grounded in research, have been emerging which lead us to question our commonly held notions about the elderly as well as our practice approaches to this segment of our population. The major sources are ego psychology, environmental psychology, and gerontology. These theoretical perspectives support a more optimistic view of the aging process and an expanded understanding of the growth potentials of older persons.

Studies of Normal Aging

Several ambitious investigations have focused on the aging process. Notable among these is the study of human aging done by an interdisciplinary team under the sponsorship of the National Institute of Mental Health (NIMH) (Birren et al., 1971; Granick and Patterson, 1971). Whereas most previous studies have been with institutionalized and incapacitated elderly, this one involved medically healthy, community-dwelling persons who were selected to maximize the opportunity of studying the effects of chronological aging itself and minimize the effects of illness, institutionalization, and social adversity (Butler, 1975). The research results having particular implications for social work intervention are summarized below.

1. Many of the attributes, such as senility, frequently attributed to the aging process reflect instead physical illness, personality factors, or the impact of social–cultural conditions.

2. In the absence of disease, persons with a mean age of 71 compared favorably with a younger population in intellectual functioning. Decline in intellectual functioning was found to be a result of specific diseases rather than the process of aging itself.

3. The healthy elderly are capable of psychological flexibility as well as new growth and development in old age. For instance, some of the subjects in this study clearly experienced aging as a time of opportunity for venturing into new careers and new successes.

4. There is a slowing in the speed of response in the elderly which affects cognitive processing. This seems to be a general characteristic of all elderly.

Old Age as a Developmental Stage

Erik Erikson (1959) describes old age as a part of the normal life cycle with its own unique, phase-specific task: the development of a sense of integrity, a basic acceptance of one's life as having been inevitable, appropriate, and meaningful. Other psychologists (e.g., Peck, 1972) have expanded this notion beyond a passive acceptance of one's life to active attempts to make life more secure, meaningful, or satisfying:

> The "successful ager" at this final stage would be the person who is purposefully active as an ego-transcending perpetuation of that culture which, more than anything else, differentiates human living from animal living. Such a person would be experiencing a vital, gratifying absorption in the future. He would be doing all he could to make it a good world for his family or cultural descendants. [Peck, 1972:91]

Similarly, Butler (1975) emphasizes the continuing possibilities in the lives of older people, further modifying the passive view of life posed by Erikson. Older people continue the desire to have an impact upon life. Their drive toward effectance (White, 1959) is as strong as ever, although it may be expressed in different ways than among younger persons.

In short, the elderly have the capacity for continued development as well as for adaptation and coping as they go through another transition in the life cycle.[1] Indeed, some aged persons demonstrate tremendous coping skills even while in living situations characterized by personal and environmental obstacles. As Lawton (1974) shows through his extensive research, the elderly population *is capable* of acquiring new information and learning new problem-solving skills to add to their lifelong repertoire and to help them in negotiating the unique adaptational tasks of aging.

Threats to Satisfying Aging

While old age has the potential for being an interesting and emotionally satisfying time of life, it also is a time when there are many forces posing threats to the person. Two major ideas agreed upon by the elderly and professionals alike are: (1) the process of aging is inextricably linked to change, change which almost always involves loss; and (2) the elderly are significantly affected by their environments while at the same time having less and less control over them (Schwartz, 1974).

The Impact of Loss.   The elderly are potentially subject to both natural losses as well as culturally determined and situational losses. Natural losses are those associated with physiological changes such as problems in vision, hearing, body image, etc. The number and intensity varies from individual to individual but every older person experiences some loss of the natural kind. Circumstantial losses include death of spouse and friends and losing familiar social network and economic security. These losses reduce the older person's options; the aging person will feel less and less able to cope with his environment and to be effective within it. Self-esteem declines to seriously low levels (Schwartz, 1974).

In short, aging is a time of change frequently associated with multiple loss. Such loss and change have the potential for causing a downward spiral in one's sense of competence and self-esteem which may bring on deterioration, both psychological and physical, and may in fact contribute to increased death rate (Birren et al., 1971).

The Impact of Environment.   Lawton (1974) states that the greater the overall deprivation of the aged person, the more he or she is subject to and affected by environmental forces. In formulating the "environmental docility hypothesis," Lawton (1974) also notes that the less competent the individual is in terms of personal disability or deprived status, the more susceptible is his behavior to the influence of immediate environmental situations. Various investigations bear out this strong correlation between environmental deprivation and a downward spiral in functioning (cf. Birren et al., 1971).

But the environment also contains a therapeutic potential. The previously mentioned NIMH studies uncovered examples of the positive influence of supportive environments (Birren et al., 1971; Granick and Patterson, 1971). For instance, some older people were found living independently within the community even though psychological tests indicated that they had cognitive detriments so severe that without environmental supports institutionalization might have been the only choice.

We have highlighted two related streams of thought with respect to promoting competence in clients:

1. Research and developmental theory support the notion that continued competence is possible among the elderly population. The older person possesses the same innate capacity as other age groups for adaptation to an average expectable environment (Hartmann, 1958).

2. Many older persons do not have average expectable environments because of rapid and cumulative changes and losses, both natural and circumstantial, which threaten their adaptation and coping.

Adaptation and coping are transactional concepts that can be understood only by simultaneous attention to the interface of person–environment. This premise leads us toward an ecological conceptual

base for planning social work intervention that provides the prerequisite and environmental conditions for effective functioning in aged persons.

An Ecological Model for Social Work Intervention

Social work practice with and on behalf of the elderly should in our
view be based on a model that stresses intervention with both person
and environment. Such a model is provided by the ecological perspective on social work (Germain, 1979; Germain and Gitterman, 1979),
which takes into account the complexities of the environment and its
effects on people in more dynamic ways than was previously possible.
These ideas complement and deepen our respect for the complexities of
people. People are not viewed as static and passive victims of environment on the one hand or hapless and helpless responders to internal
drives and needs on the other. Person and milieu are considered a
transactional unit in which each part affects the other.

An ecological model includes interventive strategies that promote
competence by working directly with individuals to strengthen their
coping skills. In addition, it includes interventive strategies that modify
the environment so as to make it more supportive of the adaptive potential of individuals.[2] The focus of attention is the total transactional
unit of person–environment. Intervention proceeds through: (1) providing prerequisite conditions in the environment; (2) providing prerequisite conditions in the individual; and (3) focusing on the interface
between person and environment.

Providing Prerequisite Conditions in the Environment

Competent functioning is fostered when the individual lives in an
environment that is both nurturing and challenging. Since old age is
characterized by change and losses, the environment of elderly persons
must be prosthetic; it must compensate for the deficits associated with
the losses that they experience. For example, eye glasses compensate
for the loss of visual acuity and in most cases restore adequate visual
functioning (Schwartz, 1974). The notion of compensatory intervention
may be extended to include prosthetic mechanisms which change the
physical, social, economic, vocational, and psychological environment
of the elderly. The key task is to tease out the proper level of compensatory intervention which prolongs competence without destroying initiative.

In addition, the environment should be mildly challenging. The
ecological theory of aging posits that the individual is operating at his

best when the environmental press is moderately stimulating. If the environment offers too little challenge, the individual adapts by becoming lethargic and thus operates below capacity (Nahemow and Lawton, 1976).

Intervention that provides environmental prerequisites is particularly important in working with the elderly because of the impact of multiple losses and stressful environments. Environmental restructuring helps to create the "average expectable environment" (Hartmann, 1958) which can set in motion natural adaptive processes in the person and thereby mobilize opportunities for growth and competence (Maluccio, 1979b). An expanded repertoire of environmental strategies therefore is essential in work with this client population.

Providing Prerequisite Conditions in the Individual

Competent functioning also requires that the individual have adequate information about the problems being faced. It requires that older persons have capabilities and skills to deal with the problematic demands of their life situation. It requires that they maintain satisfactory internal states including a modicum of self-esteem and some control over anxiety and other paralyzing affects. Finally, the older person must have a measure of autonomy with sufficient time and space to deal adequately with stressful situations.

Intervention at the Interface between the Person and the Environment

As reviewed by Maluccio (Chapter 1 in this volume), the ecological perspective stresses that successful coping requires mutuality of fit between people's adaptive capabilities and the environment's qualities and demands. Social work intervention therefore occurs at the interface of this dynamic transactional unit. Its purpose is to enhance the adaptive capacity of the individual while simultaneously modifying environments so that they become more supportive of the elderly person's efforts to cope.

The diagram in Figure 11–1 shows how interventions intersect at the person–environment transactional unit. It specifies some of the prerequisite conditions at the individual as well as the environmental levels associated with promoting competence in elderly clients.[3]

The intersecting circles reflect our theoretical perspective and practice experiences with older persons: The helping process usually involves the social worker and client in multiple activities related to both individual and environment. The dual, simultaneous focus on person

FIGURE 11-1.   Intervention in the person–environment transactional unit.

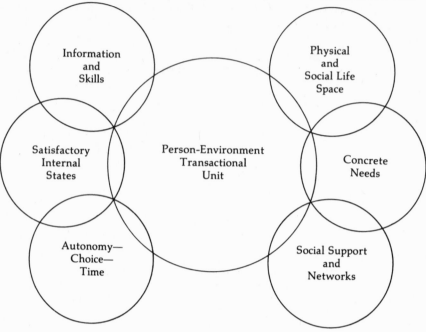

and environment is the essence of ecologically oriented practice with older persons—as with other client populations.

Practice Applications

The vignettes and discussion that follow illustrate how the ecological approach may be applied to practice with older persons. While the dual focus on person and environment is evident in these vignettes, for conceptual clarity we shall discuss separately intervention aimed at the environmental and individual levels.

Providing Prerequisite Conditions at the Environmental Level

The range and variety of interventive strategies that provide the prerequisite environmental conditions associated with the promotion of competence are numerous. In this section, we will concentrate on three major ones: (1) restructuring physical and social life space; (2) meeting concrete needs; and (3) facilitating social networks. Several variations of these activities will be presented. In some, the worker is the major actor or doer in creating prosthetic environments. In others, the clients themselves bring about changes in their own environments with little or no assistance from the worker. In still others, the worker and the client may work together to bring about environmental changes. Such variations in worker–client roles and activities characterize social work with the elderly as with other clients. The elderly are encouraged to participate in the helping process to the fullest extent possible.

Restructuring Physical and Social Life Space.   In order to promote and maintain competence among the elderly, restructuring life-space situations is often necessary because of physical changes, social losses, and environmental deprivation. As Germain (Chapter 5 in this volume) has indicated, the physical environment is particularly significant.

Mrs. Jackson had been hospitalized for amputation of her right leg just below the knee. During hospitalization she had learned how to use her wheelchair, and the discharge planning team suggested that she go to a nursing home for a period of time until her stump had healed and she could be fitted for an artificial limb. Mrs. Jackson refused and finally convinced the planning team that if they could get her and her wheelchair to her third-floor apartment, they would not need to worry about her since she had good friends and could manage. Reluctantly, the discharge planning team agreed to this.

A few days later the social worker called on Mrs. Jackson and found her wheeling around on a little stool with wheels cleaning out her cupboards. As she said, "I want to be able to keep my house like I always have." She had enlisted the assistance of a teenager in the neighborhood who built her the little stool on wheels. She then learned to manipulate herself from her wheelchair to the stool and from the stool to the wheelchair. She seemed to be managing very well and was in fine spirits. When the worker reported this back to the team, she concluded that she expected that Mrs. Jackson would soon discover a way of cleaning out her upper cupboards.

This vignette illustrates creative restructuring of physical life space by one aged client. It emphasizes that our stereotypic view of the elderly as dependent, passive, and incapable of taking action on their own behalf needs to be rethought. The environmental docility hypothesis (Lawton, 1974) cannot be generalized to the entire population. The elderly are capable of making changes, on their own, in their living environments for better adaptation and fit. Such client activity is not only a means for restructuring environments to facilitate coping but may also have "therapeutic value" because it enhances self esteem, competence, and mastery. A major task of the social worker is to support and encourage such independent coping (Maluccio, 1974).

There are other more subtle ways in which people restructure their life space. In institutional settings where privacy and space are scarce resources, individuals often stake out particular spots or chairs for themselves. Frequently these actions have high adaptive value; for example, people hear better, see better, and avoid noise and bright light. One of the ways in which people use space as an adaptive strategy is illustrated by the following:

Mr. Davis, a 95-year-old gentleman in a nursing home, was unable to communicate verbally because of a stroke which left him aphasic. Efforts by staff members to have him intermingle with other patients as a way of keeping him from withdrawing had the opposite effect. When in close proximity to other patients, he withdrew completely, refused to look at them, and would slump in his chair. However, it was noted that when he could observe others from a distance, Mr. Davis was much more attentive and seemed to be absorbing a great deal from his environment. He sat very erect and watched others closely. One can imagine that his condition caused him embarrassment when he felt forced to communicate and that his preferred arrangement of space allowed him a modicum of control over his life.

Restructuring life space sometimes requires joint client–worker activity. As seen in the next example, problems in life-space environments can provide opportunities for client and worker to engage together in tasks which bring about necessary changes and also enhance competence (Maluccio, 1979b). Life itself can be an arena where significant change and growth take place (Maluccio, 1979b). In this illustration the task of the worker is not only to support and encourage but also to facilitate client action by providing information and support enabling the clients themselves to restructure a stressful situation.

A group of senior center members were discussing the latest in a series of events indicating that the security patrol in their low-cost housing project would not be refunded. Some were angry, others fearful. They recounted many of the crimes that had been committed against them before the security patrol had been there. The social worker had been listening and recognized that this was a serious crisis for them. She asked what they wanted to do about it. Responses varied; some wanted to do nothing, while others suggested storming the mayor's office.

A process ensued that consisted of four phases. The senior center members prepared a petition to the mayor. This was typed by the worker and returned to them to collect signatures from other residents. The second phase consisted of daily meetings to draw up systematic plans for getting the mayor, city councilmen, and police to attend an open meeting. TV and other media coverage was obtained.

As the day of the meeting with the mayor approached, some people began to have qualms about talking in public. In the third phase, people wrote up speeches which were rehearsed. Role-plays were enacted to anticipate as many contingencies as possible. The fourth and final phase involved carrying out the event itself. Two large buses were required to take seventy or so persons to city hall. According to the worker, canes and walkers were necessary for many of these people but did not detract from their energy nor their success in convincing their audience, which contained many local dignitaries, that funds must be budgeted for security in the area.

Social work practice with older, sicker, and terminally ill people requires the same attention to building competence but within a narrowed life space. Special attention must be paid to selected aspects of aging, such as intellectual impairment and losses of sight and hearing. All of these may impede communication. People's competence in communicating in spite of these handicaps can be enhanced by making minor conpensatory changes in the environment that do not require the active participation of the client. Older people's ability to communicate despite severe disability has been noted when professionals allow more time for responses and when spatial arrangements are used so that eye contact and proximity are maintained. Touching and eye messages can help people feel in contact, respected and understood. So-called noisy clients in institutional settings have responded dramatically to a milieu where all staff take time to call the person by name, put a comforting hand on his or her shoulder, and say a few words in passing. While we cannot fully know the inner states of such people, one can imagine a desperate need to communicate and remind others of their existence.

The notion of prosthetic environments to compensate for physical, mental, and psychological handicaps can be further expanded in a variety of ways. Just as nursery schools need furniture, bathroom fixtures, water faucets and doorknobs particularly adapted to children, should we not also assume that older people with physical deficits need furniture and other special arrangements to compensate for their age-related problems? People with mental and intellectual problems associated with aging can be assisted to stay in touch with their environments by the use of large calendars, clocks, color-coded doors, and name plates in large print at eye height. Environmental interventions such as these extend older people's capacity to do for themselves, thereby promoting a sense of competence, even among the severely ill.

Mrs. Baymon, an 85-year-old bedridden nursing home patient, occasionally awoke during the night in a state of extreme agitation, which at first was dismissed as having been due to bad dreams. The attending nurse soothed Mrs. Baymon and turned on the night light for her. But Mrs. Baymon complained that this made her feel like a baby, and besides it kept her from going to sleep again.

A geriatric physician then noted that perhaps the agitation, whether or not stimulated by bad dreams, might involve disorientation. He suggested that the bed light be placed closer to the patient's bed, where she could turn it on or off, and that photographs of her family be placed near enough for her to touch them. These very minor alterations in Mrs. Baymon's milieu had two effects: Simply being able to manage this small area of her life in an active way enhanced Mrs. Baymon's self-image and reduced to some extent her dependency on others.

Psychosocial handicaps are frequently exacerbated by inattention to physical environments. This is true not only within the institutional setting but also within the community. Without proper attention to environments, the capacity of the elderly person to maintain social contact may be greatly diminished. Access to transportation, ramps, and walking areas free from curbs and other dangers can compensate for disabilities. By removing minor barriers to mobility, the social life of the older person will be enriched, thus positively affecting his or her psychological state.

Meeting Concrete Needs.   There are many instances when older persons must cope with completely new physical environments, as when they are forced to live on reduced incomes and move to public low-cost housing. In addition to incurring loss of familiar neighborhoods and old friendship ties, they face the simultaneous task of coping with strange and often hostile living situations. The prevalence of crimes against the elderly in low- and middle-income housing is well documented, and in many cases the elderly have to take extreme precautions to avoid muggings, assaults, and even rape. One man in such a project kept a loaded rifle by his side at all times; others have as many as five locks of various kinds on their doors.

Mrs. Allen had moved to a low-income housing project about two years previously. She brought with her a pet cat. Whereas in her old middle-class neighborhood she had been able to walk the cat for exercise, in the project the muggings and assaults frightened her. She stayed inside as much as

possible and allowed the cat to roam. Within two years the cat had produced several litters of kittens which were at various stages of growth, some
now producing litters themselves. They were literally swarming over the
small apartment as well as the neighborhood. Many complaints were lodged
against Mrs. Allen to which she did not respond. She was shunned by other
residents who considered her bizarre and was threatened with eviction.

Follow-up by a social worker revealed that Mrs. Allen was overwhelmed by the cats and wanted to get rid of all but the original one.
However, she was arthritic and was unable to catch them since they were
almost wild, hiding beneath the bathtub and in other hard-to-reach places.
Mrs. Allen's arms and hands were covered with scratches. The social worker
then enlisted the assistance of the project manager and together they col-
lected eighteen cats and took them to the local animal shelter. Mrs. Allen's
original cat was spayed and returned to her. Her chaotic living situation
soon improved radically and she was able to do her housework. Moreover,
her neighbors gradually began to take an interest in her.

Providing a concrete service can set in motion a positive spiraling
process which, as in the above case, can help the client to regain self-
esteem and ability to practice old competencies. Many such examples
from practice with older people are available to support the use of
concrete activities on the part of the social worker as a means of providing prerequisite conditions conducive to increasing the person's capacity to cope. However, as shown in the following vignette, not all
concrete needs are as obvious.

Mrs. King was a very obese lady with diabetes. Her doctor had prescribed a
diet for her several months earlier but she was not following it and had not
lost weight. A social worker who had been visiting her at the suggestion of
the doctor became aware that Mrs. King could not write anything but her
name. The worker immediately suspected that she was also unable to read.
In discussing this with her, the worker realized that she was greatly embarrassed by her inability to read or write.

Following further sessions, Mrs. King agreed to have the worker cut out
pictures of the foods she was allowed to eat and those that she was not.
These were posted on cardboard and attached to her refrigerator. This small
concrete service assisted Mrs. King to stick to her diet; over the next four
months, she lost thirty pounds.

Sometimes providing a concrete service can serve several purposes
and have unexpected but desirable consequences.

Social workers placed within a low-income housing project discovered that
one of the major problems for the elderly was dingy and drab apartments,

many of which had not been painted for twenty years. Exploration with the housing authority revealed that painting was only done when a change of tenants occurred. The elderly moved infrequently and therefore were ineligible for painting services. It was further discovered that there were many young people within the same housing project without jobs. The elderly feared these young people as the perpetrators of muggings and robbery. Mobilization of a number of public and private agencies produced money to pay workers to paint the apartment as well as the promise of paint and supplies from the housing authority. A youth agency was approached to bargain with the young people around contracting for the jobs. The young people were delighted, and with much support from the social workers painted the apartments of a number of residents. The physical environment of the elderly was greatly improved through this concrete service. However, an unexpected consequence was the development of a new relationship between the elderly and the young people, which made the elderly feel more secure in their living environment.

Facilitating Social Networks.   Swenson (Chapter 6 in this volume) has carefully examined the role of social networks and natural helping systems in people's functioning. For the elderly, one of the most deleterious experiences is the loss of meaningful relationships. Many aged persons are widowed and live out their days alone. In addition, their network of friends usually diminishes. This is a loss that has direct relationship to psychological and emotional well being, as discussed in research studies presented earlier in this chapter. Therefore, an important activity in environmental intervention is to find or construct supportive social networks. Worker activity is often paramount, especially among the older elderly, because many of them are fearful and apprehensive about moving out into a new social world. The following example shows how a small network was developed within a housing project for the elderly.

The social worker first made contact with all the residents of the targeted housing unit. The aim was to get acquainted with each one and to find out some of their individual concerns and interests. The information gathered in the initial visits was used by the worker to link people together in meaningful ways around mutual interest and need. For example, the worker discovered that several of the apartment dwellers were avid readers. They preferred reading to television. The worker brought magazines to each of them and then asked if they would exchange their magazines with each other when they were finished. There were two women living within the same building who had never talked before. Several days later, it was gratifying for the worker to see these same women standing outside conversing.

The worker discovered that two other women were avid plant enthusiasts. She shared this information with each of them and suggested that they might share clippings from the various plants. In addition, in other cases, the worker attempted to enlarge the elderly's concern for each other by sharing information. For instance, the worker would say, "Mrs. Jones is not feeling very well this week. Her arthritis has really got her down. I know she could use some cheering up. Why don't you give her a call?" Gradually, the mutual concern and interest grew within the residents themselves until they were, indeed, forming an informal support group.

This attempt to build social networks is an example of planful worker activity to intervene in environments of older people to reduce loneliness associated with the losses of old age.

Thus far, we have presented examples of interventive activities primarily aimed at changing environments. These activities are only suggestive of the range of possibilities for social work practice that shape an environment which promotes competence. Others are delineated by Grinnell, Kyte, and Bostwick (Chapter 7 in this volume) in their discussion of environmental modification. We now turn our attention to interventions that illustrate providing prerequisite conditions focused on the individual within the transactional unit.

Providing Prerequisite Conditions at the Individual Level

White's (1974) views on how competence is acquired as people face novel and unfamiliar situations are particularly useful with respect to the aged. White postulates that human beings share with all animals the need to have adequate information about the self and environment; they also need to maintain satisfactory physiological and psychological states and to have a measure of autonomy, that is, options and choices. And they need time for scanning, processing, and testing the environment and their relationship to it.

These are ideal conditions for optimal problem-solving and competence that are frequently lacking in the real-life situation of the elderly. Changes and losses tend to come in unremitting doses and to put the older person at a disadvantage in maintaining satisfactory internal conditions, securing adequate information or having options and choices.

Satisfactory Internal States. Satisfactory internal states require that people have some minimal freedom from physical and emotional pain that drains energy necessary for developing competence. Working with —and advocating for—clients with professionals from other disciplines is frequently necessary in order to ensure that older people receive the best medical treatment based on up-to-date knowledge in the field of geriatrics.

In addition, social work intervention directly with the elderly is required in order that they become aware of medical technology and are supplied with the means to take advantage of it. Also, it takes a practitioner sensitive to the needs and problems of older clients to help them explore and work through doubts and fears about changing from familiar ways of doing things to unknown ones, such as changing doctors or medication. The use of occupational or physical therapy or of prosthetic services such as hearing aids and wheelchairs can stir up anxiety if these affect the self-image of the older person.

Mrs. Delano, in her 60s, had become virtually a recluse during the last years of her marriage. When her husband died, she faced the dual problem of adapting to his being gone and maintaining her independence. The social worker from the neighborhood community center called on her a few days after her husband's death. She listened to Mrs. Delano's expressions of grief and helplessness over several weeks.

When it appeared that Mrs. Delano had begun to consider ways to pick up the pieces of her life and go on, the worker encouraged her to get out and meet people. Mrs. Delano was finally able to confide that, due to a prolapsed abdomen which hung in folds to her knees, she had stopped going out years ago; partly because it was impossible for her to use public transportation and partly because she felt grossly unattractive.

After considerable effort, the worker located a physician willing to examine Mrs. Delano in her home. The physician recommended surgery to correct the condition. Several more weeks of visits were needed for Mrs. Delano to work out questions and fears she had about the operation. Finally, her wish to improve her own body image and her determination to remain independent prevailed and she agreed to the operation.

In addition to showing the need for worker attention to the physical bases of a client's social withdrawal, the above example underscores a common reaction that the elderly have to changes in their physical appearance that represent assaults to their self-concept. It also suggests that clients should not be assumed to be deficient because they have problems in coping with difficult environments. The rapid changes taking place within and without the person often cause temporary inability to make functional adaptation. The level and quality of the individual's competence should be assessed and clarified (Maluccio, Chapter 1 in this volume).

The client–worker relationship is crucial in helping clients maintain self-esteem as they seek to cope with these difficulties. The relationship offers a means of providing psychological support but requires that workers be knowledgeable in the substantive area of aging and have a broad repertoire of helping approaches and skills.

There are some special dynamics to consider with respect to the professional relationship in working with older clients. The elderly person will frequently see the worker as a friend, teacher, or a mature older son or daughter and tend to respond more comfortable in relationships which reduce social distance and the authority of the worker. Contacts are characterized by informality, having tea or lunch in the client's home, taking walks and rides, or sharing mutual interests such as hobbies. The following example illustrates some of these points. First, a worker writes:

I found that my client, Mrs. Peters, treated me more like a daughter than like her caseworker. She chastized me one day for not wearing my boots! At other times she inquired about my personal life—advised me to get married soon before the eligible bachelors were "scooped up," etc. At first this bothered me. I wondered if this was resistance to being dependent on me. When she said one day that she had always wished for a daughter who would be company in her old age and help her with things she couldn't do herself, it occurred to me that this positive identification somehow helped her to rely on me for her real needs.

This worker showed sensitive appreciation of Mrs. Peter's need for a more mutual relationship with her. The example also suggests that starting where the client is, eliciting client participation, and supporting client self-determination are as essential for effective practice with the elderly as they are with younger populations. The worker coming with her own agenda, no matter how well intended, will not be perceived by the older client as helpful. When people are uncertain about their usefulness and worth, being pulled or pushed or even gently coaxed against their grain will reinforce a sense of helplessness. Under such circumstances some clients may continue to use social work services in spite of lowered self-esteem because they must obtain concrete services for survival. Others will drop out. More resilient older persons may take matters into their own hands.

Miss Brown, an 82-year-old unmarried woman, dropped into a family service agency requesting help in locating some proof of ownership of a burial plot she purchased several years ago in a cemetery close to a neighborhood she had lived in most of her life. She cried softly as she described her efforts to deal with cemetery officials, who reported that they had no record of this transaction. A young worker, while responding sympathetically to Miss Brown's feelings, ignored the overt content of the client's message and tried to get at her underlying fear of death.

Miss Brown responded to the worker's gentle probings over several contacts by sharing her personal philosophy of life and death and relating humorous anecdotes about funerals of friends she had attended; but she did not change her original request for help in finding her burial plot. Finally, in an exasperated tone, she said, "Young lady, you ask me how you can help but all we do is talk about how I feel about dying. I'm not scared of dying, not anymore, I'm just plain mad that something that belongs to me, that I planned a long time for, people are now saying isn't mine. I don't have any choice over whether I die or not, but I do want a choice as to where I'm buried."

This vignette illustrates the importance of starting where the client is. It also highlights two commonly held stereotypic assumptions: that elderly people are preoccupied with thoughts and fears of death and that changing the client's feelings will automatically result in some desired alteration in behavior. As White (1974) indicates, paying attention to what people can do or can be encouraged to do is as important as how they feel, since the successful completion of a task that has been causing doubt and anxiety reinforces self-esteem and builds competence.

When the worker understood that Miss Brown's depression was related to underlying feelings of anger at her helplessness in maintaining control over her current life and her future, she began to plan how together they could find out where her burial plot was. They made an excursion to the cemetery, talked with the caretaker, and finally prevailed upon an official to recheck the files. The deed, which had been misfiled, was located. During the two weeks that this process took place, Miss Brown became energized and often laughingly commented about herself and the worker being Sherlock Holmes and Watson, in that order.

Another strategy for maintaining satisfactory internal states in older people is the use of the life review process (Butler, 1974) or the process of reminiscence, which encourages older people to integrate their present and past experiences in anticipation of the future. This is what Butler (1975) calls acquiring a sense of completion, a conviction that one's life cycle, despite ups and downs, is worthwhile. This kind of integration and sense of completion is congruent with Erikson's (1959) concept that the task of aging is to feel a sense of integrity rather than despair. The life review cited in the literature as a natural means for integration and completion can be creatively used by workers. Family albums, scrapbooks, portraits, old adages and prayers, as well as familiar music, old movies and cartoons are useful with individuals or groups to stimulate both happy and sad memories and to work through unfinished business as well as deal with present and future concerns (O'Brian, 1979).

A group of aged persons in a community center were watching the old version of *Dark Victory*. An elderly gentleman said that he had watched it with his wife many years ago and that later, when his wife became blind, he had felt many of the helpless feelings of the husband in the movie. He had often felt guilty that he had not been able to be more supportive and prevent her from so much suffering but, as he said, "I'm just realizing that it's hard on the people who have to watch other people suffer—you're not at your best."

As people grow older, another avenue to maintain satisfactory internal states is to alter one's level of aspiration. This may conserve physical and psychic energy for completing necessary tasks. At the same time self-esteem is maintained. For instance, an elderly man was recently telling us how he had made up his mind to sell his car because of failing eyesight and a tendency to become disoriented when driving. As a "driver of a car" his sense of competence was reduced; on the other hand, when he explained that he was giving up driving because he did not want to endanger other people, one could see that his sense of competence as a responsible human being was enhanced. As we commented to this effect, he thought a few minutes and said, "You're right." Other older people, for whom changing one's level of aspiration is psychologically threatening, may risk unnecessary physical danger to themselves and to others.

Information and Skills. Obtaining and processing information about one's environment and one's self in relation to it is a cognitive process that serves as a guide to action and to adaptive behavior. In the lives of older people who are bombarded with changes, both internal and external, too much information can be compared to an overload on an electrical system; there is apt to be a temporary short circuiting in the person's ability to process data about his environment. In other instances the older person may not have enough information upon which to make judgments regarding appropriate actions to take.

Too much information to be absorbed is likely to occur when aged persons are suddenly thrust into novel situations for which their coping skills are inadequate. People adapt to such changes in different ways.

Mrs. Wilson was known as the "old witch" by her neighbors in a low-cost housing project. She had adapted to her changing, unfamiliar living situations by becoming aggressive and hostile to those around her. She was accused of attempting to set fire to an adjoining apartment. Although this was never proved and she was not prosecuted, her continued threats of bodily harm to others were disruptive.

Housing officials then began to consider eviction. A student worker, at this crisis period, was able to engage the client in a positive relationship by intervening for her with the housing authority. Over time, the worker was able to discuss Mrs. Wilson's outbursts, which invariably got her into trouble. At one point he said, "I bet you had a temper when you were younger, too. Since you were a nurse for so many years, how did you manage it then?" Mrs. Wilson thought about this for a bit and said that she now had too much time on her hands and every little thing bothered her a lot more.

Further discussion in subsequent sessions revealed that much of Mrs. Wilson's anger was related to the loss of autonomy she experienced when she was forced, at retirement, to move to her present neighborhood. Her previous life experience had not prepared her for these changes in her life. Skills she had relied on were mainly instrumental ones: cooking, cleaning, and nursing. The worker and Mrs. Wilson talked about roles she might still play using these old skills. But they also worked on new skills by anticipating situations that would be likely to upset her and by role-playing different ways of responding.

Another means of adapting to strange and hostile environments is by withdrawing. Some elderly people withdraw temporarily into the safety of their small apartments or, if institutionalized, to the safety of a room. Protracted periods of withdrawal may result in too little information for developing competence and adapting to their life situations.

Mrs. Taska had spent most of her life in a small ethnic neighborhood where she, her husband, and son belonged to a Polish club. Both Mr. and Mrs. Taska worked in a local factory. Her son married and moved away and later died. Shortly afterward her husband died. At about the same time, Mrs. Taska turned 62 and was forced to retire. She could not manage on her small social security income to remain in her old neighborhood and was forced to move to a low-income housing project.

Mrs. Taska spoke very broken English and her inability to communicate with her new neighbors or to manage resulted in her increased isolation. There were many kinds of information that her isolation prevented her from obtaining. For example, she did not apply for increases in her social security payments since she did not hear or read about these through news media or friends. When Mrs. Taska was forced to shop for food, she did not have information about the protective measures other elderly engaged in to ward off muggings and assaults by neighborhood teenagers. On three occasions she was robbed and once she was mugged and raped. Her increasing suspicion led to further isolation, narrowing the possibilities for obtaining knowledge about health care resources that she badly needed.

By the time Mrs. Taska's plight was discovered by an outreach social worker, her health had deteriorated to the point where she needed to be hospitalized and later, against her will, placed in a nursing home. This kind of negative spiraling effect is not atypical of what occurs in the lives of many aged persons. Only vigorous and consistent outreach work can prevent these consequences. Although there were many other factors contributing to Mrs. Taska's problem, a lack of adequate information about her environment was a strong contributing factor.

Providing information for increasing competence and mastery takes many forms.

Mr. Taylor, who had been a regular participant at the senior center, had been absent for several days when the social worker called at his home. She found him in low spirits and noncommunicative. After several minutes Mr. Taylor blurted out: "You can't get blood out of a stone." Follow-up on this comment revealed that Mr. Taylor felt he that he was losing his touch as a manager because he was old. He emphasized that he used to be able to stretch his social security checks to cover basic living expenses and have something left over to pay the dues at the center. However, recently he had not been able to manage and was ashamed to admit it, feeling that his mind wasn't working as well as it used to. The worker responded to this by saying that he guessed that the high cost of food was affecting not only him but other people at the center.

This "renaming" of the problem as one of inflation is a special instance of giving information that makes it possible for clients to feel better about themselves. Mr. Taylor, with his inner state in a somewhat more satisfactory condition, was able to meet with the center director and together they worked out a plan to waive dues and also arrange for him and other members to shop at a less expensive market.

Autonomy, Choice, and Time.   Even when their internal states are satisfactory and their cognitive grasp of their situation is adequate, the adaptive behavior of elderly persons may be upset if they are suddenly thrust into new situations over which they have no control. Autonomy is having choices and options from which to select; it also requires time for scanning and rehearsing for contingencies before committing oneself to a course of action. Providing autonomy, choice, and time often go hand in hand with information-giving.

Mr. Brown, 76, had been hospitalized for a fractured ankle. Since he was no longer in need of skilled nursing care, the discharge planning team, meeting in Mr. Brown's room, was discussing his poor progress in using his walker. They had concluded that he was not able to return to his apartment and that, since his only daughter worked, a convalescent home was the only answer. Mr. Brown knew that he was being discussed, even though his hearing impairment prevented him from getting all the conversation. He finally said in a forthright way: "Will you please speak up so I can hear you? This is my life you're talking about." The social worker apprised him of the team's conclusion and their reasons.

Mr. Brown then agreed that he could not safely return home until he could manipulate enough to care for himself and he began to engage in a process that he had used all his life when faced by problems: He looked at possible alternatives, checked these out with his friends and daughter, and eventually decided to spend his convalescence in the latter's home, since she would be on vacation from her teaching job.

With adequate information and a measure of autonomy, Mr. Brown thus drew on existing competencies. Also, he used the time at his daughter's home to learn new competencies, such as using his walker to get to the bathroom, making himself light meals, and getting in and out of bed with his heavy cast. Since his functioning was complicated by a progessive condition that affected his balance, he engaged in another coping mechanism, that of contingency planning: What would he do if he fell down when all alone? The next time he noticed his balance problem getting worse, should he consider a nursing home? Where would he most like to be? These were not happy thoughts to consider; however, through the process of thinking and planning, Mr. Brown was able to maintain a measure of control over his life rather than becoming a docile reactor to changing circumstances.

Time is a significant dimension in competence and provides guidelines for practice. With the elderly, as with other age groups, the adaptive process is extended over time. As White (1974) has pointed out, it is common in clinical assessments to consider the initial behaviors of clients as characteristic of their general way of meeting problems. We do not always take into account the importance of time in mastering new situations and developing new competencies.

Miss Yacko, 80 years old, recently entered the Hill Convalescent Home when her elderly sister died. She was nearly blind, had suffered the loss of her right foot due to diabetes, and had no other place to stay. For many years she had been an independent and successful businesswoman and saw this move as a real threat to her autonomy. She acted in an imperious manner with staff and patients, refusing to mingle and rejecting their efforts to make her comfortable.

At first, Miss Yacko sat for long periods, watching other residents and staff going about their daily routines without having to become personally involved. Her first step in mastery of her new situation thus involved her in quiet observation. Then she began to gather additional information, gingerly asking questions about staff. For instance, she wanted to know who made certain management decisions. She asked about the background of various residents, their level of education and previous occupations. Her next phase in this adaptive process consisted of starting a conversation with a gentleman who had been a professor from a large university. Miss Yacko later told the social worker that she had expected some interesting conversations from this man but instead his only concern was with his kidneys.

Miss Yacko continued brief forays into her new environment, testing out staff and residents' responses to her under a variety of conditions. Sometimes she was curt and snappish, sometimes sarcastic and autocratic, but increasingly she became more humorous and friendly. It was several weeks before she seemed trustful enough to engage spontaneously in conversation and activities of the home and to share information about herself.

This vignette shows that time is necessary in adaptation when people are faced with new and strange situations. Miss Yacko used various strategies to gain information and to process cognitively what she saw and heard, while simultaneously avoiding situations that would increase her anxiety. She maintained a measure of autonomy within the limitations of her new setting and her physical impairment by carefully checking out her options before making commitments. Miss Yacko had probably used similar coping mechanisms in her role as a successful businesswoman. It can be predicted that she would meet the challenges in the new environment by adding new coping skills to those she has already acquired.

Time as a variable in developing competence expands the usual view of autonomy: autonomy is gained by degrees over the life cycle. There has been an extended period of time preceding old age in which the person has acquired adaptive strategies "to become ready—but not in a hurry for—death."

Mr. Brown told his worker that he had just read something in a magazine that made him mad, although he supposed it was meant to be funny. Someone had written that the elderly worry about only two things when they go to bed at night: dying and what they will have for breakfast. He acknowledged that he often "planned" his breakfast after going to bed and sometimes he thought about the time ahead if he shouldn't be able to care for himself. He said, "And that's planning too!"

Coping with Death—the Final Autonomy.   There is much that social workers can do to support clients' adaptive strategies even in the very last task of life, that is, to face death with competence. One of the most difficult and painful tasks facing practitioners is offering help to a dying patient. Perhaps this is because we overlook the cumulative competence that older people have acquired in the process of living. Experience shows that one can be ready to die and in some cases welcome death but this does not mean the dying person does not appreciate the worker's attentiveness and caring (Kubler-Ross, 1969).

Competence in facing death can be reinforced by knowing that one is cared about; internal conditions of pain and isolation can be reduced; and the autonomy of the client will be reflected, in the final analysis, in how he or she cares to use such support.

A social work student writes as follows from her experience with an aged client.

Mrs. Roberts was dying and I knew it. I would go in every day thinking that she might like to talk, but she wouldn't or couldn't. I read in Dr. Butler's book that when a person is physically unable to talk the worker can use her intuition as to what the client may be thinking and feeling. The next day I again visited Mrs. Roberts. She opened her eyes ever so briefly. I took her hand and said, "It must be very tiring to talk but if you would like, I'll just sit here beside you." She squeezed my hand lightly, and continued to hold it for the next twenty minutes or so. When I said good-bye for now, she squeezed my hand again. I visited this way until one day I came in and she had died. This experience for me was one of the most gratifying ones in my life. Those moments with Mrs. Roberts were so serene and peaceful and I imagine will help me to prepare for my own death.

Terminal illness and approaching death are likely to be viewed by professional helpers as times when people should not or cannot be involved in making decisions or taking responsibility, thus reducing the possibility for maintaining and enhancing competence. However, movements such as Hospice are recognizing the rights of dying patients for options, choice, and autonomy in using the time remaining to them.

In the above vignette, Mrs. Roberts was provided the information that the worker cared but also was given a choice as to how this caring would be communicated, thus allowing her to have some measure of control over her final life task. Social work practice that encourages client participation and self-determination is a means of promoting competence in work with the very ill or dying person.

Conclusion

In this chapter we have focused on the aging process and the potential for social work practice to promote competence and self-esteem in elderly persons. We have integrated theory and research from gerontology with contemporary ego psychology. Out of this integration emerges an optimistic view of the possibilities and challenges that exist throughout the life cycle.

We have described social work practice with older persons from an ecological perspective, which focuses on the person–environment transactional unit and enriches the repertoire of strategies available to us in work with older persons. In particular, notions of compensatory and prosthetic interventions suggest many ways through which the environments of people can be made more nourishing and stimulating. Further, knowledge of the personal components necessary for adaptation expands the range of activities available to us in working with each person.

Promoting competence requires attention to the inner conditions of people as well as the environmental context in which they strive for adaptation and fit. Attention to this total ecological unit makes work with the elderly a challenging and promising area of practice.

Notes

1. Golan (Chapter 4 in this volume) discusses principles and techniques for building competence in transitional states that are also useful in work with clients going through the aging stage of life.
2. Lawton and Nahemow (1973) and Nahemow and Lawton (1976) propose a similar ecological change model that has evolved out of their work specifically with the elderly. Their major premise is that change which promotes coping and adaptation may be facilitated through intervention aimed either at the individual or at the environment.
3. This diagram was suggested by the schema presented by Brown (Chapter 9 in this volume).

CHAPTER 12

Promoting Competence in Involuntary Clients

Genevieve B. Oxley

To seek help requires a recognition of loss of competence in some area of functioning. At the same time the person who seeks help demonstrates considerable competence in the very act of finding and eliciting appropriate intervention. That person has already taken several steps that require basic abilities and resourcefulness: He or she has recognized a problem; defined it sufficiently to have some idea of the needed resource; located, often with ingenuity, a possible resource to meet that need; made an appointment; come to an office; handled the anxiety of waiting and uncertainty; and verbally made a request. This self-initiated, competent action establishes a base for developing further competencies.

In contrast, the involuntary client has suffered some loss of competence but has not demonstrated recognition of a problem or capacity to find a possible resource for help. We can assume that this person is immobilized by a feeling of failure, uncertainty, or incompetence; unaware of social work resources; or not sophisticated in the use of community services.

An involuntary client is often viewed as a member of a poor, multiproblem family or as a resident of an institution. However, there are many other groups of clients who are involuntary in the sense that, although possibly aware of a problem, they are not aware of—or actively seeking—social work help as offered by an agency. With this definition, there are more involuntary than voluntary clients. There is

290

the child brought in by the parent for help. There is the parent who brings the child to be "changed" and does not anticipate or want any personal involvement. There is the husband who brings his wife into the agency to be "made over" and finds that he is expected to participate in the process. There is the patient hospitalized for a medical procedure and asked to see a social worker. There is the person in crisis brought in by a friend or relative. The list goes on and on, and contrasts dramatically in number with the clients who come to social agencies aware of a problem and with a degree of realistic belief and hope that the agency can help.

One might say that such a broad definition of "involuntary" loses any meaning for practice. On the contrary, I believe that it is important to recognize those clients who feel tentative, confused, or reluctant and to offer them effective help. In this chapter I shall focus on social work intervention to promote competence in these clients. I shall classify involuntary clients in the following general groups and discuss practice with each:

1. *Clients from low status groups:*   persons who come to the attention of agencies through schools, visiting nurses, crisis hot lines, housing authorities. They are often members of minority and low socioeconomic status groups. In the context of the majority culture they may be described as multiproblem, uncooperative, or hard to reach; they do not define their situation as it is defined by the majority culture agency.

2. *In-patient clients:*   involuntary clients in settings such as hospitals, psychiatric centers, or detention facilities. The nature of these settings tend to undermine confidence; normal role assignments are confused and the patient/client is usually placed in the role of someone who is sick, helpless, dependent, wrong, or bad. The adjectives could go on; but they do not include "competent."

3. *Parents of the identified patient child:*   parents who seek or have forced upon them child care or child protective services and are then expected to submit to treatment. The person to whom society assigns the role of inadequate or bad parent feels overwhelming incompetence.

4. *Child clients:*   the child who is brought to the agency by parent or guardian. The child may know that he is unhappy or feel that he is bad; however, he rarely understands the meaning of social work help.

5. *Crisis-immobilized clients:*   the individual in crisis who is immobilized and is physically accompanied to an agency by relative or friend.

Life Model/Competence Development Framework

As background for the consideration of the concept of competence, I refer the reader to Maluccio's introductory chapter in this volume. Here I would emphasize the idea of competence as a transactional interchange. Maas (1979:6) defines competence as "marked by behavior aimed at effecting the environment and which thus arises in interaction with an effectible environment. . . . Competence is contextual—it grows in effectible environments." Snowden also speaks of

> competence as a *transaction*, defined as an effective coping response to a culturally imposed expectation. This recognition of the role of social expectations serves to broaden the scope of competence. So conceived, competence becomes a phenomenon of both persons and situations, whose appraisal allows for explicitly considering cultural requirements and culturally based interpretations of behavior. Adopting this perspective also weakens the tendency to accept reflexively the interpretation of a situation which forms the understanding of the dominant culture. [Snowden, in press]

For example, the Vietnamese refugee who was successful and competent in his homeland is transplanted to the United States. Without the familiar supports of culture, extended family, financial security, and language, he appears incompetent and bewildered in the context of a strange environment. Or consider the mother who is reasonably competent in her neighborhood and is required by the judge to go for counseling when a son has been arrested for shoplifting. Her sense of competence falters. Moreover, the agency to which the referral is made is in a large austere office building several miles from the home community. As this person finds herself in such an unfamiliar context, her sense of competence is threatened further.

An interactional–transactional view of competence places responsibility for its development not alone on the individual but equally on the environment. This perspective is particularly useful in work with the involuntary client, where so often the individual's competence is "out of context" in a majority culture, in a social agency setting, or in a new or crisis situation.

I would like to distinguish two aspects of competence that are especially important in working with involuntary clients: interpersonal or object relationship competence and competence in task performance. To achieve competence the individual should bring to the encounter with the environment a degree of innate ability, positive experiences on which to build, and practice in enhancing skills. The environment should offer nurturance, opportunity for growth, encouragement and positive feedback in achievement.

Interpersonal or object relationship competence is strongly influenced by events in infancy, within the family and between the infant and the mothering figure. Hartmann (1958:35) speaks of the ego developing in what he terms the "average expectable environment." Mahler's (1968) research has further emphasized the importance of early childhood in the normal development of the human being. Her emphasis is on the process whereby a child becomes an individual, a process that requires a relatively stable and available mother figure during the first two years of life. This necessitates a societal and environmental context in which mothers can be free from unnecessary strain and anxiety; adequate food, health care, housing, and respect for the mothering role are essential. The provision of services to enhance the mother's self-confidence and feeling of competence will have beneficial effects not only for the mother but for her children as well.

Competence in task performance begins later but often develops parallel to competence in interpersonal skills. According to Erikson (1963), the drive for achievement in work is strongest in latency years and the school is a crucial context in which the child develops task competence. The parallel development of the two aspects of competence does not always follow, and we see some individuals who are competent in relationships yet not in task accomplishment, or vice versa. Other influences are the expectation of parents and the modeling of the work ethic which emphasizes task performance over the ability to relate easily with one's fellow man. I am reminded of the recent autobiography of Isaac Asimov (1970). Without question his production of two hundred books by the age of 59 is indication of a high degree of task competence. Yet his autobiography describes a man gauche, alone, never making a good first impression. The task orientation of his immigrant parents running their candy store fourteen hours a day, seven days a week modeled the value of task competence. It also left no time for relating to the emotional needs of a child.

In discussing the challenge of creating competence in the involuntary client, I would like to turn to the ecological or life-model approach to change, which stresses that change takes place as a natural phenomenon (Germain, 1979; Maluccio 1979b). The involuntary client may experience positive change facilitated by relatives, support groups, and normal maturation.[1] The social worker can often give an important "assist" to the client's utilization of his own environment. Such an approach frequently makes sense to the client who has not voluntarily sought the services of "talking" therapy.

In 1971 I proposed a summary of ways in which positive change occurs in life, with suggested modes of approach which could be used by social workers to enhance that change (Oxley, 1971). In this chapter I would like to modify that schema and use it as background for discussion of competence and involuntary clients.

This approach emphasizes the worker's responsibility to view the client in his context and to serve as an instrument of environmental as well as client change. A major role of the worker is to assist the involuntary client in experiencing success and becoming appropriately assertive in seeking out resources to fill needs and more sophisticated in using society's supports. At the same time the worker focuses on enriching the environmental opportunities for the client's growth and achievement of competence.

The life-model/competence-development schema (Table 12–1) will be used in the rest of this chapter to discuss and illustrate practice with each group of involuntary clients.

Clients from Low Status Groups

Members of minority and low socioeconomic status groups are often reluctant to seek the services of social workers. However, many children and families with multiple needs are attending public institutions. Schools, day nurseries, and Head Start programs are examples of society's provision of a context in which children can learn both interpersonal and task competence. Parents can be supported in their efforts at good parenting.

Head Start Program

An interesting setting that illustrates the life-model/competence-development framework is the YWCA-administered Head Start program in San Francisco. Important needs of families with low socioeconomic status (mostly single parent and 90 percent minority) are met by the child care and educational aspects of the program. In addition, the program provides an opportunity for imaginative social work outreach to parents and children with special needs. It offers a setting in which problems can be identified early. The central challenge for the social worker is to break through the parents' suspicion and reticence in sharing their problems and fears. Too often parents' recollections of negative encounters with persons calling themselves social workers inhibit their asking for help. Many confuse "social worker" with "eligibility worker" or with the public assistance worker who had been perceived as punitive or investigatory. In this program, the social workers chose to call themselves by titles representing other roles they carried—one an administrator, another an assistant teacher. What we call ourselves and how we interpret our role presents a particular challenge with the involuntary client.

How did the social workers engage these parents? First of all, the expectation of Head Start that the parents direct the program gives mothers an opportunity to experience competence and mastery. It provides an "effectible" environment (Maas, 1979). The involvement of parents in this active fashion enhances their interest in the program and their children. The message to the parents is: "We respect you and expect you to be competent in directing this—your program." On request, the social worker attends and participates in parent meetings, thus making herself available as a resource but not an authority figure. The social worker first meets the parents and children through the intake interview and later through life-space interviews as the parent brings and picks up the child each day. She gets acquainted with the children as they engage in the Head Start program activities and offers individual attention as needed.

Social workers in this setting offer other needed and concrete services, such as a health and nutrition program. They offer vision screening as a way of early identifying any visual problems and assisting the parent with appropriate referrals. They survey parents about their interests and start programs to meet their special needs. Gradually, by concrete help and demonstrated respect, the social workers win the confidence of the parents so that they are more ready to share economic, employment, family, health or emotional needs. For all parents and children, the social workers are attempting to facilitate positive interaction between the client and a nurturing environment.

In terms of the life-model/competence-development approach, the clients are aided in normal *maturation* through the provision of an environment for growth. *Interaction* is facilitated through positive relationships, corrective emotional experiences, expectations, and role modeling. The opportunity for successful *action* is perhaps the most important feature of the total environment. The mothers' opportunity to direct the program and the children's experience with age-appropriate activities enhance the development of competence. *Learning* is closely related to action (cf. Maluccio, 1974: Oxley, 1971).

School Environment

The school is an environment to which all children are exposed. School social workers can have an impact on that environment; they often serve as facilitators of interaction among pupils, teachers, administrators, and parents. All members of these groups may begin as involuntary clients. The pressures of a school system are such that

TABLE 12–1. Casework Treatment—A Life-Model/Competence-Development Framework

Ways in which Change Occurs	Requirements for Positive Change and Development of Competence	Facilitating Social Institutions	Facilitating Treatment Interventions	Social Work Role
Maturation	Emotional and material environment for growth (nurturance, stimulation) Physical and emotional health	Family/caretaker Community Schools Medical facilities Day nurseries	Client–worker relationships encouraging growth and competence. Provision of resources necessary to growth	Enabler Advocate Therapist Parent Institutional change agent
Interaction	Sustaining and caring individuals Supporting social group Validation by significant others	Family/caretaker Peer group	Relationship Corrective emotional experience Expectations Positive sanctions Role modeling Use of interaction in interview Family and group Rx. Experience of competence	Therapist Friend Enabler Parent

Action	Opportunity Emotional freedom to act Validating experience	Schools Social clubs Employment Activity groups	Provision of opportunity for action Assistance in carrying out appropriate tasks Preparation (community, resources, client, family) Experience of competent action	Enabler Advocate Therapist Teacher Institutional change agent
Learning	Information available Emotional freedom to understand and gain insight Opportunity	Schools Free press	Provision of information Reflective discussion Clarification Insight development Behavior modification Experience of mastery	Therapist Teacher Advocate Institutional change agent
Crisis Resolution	Material and emotional means of solution	Support groups Crisis centers Family	Immediate intervention to take advantage of heightened emotional readiness to change Connecting with family and community supports Increase mastery and competence	Enabler Advocate Therapist

teachers have little time to consider matters beyond learning plans and classroom duties, while administrators are pressed for time, and children and parents may be unaware or suspicious of any special service.

As shown by the case examples that follow, social workers can positively influence the school experience through helpful support and consultation with teachers and staff, while directly or indirectly helping individual students and parents. The examples are drawn from a worker's experience in an elementary school, where the worker first made herself available to teachers by seeking them out and meeting them informally in the lunchroom, between classes, or in her "open door" office. She clarified her role, talked informally with teachers about their classroom problems, and offered helpful suggestions, always remembering the very difficult role of the teacher who carries the ongoing classroom responsibility. Teachers clearly appreciated having an attentive ear.

The next step was to establish a useful role with the students. To this end, the worker spent time on the playground, clarifying her role as someone who was there to help make the school experience successful and pleasant. She also had an "open-door" policy for students and encouraged drop-in visits. In this way the social worker established herself as someone who was a friend of all students: "Seeing Su" became a sought-after treat which reduced the stigma and anxiety that might be attached to intervention with troubled children.

When a child in this school presents learning or behavior problems in the classroom, he or she is discussed at a weekly "staffing". If it is decided that the child and family could benefit from individual help, a collaborative model of intervention is used. The approach to the child and family is important, since neither specifically requested help, although it could be said that the child is calling for help by his behavior. The child and parents are first invited to attend a meeting with the teacher and social worker. Here the participants discuss the observed problem and decide on intervention. This step has the benefit of clarity, a sense of collaboration, and participation of the child and family in their own destiny. It seems reassuring to children engaged in this process to know that significant others are caring and cooperative on their behalf. Areas of strength are discussed along with specific concerns. It is a rare experience for most children to be included and respected and heard. Together the group works out a contract, spelling out the services that the social worker and school will offer. The parent's and child's continuing cooperation in joint meetings is established. Expectations, consequences, and rewards are mutually understood. Perhaps most important, a new relationship has begun among child, parents, and school that impacts in areas other than the specific referral problem. Parents begin to view the school as a helpful, supportive place; teachers begin to view the parents as concerned people who are often struggling with overwhelming problems; and, as the child responds to intervention, both begin to view the child more positively and with more respect. The child senses the changed attitudes of the adults and is able to respond differently in all areas of functioning. This process, focused on an individual child, can also have positive ramifications for other children in the school.

Counseling with the child is similar to that in other settings, with perhaps more emphasis placed upon responsibility and limit setting. Responsibility rests with the child to remember the appointments and to attend. After the first few sessions, the child usually reminds the teacher that it is time to leave the class. The child is responsible for choosing activities in the playroom, which marks this part of the school system as different. For most children referred to the social worker, the classroom is not a happy place; therefore, spending time outside the class is welcome. Since classes are large, counseling sessions provide a singular place where the child receives intensive one to one attention. Work with these children is supportive and task oriented—an approach that reduces initial anxiety and provides specific opportunity for the development of task as well as interpersonal competence.

The Peter Jackson Case

Peter is an 11-year-old black boy who was referred because of a five-year history of increasingly hostile and aggressive behavior with staff and peers. His academic performance was satisfactory. He spent a great deal of time in the office as a result of his physical attacks on peers and had become intensely disliked by all staff members. Peter's parents are upwardly mobile, well educated middle-class people, both of whom work. An older brother just left the home and a younger brother is at home.

A conference was arranged with teacher, parents, social worker, and Peter to discuss his difficulties and the recommendation that he enter counseling. Peter remained sullen and silent throughout the session. The discussion centered around his problems at home and school. The worker sensed that the parents believed that Peter was being picked on and selected out for discipline by school staff and inquired directly as to a possible racial issue. The parents seemed surprised to hear this comment and visibly relaxed and became more open in verbalizing their concerns and caring for their child. It was agreed that Peter would meet twice a week for one half hour with the social worker and that all of them would keep in touch through regular conferences. Peter has now been seen for six months.

Peter arrived on time for the first two sessions, after being reminded by the teacher. He was sullen and unresponsive to what turned out to be the worker's monologue. He remained standing with his back to her, arms crossed, and obviously fighting tears. He left on time without ever speaking.

In the third session, he sat facing the worker, but still remained verbally unresponsive, with no eye contact. She suggested that he seemed to want to spend his time quietly and respected his wishes, explaining that she was there if he chose to do something else. She shuffled papers, still facing him. He became somewhat anxious but his squirming resulted in his facing the worker more directly. He finally asked how much time was left and was told five minutes.

The next session and every session thereafter were on his own volition, with his reminding the teacher. He came into the room, sat down, and responded shakily and in a hoarse voice to the worker's comments about his sports jacket, football, and baseball games. He chose to play checkers, which began a continuing pattern of beating the worker shamelessly and legitimately. In each of these action-oriented sessions, Peter experienced competence; but his affect for approximately three months remained impassive. Meanwhile the social worker served as Peter's advocate by talking with the staff, reframing his being "aggressive" into "frightened and unsure," and arranging ways that Peter could gain recognition for positive interactions. She worked with the parents to sort out how they let Peter know that he was important to them. She helped them arrange for adequate child care after school and recreation activities for Peter.

The aggressive behavior and verbal defiance ceased both at home and at school almost from the initial conference. Peter now speaks in a clear, audible voice and staff members are surprised to note that he has dimples. When disciplinary action is needed, which happens infrequently, the principal reports that Peter's attitude is no longer sullen and defiant, and that they have normal conversations. His academic abilities are above grade level and his relations with staff members are more positive and pleasant. He is part of a small group and is learning more successful ways of interacting with peers. He has recently been heard laughing at himself in tense situations where he would previously have escalated into physical confrontation.

The Robert Moore Case

Robert is a 10-year-old black child referred due to poor academic performance (three years below grade level), an unhappy demeanor, and few social contacts with peers. Psychological testing revealed no physiological or conceptual handicaps. Robert and his single mother have recently moved from the rural Deep South and live as an extended family household. The home is crowded and seems chaotic. Ms. Moore is supported by AFDC and is trying to find employment. At the initial conference she appeared to be fearful and reluctant to give any family information; she seemed concerned about her child and reported there were no problems at home.

Robert arrived at his first session on his own volition and chose to build a model, which provided a way in which he could be active and develop task competence. Robert seemed hesitant to talk, his communications were inaudible, and there was no eye contact. This was his first model and he asked to take it home. He was told that he must work on it in the office but that he could take it home when it was finished. He appeared to accept this limit.

The worker arranged to talk with Robert and his mother after the second session, when the boy expressed some lack of trust. She explained to them that her services were voluntary and could stop at any time they wished. She then focused with the mother on the difficulties of single parenthood and AFDC problems and acknowledged how well Ms. Moore seemed to have done for herself and her child against great odds. The mother described problems in finding a job and the worker was able to refer her to a vocational agency through which she found a job that she continues to hold.

The next session with Robert seemed to be the turning point in the treatment relationship. He intensely tested the limit of taking the model home unfinished. He argued, yelled, cried, and refused to leave. The worker knew he was a socially and materially deprived child but decided to remain firm. She carried him out of the room, saying that she would see him the next day. He returned for his appointment the following day and never tested any limit again, although he systematically tested other staff working with him. As he finished seven models and became more independent and proficient, his self-image improved. He began to relate his new found model-building skill to academic learning and verbalized his discovery that he *could* learn things!

Robert has become one of the more popular students in his age group. His speech is clear and understandable. He perceives himself realistically —behind the other kids, but catching up slowly. Reports from teachers now center around how to control his incessant chatter and how to modify his speaking out in class. His mother remains aloof as far as family information goes, but shares her plans and hopes for a better future for herself and her son.

Clarity of expectations and a clear contract seem particularly important in the school setting (Maluccio and Marlow, 1974). Children appear to interpret successful limit setting as caring in a very real sense. Limits revolve around keeping appointments, time of sessions, and removal of items from the playroom. These limits are tested by the child almost immediately and further progress and behavioral changes seem to depend on the social worker's capacity to respect and enforce the contract.

In terms of the life-model/competence-development approach, the school social worker in these examples relied most heavily on *action* and *learning*. In her work with individual children she structured the interviews around skill-development activities, thus providing an opportunity for positive action and assisting when necessary in carrying out tasks, as in the beginning of model work with Robert. Robert made a direct association between his ability to learn model building and learning in the classroom. He experienced mastery and competence.

Maturation was stimulated by the attention of a positive one to one relationship and the provision of special resources necessary to growth. *Interaction* also was growth-producing, particularly in setting up the structure for mutual concern and discussion among parents, school, and child. *Crisis resolution* played a part in the school setting. Very often the child is referred following a classroom crisis. The tension around such a precipitating incident can be used to mobilize action and change (cf. Golan, Chapter 4 in this volume).

The social worker in the school serves as broker and advocate, friend and enabler with children. Perhaps of greatest importance is her influence in improving communication and understanding among administrators, teachers, students, and parents and thus positively influencing the institutional environment, i.e., the context for growth, for all children.

Inpatient Clients

The person involuntarily admitted to a psychiatric hospital is an extreme example of someone who has lost all feeling of competence and control over his life situation. The following case of a 28-year-old man in these circumstances illustrates what can be done by a social worker to assist in the restoration and building of competence and control.

The Bob Smalley Case

Bob was brought to the psychiatric emergency service by his mother and girlfriend and placed on a seventy-two-hour hold that was later extended. He presented psychotic symptomatology—loose, rambling, tangential speech, disorientation, extreme self-preoccupation indicative of internal stimulation and ideas of reference. His mother and girlfriend gave a history of steady decompensation of mental functioning over the preceding week. Although this was the first episode of frankly psychotic behavior, Bob had a premorbid history of isolation and extreme dependence on family and girlfriend as well as severe obsessive-compulsive behavior dating back to the onset of puberty. The present break had been precipitated by the coincidence of three losses: his job, his girlfriend, and his car in an accident.

Bob's expectations and those of the hospital were in contradiction—Bob strongly wished to leave; the hospital staff believed that he needed inpatient care. He became somewhat more aware of his external environment with the help of antipsychotic medication, but continued to be disturbed and in great mental anguish.

The task of the social worker assigned to Bob was to find ways to engage him toward the goal of restoring his reality testing and building his competence. First, it was necessary to find a way to relate to Bob. The worker began with brief but frequent contacts, letting him know that she was there and who she was. She tried to make the contacts of a length tolerable to him in his guarded, frightened state and also to help continually to reorient him to his external environment. After a while Bob began to approach his worker and other staff, indicating his increasing comfort with contact. As Gendlin (1967) points out, it is important to believe that inside the patient is a sensible person, even if he is confused or not responsive at the moment. The worker took extra care to be concrete and clear in her messages to Bob, but at the same time did not talk "down" to him or assume that he was not capable of understanding her. She also took care to acknowledge her own feelings and statements, making clear her boundary and that of Bob.

The worker further took responsibility for keeping Bob on the ward against his own wishes. She explained to him that he was on a hold and that she did not feel he was ready to leave because he was in the throes of a process necessitating his hospitalization and from which he would in time recover with treatment. She stressed that he did not need to be anxious around the decision to stay or leave nor feel guilty about it, as the decision had been made by the worker.

The worker provided structure to help Bob establish a firmer connection with reality and a return of competence through engaging him in ward activities. As he became more verbal, she tried to help him become clear in his communications—pointing out when she could and could not follow him. She also tentatively explored his feelings of sadness and loss and he began to acknowledge and discuss his sad affect.

Another very important part of the therapeutic intervention was the involvement of those who were a part of his life. Bob had many issues of anger and dependency with his parents. He was struggling between a desire to be infantalized and a wish for independence. Several family sessions were arranged with Bob and his parents. From a diagnostic viewpoint, the relationship patterns and interaction between parents and Bob became clear. As mother stroked the forehead of this young man, father paced impatiently about the room saying that Bob should act like a man. In the family sessions Bob was able to communicate some of his feelings and desires to his parents and talk more openly with them. Conjoint sessions were also arranged with Bob and his ex-girlfriend; the purpose was to help them clarify the mutually agreed-upon boundaries of their friendship and to explore his feelings, particularly of sadness and anger, around the breakup of their three-year living together arrangement.

In the joint family sessions Bob was generally more in touch with external realities even though they were difficult for him. The worker watched with satisfaction as Bob slowly but steadily returned to reality and showed signs of increased competence in handling his relationships with parents and girlfriend.

Bob did not return to the hospital from a pass issued the Saturday before his scheduled Monday discharge. Despite lack of medical authorization, his departure was seen as a positive step. He telephoned his parents and calmly told them that he was staying with a friend. Also, he immediately telephoned a psychiatrist whose name had been given to him prior to his hospitalization and arranged and kept an appointment for ongoing treatment. The social worker who had facilitated his emergence from a psychotic state was pleased that he had taken a health-oriented step by seeking continuing treatment outside the hospital setting. The initiative he demonstrated in finding a living plan away from his parents and calling the psychiatrist reflected his improved level of competent functioning.

In this case several behaviors on the part of the worker are particularly significant. She assumed responsibility for his being in the hospital—thus establishing a reality-based boundary and protection of the client at a time when he could not protect himself. At the same time she held realistic expectations of Bob that he was a sensible person whose competence was temporarily suppressed and would return. She instilled reality and hope of change. She listened and credited past, present, and potential strengths in the client and his environment. Working with Bob in his ecological context of family, girlfriend, and hospital proved to be especially beneficial (Germain, 1979). The worker enlisted the help of family and girlfriend and facilitated interchange between Bob and these significant others. As discussed in further detail by Goldstein (Chapter 13 in this volume), the family of a psychiatric patient constitutes an important resource that can be mobilized to promote competence.

In the life-model/competence-development schema, the worker utilized *interaction*—with herself, with family, and with girlfriend. She was clear and set appropriate expectations for the client; she worked with family and community and took advantage of the client's own step into health by supporting his premature departure from the hospital rather than reinstitutionalizing him. *Crisis resolution* also played a part in this case, as the client and his family and girlfriend experienced a heightened emotional readiness to change.

Parents of the Identified Patient Child

When a parent brings a child to a clinic or residential center, it may be assumed that the parent is coming voluntarily for help. This is generally not the case. First of all, the parent is often responding to pressure from a school or some outside source before he approaches an agency. When he does approach the agency, he expects the worker to cure his child. The parent may feel guilt, sadness, and shame that he has produced a child who is not conforming to society's expectations.

The parent may also feel gratitutde for the agency which agrees to attempt to help his child. That was certainly one reaction reported in a follow-up study by parents who placed their children at Edgewood, a residential treatment center in San Francisco (Oxley, November 1977). What most parents did not expect was that they too would be required to participate weekly in treatment while their child was in residence.

> The basis of the treatment contract was the requirement of parent participation in return for child-care service. A basic question is whether this kind of mandatory involvement can be effective. This contract assured the bodily presence of parents. It assured no more. The transformation of a required presence into an involved and goal-directed commitment to growth and change rested with the skill and creativity of the social worker or psychiatrist. [Oxley, December 1977:609]

A parent who requests placement of a child in residential treatment feels a failure as a parent. By agreeing to accept the child and take over the parenting role, the agency reinforces the parent's feelings of failure and incompetence. The implicit message to the parent is that "we can do what you failed to do." Counteracting this message in the Edgewood program was the expectation and indeed requirement that the parent be involved with the center in its efforts to help the child.

As seen in the follow-up study, the first message to the parent which seemed to have a positive effect on outcome was: "You, parent, are important to your child." The second significant message was: "You are important as a person, a separate individual with your own needs, hopes, and abilities." A mother described her perception of this attitude: "Of course their goal is more strengthening of yourself so you'll be happier too. You're not just a mother, you're a person. You're a woman. If you're happier, of course then you will make your kids happier" (Oxley, December 1977:610).

An active give-and-take exchange between worker and parent seemed to be more valued by parents than a more passive approach. One father told the interviewer that his social worker was responsible for his ownership of a very comfortable home, which evidenced much skillful remodeling accomplished with the help of his son. His comment about the worker was, "She helped us set goals—how to spend money and not go into debt. It was one of our big problems and she helped us out. She taught us how to work out problems for ourselves" (Oxley, December 1977:611). He might have summarized by saying that "she increased our competence and control over our own life."

The findings of the follow-up study suggest that a deliberate self-focus enhanced treatment outcome; the sons of parents who had in treatment focused on changing themselves were doing significantly better at follow-up than sons of parents who continued to see their boy as the only problem. It appeared that the skill of the social worker was the key factor in guiding parents from a focus on the identified patient to the self or family.

In relating these findings to the life-model/competence-development approach, I would like to emphasize the social worker's role as an institutional change agent working to provide a context in which parent and child are supported in the tasks of *maturation*. Specifically, the institution that validates and recognizes the crucial importance of parents in the treatment of children was found to have better follow-up results than many institutions which did not have such an emphasis. The social worker who constantly and vigilantly encourages staff members to involve parents—even at the cost of time, frustration, and extra effort—will have made a substantial contribution to effective child care.

Learning and *action* are two important ways in which parents were helped by their involvement in treatment. The feedback of parents of children in residence supported the view that their active involvement was important to them. They expressed appreciation for treatment modalities that emphasized learning and doing rather than a more passive, "talking" therapy style.

Child Clients

Many children are seen in outpatient and residential centers. Most are involuntary clients; it is not the child but someone else who sees a need for change. The child may feel unhappy or be aware that he is not meeting the expectations of the adults around him but it is indeed rare for a child in Anna Freud's (1946) terms to initially recognize a problem and choose the therapist as someone who can help toward its solution.

The issue of competence is particularly important with children.

The facilitation of growth and change and the freeing of the child to use his or her native ability and creativity will have lifelong effects on adaptation. Often the problem for which the child is referred is first recognized in the school setting. Lack of competence in task accomplishment and in interpersonal skills precipitates a high percentage of child referrals. In the Edgewood study described earlier, schools were the largest source of referral. Treatment which can directly influence school performance will increase competence.

Two factors are of particular importance in working with children. The first is the challenge of engaging the child in a process of relationship and discovery, and the second is the challenge of finding creative ways to assist the young client in developing competence. Perhaps of even greater significance is the need to view him or her in the total context of family, school, and neighborhood and to be prepared to intervene in these systems. The earlier examples from school social work demonstrated the validity of this principle. In the following example the intervention was made by a child guidance clinic:

The Fred Painter Case

Fred was a 10-year-old boy of mixed racial parentage who was brought to a child-guidance clinic by his grandmother, with whom he was living. She had been pressured by the school to do something for Fred, who was failing despite good intelligence and so disruptive in the classroom that the school was threatening to expel him.

Fred's life at home was complicated. When he was 2 his parents separated and he went to live with his mother and maternal grandparents. The parents reconciled and have since lived in the same neighborhood. Three siblings were born and have remained with the parents, while Fred has continued to live with his grandparents. Fred's father has little to do with him, yet in subtle ways he has encouraged his son to fight and act-out some of his own repressed anger. Fighting is one way in which Fred can get some positive recognition from his dad. Fred is very fond of his grandparents and wants to please them; but he also wants to live with his parents. His identity confusion and contradictory messages from school, parents and grandparents have prevented him from using his real abilities. The school has placed him in a learning-disability class.

The first task of the worker was to develop a relationship with Fred, clarify the reasons for his coming to the clinic and discuss ways they might work together to bring about some change that could make him happier. Fred was aware of his troubles and told the therapist: "I hate myself. I'm crazy." The worker also involved the family in various treatment combinations, sometimes seeing the parents together and at other times the mother, grandmother, and Fred. In addition, she visited the school to assist in making the best educational plan.

The first major confusion and source of identity diffusion for Fred was his living situation. After clarifying with all members of the family that it would be possible for Fred to return to his own home to live, the worker had the choice of arranging for a change in living plan or involving Fred in the process. She chose to help Fred act on his own in this crucial aspect of his life. Together they planned a joint family interview during which Fred would request to move home. In preparation the worker suggested that Fred role-play what his mother and grandmother might say—and how he would respond, using chairs to represent different family members. From a timid and apprehensive start, Fred gradually gained confidence as he played out the scene in preparation for the coming meeting. Convinced that he was ready, he excitedly urged the worker to get everyone to the office so they could begin. The session went well, with his own parents agreeing that they would like to have him home and would immediately look for a larger house to make this possible. The grandparents were equally supportive and recognized that Fred still loved them and would continue to see them. This session gave Fred new confidence in himself and new commitment to the worker, who had proven her usefulness.

Fred is an unusually creative child and, once he was introduced to the idea of role-playing, he frequently used this mode to work out a relationship or to practice for a feared encounter. The worker was resourceful in engaging this child in treatment. One ongoing activity was to write a story about Fred and add to it during each session. Fred also enjoyed games such as "what would Fred say to Fred?". "What I like/don't like" list had particular appeal and he never failed to bring this list up to date. He was able to identify his good moods and his bad ones. For instance, he indicated: "When I feel happy I don't need so much attention—I feel joyful. Oh, yeah, maybe that's why I'm bad—I need more attention." Fred seemed relieved to be able to put words to his feelings and bad behavior and acted on his new awareness. At one point, he went home and asked his mother to give him more attention!

The worker also saw the grandparents specifically to help them understand the importance to Fred of respect for his own father and his Latin origin, which meant of course respect for the Latin heritage of Fred.

This case illustrates the complexities and rewards of working with the child in his ecological context. The multifaceted work with Fred, his extended family, and school was successful in assisting this bright child to begin to use his potential and demonstrate his competence in school and in his relationships with peers and siblings.

Action and *learning* are the dominant ways in which positive change took place for Fred. The worker structured active role-playing rehearsal for real-life situations and enabled this boy to gain mastery over his own destiny. She served as a therapist, as a teacher, and as a broker/advocate with the extended family and the school. She helped Fred to *interact* within his ecological environment and to facilitate change in a living plan that reinforced his identity and competence.[2]

Crisis-immobilized Clients

Often individuals in crisis are unable to take the initiative in seeking help. If their behavior is such as to cause alarm in others, they may be brought to a mental health clinic, a psychiatric inpatient or outpatient facility. As is seen in the next example, they are often in a role similar to that of a child whose problem and source of possible solution is recognized only by others.

The Jean Lowry Case

Jean was a 35-year-old wife and mother of three young children. She was immobilized by the terminal illness of her husband. Suffering from a brain tumor, he was moody, unwilling to have his wife get assistance with his care or share the nature and seriousness of his illness with relatives and friends who could have offered support. The seriousness of his illness was withheld from the children as well. Under this strain, Jean broke down, was unable to sleep or eat, lost energy, and finally left her home and went to a neighbor's, where she stayed for four days while the latter took food and gave necessary medicine to her husband.

When Jean seemed totally unable to return to her home, the neighbor brought her to the clinic. Jean was seen for one interview in the immediate-treatment center. She was helped to share and ventilate her feelings of anger, resentment, guilt, helplessness, and, finally, fear. She feared her husband's death and expressed her anxiety about the adequacy of her nursing care. She found relief from this interview and at its conclusion said that she felt able to return home. A second appointment was offered for the following week and she was encouraged to telephone earlier if she wished to talk.

The clinic service had been useful to this client in helping her return to meet her responsibilities to husband and children. It might have ended there, but for the caring, concern, and interest of the worker. It is the process beyond the initial interview which I wish to emphasize. Engaging and reaching out to the involuntary client can often mean the difference between a minimal service and one which offers the opportunity for growth and the freeing of the individual and family for the development of coping skills and the competence that comes with successful problem-solving. Jean did not keep her second appointment but called to say that her husband was too ill to be left alone. She requested an appointment for the following week. The worker then took the initiative in calling every day to inquire how Jean and her husband were. The morning of the second scheduled appointment, her husband died.

A week after the husband's funeral, Jean called to request an appointment. She said she was in great pain and hoped that she and the worker could work together to alleviate it. The worker commended her for seeking help and told her that her feelings were only natural following the death of her husband. She expressed concern about her and her children. Jean described her inability to talk with friends, relatives, or her children. She wanted to isolate herself from the living, yet she expected to feel better if she could discuss her husband's death and her reactions to it with someone who cared. She said she had not intended to see the worker again, *but her daily phone calls expressing concern not only for her husband but for her* enabled her to call for this appointment. The worker and Jean made a plan for six interviews, with the goals of helping Jean work through the death of her husband and discuss his death with the children. The worker geared her approach to Lindemann's "grief work" (1944) and defined in simple terms the steps of: (1) emancipation from the bondage of her husband; (2) readjustment to an environment without her husband; and (3) forming other satisfying relationships.

In succeeding sessions, Jean was able to talk about her feelings of guilt for not giving her husband adequate care so that he had to go to the hospital the day before he died. The worker helped her sort out the reality of the doctor's recommendation and her husband's choice to go to the hospital. Jean recognized·that it was realistically beyond the capacity of the home setting to care for him at the end of his illness. The worker helped Jean to discuss her feeling of abandonment by friends and relatives following his death and begin to be able to ask for help and find it enthusiastically given. Positive feelings and a review of life with her husband were also explored and gave relief and validation to the many good things in their marriage.

The most difficult task for Jean was to bring herself to talk with the children about their father's death. The pattern of denial initiated by her husband and adopted by her with a front of make believe cheerfulness during his terminal illness made it hard now to change. Between the fifth and sixth interviews, Jean was able to talk with the children. They cried together and shared their feelings for the first time. She said that sharing their pain and loss diminished their guilt and fear and brought the family closer.

Jean accepted a part-time job which fit with the children's school hours. She also took over an office in the Parent Teachers Association which her husband had held. She joined an ongoing support group suggested by the worker and in the following weeks and months reported by phone that she and the children were getting along well.

In this situation I am struck with the importance of the worker's outreach, which enabled an involuntary client to make use of a brief treatment service to begin to work through the tragic death of a husband. The literature on unresolved grief reactions (Lindemann, 1944) places particular emphasis on the importance of assisting individuals and families in coping with loss. Although only the mother was seen, three children were also positively affected; they were freed to use their competence in school and to continue to grow and learn rather than being slowed or arrested in their development because of the energy involved in continued denial of pain. Jean responded to the encouragement of the worker to make use of relatives and friends for support (Swenson, 1979, and Chapter 6 in this volume). Jean responded to the brief treatment model based upon strengths and positive expectations of problem resolution.

In the life-model/competence-development framework, the worker took advantage of a very real *crisis* to reach out and offer specific and concrete help in coping with loss (cf. Golan, Chapter 4 in this volume). She enabled the client to use again her natural support systems. She modeled caring and *interacted* with the client in a supportive and expectant way. The client gained useful, specific knowledge about loss and *learned* to understand and accept her normal feeling of bereavement. She translated her understanding into *action*, discussing their father's death with the children and finding a part-time job.

Practice Principles

As we review these diverse case situations, various common themes and principles emerge as important in assisting involuntary clients to develop competence.

Engaging the Involuntary Client

Engaging the involuntary client stands out as the prerequisite for any helpful encounter. There are specific worker attitudes and skills necessary to the successful engagement process. The worker must be aware that the client is involuntary. He must be finely tuned to the fact that the client is not seeking help. This most often means that the client is not clearly cognizant of the type of help offered or available. If a worker makes the opposite assumption that the client knows and fails to seek help only because of lack of motivation, he is doing the client a rank disservice. The vast majority of people in our population either are not aware of the potential helpfulness of social agencies or they are positively averse to sharing a problem with a stranger. The latter attitude may develop from a strong belief in solving one's own problems, with the concomitant shame and weakness that accompanies the notion of seeking help. Or the client may have had specific negative experiences with the helping professions. Too often negative connotations accompany "social work" because of the confusion with eligibility worker and the rather loose way in which the term social worker has been used.

Essentially the worker with the involuntary client must be especially aware of the edict "Begin where the client is." All of us tend to give enthusiastic lip service to this dictum. Yet, in reality all too often our own perception of what we offer clouds our awareness of where the client is. For example, a director of a residential treatment center expressed a new awareness that a parent could be an involuntary client. She had seen only the positive, helpful aspect of the service to parents. In a few agencies, the same intake process is used with voluntary or involuntary clients, without sufficient explanation, discussion, and engagement behavior on the part of the worker with the involuntary client. The uninitiated client may not follow through with an extensive intake work-up. Or such a process may lead to expectations of ready solutions, serious disappointments, and early withdrawal when they are not forthcoming. A few psychoanalytically oriented therapists approach the involuntary client with an unstructured, stressful interview that is completely bewildering to the uninitiated.

Once recognized, what steps and skills are useful in engaging the involuntary client?

1. Make clear the available service in terms the client can understand. The social worker must reach out and take the initiative in offering services to clients in a way which is meaningful to them. There has been some debate in the profession about self-determination and the right of individuals to make their own decisions, including whether to seek or not to seek help (Miller, 1968). I agree that individuals should have that right—but only when they know and understand that they have a choice, and the nature of that choice.

2. Clarify the client's initial understanding of his or her needs in relation to the agency, and his positive and negative expectation of how his situation might be changed. Any discrepancy between the client's and the agency's or worker's expectations needs to be clearly addressed if the client is to make positive use of the encounter with the agency (Oxley, 1966). Maluccio's (1979a) follow-up study of clients' perceptions of service underscores the importance of an early focus on client expectations. If the early fears and realistic lack of knowledge of what the

agency can offer are not handled, the client will soon be lost to the label "Case closed because of lack of motivation."[3]

3. Discuss with the client ideas, previous experience, and fantasies about talking with a social worker. In the earlier example of the Head Start program, when "social worker" was used, it was necessary to talk with the client about other experiences with social workers and to clarify the difference in roles between the eligibility worker and the Head Start social worker. When a marital partner brings in a spouse, it is essential to dicuss with the partner his or her thoughts about coming in. In a case from my own practice, this was a crucial issue when a wife brought her husband in for counseling. It was only after I kept asking about his own ideas that he shared great apprehension and anxiety that were unknown to his wife. He disclosed that his first marriage had ended very abruptly when his wife asked him to go with her to a marriage counselor and used the session to tell him for the first time that she was unsatisfied with the marriage and wanted a divorce. It is clear that without the open sharing of this information, the resistance of her husband would have prevented any significant work together. The outcome of the counseling that followed was positive for both partners.

4. Demonstrate "usefulness' to the client. This may be accomplished through the crucial skill of attentive listening and expression of interest. The qualities of genuineness, empathy, and positive regard (Rogers, 1970) can be experienced as very useful by a client in stress. However, often a worker can be more specifically and practically useful to a client. For instance, in the case of Fred, the worker enabled Fred to talk with his parents and grandparents about moving to his own parents' home. In the case of Robert, the social worker made herself useful to a parent by an appropriate referral to an employment agency.

5. Assume responsibility and direction when the client is physically or emotionally unable to act. The worker should use his or her competence until it is possible for the client to assume a competent and self-directing role. The case of Bob illustrates this point; the worker and the psychiatric team assumed responsibility for Bob's remaining in the hospital and openly shared that fact with him.

6. Remove as much as possible the "ambiguities" from the treatment encounter. Involuntary clients need clear, specific knowledge as to what is expected of them and what they can expect of the worker. It is only with that kind of openly shared information that the client can begin to trust a process about which he either knows little or already has negative associations.

7. Establish with the client a focus and goal geared to the direction in which the desired change may occur. It is important to look forward to health rather than backward to pathology. The case illustrations in

this chapter have used a health model. In the Edgewood study it was clear that treatment outcome was improved when the boys and the parents established with the worker a specific focus and goal. It is also important that the goal include activity that is meaningful to the client.

8. The engagement process must include the worker's awareness of—and sensitivity to—the client's culture. In the beginning of the case of Fred, it would have been easy for the worker to miss the importance of his bicultural heritage and its ramifications for this boy. With Latin families, it is crucial that the worker greet the family members with the formality that is expected in that culture. In agencies where first names are typically used, the use of a first name addressed to a black man may be viewed as a put-down or infantalizing gesture. It was particularly useful in the case of Peter for the social worker to verbalize her impression that the parents might feel that the school staff was picking on Peter because he was black; bringing this issue out in the open seemed helpful and therapeutic for the family. These are illustrations of small and sometimes subtle issues that can have a large, significant impact on minority clients in a majority culture agency.

Assisting the Involuntary Client in Developing Competence

Many of the same skills and principles are needed to assist the involuntary and the voluntary client in developing competence. I shall delineate a few that are particularly useful with the involuntary client.

1. The setting of realistic expectations. As the involuntary client becomes engaged in the helping process, it is essential that the worker assist him in setting realistic goals and expectations for himself that are geared to his life stage and competence level. For example, Bob initially required the protection of the hospital's decision to hospitalize him. Later he was ready for the worker's encouragement to involve him in family therapy sessions with his parents and girlfriend. The flexible worker will be able to ascertain when she needs to "do for" the client, and when she needs to encourage and sometimes insist that the client accomplish a task for himself. Both actions, administered at the right time, will promote task competence in the client.

2. The importance of relationship. Relationship is a key factor in any therapeutic encounter. It takes on added meaning for the involuntary client whose relationship skills are often in deficit. The establishing of a strong, positive relationship with a client will have a major impact on his development of interpersonal competence. In several of the cases cited earlier, the individual attention, concern, and interest of the school social worker enabled the children to transfer their experiences with the worker to their interpersonal skills with teachers and peers.

3. The setting of realistic limits tends to provide supportive and reassuring structure to the involuntary client. The cases of Robert and Peter in the school setting illustrate this point. The structured setting with the worker provided an environment for the development of task competence.

4. The use of action and practice provides specific teaching in task accomplishment. This treatment intervention was successfully used with Fred in role-play to try out ways in which he might ask to have his needs met. With Robert, his achievement of skill in model building carried over directly to his awareness that he was capable of learning in the classroom situation as well. In the Head Start setting, mothers actively directed the program.

Working with the Ecological System of the Client

In all of the illustrations we have used in this chapter, the worker was aware of the importance of the family, the community, the total context of the client. Along with individual counseling and therapy, the worker actively involved parents, relatives, friends, schools, and community resources. Competence develops in context, and it is essential that both individual and context be viewed as targets for intervention. The environment often needs to be modified so as to become more conducive to a client's growth and problem-solving (cf. Grinnell, Kyte, and Bostwick, Chapter 7 in this volume).

1. It is important to understand the context of the client if one is to understand the client. For example, the fact that Robert and his mother had recently come from the rural Deep South explained his initial suspicion and lack of trust of the white social worker. In the case of Jean, her flight from home and a terminally ill husband needed to be understood in terms of a reaction to crisis, not the irresponsible desertion of husband and children.

2. Intervening in family and community were essential aspects of treatment for Fred. The complications of a several-generation, cross-cultural family might well have seemed overwhelming to the traditional child therapist. Had Fred been seen in play therapy without the focus on parents and extended family, it is unlikely that he could have made the dramatic strides toward health and competence that were evident in his case. The children seen by the school social worker were equally helped by active involvement of parents and teachers. In the case of Bob, having parents and former girlfriend meet in family sessions provided a significant turning point in his progress to health.

3. Knowing and using community resources is an essential aspect of treatment. In the case of Robert the worker was helpful to his mother by referring her to an employment service through which she secured

a desired position. Jean's worker referred her to an ongoing support group at the end of the brief treatment contract for individual work. In each instance the referrals had the effect of contributing to the development of client competence.

Conclusion

In addition to our responsibility for individual clients and their families, we should constantly emphasize attitudes and services that provide a societal context in which people can develop maximum competence. Equal opportunity has a long way to go to be an actuality. We need to work to that end. Racial equality has a long way to go to be realized. We need to work to that end. Equal education exists only on paper. We need to work to make it a reality. Adequate food, housing, child-care facilities, and schools are all essential to an environmental context in which competence can develop and flourish. These issues may be approached from the national political perspective; they may also be approached and influenced by the daily concern and interest at the local community level of social workers' identifying needs and developing ways of meeting them.

Social work has a unique opportunity to look to the development of individual competence in relationships and in task performance. And it has a demand to look to the environment to facilitate the opportunities for the development of individual competence. In an interactional fashion, each will enhance the other. This will occur only when the focus is on the development of opportunities as well as the motivation of the individuals to make use of their idiosyncratic abilities within the environmental context.

Notes

Acknowledgment: Case illustrations have been provided by David Hollands, Peel Leifer, Sue Sawatzky, Julie Ball, Sandy Trimble, and Marian Subee.

1. See Swenson (Chapter 6 in this volume) for consideration of the role of social networks and natural helping systems in social work practice.
2. See Lee (Chapter 10 in this volume) for further discussion of practice designed to promote competence in children.
3. Moore-Kirkland (Chapter 2 in this volume) formulates various approaches to increasing and mobilizing motivation, particularly with involuntary clients.

CHAPTER 13

Promoting Competence in Families of Psychiatric Patients

Eda G. Goldstein

"Our son, Bobby, was an outgoing, popular and intelligent boy," Mr. Joseph explained. "His mother and I were shocked when he dropped out of college. We have always been so proud of him." Mrs. Joseph chimed in. "When he returned home to live with us, we knew something was wrong. He barely left his room and refused to eat. We were desperate. Our family doctor recommended that we hospitalize him. All we could think of was getting him help. We couldn't handle him at home; but when our insurance ran out after a month, the hospital discharged him. He began seeing a psychiatrist privately and was improving but he has been getting worse recently. We're beside ourselves and just don't know what to do or how to help. We have so many questions, but there hasn't seemed to be anyone to answer them. His doctor was highly recommended, but he has not wanted to talk with us in order to gain Bobby's confidence. Now he's recommended we try a longer hospitalization, but we have very little money. We've tried our best as parents, and feel like such failures. There must be something we can do."

Mr. and Mrs. Joseph spoke with emotion to the social worker about their son, Bobby, in a research-oriented admissions interview of a specialized treatment program (Goldstein, 1978; 1979). They felt alone in their efforts to help him, unaware that their words echoed those of an ever-expanding group of families facing severe emotional problems in their close relatives. The needs of such families and the importance of

317

their role in rehabilitative efforts have been addressed by many social workers. Yet social work services to families like the Josephs have been inconsistent in their development and focus and poorly integrated with the treatment of the identified patient. In the absence of a clear model for social work with families of psychiatric patients, professional practices as well as institutional arrangements often have fallen short of a broadly defined therapeutic task with this population. While many families have received individualized services, others have been abandoned to a helpless and hopeless state.

This chapter first will examine practices in psychiatric settings and their underlying theories in order to suggest some of their dysfunctional elements in meeting the needs of families coping with the burden of severe emotional disturbance in a member. The main thesis of this review is that our dominant theories and practices have emphasized family pathology rather than the family's adaptive capacities, or they have narrowly focused on the family as a material resource rather than as a potent emotional support system for the patient. Moreover, they have ignored the family's growth needs in its own right as well as the importance of the social environment, including the institutional setting, in providing supports to the family that help it to be effective in its coping.

The chapter then will suggest the elements of a broader conception of social work practice with families of psychiatric patients that has the goal of promoting competence and self-esteem in family members at its core. Such a model expands its theoretical base in order to do justice to the complexity of the adaptive as well as pathological characteristics of family members. It also views the family as having needs in its own right; as a unit that is stressed considerably in having an emotionally disturbed member; as a crucial support system for the patient; as a possible locus of maladaptive patterns that influence patient behavior and diminish family functioning; and, more importantly, as having the potential for positive impact on treatment outcome and on the rehabilitative process. It recognizes the importance of the mutual and dynamic interplay between the family and the treatment setting and its staff, as well as the crucial role of the social worker at the interface between the setting and the external environment. Such a model enlarges upon the various roles that social workers have carried traditionally in psychiatric settings, challenges some of the usual institutional arrangements and practices, and recognizes and utilizes the institutional and the social environment as a potent force in enhancing coping and mastery.

Historical Developments

The Impact of Psychoanalytic Theory

Freud voiced his pessimism regarding the treatment of families of neurotic patients:

> Let me express a hope that the increasing experience of psychoanalysts will soon lead to agreement on questions of technique and on the most effective method of treating neurotic patients. As regards the treatment of their relatives, I must confess myself utterly at a loss, and I have, in general, little faith in any individual treatment of them. [Freud, 1912:120]

The psychoanalytic treatment of the neuroses focused on the patient's internal conflicts and defensive structure. It viewed drives, fantasy life, unconscious processes as primary, relegating reality and the interpersonal field to a position of little significance. The only contemporary relationship of importance was that of analyst and patient, and it was viewed as a screen upon which the conflicts of the past were projected.

When psychoanalytic theory and technique were applied more extensively to the treatment of hospitalized psychiatric patients, differing views of the role of the family were reflected in hospital practices. Many psychiatrists saw no role for the family and thought it was critical to keep the family away from the patient's therapist in order to safeguard the transference relationship, postulated as essential to the therapeutic process. Others identified individual family members as pathological agents and consequently excluded them from the treatment process. In child guidance settings, individual parents often were seen as having an ongoing negative effect on their children due to the personality pathology of the parents, who themselves required intensive psychotherapy.

Social workers' roles with families varied also, as the social worker could be the solicitor of money, clothes, and other material resources, the person who contacted the family at discharge, or the history-taker. In many instances, the family was kept from intruding on the psychiatric staff by the social worker, who kept them informed about the progress of the patient, while "therapeutically oriented" social workers treated the pathology of the individual relative.

The social work literature began to suggest alternative views of the family as early as the mid-1940s, when articles appeared calling for greater attention to the impact of mental illness on the family and to the family's role in enhancing or obstructing therapeutic progress. Richardson (1945) was the first to consider the stress of emotional disorder on family members. He and numerous other authors recommended social work services to help families express themselves and to lessen their anxieties and fears (e.g., Faris, 1955; Hughes, 1958; and Levinson and Withey, 1955).

The coping patterns and the obstacles to effective coping that such families manifest were documented vividly in a pioneer study conducted by Yarrow, Clausen, and Robbins (1955:33–48). Echoing these findings, Nealon (1964:302–22) and Grob and Edinburg (1972:14–22) described family members' anxiety, guilt, low self-esteem, depression, feeling of social stigma, shame, and concern about hospitalization. The disorganizing effects of emotional disturbance on family members always were in evidence in the population they studied. Identifiable stages in the responses of the family to the psychiatric illness of a member were noted by Raymond, Slaby, and Lieb (1975:495–98). All of these authors linked their findings to the need for social work services to such families in order to help them cope with the impact of illness and hospitalization. The importance of the family in the rehabilitative process was also addressed by numerous authors (e.g., Beutner and Branch, 1959; Freeman, 1947; and Muncie, 1950). Others described the crucial connection between successful treatment of emotional disorder and family involvement (e.g., Burgum, 1942; Polskin, 1961; and Szurek, 1952).

The practice model stemming from psychoanalytic theory is still used widely by social workers in psychiatric settings; thus, social work practice continues to be wedded to a restrictive model, even though alternative approaches exist that stress the importance of human beings in transaction with their environment, the more adaptive capacities of individuals, and a more complex conception of causality. As recently as the late 1970s, numerous articles drew attention to the lingering presence of dysfunctional attitudes and practices with respect to families and described the difficulty of integrating an approach to the family with the treatment of the identified patient (e.g., Anderson, 1977; Goldstein, 1979). Many social workers continue to view the modification of individual intrapsychic conflict as the best form of treatment and stress the pathological effects of the family and social environment on the patient rather than the importance of promoting problem-solving, competence, and self-esteem.

The Impact of Family Systems Approaches

A second major theoretical perspective on the family of the psychiatric patient that has had widespread impact on practice arose in the late 1950s. It focused on the structure and process of family life as it causes and perpetuates symptomatology in family members. The clinical impetus to this view came from attempts to deal with treatment failures through individual psychotherapy of hospitalized persons.

When a patient's treatment was stalemated, the family was called in to discuss future plans. Often there was a marked and surprising change in the condition of the patient. Moreover, practitioners began to accumulate clinical experience with families who appeared to sabotage treatment efforts just when they seemed successful and with family members who were themselves disorganized or became symptomatic when the identified patient seemed to improve (e.g., Ackerman, 1965; Burgum, 1942; Fleck, Cornelison, Norton, and Lidz, 1957; and Szurek, 1952:296–302). These observations focused attention on the mutual reverberations of patient and family that might explain the lingering presence of certain types of symptomatology, provide the key to understanding causality, and point to new directions for successful treatment.

While differing in their special foci, family system approaches defined the family as a well-regulated unit charaterized by a homeostatic principle, always in a process of dynamic reequilibration, and composed of a set of interfaces with its surrounding environment, with which it is also in a state of continuous transaction and regulation. Each family was viewed as unique in the way it organized to meet the needs of its members and in the conscious and unconscious rules it lived by. Symptoms in an individual family member served to balance forces within the family as well as the individual's internal needs, so that one could not understand psychiatric disorder as occurring in an individual apart from his total familial context. Moreover, the disorder itself was symptomatic of a larger disorder located in the family system (Bateson, et al., 1956; Bowen, 1960).

In contrast to psychoanalytic theory, this perspective broadens the locus of intervention to include the family unit and has been adopted by many social workers. However, it is still a model that focuses on pathology, merely substituting the internal world of the family for the intrapsychic life of the individual. It prescribes intensive treatment to modify family pathology, does not address the full range of needs of the families of psychiatric patients, and does not link the family with the surrounding social environment. Moreover, the practices associated with diagnosing and treating family pathology continue to obscure an appreciation of the positive forces in families and in other aspects of the social environment that can be mobilized to help both patient and family in meeting their needs, enhancing their growth functioning, and promoting their competence.

The Growth of the Biological Perspective

A resurgence of interest in genetic and constitutional determinants of severe emotional disorder has been buttressed by an accumulation of research evidence linking hereditary and other biological factors to the incidence of mental illness. Profound changes in treatment philosophy and services and in governmental funding have accompanied these developments. The use of psychotropic medication—specifically the major tranquilizers and the antidepressants—is rampant in both acute and chronic cases. Research has supported the efficacy of such drugs in alleviating many conditions, while revealing less than impressive effects for the various forms of psychotherapy when used in comparisons to such drugs (Arieti, 1974; May, 1969). The idea that "bad genes" or a chemical imbalance really do cause mental illness and that drugs are the treatment of choice is pervading psychiatric practice.

While this approach does not preclude various forms of psychosocial intervention, its proponents minimize and criticize nonbiologically oriented methods. Patients and families are advised that appropriate medication and dosage will provide the cure. Diagnostic work-ups focus not only on the development of the patient's symptoms but also on mental illness in the entire family, going back several generations. The family is enlisted to monitor the patient's medication, to participate in genetic and biochemical family studies of mental disorder, and in some cases to consider genetic counseling with respect to future offspring. The family's needs during the treatment process are not addressed, nor is the possible interrelatedness of patient symptomatology and improvement with family functioning.

Far from eliminating the need for supportive services to families, this approach creates new problems, as families require help in dealing with the relative who is maintained at home and in coping with the implications of hereditary illness. For instance, parents can be guilty for having passed on "bad genes." Families may manifest severe conflict that may be sustaining symptomatology in a member. They may need help in enhancing their problem-solving capacity, in repairing injuries to self-esteem, in alleviating anxiety, depression, and guilt, or in locating and using appropriate resources. Social workers in settings that emphasize the biological perspective or who are involved in any case where such an approach is indicated need to individualize the family members involved and bring an integrated conception to their practice.

The Community Mental Health Perspective

In the 1960s the advent of medications that reduced symptomatology in severely disturbed patients, enabling them to be discharged and maintained outside of hospitals, joined with a humanitarian and idealistic sociopolitical thrust and eventually with economic necessity to create an enormous population of patients living in the community near or with their families. Hospital stays were reduced, hospitalizations were prevented, and short-term solutions to address long-term suffering were emphasized. Ego psychology, crisis theory, social role and social deviance theories, and community and organizational theories were used as underpinnings to various therapeutic efforts.

These changes in public mental health policy drew attention to families of patients as "agents of rehabilitation and bearers of burden" (Kreisman and Joy, 1974). One repercussion of this policy was that the burden of treatment was placed on the family, since rehabilitative services in the community emerged in a fragmented and uncoordinated fashion and have fallen far short of keeping pace with needs. In principle it was assumed that the family might serve as a support system for the patient in the community. In practice, the nature of the positive forces in families that can enable successful rehabilitation was poorly understood, and services to help families carry this role have not been forthcoming (Doll, 1976).

Toward a Social Work Practice Perspective

Each of the perspectives reviewed so far in this chapter exists in our current armamentarium in dealing with the problems of patients with severe emotional disorder. Each embodies a particular view of the family's role in causing mental disorder and of intervention with families. But there is a lack of integration of these approaches and polarizations have evolved and rigidified. To make an optimal professional contribution, social workers should be guided by a practice framework that encompasses the diverse needs of this population of patients and families and an individualized approach to intervention that does justice to the adaptive as well as pathological capacities of people.

Such a framework is suggested by the ecological perspective (Germain, 1973; Germain, 1979; and Maluccio, Chapter 1 in this volume). This view embodies a multicausal explanation of human development and human problems. It emphasizes the growth potential of people, their creative and adaptive capacities and struggles, mutuality between people and environments, and the therapeutic potential of life events. It advocates an individualizing role for social work intervention (Meyer, 1970). It stresses the need for understanding all the transacting forces in a person's total life space and for interventions aimed at promoting positive changes in the various systems impinging on individuals. It highlights the importance of the social worker's location at points of crisis in people's lives, along with the need to help people "match their coping patterns with qualities of impinging environment" in order to effect positive changes in both people and environments

(Gordon, 1969). The approach to families also draws on Maluccio's writings (1979b:282–304; and in press), which identify the promotion of competence as a central feature of social work practice.

In this section we will discuss and illustrate the practice principles stemming from such a perspective when it is applied to the population of families of individuals with severe emotional disorder in outpatient as well as inpatient settings.

Biopsychosocial and Contemporaneous View of Causality

Both assessment and choice of intervention reflect a broadened view of the nature of causality that encompasses biological, intrapsychic, interpersonal, and environmental factors and that reflect current person–environment transactions as well as past development. This view moves away from a linear concept of causality and from one that isolates problems either within the person or in the environment. Rather, manifest "pathology" may stem from a mismatching of needs and available resources, with the past being important as it is reflected in the here and now (Goldstein, 1979).

It is crucial to locate the cause of a particular problem and determine the features of the biopsychosocial field that may be mobilized as part of the solution. To do this, the practitioner needs to evaluate the transacting forces operative at a given point in time in an individual's life space. Siporin (1972:91–109) has described the nature of this broader-based assessment in his work on situational diagnosis. The focus of intervention is to improve the person–environmental fit. The nature of the therapeutic task has been suggested by Bandler (1963:27–44): "First we must identify and help remove blocks and obstacles . . . second, we must mobilize the progressive forces with which we ally ourselves and which at the appropriate time we can mobilize."

Assessment of the Family Environment and Family Coping

In applying this multicausal perspective to social work intervention with the families of severely disturbed individuals, the nature of the fit between family and patient is assessed and the ways in which a more positive fit can be effected is considered. It is important to assess the inner and outer stresses with which family members are coping; the ways in which they are coping; the internal and external resources available to them; the positive and negative effects of their coping on the patient and on one another; the obstacles to effective coping from inside and outside the family; and the mutual impact of the family, patient, and the social environment. Moreover, a broader-based assessment identifies specifically the internal and external factors that are inhibiting effective problem-solving and that lower self-esteem and competence in family members. Diminished problem-solving capacities and profound feelings of shame and guilt at having an emotionally disturbed relative may stem from deep-seated individual conflicts or may be induced or reinforced by social or institutional environments.

The following three examples illustrate the multicausal perspective in which family coping is viewed and the varied responses to the stress of emotional disorder in a relative.

The Nesbitt Family

Rita, an artistically talented, Protestant, 22-year-old daughter of Mr. and Mrs. Nesbitt, made two suicide attempts in the past two years and another four years ago, each when Dr. Young, her outpatient psychiatrist, went on vacation. The Nesbitts became concerned about Rita when at 15 she cried inconsolably, had severe headaches, daydreamed, and cut classes. The guidance counselor in the private school she attended recommended psychiatric help for her, and the parents consulted Dr. Young, recommended by Mr. Nesbitt's brother, who had sought psychiatric help over many years. After an extensive evaluation, Dr. Young told the Nesbitts that Rita was very disturbed, might never be able to fulfill her ambition to have a successful artistic career, and that she would need their emotional support as well as long-term psychotherapy to help her cope with everyday life. They were very upset initially, but had confidence in the doctor, whom Rita seemed to like. They admired her for the courage she showed in trying to help herself and paid for rather costly psychiatric sessions for seven years.

Alarmed by her recent suicide attempts, the Nesbitts sought consultation from Dr. Young, who feels that Rita makes these attempts at critical phases in her treatment, and this does not mean she is getting worse. The Nesbitts do feel that Rita has made enormous progress with Dr. Young. Wanting to be sure that they were not being blinded by their high opinion of him, the Nesbitts sought a second opinion from an eminent psychiatrist who concurred with Dr. Young. Married twenty-nine years, the Nesbitts feel they have also made progress. They sought marital counseling when Rita was 16, when arguments and misunderstandings at home escalated. They feel that they blamed each other for Rita's problems, allowed her to manipulate them with her difficulties, and permitted divisiveness. Mrs. Nesbitt became overly involved with Rita while Mr. Nesbitt withdrew into his successful career.

After several months of counseling they realized that they were letting Rita's problems affect them and that they could not continue doing so, especially with two other children at home. While the past years have been stressful at times, they enjoy their family, feel close to one another, and generally are able to ride out difficult periods together.

The Gould Family

Mr. and Mrs. Gould are middle-aged, Jewish, foreign-born parents of a 21-year-old daughter, Francine, who was hospitalized psychiatrically after a life-threatening weight loss, with no known organic basis. The Goulds denied the severity of Francine's problems, coming slowly to the appreciation that she needed psychiatric help. No one in their close-knit family and friendship groups had ever seen a psychiatrist, and acquaintances offered numerous home remedies for curing Francine's problems. When she became worse, Mr. and Mrs. Gould became panicky, consulted their internist who, after several weeks of unsuccessful efforts to curb Francine's serious weight loss, recommended psychiatric hospitalization. Seeing no other alternative, the Goulds agreed, wanting desperately to help their daughter but still feeling that they should be solving the problems themselves.

The Goulds experienced the first few days that Francine was in the hospital as a nightmare. No visiting or telephone calls were allowed. They felt guilty for having hospitalized her and fearful about her condition and called the social worker every day. Significant in their background was that they had fled Germany in 1938 and lost several relatives during the Second World War in concentration camps. They physical separation from—and institutionalization of—Francine evoked recollections of their earlier life experiences. Shortly after visiting her the first time a week after she was admitted, the Goulds' panic subsided. They were more relaxed in seeing her surroundings and that she was looking better. When a longer hospitalization was recommended several weeks later, the Goulds agreed. They wanted to do anything they could to help Francine.

It became apparent that, in the year preceding the hospitalization, family life was centered on Francine to the detriment of what otherwise seemed a solid marriage of twenty-eight years. While a value was placed on close family ties and a somewhat overinvolved parent–child relationship pattern existed, both Mr. and Mrs. Gould expressed relief that they now could share the burden of Francine's problems with professionals, as they each felt emotionally drained and aware of growing conflict in their own relationship. They agreed to attend weekly sessions with the social worker to discuss their concerns about the present and future and what they could do to help Francine.

The Silver Case

Mitchell, an 18-year-old boy, was admitted to the hospital after almost dying from an overdose of sleeping pills. His parents revealed a stormy account of serious marital and family discord, predating Mitchell's birth but frequently centering on him. The parents disagreed about almost every detail of history about Mitchell and in their perceptions of him as well as about their views of child-rearing. However, they considered themselves overprotective, worrying constantly about their children but not knowing how to set limits. Both Mr. and Mrs. Silver's parents were poor and died at an early age. The Silvers were self-conscious about not having finished college and about their meager finances. They sacrificed to put Mitchell through private school and give him material things so that he would not feel inferior to the other boys with whom he associated. They agreed on how important Mitchell was to each of them.

Both were devastated by his suicide attempt and, despite their chronic and pervasive marital discord, agreed to hospitalization. Aware of Mitchell's difficulties for a long time, they had sought advice from their family doctor, who began to see him on a regular basis and treated him with medication. The Silvers followed the doctor's recommendations (which seemed ill-advised) until they saw that Mitchell was not improving. Having difficulty concentrating at work, Mr. Silver confided in his employer, who recommended a psychiatrist for Mitchell. The latter attended weekly sessions for a month, when the doctor went on vacation and the suicide attempt occurred.

In their initial session with the hospital social worker, the Silvers shared their feelings that their problems had affected Mitchell. They then became willing to engage in family treatment in an effort to try to resolve long-standing difficulties.

In the first of these examples, the Nesbitt family acknowledged their daughter's problems realistically, seemed to do everything possible to help her, and managed the emotional stresses resulting from Rita's problems and from other aspects of their family life fairly well. They had abundant financial resources and were able to mobilize and use professional help when necessary. The Nesbitts reflected a sense of self-esteem and competence. Social work services were offered to them as needed to keep them informed of Rita's progress and to maintain their positive involvement in her rehabilitation, an important element not only for Rita but also for the family's sense of competence.

In the second example the Goulds tried to help their daughter but denied the seriousness of her problems and avoided seeking appropriate professional help until a crisis occurred. When their panic subsided, these difficulties seemed to be related as much to special factors in their life experiences and to the impact of attitudes and mores of their reference groups as to pathological family patterns. Their genuine motivation to help their daughter, their emotionally drained existence, and their need for help in dealing with Francine were apparent. They felt like failures, were guilt-ridden, and demonstrated diminished problem-solving capacities. Weekly meetings with the social worker were offered, initially aimed at enabling the Goulds to share their concerns, to diminish their sense of guilt and failure, and to restore their capacity for problem-solving. Later the goals were to enable them to cope more effectively with Francine and to strengthen their marital relationship.

Finally, the Silvers reflect more chronically maladaptive marital and family relationships in people who had few external supports but who were willing to engage in treatment themselves. Weekly marital sessions with the social worker and weekly family sessions with Mitchell and his therapist as well as their social worker were offered to modify the ways the Silvers dealt with each other and with Mitchell, to develop problem-solving capacities in areas in which they seemed deficient, and to enable the Silvers to experience themselves as more effective in managing their family life.

As these cases suggest, the individualized assessment of families leads to planning differential interventions that can enhance the family's capacity to cope with its internal needs and external stresses and also to improve the fit between the family and the patient.

Positive Emphasis on Growth and Adaptation throughout the Individual and Family Life Cycles

Individuals have the capacity to grow and change throughout life. The motivation and capacity for growth, successful adaptation, ego mastery, and enhanced coping do not stop at a prescribed age but continue through all developmental phases (Erikson, 1959:50–164; Hartmann, 1958; White, 1963).[1] The interplay of contemporary events, needs, resources, and coping mechanisms is crucial; at any given phase of development, when the personality may be in greater flux, individuals may resolve previous difficulties in mastering current tasks or may develop new ways of coping with internal and external factors. Despite the presence of stable personality features or of limiting factors within individuals, certain characteristics may be more open to influence at times of crisis or disequilibrium. As emphasized by Golan (Chapter 4 in this volume) in her discussion of transitional and crisis states, at these times the person may be particularly open to change.

The life-cycle concept has been extended to our understanding of the family. The family unit itself has been described by several authors

(Rapoport, R., 1965:75–87; Rhodes, 1977:301–11; Rodgers, 1973) as having specific developmental phases. Thus, major tasks for the family include coping with the internal and changing needs of its members, with its changing needs as a unit, and with multiple stresses from the external environment. These factors, both internal and external, require that the family learn new means of coping and thus provide the impetus for positive changes in family functioning. Maluccio (in press) has built on these ideas in relating a life-model perspective on the family to social work practice. Elsewhere (Goldstein, 1979), I have applied this perspective to work with families with emotionally disturbed offspring. As I have written, it is crucial to assess the phase-specific needs of the family and of key family members as well as those of the identified patient in efforts to understand patient symptomatology and in determining intervention. The patient's manifest problems and the family's "pathological" patterns may reflect difficulties in the mesh between the patient's and family's ways of coping with developmental tasks. The obstacles to achieving a more adaptive fit may stem not only from intrafamilial or intrapsychic factors but also from a mismatching between family needs and available environmental supports. The goals of intervention therefore become those of identifying and modifying both internal and external factors that are obstructing successful mastery of developmental tasks in the patient, in the family, and in the fit between patient and family.

One of the most frequently encountered examples of the mismatching between family needs and individual needs pertain to the clash between maladaptive coping mechanisms developed to deal with the needs of middle-aged parents and those developed by adolescents and young adults in their efforts to emancipate from parental ties, to consolidate identity, and to form intimate relationships outside the family. It has been customary to view these problems as stemming from individual or parental "pathology" and to direct treatment efforts at helping the patient separate from the family by means of intensive individual psychotherapy and/or intensive family therapy. While in some cases it may be necessary to employ these modalities, often families may not be as "pathological" as they seem. Social work intervention can be directed toward helping family members to identify their own phase-specific needs and to find more adaptive ways of meeting them both inside and outside the family.

In the Gould case described earlier, the parents were in their late forties when their daughter Francine, in her late teens, began to have serious difficulties. Although Francine was 21 at the time she was hospitalized, difficulties around autonomy were prominent in her clinical picture. Her parents' concerns reflected anxiety around issues of separation that seemed to escalate when Francine entered her teens, but initially they described their relationships with her as "normal."

We have good, close family relationships. That has been very important to us. We don't think it's abnormal to be close to your children. We do worry a lot, and we've always done a lot for Francine. We did her laundry, her cooking, and we even got an A for her course in German. We had misgivings about her going away to college. We missed her terribly. In a way, we were relieved when she came home after a year, decided not to return, and went to a city school. With Francine in the hospital, we feel that there's a void, and it's lonely. We wish we weren't so dependent on her and so lonely now, but it seems natural when you have raised a daughter to feel this way.

Several months later, the Goulds described the overinvolvment with their daughter to the social worker somewhat differently, reflecting on some of the possible sources of it, identifying needs that currently existed in the family.

We don't think it would be good for us or for Francine to have as much closeness as before. It will be hard, but we would like to see her living on her own when she leaves the hospital. She really needs to have her own life. We've had our chance. She needs hers too. We're trying not to do too much for her. If she says she doesn't want to eat, we say, "Don't eat," and we stay calm. She responds better to that. We have to admit that we have been too dependent on Francine. We did our best—our ignorant best. You don't take courses on being parents, but we looked to her as a companion. Maybe we were disappointed in each other, and Francine filled in the void. The year she was away at college was hard on us. We fought more. We had some serious problems early in our marriage, but divorce was unheard of, and we did love each other. We still have a lot of feeling for one another, but we haven't been focused on ourselves—just on Francine. We're not getting any younger. We haven't wanted to face getting older. We both need to get outside of ourselves more, but also to do more together without Francine. We don't have to work at our own relationship when she is the focus of our attention.

The Goulds were able to use supportive social work intervention to identify their needs and maladaptive coping. But there are other cases in which deep-seated familial pathology does exist and therapeutic efforts may need to be much more intensive in order to modify serious blocks to phase-appropriate separation. Nevertheless, we need to ask whether we do the utmost to identify and mobilize strengths that exist and to utilize the power of developmental processes in working with families. Frequently, self-fulfilling prophecies about the resilience of familial pathology are created and maintained.

Therapeutic Potential of Life Events and the Strategic Location of Social Work Services

Closely related to the concept of developmental phase is the idea of crisis. Many authors have described the potential of individuals for growth as a result of traumatic events, developmental phases, and role transitions (Erikson, 1959:50–100; Golan, 1979, and Chapter 4 in this volume; Goldstein, 1973; Lindemann, 1944; Rapoport, L., 1965:22–31; Rapoport, R., 1965:75–87).

Families too confront crises, and the need to cope with severe emotional disturbance in a close relative may create a crisis for the family. Such an event, in upsetting the family's equilibrium, also presents it with new challenges. The ways families have dealt with stress in the past and the nature of family relationship patterns, strengths, and difficulties may have bearing on how families will cope with the crisis of psychiatric disturbance in a member; but family members may be able to use the crisis itself to enhance coping and mastery in the here and now.

The Jackson Case

Mr. and Mrs. Jackson, a Catholic couple in their early fifties, sought family counseling reluctantly at the urging of a priest whom they consulted about their 14-year-old son, Peter, after learning about his truancy from high school and probable drug abuse. When the Jacksons tried to enforce the punishment of a week-long restriction on Peter's outside activities, he ran away, returning twenty-four hours later drunk. Meanwhile, his parents searched his room, finding a supply of marijuana and associated paraphernalia. This episode followed a year of Peter's resistance to his parents' efforts to regulate his behavior, which was becoming increasingly rebellious. The Jacksons no longer trusted Peter, feeling that he lied to them. Peter accused his parents of controlling him like a puppet on a string and wanting him to be a "goodie-goodie" like his sister, the Jacksons' 19-year-old adopted daughter, currently away for her second year of college.

The parents agreed that Peter, their only natural child, was special but that both children had filled a long-standing void in their marital relationship. Each parent felt emotionally isolated from the other, had a civil but strained, noncommunicative relationship, and had given up on changing it. Mrs. Jackson earlier had sought psychotherapy, but her husband refused to attend. She frequently threatened separation, but held back because divorce

was against her religious and family values. Mr. Jackson described his relationship with Peter as a close one, in contrast to his relationship with his
own father, a stern disciplinarian, who sent Mr. Jackson to military school.
Mrs. Jackson alternated in feeling very close to Peter on the one hand,
envious and angry at his freedom on the other, connecting these reactions to
a turbulent relationship with her own brother, who was the favorite child of
her parents. Mr. Jackson had high expectations of Peter, but was laissez-
faire in setting limits on him, while angry at him for not doing "what he
should be doing." Mrs. Jackson was the stern disciplinarian, but under the
impact of her son's and husband's accusations that she was mean she would
reverse her "rulings" and try to make up for their punishing quality.

Despite their chronic marital problems, the Jacksons had developed an
equilibrium, albeit an unhappy one, until Peter's behavior escalated to crisis
proportions. They were unable to work together in coping with Peter, whose
difficulties intensified their interpersonal tensions and their long-standing
differences about child-rearing. In early sessions with the social worker who
saw them for a family evaluation, the Jacksons were skeptical about and
fearful of ongoing therapeutic involvement and focused on their son's rebellious behavior as their main problem. They were ashamed and resentful at
the priest's strong recommendation that they seek family counseling, feeling
they were being blamed for Peter's problems and that they had failed. They
also felt humiliated at having to discuss their family problems with a
stranger. The social worker supported their efforts to do the right thing in
following the priest's suggestion despite their reservations and their parental
concern for their son, and addressed their confusion and bewilderment
about their son's difficulties when they had tried to do their best as parents.

As the family discussed their past and current relationships, the chronic
disharmony between the Jacksons emerged directly in the sessions. The
parents volunteered that they felt their marital problems had affected Peter,
but that they saw nothing that they could do now to make up for that. The
social worker suggested that Peter's behavior might be a cry for help not
only for himself but for the entire family and that at such a time of turmoil
perhaps new solutions to long-standing problems might be possible. While
Mrs. Jackson was pessimistic about her relationship with her husband
changing, Mr. Jackson said he wanted to try to work things out and that he
had not fully appreciated how much he had "put his head in the sand" for
so many years. Mrs. Jackson, startled by her husband's willingness to attend
family sessions, stated that "I'll believe it when I see it," but then softened
and tearfully said that she wanted to have hope.

As Perlman (1968:149–228), Meyer (1970:158–61) and others have
emphasized, since clients seek social work assistance during such crucial moments in their lives, practitioners are in optimal positions to be
catalysts of growth. Furthermore, social workers have an unique posi-

tion "at the crossroads of life": a "location on the scene of the natural life event [that] will in itself make help available and more possible" (Meyer, 1970:160). In their various roles within mental health settings social workers are at the interface between people and environments. The challenge is to find ways of using this strategic location to provide services that promote the improvement of the identified patient as well as the coping of the family.

Restructuring the Institutional Environment

Social workers practicing within a therapeutic orientation generally have focused on changing the person rather than the environment or the transactions between the two. In contrast, in formulating a life-model approach to social work practice with families, Maluccio (in press) cites the major task of social systems and institutions as facilitating the family's adaptive tasks by enhancing the mutual fit between the family and its impinging environment. Central to this task is the promotion of competence, which Maluccio (1979b) defines as the network of skills, knowledge, and talents that enable a person to interact effectively with the environment. In addition, in applying an ecological perspective to social work practice in health care (Germain, 1977:67–76) describes four aspects of the environment required by patients for effective coping with the stress of illness and disability: (1) opportunities for taking action, exercising judgment, and making decisions; (2) staff behavior and patient services that support patients' self-esteem and reward patients' coping efforts; (3) organizational policies and procedures that respect patients' life-styles, cultural values, and social supports; and (4) the provision of information in the appropriate amount at the appropriate time. She notes various ways in which health organizations and services create obstacles to successful coping when they deprive patients of these necessary nutriments.

So too with the families of patients, the nature of the setting itself and its policies are an integral part of the therapeutic program. Families to whom positive roles in rehabilitative efforts are not allocated, who are not included in decision-making, who are deprived of necessary information, who are treated insensitively by bureaucratically efficient procedures developed for the benefit of staff, who are expected to conform and to comply with organizational necessities or labeled as obstructive, and who are viewed as worthy of blame are systematically robbed of opportunities for enhancing competence. Attention to aspects of the institutional environment that may provide a more human experience for people can provide such opportunities.

Families can become collaborators in the treatment process. Involving them as early as possible, even prior to hospitalization, is advisable. Arranging a conference with the family and the staff may provide them with needed information as well as allow for a sharing of mutual expectations that can enable more effective decision-making. Obviously, when there is a sudden or emergency hospitalization, this may not be possible, but arranging for meeting with the family at the point of admission or soon after can be done. The family also can be brought onto ongoing treatment planning by members of the treatment team rather than viewed as outsiders.

Families are consumers of services. There is a value in—and a necessity for—providing them with as much information as possible about psychiatric illness in general and the problems of their members in particular. This is not an easy task as there is so much that is unknown in psychiatry. Perhaps the most important questions cannot be answered. Moreover, questions regarding diagnosis, prognosis, and the specific nature of treatment may be repetitive, despite answers given, because of the complex meanings attached to them. Nevertheless, even putting aside the accountability issue involved, provision of information enables people to perceive situations more realistically and enhances problem-solving capacities.

A useful approach in the beginning phase of work with a family is to have orientation groups, which serve a threefold purpose: They provide the families with an opportunity to air questions as well as to receive information; they allow families the opportunity to meet one another; and they allow the families to meet members of the staff who will be involved in the care of their relative. The use of other task-oriented groups during the treatment process can be valuable. Scheduling family meetings with staff after visiting hours may make visiting a part of the therapeutic program as well as bring the families into closer and regular contact with staff members. This allows the hospital staff to become real to the families and the families to become real to the hospital staff. Regularly scheduled sessions with the treating psychiatrist or other key treatment personnel are also helpful.

Providing information and allowing for greater participation in decision-making increases demands upon staff for explanations of the why and what of the treatment program. The value of this in terms of the positive effects on the rehabilitative process and in sensitizing staff and families to each other far outweighs the strains involved; but there need to be mechanisms and structures established whereby staff can discuss their impressions of and concerns about the family's more active participation with staff.

From a broader perspective, such involvement challenges the ways roles and decision-making generally are conceived of in psychiatric settings. The medical staff view themselves as experts, and a mystique often exists around decision-making. It has been argued that this enables the experts to do what is necessary, unhampered by the interference of lay people whose knowledge, even if sophisticated, is tinged by their emotional involvement. The potential dangers of this view have been pointed out in recent years. On the other hand, the advocacy of a swing to consumer control of mental health settings is not the purpose of this suggestion. Rather, there is a middle ground that enables professionals who do have certain types of expertise to perform their functions while sharing their thinking in honest, direct ways with people who depend on them for help. Further, with those families who must change in order for treatment to be effective, their successful engagement in the program is more likely to occur if they are active and full participants.

The following comments came from a family member of a hospitalized patient after a meeting was held with the families of the patients and the treatment staff in an effort to engage the families in a more collaborative relationship with the hospital.

I have been appointed a spokesperson for many of the families who attended last week's meeting with your staff. As you know, we have felt that the hospital has kept us in the dark unnecessarily and thus found the meeting very helpful. We hope you will continue to have such meetings with us and with other families. We really are capable of understanding your terminology, and more than anything else want to be helpful. We resent being treated as if we have neglected or abused our children deliberately, or that we are so fed up that we don't want anything to do with them. Most of us realize what a long-term prospect is ahead of us and our children for there to be some repair, and want to know what we can do. There is so much written and described these days in the media about mental illness, it is easy to become bewildered and confused as to what is good treatment. It was very helpful to get the opinions of those who are caring for our children directly. We are all impressed with the high caliber and sensitivity of your staff and want to thank you again for talking with us.

Engaging the "Resistant Family"

What about those individuals who do not wish to avail themselves of such social work services? Labeling these people as unmotivated, resistant, or unworkable may be dysfunctional to our work. In a study by Goldstein (1979:350–59) on the impact of parental attitudes on psychiatric treatment outcome, parental willingness to be involved in the treatment of the identified patient was a key factor in how much service the family received, in patient improvement, and in parental change. These findings point to the challenge of discovering ways of engaging individuals who are not reachable by our usual methods (cf. Moore-Kirkland, Chapter 2 in this volume).

The social worker located in a psychiatric setting encounters family members' intense feelings of anxiety, blame, and guilt. These feelings may result in avoidance of meaningful involvement. Efforts to reach such people require a respect for their coping needs and sensitive attempts to establish connections with strengths rather than a focus on pathological patterns. This is not to suggest that there is no such pathology, but that the path to meaningful engagement lies in tapping positive motivations, attitudes, and characteristics. We should eliminate the practice of trying to keep a family that has been labeled as destructive or resistant away from the treatment of the identified hospitalized or nonhospitalized patient. Such an effort only masks the harmful effects that reassert themselves later in the treatment process. These consequences are seen time and time again, when patients who do not improve must be discharged, often back to their families of origin, because there is nowhere else for them to go; or when patients do not improve, and it becomes clear that their interactions with family members seem to be sustaining the problems. In both instances, not only is there a treatment failure of the patient but a failure in efforts to help the family to cope in more adaptive ways that are critical to patient improvement as well as to enhancement of family functioning.[2]

The Whiteman Case

Mr. and Mrs. Whiteman, a Jewish couple in their late forties, were referred to the social worker for a family evaluation by Dr. Horne, the new private psychiatrist seeing their 20-year-old daughter, Nancy. She had seen three psychiatrists previously in the past two years for her agoraphobic symptoms. Nancy was fearful of leaving the house alone and had become dependent on the company of one or both of her parents when she did. These fears had worsened to the point that she could not even walk her dog around the block near her suburban home. Each of the three psychiatrists who had seen Nancy before had advised the parents that they were overprotective and suffocating their daughter, who needed to become independent of them. Each had recommended individual treatment for Nancy, along with making her live away from home.

With each recommendation, the Whitemans, in a seemingly cooperative way, agreed to the plan. Nancy would move out, only to call her parents to take her to psychotherapy sessions or to accompany her wherever she wanted. She would continue in therapy for a time until a crisis would ensue between her and her parents over her constant demands on them for companionship. They would become convinced that the therapist was not helping and seek another psychiatrist. At age 20, Nancy, a talented and intelligent young woman, had not worked, attended school, or socialized other than on the telephone and with family for over two years since graduating from high school and dropping out of college.

When the social worker met with this family initially, the parents were contemptuous of the professionals with whom they had been associated, feeling that psychiatrists were interested only in breaking up families. While they stated that Dr. Horne and the social worker were highly recommended and worthy of trust, it was clear that they expected to be disappointed again. It also became clear during the evaluation why other psychiatrists felt that Mr. and Mrs. Whiteman were overprotective: Each parent found Nancy's companionship preferable to that of the spouse; each had come from lonely family backgrounds, fraught with the tensions and terrors associated with Europe during the Second World War; and each valued a close family that could be a cushion against the dangers of the outside world. It seemed likely that, despite their seeking of psychiatric help whenever Nancy's problems became extreme, the Whitemans were threatened by the prospect of her becoming an adult and leaving home; they communicated this to Nancy in subtle ways and opposed the very psychiatric help they sought. It was evident that each psychiatrist's direct efforts to separate Nancy from her parents intensified the anxiety of all family members and doomed the treatment recommendations from the start.

Following a period of evaluation, the social worker recommended that Nancy stay with the family, and that, rather than her seeing her individual therapist only, the whole family be seen in sessions regularly. The Whitemans were surprised and relieved at this recommendation, which seemed to diminish their intense anxiety about losing their daughter. They began to feel a part of the treatment, since Nancy's psychiatrist supported the plan. It became apparent that they thought in extremes; either Nancy was independent, in which case she would not want to associate with them, or she would be their "little girl" forever.

Treatment sessions were used to explore these issues, to find middle-ground areas in which Nancy could do more with the support of her family, such as working in the family business, and to air the parents' and Nancy's anxieties about each other, the past, and the future. Meanwhile, the psychiatrist worked with Nancy around more individually oriented dynamic conflicts. After one year Nancy was able to navigate outside the home alone to some extent, was working, and had developed a number of friendships; the parents were beginning to explore aspects of their own relationship that might bring them closer together and activities in which each could engage that would enhance their sense of connection to life. The parents' self-esteem was enhanced, as they saw some positive movement in their daughter to which they had contributed.

In working with families such as this one, the challenge is to find creative ways of using ourselves and resources available to us and to promote "growth-inducing" and "environment-ameliorating transactions" for all clients rather than only the ones who are the most highly "motivated."

Utility of Self-help Groups

The range of needs that families demonstrate has already been discussed. These needs require a flexible use of interventive modalities with a variety of goals. In addition to individual, marital, or family intervention, treatment groups involving multiple sets of families can be valuable in mobilizing their positive involvement, particularly with families who are difficult to engage. In addition, the self-help nature of such a group (even though it is led by professional staff) is an important vehicle for the enhancement of coping. Anxiety, shame, and guilt associated with exposing oneself to others are counterbalanced by the knowledge that everyone is in the same boat. Yet, family members have different solutions and different strengths and can serve as important sources of empathy, support, identification, and resources for problem-solving. As suggested by Swenson (Chapter 4 in this volume), family members also can use one another as support systems that can continue once the patient leaves the hospital and the formal therapeutic relationship with the staff may terminate.[3]

Use of the Social Environment

The location of environmental resources and the linkage of families and patients to these resources are critical functions of social work (Grinnell, Kyte, and Bostwick, Chapter 7 in this volume; Maluccio, Chapter 1 in this volume). This refers not only to attempts to find aftercare services but also to helping the family and patient locate supports in the environment that help to foster its functioning. For instance, families may need to find increased leisure-time activities or outlets for interests and talents that have not been developed or that have ceased due to illness. Services that can help relieve additional child-care responsibilities may need to be located. These social work functions have tended to be de-emphasized or undervalued in psychiatric settings because of their association with a nontherapeutic emphasis. The therapeutic value of real life has been little appreciated. It is very easy to lapse into the more traditional therapeutic mentality in the face of dominant psychiatric practices, professional status concerns, and the frustrations of limited resources in the social environment. However, promoting a better fit between family needs and available resources not only enhances the coping of families but may also free them to become more effectively engaged in the rehabilitative process itself.

Continuity of Care and Follow-up

Intervention does not stop when the patient leaves the hospital. Moreover, while this chapter has focused largely on hospitalized patients, services in the community before and after hospitalization are critical. Optimally, there should be continuity between hospital programs and community services for patients and families. However, even in the absence of continuity of care, a continuity of interest in what happens to the patient and family after discharge is important. Such follow-up can be part of a formalized and systematic research program or it can involve asking patients and families for feedback about what has occurred in more informal ways.[4]

Social Policy and Research

This perspective on social work practice with families of psychiatric patients leads to various implications for social policy and research.

To begin with, we are faced with a lack of theoretical and practical integration of our approaches to the treatment of the mentally ill and are witnessing the erosion of public commitment to psychosocial treatment methods. We see chronically ill patients in the community, maintained through public funds, who are functioning barely if at all on medication. They rarely receive other kinds of necessary services and often burden their families financially, physically, and emotionally, while the families themselves get little, if any, help in coping with these problems. It is not that services, and creative ones at that, do not exist, but that they are too few and too uncoordinated to meet the demand. We see other individuals who can afford private insurance and outpatient psychiatric services but only several weeks or several months of psychiatric hospitalization at most. While there is still a two-track system in the mental field, these tracks are converging as the cost of care becomes prohibitive and as the need for services escalates in relation to available resources.

For those patients whose symptomatology is life threatening to themselves or to others or who are so enfeebled physically or emotionally that they cannot live in any autonomous living situation, there are still city and state mental hospitals, although these specialize in short-term hospitalizations. However, because the thrust of mental health policy is toward returning patients to the community, these facilities are operating on even lower budgets currently than was previously the case. Thus, we see that services have been cut on both sides—in hospitals and in the community.

The situation is grim and it is not getting better. Consequently a crucial task before us as social workers is to join with other mental health professionals in fighting for the kinds of services that will support the quality of life for patients and families. In order to do this, ideological struggles have to be overcome among professions and within professions. The need for intra- as well as inter-professional collaboration is essential for a successful struggle to make services available for people who need them. Although conflict is healthy and potentially creative, there are times when it must be transcended sufficiently in the service of a broader, more overriding commitment. While there is reason for optimism about the potential for successful rehabilitation of many patients, this "therapeutic optimism" has to be converted into collective action on behalf of those who need our services. Such is the task before us. In this respect, the social work function must be connected to the social work cause.

One of our strongest allies in promoting our cause is our ability to research our practice. Clinical research, to be relevant, must be designed, at least in part, by practitioners. This presents a challenge to those of us engaged in clinical social work. It is essential to move beyond our belief in the significance and complexity of what we do and to embrace the task of documenting its efficacy.

Conclusion

This chapter first reviewed the theories underlying many current practices in psychiatric settings, suggesting their dysfunctional elements in meeting the needs of families coping with severe emotional disorder in a relative. The main conclusion was that family pathology has been emphasized to the detriment of appreciating the family's adaptive capacities, its crucial role in rehabilitative efforts, and the importance of the social environment in providing supports to the family that enable it to cope more effectively and which enhance self-esteem and competence.

The chapter then outlined a perspective on social work practice with families of psychiatric patients that emphasizes the family's adaptive capacities and that identifies the promotion of competence as a central feature of social work practice. This perspective can help practitioners in mental health settings to identify and mobilize the resources and strengths existing in families and thus enhance the functioning of the families as well as of the patients.

Notes

1. See Moore-Kirkland (Chapter 2 in this volume) for analysis of ways of mobilizing motivation to promote competence.
2. In her examination of practice with involuntary clients, Oxley (Chapter 12 in this volume) also stresses the importance of working with the families of psychiatric hospital patients.
3. See Swenson (Chapter 6 in this volume) for further discussion of social networks and natural helping systems in social work practice.
4. See Maluccio (1979a) for research concepts and methods on obtaining client feedback.

References

ACKERMAN, NATHAN. "Interpersonal Disturbances in the Family: Some Unresolved Problems in Psychotherapy." *Psychiatry* 17 (1965):359–68.

ALISSI, ALBERT S. "Social Group Work: Commitments and Perspectives." In *Perspectives on Social Group Work Practice,* edited by Albert S. Alissi. New York: The Free Press, 1980, pp. 4–35.

ALLPORT, GORDON W. *Pattern and Growth in Personality.* New York: Holt, Rinehart, and Winston, 1961.

ALTMAN, IRWIN. *The Environment and Social Behavior.* Monterey, California: Brooks/Cole, 1975.

AMERICAN PSYCHOLOGICAL ASSOCIATION. "Report on the Task Force on Sex Bias and Sex-role Stereotyping in Psychotherapeutic Practice." *American Psychologist* 30 (December 1975):1169–75.

ANDERSON, CAROL M. "Family Intervention with Severely Disturbed Patients." *Archives of General Psychiatry* 34 (June 1977):679–702.

ANDERSON, RALPH, and CARTER, IRL. *Human Behavior in the Social Environment: A Systems Approach.* Chicago: Aldine Publishing Company, 1974.

ANGYAL, ANDRAS. *Foundations for a Science of Personality.* New York: Commonwealth Fund, 1941.

ARGYRIS, CHRIS. "Conditions for Competence Acquisition and Therapy." *Journal of Applied Behavioral Science* 4 (April, May, June 1968):147–79.

ARIETI, SILVANO. *The Interpretation of Schizophrenia.* New York: Basic Books, 1974.

ASIMOV, ISAAC. *In Memory Yet Green.* Garden City, New York: Doubleday, 1979.

ASLIN, ALICE L. "Feminist and Community Mental Health Center Psychotherapist's Expectations of Mental Health." *Sex Roles* 3 (1977):537–44.

ATTNEAVE, CAROLYN. *Family Network Map.* Seattle, Washington, 1975 (privately printed).

AUSTIN, LUCILLE N. "Trends in Differential Treatment in Social Casework." *Social Casework* 29 (June 1948):203–11.

AUERSWALD, EDGAR H. "Interdisciplinary vs. Ecological Approach." *Family Process* 7 (September 1968):202–15.

BAKER, FRANK. "The Interface between Professional and Natural Support Systems." *Clinical Social Work Journal* 5, no. 2 (Summer 1977):139–48.

BALL, PATRICIA, and WYMAN, ELIZABETH. "Battered Wives and Powerlessness: What Can Counselors Do?" *Victimology* 2 (1978):545–52.

BARNES, JOHN A. "Class and Committees in a Norwegian Island Parish." *Human Relations* 7 (1954):39–58.

———. "Social Networks." Reading, Massachusetts: Addison-Wesley Modular Publications, no. 26, 1972.

BARNETT, ROSALIND, and BARUCH, GRACE. *The Competent Woman*. New York: Halsted Press, 1978.

BARTLETT, HARRIETT M. *The Common Base of Social Work Practice*. Washington, D.C.: National Association of Social Workers, 1970.

BATESON, GREGORY, et al. "Toward a Theory of Schizophrenia." *Behavioral Science* 1 (October 1956):251–64.

BEATT, EARL J. "The Family Developmental Approach: A Program for Coping with Transitional Crises." In *Emergency and Disaster Management*, edited by Howard J. Parad; H.L.P. Resnik; and Libbie G. Parad. Bowie, Maryland: Chalres Press, 1976, pp. 395–406.

BEAVERS, ROBERT W. *Psychotherapy and Growth—A Family Systems Perspective*. New York: Brunner/Mazel, 1977.

BEM, SANDRA. "Sex Role Adaptability: One Consequence of Psychological Androgyny." *Journal of Personality and Social Psychology* 31 (April 1975):634–43.

BEM, SANDRA, and LENNEY, ELLEN. "Sex Typing and the Avoidance of Cross-sex Behavior." *Journal of Personality and Social Psychology* 33 (January 1976):48–54.

BENEDEK, THERESE. "The Psychobiology of Pregnancy." In *Parenthood: Its Psychology and Psychopathology*, edited by E. James Anthony and Therese Benedek. Boston: Little, Brown, 1970, pp. 137–51.

BERGER, PETER L., and KUCKMAN, THOMAS. *The Social Construction of Reality*. Garden City, New York: Doubleday, 1966.

BERLIN, SHARON. "Better Work with Women Clients." *Social Work* 21 (November 1976):492–97.

BERNARD, JESSIE. *The Future of Marriage*. New York: World, 1972.

———. *The Future of Motherhood*. New York: Dial Press, 1974.

BERTALANFFY, LUDWIG V. *General System Theory: Foundations, Development, Applications*. New York: George Braziller, 1968.

BEUTNER, KARL, and BRANCH, RUSSELL. "The Psychiatrist and the Patients' Relatives." *Psychiatric Quarterly* 33 (January 1959):1–8.

BIBER, BARBARA. *Schooling As an Influence in Developing Healthy Personality*. New York: Bank Street College of Education, 1967a.

———. *Teacher Education and Mental Health: From the Perspective of the Educator*. New York: Bank Street College of Education, 1967b.

BIBER, BARBARA, et al. *Promoting Cognitive Growth: A Developmental-Interaction Point of View*, 2d ed. Washington, D.C.: National Association for the Education of Young Children, 1977.

BILLINGSLEY, DONNA. "Sex Bias in Psychotherapy: An Examination of the Effects of Client Sex, Client Pathology, and Therapist Sex on Treatment Planning." *Journal of Consulting and Clinical Psychology* 45 (April 1977): 250–56.

BIRREN, JAMES; BUTLER, ROBERT N.; GREENHOUSE, SAMUEL; SOKOLOFF, LOUIS; and YARROW, MARIAN, editors, *Human Aging—A Biological and Behavioral Study*. Washington, D.C.: Department of Health, Education and Welfare, 1971.

BLANCK, GERTRUDE, and BLANCK, RUBIN. *Ego Psychology: Theory and Practice*. New York: Columbia University Press, 1974.

BLAU, PETER. "Interaction: Social Exchange." In *International Encyclopedia of Social Sciences*, vol. 7, edited by David L. Sills. New York: Macmillan & The Free Press, 1968, pp. 452–58.

BLOCK, JEANNE. "Another Look at Sex Differentiation in the Socialization Behaviors of Mothers and Fathers." In *Psychology of Women: Future Directions of Research*, edited by Florence Denmark and Julia Sherman. New York: Psychological Dimensions, 1979.

BOTT, ELIZABETH. *Family and Social Network*. Second edition. New York: The Free Press, 1971.

BOWEN, MURRAY. "A Family Concept of Schizophrenia." In *Etiology of Schizophrenia*, edited by Don Jackson. New York: Basic Books, 1960.

BRADBURY, RAY. *Dandelion Wine*. New York: Bantam Pathfinder, 1964.

BRAGER, GEORGE, and HOLLOWAY, STEPHEN. *Changing Human Service Organizations: Politics and Practice*. New York: The Free Press, 1978.

BRAGINSKY, BENJAMIN M., and BRAGINSKY, DOROTHEA D. "Mental Hospitals As Resorts." *Psychology Today* 6 (March 1973):22–32.

BRIAR, SCOTT, and MILLER, HENRY. *Problems and Issues in Social Casework*. New York: Columbia University Press, 1971.

BRILL, NAOMI I. *Working with People: The Helping Process*. New York: J.B. Lippincott, 1973.

BRODKSY, ANNETTE. "Therapeutic Aspects of Consciousness-raising Groups." In *Psychotherapy for Women*, edited by Edna Rawlings and Diane Carter. Springfield, Illinois: Charles Thomas, 1977.

BRONFENBRENNER, URIE. "The Disturbing Changes in the American Family." *Search* (State University of New York) 2 (1976):4–10.

———. "Lewinian Space and Ecological Substance." *Journal of Social Issues*, vol. 33, no. 4 (1977):199–212.

BROVERMAN, INGE; BROVERMAN, DONALD; CLARKSON, FRANK; ROSENKRANTZ, PAUL; and VOGEL, SUSAN. "Sex-role Stereotypes and Clinical Judgments of Mental Health." *Journal of Consulting and Clinical Psychology* 34 (February 1970):1–7.

BRUNER, JEROME S. *On Knowing—Essays for the Left Hand*. New York: Atheneum, 1970.

———. *Beyond the Information Given*. New York: Norton, 1973.

BUCKLEY, WALTER. *Sociology and Modern Systems Theory*. Englewood Cliffs, New Jersey: Prentice Hall, 1967.

BURGUM, MILDRED. "The Father Gets Worse: A Child Guidance Problem." *American Journal of Orthopsychiatry* 12 (July 1942):474–85.

BUTLER, ROBERT N. "The Facade of Chronological Age: An Interpretative Summary." In *Middle Age and Aging*, edited by Bernice L. Neugarten. Chicago: University of Chicago Press, 1972, pp. 235–44.

―――. *Why Survive.* New York: Harper & Row, 1975.

BUTLER, ROBERT N., and LEWIS, MYRA I. "Life Review Therapy." *Geriatrics* 29 (November 1974):165–73.

―――. *Aging and Mental Health.* Second edition. St. Louis, Missouri: C. V. Mosby, 1977.

CAIN, LILLIAN P. "Social Workers' Role in Teenage Abortion." *Social Work,* vol. 24, no. 1 (January 1979):52–56.

CAMMAERT, LORNA, and LARSEN, CAROLYN. *A Woman's Choice.* Champaign, Illinois: Research Press Company, 1979.

CAPLAN, GERALD. *The Theory and Practice of Mental Health Consultation.* New York: Basic Books, 1970.

―――. *Support Systems and Community Mental Health.* New York: Behavioral Publications, 1974.

―――. "The Family As a Support System." In *Support Systems and Mutual Help: Multidisciplinary Explorations,* edited by Gerald Caplan and Marie Killilea. New York: Grune and Stratton, 1976, pp. 19–36.

CAPLAN, GERALD, and KILLILEA, MARIE. *Support Systems and Mutual Help.* New York: Grune and Stratton, 1976.

CATALDO, CHARLES. "Wilderness Therapy: Modern Day Shamanism." In *Social Work Practice: People and Environments,* edited by Carel B. Germain. New York: Columbia University Press, 1979, pp. 46–73.

CHAFETZ, MORRIS. "The Effect of a Psychiatric Emergency Service on Motivation for Psychiatric Treatment." *Journal of Nervous and Mental Disease* 140 (June 1965):442–48.

CHERNESKY, ROSLYN. "Women Administrators in Social Work." In *Women's Issues and Social Work Practice,* edited by Elaine Norman and Arlene Mancuso. Itasca, Illinois: F.E. Peacock, 1980, pp. 241–62.

COHEN, GENE D. "Mental Health Services and the Elderly: Needs and Options." *American Journal of Psychiatry* 133 (January 1976):65–68.

CLARK, FRANK W.; ARKAVA, MORTON L.; and ASSOCIATES. *The Pursuit of Competence in Social Work.* San Francisco: Jossey-Bass, 1979.

CLARK, KENNETH B. *Prejudice and Your Child.* Boston: Beacon Press, 1963.

CLARK, KENNETH B., and CLARK, MAMIE P. "Emotional Factors in Racial Identification and Preference in Negro Children." *Journal of Negro Education* 19 (1950):341–50.

COLLINS, ALICE H., and PANCOAST, DIANE L. *Natural Helping Networks: A Strategy for Prevention.* New York: National Association of Social Workers, 1976.

COMMISSION ON MENTAL HEALTH. *Report to the President* and *Task Panel Report, vol. 2.* Washington, D.C.: U.S. Government Printing Office, 1978.

COMPTON, BEULAH, and GALAWAY, BURT. *Social Work Processes.* Homewood, Illinois: The Dorsey Press, 1975.

CONNOLLY, KEVIN, and BRUNER, JEROME. "Competence: Its Nature and Nurture." In *The Growth of Competence,* edited by Kevin Connolly and Jerome Bruner. London and New York: Academic Press, 1974, pp. 3–7.

COSTIN, LELA. "School Social Work Practice: A New Model." *Social Work* 20 (March 1975):135–39.

CREMIN, LAWRENCE. *Public Education*. New York: Basic Books, 1976.

CUMMING, ELAINE, and HENRY, W.E. *Growing Old: The Process of Disengagement*. New York: Basic Books, 1961.

CUMMING, JOHN, and CUMMING, ELAINE. *Ego and Milieu*. Chicago: Aldine-Atherton, 1962.

DANSEREAU, PIERRE. *Inscape and Landscape: The Human Perception of Environment*. New York: Columbia University Press, 1975.

DAVIS, MARTHA. "Women's Liberation Groups As a Primary Preventive Mental Health Strategy." *Community Mental Health Journal* 13 (Fall 1977):219–28.

DEAUX, KAY, and FARRIS, ELIZABETH. "Attributing Causes for One's Own Performance: The Effects of Sex, Norms and Outcome." *Journal of Research in Personality* 11 (1977):59–72.

DECI, EDWARD L. *Intrinsic Motivation*. New York and London: Plenum Press, 1975.

DE LONG, ALTON J. "The Micro-Spatial Structure of the Older Person: Some Implications of Planning in Social and Spatial Environments." In *Spatial Behavior of Older People*, edited by Leon A. Pastalan and Daniel H. Carson. Ann Arbor: University of Michigan Press, 1970, pp. 68–87.

DEWEY, JOHN. *Experience and Education*. Toronto: Collier Books, 1963.

DOLL, WILLIAM. "Family Coping with the Mentally Ill: An Unanticipated Problem of Reinstitutionalization." *Hospital and Community Psychiatry* 27 (March 1976):183–85.

DRUM, DAVID, and KNOTT, EUGENE J. *Structured Groups for Facilitating Development*. New York: Human Sciences Press, 1977.

DUBOS, RENÉ. *So Human an Animal*. New York: Charles Scribner's Sons, 1968.

DUMONT, MATTHEW P. *The Absurd Healer: Perspectives of a Community Psychiatrist*. New York: Science House, 1968.

EASTMAN, PAULA. "Consciousness-raising As a Resocialization Process for Women." *Smith College Studies in Social Work* 43 (June 1973):153–83.

EGAN, GERARD. *Interpersonal Living: A Skills/Contract Approach to Human-Relations Training in Groups*. Monterey, California: Brooks/Cole, 1976.

EISMANN, EDWARD. "Children's Views of Therapeutic Gains and Therapeutic Change Agents in an Open-System Therapeutic Community." Bronx, New York: Lincoln Community Mental Health Center, 1975 (Mimeographed).

ELLIS, ALBERT. *Reason and Emotion in Psychotherapy*. New York: Lyle Stuart, 1962.

———. "The Treatment of Sex and Love Problems in Women." In *Women in Therapy*, edited by Violet Franks and Vasanti Burtle. New York: Brunner/Mazel, 1974.

ERIKSON, ERIK N. *Childhood and Society*. New York: Norton, 1950.

———. "Identity and the Life Cycle." *Psychological Issues*, vol. 1, no. 1. New York: International Universities Press, 1959, pp. 50–164.

———. *Childhood and Society*. Second edition. New York: Norton, 1963.

ESTES, RICHARD J., and HENRY, SUE. "The Therapeutic Contract in Work with Groups: A Formal Analysis." *Social Service Review* 50 (December 1976):611–22.

EUSTER, GERALD. "Group Work Revisited: Directions for the Third Century." *Social Work with Groups* 1 (Summer 1978):207–14.

FABRICANT, BENJAMIN. "The Psychotherapist and the Female Patient." In *Women in Therapy*, edited by Violet Franks and Vasanti Burtle. New York: Brunner/Mazel, 1974.

FANSHEL, DAVID. "Status Differentials: Men and Women in Social Work." *Social Work* 21 (November 1976):448–54.

FARIS, MILDRED. "Casework with Mentally Ill Patients and Their Relatives." *Journal of Psychiatric Social Work* 24 (January 1955):108–12.

FEIN, GRETA G., and CLARKE-STEWART, ALISON. *Day Care in Context.* New York: John Wiley & Sons, 1973.

FEINBERG, MORTIMER, R.; GLORIA FEINBERG; and JOHN J. TARRANT. *Leavetaking: When and How to Say Goodbye.* New York: Simon & Schuster, 1978.

FINE, SIDNEY A., and WILEY, WRETHA W. *An Introduction to Functional Job Analysis.* Kalamazoo, Michigan: The Upjohn Institute, 1971.

FISCHER, JOEL. *Effective Casework Practice: An Eclectic Approach.* New York: McGraw-Hill, 1978.

FLECK, STEPHEN; CORNELISON, ALICE; NORTON, NEA; and LIDZ, THEODORE. "Interaction between Hospital Staff and Families." *Psychiatry* 20 (November 1957):343–50.

FONTANA, VINCENT J. *Somewhere a Child Is Crying: Maltreatment Causes and Prevention.* New York: Mentor Books, New American Library, 1976.

FOOTE, NELSON N., and COTTRELL, LEONARD S., JR. *Identity and Interpersonal Competence.* Chicago: University of Chicago Press, 1955.

FRANKS, VIOLET. "Gender and Psychotherapy." In *Gender and Disordered Behavior*, edited by Edith Gomberg and Violet Franks. New York: Brunner/Mazel, 1979.

FREEMAN, HENRY. "Casework with Families of Mental Hospital Patients." *Social Casework* 28 (March 1947):107–13.

FREUD, ANNA, *The Psycho-Analytic Treatment of Children.* New York: International Universities Press, 1946.

———. *The Ego and the Mechanisms of Defense.* New York: Mentor Books, New American Library, 1976.

FREUD, SIGMUND. "Recommendations to Physicians Practicing Psychoanalysis." In *Standard Edition of the Complete Psychological Works of Sigmund Freud*, edited by James Strachey. London: Hogarth Press, 1912.

———. *The Ego and the Id.* New York: Norton Library, 1960.

FRIED, MARC. "Grieving for a Lost Home." In Leonard J. Duhl. *The Urban Condition.* New York: Simon & Schuster, 1969, pp. 151–71.

FRIEZE, IRENE; PARSONS, JACQUELYNNE; JOHNSON, PAULA; RUBLE, DIANE; and ZELLMAN, GAIL. *Women and Sex Roles.* New York: Norton, 1978.

GAGNE, ROBERT M., and BRIGGS, LESLIE J. *Principles of Instructional Design.* New York: Holt, Rinehart and Winston, 1974.

GARLAND, JAMES; KOLODNY, RALPH; and JONES, HUBERT. "A Model for the Stages of Development in Social Work Groups." In *Explorations in Group Work*, edited by Saul Bernstein. Boston: Charles River Books, 1975.

GARRISON, JOHN. "Network Techniques: Case Studies in the Screening-Linking-Planning Method." *Family Process* 13 (September 1974):337–54.

GARTNER, ALAN. "Services: Do the Poor Use Them?" *Social Policy* 1 (November-December 1970):71–72.

GENDLIN, EUGENE. "Therapeutic Procedures in Dealing with Schizophrenics." In *The Therapeutic Relationship and Its Impact: A Study of Psychotherapy with Schizophrenics*, edited by Carl Rogers. Madison, Wisconsin: University of Wisconsin Press, 1967, 369–78.

GERMAIN, CAREL B. "An Ecological Perspective in Casework Practice." *Social Casework*, vol. 54, no. 6 (June 1973):323–30.

———. "A Theoretical View of the Life Model: Ecosystems Perspective." In *The Ecological Approach and Clinical Practice*, by Eda Goldstein, Carel Germain, and Anthony Maluccio. West Hartford, Connecticut: University of Connecticut School of Social Work, 1975 (mimeographed), pp. 1–25.

———. "Time, an Ecological Variable in Social Work Practice." *Social Casework*, vol. 57, no. 7 (July 1976):419–26.

———. "An Ecological Perspective on Social Work Practice in Health Care." *Social Work in Health Care*, vol. 3, no. 1 (Fall 1977):67–76.

———. "Space, an Ecological Variable in Social Work Practice." *Social Casework*, vol. 59, no. 9 (November 1978):515–22.

———. "Ecology and Social Work." In *Social Work Practice: People and Environments*, edited by Carel B. Germain. New York: Columbia University Press, 1979, pp. 1–22.

GERMAIN, CAREL B., and GITTERMAN, ALEX. "The Life Model of Social Work Practice." In *Social Work Treatment—Interlocking Theoretical Approaches*, edited by Francis J. Turner. Second edition. New York: The Free Press, 1979, pp. 361–84.

———. *The Life Model of Social Work Practice*. New York: Columbia University Press, 1980.

GITTERMAN, ALEX. "Group Work in Public Schools." In *The Practice of Group Work*, edited by William Schwartz and Serapio R. Zalba. New York: Columbia University Press, 1971, pp. 45–72.

GITTERMAN, ALEX, and GERMAIN, CAREL B. "Social Work Practice: A Life Model." *Social Service Review* 50 (December 1976):601–10.

GLADWIN, THOMAS. "Social Competence and Clinical Practice." *Psychiatry* 30 (November 1967):30–43.

GOFFMAN, ERVING. *Asylums*. New York: Doubleday Anchor, 1961.

GOLAN, NAOMI. "Crisis Theory." In *Social Work Treatment: Interlocking Theoretical Approaches*, edited by Francis J. Turner. New York: The Free Press, 1974, pp. 420–56.

———. "Work with Young Adults in Israel." In *Task-Centered Practice*, edited by William J. Reid and Laura Epstein. New York: Columbia University Press, 1977, pp. 270–84.

———. *Treatment in Crisis Situations*. New York: The Free Press, 1978.

GOLDBERG, GALE. "The Dynamics of Exclusion." In *Handbook of Structured Experiences*, vol. 4, edited by J.W. Pfeiffer and J.E. Jones. San Diego, California: University Associates, 1975.

GOLDFRIED, MARVIN R., and D'ZURILLA, THOMAS J. "A Behavioral-Analytic Model for Assessing Competence." In *Current Topics in Clinical and Com-

munity Psychology, vol. 1, edited by Charles D. Spielberger. New York and London: Academic Press, 1969, pp. 151–96.

GOLDSTEIN, ARNOLD; HELLER, KENNETH; and SECHREST, LEE. *Psychotherapy and the Psychology of Behavior Change*. New York: John Wiley, 1966.

GOLDSTEIN, EDA G. "Social Casework and the Dying Person." *Social Casework* 54 (December 1973):601–08.

———. "Parental Attitudes and Characteristics, Social Work Involvement, and the Outcome of Psychiatric Hospitalization." Doctoral dissertation, Columbia University School of Social Work, New York, New York, 1978.

———. "Mothers of Psychiatric Patients Revisited." In *Social Work Practice: People and Environments*, edited by Carel B. Germain. New York: Columbia University Press, 1979, pp. 150–73.

———. "The Influnece of Parental Attitudes on Psychiatric Treatment Outcome." *Social Casework* 60 (June 1979):350–59.

GONZALES, AGUSTIN. "The Struggle to Develop Self-help Institutions." *Social Casework* 55 (February 1974):90–93.

GORDON, WILLIAM. "Basic Constructs for an Integrative and Generative Conception of Social Work." In *The General Systems Approach: Contributions Toward an Holistic Conception of Social Work*, edited by Gordon Hearn. New York: Council on Social Work Education, 1969, pp. 5–11.

GOULDNER, ALVIN. "The Norm of Reciprocity: A Preliminary Statement." *American Sociological Review* 25 (April 1960):161–68.

GOVE, WALTER, and TUDOR, JEANNETTE. "Adult Sex Roles and Mental Illness." *American Journal of Sociology* 78 (January 1973):812–35.

GRABER, LINDA H. *Wilderness As Sacred Space*. Washington, D.C.: The Association of American Geographers, monograph 8, 1976.

GRANICK, SAMUEL, and PATTERSON, ROBERT D., editors. *Human Aging—An Eleven Year Follow-up, Biomedical and Behavioral Study*. Washington, D.C.: U.S. Department of Health, Education, and Welfare, 1971.

GRINNELL, RICHARD M., JR. "Environmental Modification: Casework's Concern or Casework's Neglect?" *Social Service Review*, vol. 47, no. 2 (1973):208–20.

GRINNELL, RICHARD M., JR., and KYTE, NANCY S. "Modifying the Environment." *Social Work*, vol. 19, no. 4 (1974):477–83.

———. "Environmental Modification: A Study." *Social Work*, vol. 20, no. 4 (1975):313–18.

GROB, MOLLIE, and EDINBURG, GOLDA. "How Families View Psychiatric Hospitalization for Their Adolescents. A Follow-up Study." *International Journal of Social Psychiatry* 18 (Spring 1972):14–22.

GROSSER, CHARLES F. "Community Development Programs Serving the Urban Poor." *Social Work*, vol. 10, no. 3 (1965):15–21.

———. "Participation and Practice." In *Social Work Practice: People and Environments*, edited by Carel B. Germain. New York: Columbia University Press, 1979, pp. 305–25.

GUERNEY, BERNARD G., JR. *Relationship Enhancement*. San Francisco: Jossey-Bass, 1977.

HAJAL, FADY. "Using Tape Recorders in the Treatment of Latency Age Children." *Social Casework* 59 (June 1978):371–74.

HALEY, JAY, editor. *Changing Families: A Family Therapy Reader.* New York: Grune and Stratton, 1971.

HALL, ARTHUR D., and FAGEN, ROBERT E. "Definition of System." In *General Systems: Yearbook of the Society for the Advancement of General Systems Theory*, vol. 1, edited by Ludwig Bertalanffy and Anatole Rapoport. Ann Arbor, Michigan: Braun-Brumfield, 1956, pp. 18–29.

HALL, EDWARD T. *The Silent Language.* New York: Doubleday 1959.

———. *The Hidden Dimension.* New York: Doubleday, 1966.

HAMILTON, GORDON. *Theory and Practice of Social Casework.* Second edition. New York: Columbia University Press, 1951.

HARNACK, CURTIS. "Home." *New York Times.* Op-Ed page, August 28, 1977.

HARTER, SUSAN. "Effectance Motivation Reconsidered—Toward a Developmental Model." *Human Development* 21 (1978):34–64.

HARTFORD, MARGARET. *Groups in Social Work.* New York: Columbia University Press, 1971.

———. "Groups in the Human Services: Some Facts and Fancies." *Social Work with Groups* 1 (Spring 1978):7–14.

HARTMAN, ANN. "To Think about the Unthinkable." *Social Casework*, vol. 51, no. 8 (1970):467–74.

———. "Diagrammatic Assessment of Family Relationships." *Social Casework*, vol. 59, no. 8 (October 1978):465–76.

———. *Finding Families—An Ecological Approach to Family Assessment in Adoption.* Beverly Hills: Sage, 1979a.

———. "The Extended Family As a Resource for Change: An Ecological Approach to Family-centered Practice." In *Social Work Practice: People and Environments*, edited by Carel B. Germain. New York: Columbia University Press, 1979b, pp. 239–66.

HARTMANN, HEINZ. *Ego Psychology and the Problem of Adaptation.* New York: International Universities Press, 1958.

HASELKORN, FLORENCE. "Evolving Roles and Services in Abortion Counseling." In *Changing Roles in Social Work Practice*, edited by Francine Sobey. Philadelphia: Temple University Press, 1977, pp. 243–65.

HAWORTH, MARY R., editor. *Child Psychotherapy.* New York: Basic Books, 1964.

HEARN, GORDON, editor. *The General Systems Approach: Contributions Toward an Holistic Conception of Social Work.* New York: Council on Social Work Education, 1969.

HEATH, DOUGLAS H. *Maturity and Competence—A Transcultural View.* New York: Gardner Press, 1977.

HEBB, DONALD O. "Drives and the c.n.s. (conceptual nervous system)." *Psychological Review* 62 (1955):243–54.

HENRY, CHARLOTTE. "Motivation in Non-Voluntary Clients." *Social Casework* 39 (February 1958):130–36.

HERIOT, JESSICA. "The Double-bind: Healing the Split." Paper presented at the American Orthopsychiatric Association Meeting, Washington, D.C., March 1979.

HOFF, LEE ANN. *People in Crisis: Understanding and Helping.* Menlo Park, California: Addison-Wesley, 1978.

HOFFMAN, LOIS W. "Early Childhood Experiences and Women's Achievement Motives." *Journal of Social Issues* 28 (November 1972):129–55.

————. "Changes in Family Roles, Socialization, and Sex Differences." *American Psychologist* 32 (August 1977):644–57.

HOLLIS, FLORENCE. *Casework: A Psychosocial Therapy.* Second edition. New York: Random House, 1972.

HOLT, ROBERT R. "Ego Autonomy Re-Evaluated," *International Journal of Psychiatry* 3 (June 1967):481–512.

HUGHES, KATHLEEN N. "Resistance in Relatives of the Hospitalized Mentally Ill." *Smith College Studies in Social Work* 29 (October 1958):38–50.

INKELES, ALEX. "Social Structure and the Socialization of Competence." *Harvard Educational Review* 36 (February 1966):30–43.

ITTELSON, WILLIAM H.; FRANCK, KAREN A.; and O'HANLON, TIMOTHY J. "The Nature of Environmental Experience." In *Experiencing the Environment,* edited by Seymour Wagner; Saul B. Cohen; and Bernard Kaplan. New York: Plenum Press, 1976, pp. 187–205.

JACOBSON, GERALD F. "Programs and Techniques of Crisis Intervention." In *American Handbook of Psychiatry,* edited by Silvano Arieti. Second edition. New York: Basic Books, 1974, pp. 810–25.

JAKUBOWSKI, PATRICIA. "Self-assertion Training Procedures for Women." In *Psychotherapy for Women,* edited by Edna Rawlings and Diane Carter. Springfield, Illinois: Charles Thomas, 1977.

JANCHILL, MARY P. "Systems Concepts in Casework Theory and Practice." *Social Casework,* vol. 50, no. 2 (1969):74–82.

JONES, RUSSELL A. *Self-Fulfilling Prophecies.* Hillsdale, New Jersey: Lawrence Erlbaum Associates, 1977.

KAGAN, J. "Motives and Development." *Journal of Personality and Social Psychology* 22 (April 1972):51–66.

KANTOR, DAVID, and LEHR, WILLIAM. *Inside the Family.* San Francisco: Jossey-Bass, 1975.

KAPLAN, MILDRED F., and GLENN, ANNE. "Women and the Stress of Moving: A Self-help Approach." *Social Casework,* vol. 59, no. 7 (July 1978):434–36.

KATZ, ALFRED H., and BENDER, EUGENE I. *The Strength in Us: Self-help Groups in the Modern World.* New York: New Viewpoints, 1976.

KELLY, JAMES G. "Ecological Constraints on Mental Health Services." *American Psychologist* 28 (July 1973):535–39.

KESKINER, ALI. "The Foster Community: A Partner in Psychiatric Rehabilitation," *American Journal of Psychiatry* 129 (September 1972):283–88.

KILGUSS, ANNE F. "Using Soap Operas As a Therapeutic Tool." *Social Casework* 55 (November 1974):525–30.

KLEMP, GEORGE O. "Identifying, Measuring and Integrating Competencies." In *Defining and Measuring Competencies,* edited by Paul S. Pottinger, Joan Goldsmith, et al. San Francisco, California: Jossey-Bass, 1979, pp. 41–52.

KILLILEA, MARIE. "Mutual Help Organizations: Interpretations in the Literature." In *Support Systems and Mutual Help,* edited by Gerald Caplan and Marie Killilea. New York: Grune and Stratton, 1976, pp. 37–94.

KIRSCH, BARBARA. "Consciousness-raising Groups as Therapy for Women." In

Women in Therapy, edited by Violet Franks and Vasanti Burtle. New York: Brunner/Mazel, 1974.

KLEIN, MARJORIE. "Feminist Concepts of Therapy Outcome." *Psychotherapy: Theory, Research and Practice* 13 (1976):89–95.

KOGAN, LEONARD S. "The Short-Term Case in a Family Agency" (Part 1). *Social Casework* 38 (May 1957):231–38.

KOVACS, MARIA, and BECK, AARON T. "Maladaptive Cognitive Structures in Depression." *The American Journal of Psychiatry,* vol. 135, no. 5 (May 1978):525–33.

KRAVETZ, DIANE. "Sexism in a Woman's Profession." *Social Work* 21 (November 1976):421–26.

KREBS, DENNIS L. "Altruism." *Psychological Bulletin* 73 (April 1960):258–02.

KREISMAN, DOLORES E., and JOY, VIRGINIA. "Family Response to the Mental Illness of a Relative; A Review of the Literature." *Schizophrenia Bulletin* 10 (Fall 1974):34–57.

KRIEGER, MARTIN H. "What's Wrong with Plastic Trees?" *Science* 179 (February 1973):446–55.

KÜBLER-ROSS, ELIZABETH. *On Death and Dying.* London: Macmillan, 1969.

LADNER, JOYCE. *Tomorrow's Tomorrow: The Black Woman.* New York: Anchor Books, 1972.

LAIRD, JOAN. "An Ecological Approach to Child Welfare: Issues of Family Identity and Continuity." In *Social Work Practice: People and Environments,* edited by Carel B. Germain. New York: Columbia University Press, 1979, pp. 174–209.

LANTZ, JAMES E. "Cognition and Social Casework." *Social Work,* vol. 23, no. 5 (September 1978):361–67.

LAWTON, M. POWELL. "Coping Behavior and the Environment of Older People." In *Professional Obligations and Approaches to the Aged,* edited by Arthur E. Schwartz and Ivan N. Mensh. Springfield, Illinois: Charles Thomas, 1974, pp. 67–93.

LAWTON, M. POWELL, and NAHEMOW, LUCILLE. "Ecology and the Aging Process." In *The Psychology of Adult Development and Aging,* edited by C. Eisdorfer and M. Powell Lawton. Washington, D.C.: American Psychological Association, 1974, pp. 619–74.

LAZARUS, RICHARD S. "Cognitive and Coping Processes in Emotion." In *Cognitive Views of Human Motivation,* edited by Bernard Weiner. New York: Academic Press, 1974, pp. 21–32.

LEE, JUDITH A.B. "Group Work with Mentally Retarded Foster Adolescents." *Social Casework* 58 (March 1977): 164–73.

———. "The Foster Parents Workshop." *Social Work with Groups* 2 (Summer 1979):129–43.

LEE, JUDITH A., and PARK, DANIELLE N. "A Group Approach to the Depressed Adolescent Girl in Foster Care." *American Journal of Orthopsychiatry* 48 (July 1978):516–27.

LEE, JUDITH A., and SWENSON, CAROL R., "Theory in Action: A Community Social Service Agency." *Social Casework* 59 (June 1978):359–70.

LEICHTER, HOPE, and MITCHELL, WILLIAM. *Kinship and Casework.* Second edition. New York: Teacher's College Press, 1979.

LESY, MICHAEL. " 'Mere' Snapshots, Considered." *New York Times*. Op-Ed Page, January 16, 1978.

LEVINE, RACHEL. "Treatment in the Home." In *Mental Health of the Poor*, edited by Frank Riessman, Jerome Cohen, and Arthur Pearl. Glencoe, Illinois: Free Press, 1965, pp. 329–35.

LEVINSON, DANIEL J. *The Seasons of a Man's Life*. New York: Knopf, 1978.

LEVINSON, SEMA, and WITHEY, MILDRED Z. "Sessions with Relatives of Mental Hospital Patients." *Mental Hygiene* 39 (January 1955):118–25.

LEWIN, KARL. *Field Theory in Social Science*, edited by D. Cartwright. New York: Harper, 1951.

LEWIS, C.A. "People/Plant Interaction: Human Perspectives in Horticulture." *Hortscience*, vol. 11, no. 1 (February 1976):4–5.

LEWIS, KAREN, and WEINSTEIN, LYNN. "Friendship Skills: Intense Short Term Intervention with Latency Age Children." *Social Work with Groups* 1 (Fall 1978):279–86.

LINDEMANN, ERIC, "Symptomatology and Management of Acute Grief," *American Journal of Psychiatry* 101 (September 1944):141–48.

LOEWENSTEIN, SOPHIE F. "Preparing Social Work Students for Life-Transition Counseling within the Human Behavior Sequence." *Journal of Education for Social Work*, vol. 14, no. 2 (Spring 1978):66–73.

LOWRY, FERN. "The Client's Needs as the Basis for Differential Approach in Treatment." In *Differential Approach in Case Work Treatment*. New York: Family Welfare Association of America, 1936, pp. 1–13.

MAAS, HENRY. "Social Development and Social Loss." Paper presented at University of California at Berkeley (March 13, 1979).

MADDI, SALVATORE R. "The Search for Meaning." *Nebraska Symposium on Personality* 18 (1970):137–86.

MAGER, ROBERT. *Developing Instructional Objectives*. Belmont, California: Fearon, 1962.

MAHLER, MARGARET. *On Human Symbiosis and the Vicissitudes of Individuation*, vol. I, *Infantile Psychosis*. New York: International Universities Press, 1968.

MAHONEY, MICHAEL J. *Cognition and Behavior Modification*. Cambridge, Massachusetts: Balinger, 1974.

MALUCCIO, ANTHONY N. "Action As a Tool in Casework Practice." *Social Casework* 55 (January 1974):30–35.

———. "The Life Model As a Potential Frame of Reference for Social Work Practice." In *The Ecological Approach and Clinical Practice*, by Eda Goldstein, Carel Germain, and Anthony Maluccio. West Hartford, Connecticut, University of Connecticut School of Social Work, 1975, pp. 1–12 (mimeographed).

———. *Learning from Clients: Interpersonal Helping As Viewed by Clients and Social Workers*. New York: The Free Press, 1979a.

———. "Promoting Competence Through Life Experience." In *Social Work Practice: People and Environments*, edited by Carel B. Germain. New York: Columbia University Press, 1979b, pp. 282–302.

———. "A Life Model Perspective on the Family." In *Perspectives on the Family:*

Readings in Theory and Practice, edited by Cathleen Getty and Winnifred Humphreys. New York: Appleton-Century-Crofts, in press.

MALUCCIO, ANTHONY N., and MARLOW, WILMA D. "The Case for the Contract." *Social Work* 19 (January 1974):28–36.

MALUCCIO, ANTHONY N., and SINANOGLU, PAULA A., editors, *The Challenge of Partnership—Working with Parents of Children in Foster Care.* New York: Child Welfare League of America, 1981.

MARACEK, JEANNE. "Psychological Androgyny and Positive Mental Health: A Biosocial Perspective." In *Exploring Contemporary Male/Female Roles,* edited by Clarke Carney and Sarah McMahon. La Jolla, California: University Associates, 1977, pp. 197–208.

MARACEK, JEANNE, and KRAVETZ, DIANE. "Women and Mental Health: A Review of Feminist Change Efforts." *Psychiatry* 40 (November 1977): 323–29.

MARSHALL, ELDON K.; CHARPING, JOHN W.; and BELL, WILLIAM J. "Interpersonal Skills Training: A Review of the Research." *Social Work Research and Abstracts* 15 (Spring 1979):10–16.

MASLOW, ABRAHAM H. "A Theory of Human Motivation." *Psychological Review* 50 (1943):370–96.

———. *Motivation and Personality.* Second edition. New York: Harper & Row, 1954.

MAY, PHILIP. *Treatment of Schizophrenia.* New York: Science House, 1968.

MAYER, JOHN E., and TIMMS, NOEL. *The Client Speaks—Working-Class Impressions of Casework.* Boston: Routledge and Kegan Paul, 1970.

MCBRIDE, G., and CLANCY, H., "The Social Properties of Places and Things." In *The Mutual Interaction of People and Their Built Environment,* edited by Amos Rapoport. The Hague: Mouton, 1976, pp. 159–76.

MCCLELLAND, DAVID C. "Testing for Competence Rather than for 'Intelligence.'" *American Psychologist* 28 (January 1973):1–14.

MCCLELLAND, DAVID C.; ATKINSON, JOHN W.; CLARK, RUSSELL; and LOWELL, EDGAR L. *The Achievement Motive.* New York: Appleton-Century-Crofts, 1953.

MCGUIRE, WILLIAM J. "The Nature of Attitudes and Attitudes Change." In *The Handbook of Social Psychology,* edited by Gardner Lindzey and Elliot Aronson. Second edition, vol. 3. Reading, Massachusetts: Addison-Wesley, 1969, pp. 136–314.

MCPHEETERS, HAROLD L., and RYAN, ROBERT M. "Social Welfare Objectives and Roles." In *A Core of Competence for Baccalaureate Social Welfare and Curricular Implications.* Atlanta: Southern Regional Education Board, 1971, pp. 17–20.

MECHANIC, DAVID. "Social Structure and Personal Adaptation: Some Neglected Dimensions." In *Coping and Adaptation,* edited by George V. Coelho, David A. Hamburg, and John E. Adams. New York: Basic Books, 1974, pp. 32–46.

MEDNICK, MARTHA S.; TANGRI, SANDRA S.; and HOFFMAN, LOIS W., editors. *Women and Achievement: Social and Motivational Analyses.* Washington, D.C.: Hemisphere, 1975.

MERTON, ROBERT K.; COTTRELL, LEONARD S.; and BROOM, LEONARD. *Sociology*

Today: Problems and Prospects, American Sociological Society. New York: Basic Books, 1959.

MEYER, CAROL H. *Social Work Practice: A Response to the Urban Crisis.* New York: The Free Press, 1970.

————. *Social Work Practice: The Changing Landscape.* Second edition. New York: The Free Press, 1976.

MIDDLEMAN, RUTH R. *The Non-Verbal Method in Working with Groups.* New York: Association Press, 1968.

————. "The Skill Component of Professional Social Work Education." Unpublished paper presented at the 23rd Annual Program Meeting, Council on Social Work Education, 1977a.

————. "A Teaching/Training Specialization within the Masters Curriculum." Unpublished paper presented at the 23rd Annual Program Meeting, Council on Social Work Education, 1977b.

————. "Returning Group Process to Group Work." *Social Work with Groups* 1 (Spring 1978):15–26.

MIDDLEMAN, RUTH R., and GOLDBERG, GALE. "The Interactional Way of Presenting Generic Social Work Concepts." *Journal of Education for Social Work* 8 (Spring 1972a):48–57.

————. "The Concept of Structure in Experiential Learning." *1972 Handbook for Group Facilitators.* Iowa City, Iowa: University Associates, 1972b, pp. 203–10.

————. *Social Service Delivery: A Structural Approach to Social Work Practice.* New York: Columbia University Press, 1974.

MILLAR, MARGARET. "Modern Use of Older Treatment Methods." In *Readings in Social Case Work—1920–1938,* edited by Fern Lowry. New York: Columbia University Press, 1939, pp. 344–53.

MILLER, DOROTHY; VAUGHAN, W. TAY; and MILLER, DON E. "Effectiveness of Social Services to AFDC Recipients: Summary and Findings." In *California Welfare: A Program for Reform* Sacramento: California Legislature, 1969, part III, appendix I, pp. 1–34.

MILLER, HENRY. "Value Dilemmas in Social Casework." *Social Work* 13 (January 1968):27–33.

MILLER, JEAN B. *Toward a New Psychology of Women.* Boston: Beacon Press, 1976.

MILLER, SHEROD; ELAM W. NUNNALLY; and DAVID B. WACKMAN. *Alive and Aware: Improving Communication in Relationships.* Minneapolis, Minn.: Interpersonal Communication Programs, 1975.

————. "A Communication Training Program for Couples." *Social Casework* 57 (January 1976):9–18.

MINUCHIN, SALVADOR. "The Plight of the Poverty-Stricken Family in the United States." *Child Welfare* 49 (1970):124–130.

————. *Families and Family Therapy.* Cambridge, Massachusetts: Harvard University Press, 1974.

MITCHELL, J. CLYDE. *Social Networks in Urban Situations.* Manchester, England: Manchester University Press, 1969.

MOOS, RUDOLF H., and INSEL, PAUL M., editors. *Issues in Social Ecology.* Palo Alto, California: National Press Books, 1974.

Moos, Rudolf H., and Tsu, Vivian Davis. "Human Competence and Coping." In *Human Adaptation,* edited by Rudolf H. Moos. Lexington, Massachusetts, D.C. Heath and Co., 1976, pp. 3–16.

Mullen, Edward J. "The Construction of Personal Models for Effective Practice: A Method for Utilizing Research Findings to Guide Social Interventions." *Journal of Social Service Research,* vol. 2, no. 1 (1978):45–63.

Mullen, Edward J. "Development of Personal Intervention Models." In *Social Work Research and Evaluation,* edited by Richard M. Grinnell, Jr. Itasca, Illinois: F.E. Peacock Publishers, forthcoming.

Muncie, Wendall S. "The Therapeutic Situation As It Concerns the Family with Special Reference to the Other Marital Partner." *American Journal of Psychotherapy* 4 (October 1950):595–610.

Murphy, Lois B. "Coping, Vulnerability, and Resilience in Childhood." In *Coping and Adaptation,* edited by George V. Coelho, David A. Hamburg and John E. Adams. New York: Basic Books, 1974, pp. 69–100.

Murphy, Lois B., and Associates. *The Widening World of Childhood: Paths Toward Mastery.* New York: Basic Books, 1962.

Murphy, Lois B., and Moriarty, Alice E. *Vulnerability, Coping and Growth.* New Haven, Connecticut: Yale University Press, 1976.

Nahemow, L., and Lawton, M.P. "Toward an Ecological Theory of Adaptation and Aging." In *Environmental Psychology,* edited by Harold M. Proshansky; William H. Ittelson; and Leanne G. Rivlin. Second edition. New York: Holt, Rinehart and Winston, 1976, pp. 315–32.

Nealon, Jody. "Adolescent's Hospitalization As a Family Crisis." *Archives of General Psychiatry* 11 (September 1964):302–22.

Newman, Oscar. *Defensible Space.* New York: Collier Books, 1973.

Oakley, Ann. *The Sociology of Housework.* New York: Random House, 1974.

O'Brien, Charles R.; Johnson, Josephine L.; and Miller, Barbara. "Counseling the Aging: Some Practical Consideration." *Personnel and Guidance Journal* 57 (February 1979):288–91.

O'Leary, Virginia E. *Toward Understanding Women.* Monterey, California: Brooks/Cole, 1977.

Orlinsky, David, and Howard, Kenneth. "The Effects of Sex of Therapist on the Therapeutic Experience of Women." *Psychotherapy: Theory, Research and Practice* 13 (1976):82–88.

Osborn, Susan, and Harris, Gloria. *Assertive Training for Women.* Springfield, Illinois: Charles Thomas, 1975.

Osmund, Humphrey. "Function As the Basis of Psychiatric Ward Design." *Mental Hospitals* (Architectural Supplement) 8 (April 1957):23–30. Reprinted in Harold M. Proshansky et al., editors. *Environmental Psychology.* New York: Holt, Rinehart and Winston, 1970, pp. 560–69.

Oxley, Genevieve B. "Caseworkers' Expectations and Client Motivation." *Social Casework* 47 (July 1966):432–37.

———. "A Life Model Approach to Change." *Social Casework* 52 (December 1971):627–33.

———. "A Modified Form of Residential Treatment." *Social Work* 22 (November 1977):493–97.

————. "Involuntary Clients' Responses to a Treatment Experience." *Social Casework* 58 (December 1977):607–14.

PARKES, C. MURRAY. "Psychosocial Transitions." *Social Science and Medicine* 5 (1971):101–15.

PECK, ROBERT C. "Psychological Developments in the Second Half of Life." In *Middle Age and Aging*, edited by Bernice L. Neugarten. Chicago: University of Chicago Press, 1972, pp. 235–44.

PENDAGAST, EILEEN C., and SHERMAN, CHARLES O. "A Guide to the Genogram Family Systems Training." *Family* 5 (Spring 1978):3–14.

PERLMAN, HELEN H. *Social Casework: A Problem-Solving Process*. Chicago: University of Chicago Press, 1957.

————. *Persona*. Chicago: University of Chicago Press, 1968.

————. "Social Components of Casework Practice." In Helen H. Perlman, *Perspectives on Social Casework*. Philadelphia: Temple University Press, 1971, pp. 35–50.

————. "Once More with Feeling." In *Evaluation of Social Intervention*, edited by Edward J. Mullen, James R. Dumpson, and Associates. San Francisco: Jossey-Bass, 1972, pp. 191–209.

————. "Confessions, Concerns, and Commitment of an Ex-Clinical Social Worker." *Clinical Social Work Journal*, vol. 2, no. 3 (1974):221–29.

————. "In Quest of Coping." *Social Casework*, vol. 56, no. 4 (April 1975):213–25.

PHARES, E. JERRY. "Locus of Control." In *Dimensions of Personality*, edited by Harvey London and John Exoner. New York: John Wiley and Sons, 1978, pp. 263–301.

PHILLIPS, LESLIE, and COWITZ, BERNARD. "Social Attainment and Reactions to Stress." *Journal of Personality* 22 (December 1953):270–83.

PIAGET, JEAN. *The Origins of Intelligence*. New York: International Universities Press, 1952.

PINCUS, ALLEN, and MINAHAN, ANNE. *Social Work Practice: Model and Method*. Itasca, Illinois: F.E. Peacock Publishers, 1973.

PINES, MAYA. "Superkids." *Psychology Today* (January 1979):53–60.

POLSKIN, SYLVIA R. "Working with Parents of Mentally Ill Children in Residential Care." *Social Work* 6 (October 1961):82–89.

RAPAPORT, DAVID. "The Theory of Ego Autonomy: A Generalization." *Bulletin of the Menninger Clinic* 22 (January 1958):13–35.

RAPOPORT, LYDIA. "The State of Crisis: Some Theoretical Considerations." In *Crisis Intervention: Selected Readings*, edited by Howard J. Parad. New York: Family Service Association of America, 1965, pp. 22–31.

————. "Creativity in Social Work." *Social Service Review* 42 (June 1968):139–61.

————. "Crisis Intervention As a Mode of Brief Treatment." In *Theories of Social Casework*, edited by Robert W. Roberts and Robert H. Nee. Chicago, University of Chicago Press, 1970, pp. 267–311.

RAPOPORT, LYDIA, and POTTS, LEAH. "Abortion of Unwanted Pregnancy As a Potential Life Crisis." In *Family Planning: A Sourcebook of Readings and Case Material*, edited by Florence Haselhorn. New York: Council on Social Work Education, 1971, pp. 249–66.

RAPOPORT, RHONA. "Normal Crisis, Family Structure and Mental Health." In *Crisis Intervention: Selected Readings*, edited by Howard J. Parad. New York: Family Service Association of America, 1965, pp. 75–87.

RAYMOND, MARGARET E.; SLABY, ANDREW E.; and LIEB, JULIAN. "Familial Responses to Mental Illness." *Social Casework* 56 (October 1975):492–98.

RAWLINGS, EDNA, and CARTER, DIANNE, editors. *Psychotherapy for Women.* Springfield, Illinois: Charles Thomas, 1977.

REID, WILLIAM J., and EPSTEIN, LAURA, *Task-Centered Casework*. New York: Columbia University Press, 1972.

REISSMAN, FRANK. "Self-Help: A Strategy for the New Professional Movement." *The New Professional* 1 (May/June 1979):1–3.

RESNICK, MIRIAM. "Learned Helplessness and Women." Paper presented at the Women in Crisis Conference, New York City, May 1979.

REYNOLDS, BERTHA C. "Between Client and Community: A Study of Responsibility in Social Casework. *Smith College Studies in Social Work* 5 (September 1934):5–128.

REYNOLDS, BERTHA C. *Learning and Teaching in the Practice of Social Work.* New York: Farrar and Rinehart, 1942.

REYNOLDS, BERTHA. *Social Work and Social Living.* New York: Citadel Press, 1951.

RHODES, SONYA L. "A Developmental Approach to the Life Cycle of the Family." *Social Casework* 58 (May 1977):301–11.

RICHAN, WILLARD C. "Presto: You Are a Social Work Advocate." Unpublished paper presented at the Eastern Regional Institute, National Association of Social Workers, 1969.

RICHARDSON, HENRY B. *Patients Have Families.* New York: The Commonwealth Fund, 1945.

RICHMOND, MARY E. *What Is Social Case Work?* New York: Russell Sage Foundation, 1922.

RIPPLE, LILLIAN; ALEXANDER, ERNESTINA; and POLEMIS, BERNICE. *Motivation, Capacity, and Opportunity.* Chicago: School of Social Service Administration, University of Chicago, 1964.

RODGERS, ROY H. *Family Interaction and Transaction—The Developmental Approach.* Englewood Cliffs, New Jersey: Prentice Hall, 1973).

ROGERS, CARL R. *Client Centered Therapy.* Boston: Houghton Mifflin, 1951.

———. *On Becoming a Person.* Boston: Houghton Mifflin, 1970.

ROSE, SHELDON D. "In Pursuit of Social Competence." *Social Work* 20 (January 1975):33–39.

ROSKIN, MICHAEL. "Life Change and Social Group Work Intervention." *Social Work With Groups* 2 (Summer 1979):117–28.

RUBEN, BRENT D. "Assessing Communication Competency for Intercultural Adaptation." *Group & Organization Studies* 1 (September 1976):334–54.

RUBIN, LILLIAN B. *Worlds of Pain: Life in the Working Class Family.* New York: Basic Books, 1976.

RUSSELL, BETTY, and SYLVIA SCHILD. "Pregnancy Counseling with College Women." *Social Casework* vol. 57, no. 5 (May 1976):324–29.

SARASON, SEYMOUR B.; CARROLL, CHARLES; MATON, KENNETH; COHEN, SAUL;

and ELIZABETH LORENTZ. *Human Services and Resource Exchange Networks.* San Francisco: Jossey-Bass, 1977.

SARASON, SEYMOUR B., and LORENTZ, ELIZABETH. *The Challenge of the Resource Exchange Network.* San Francisco: Jossey-Bass Publishers, 1979.

SATIR, VIRGINIA. *Conjoint Family Therapy.* Palo Alto, California: Science and Behavior Books, 1964.

SCHERZ, FRANCES H. "Casework—A Psychosocial Therapy: An Essay Review." *Social Service Review* vol. 38, no. 2 (1964):206–11.

SCHNEIDERMAN, LEONARD. *A Critical Incident Test of the Decision to Apply for Public Assistance in Ohio.* Columbus: Ohio Department of Public Welfare, 1971.

SCHWARTZ, ARTHUR N. "A Transactional View of the Aging Process." In *Professional Obligations and Approaches to the Aged,* edited by Arthur N. Schwartz and Ivan N. Mensh. Springfield, Illinois: Charles Thomas, 1974, pp. 5–29.

SCHWARTZ, MARC D. "Situation/Transition Groups: A Conceptualization and Review." *American Journal of Orthopsychiatry,* vol. 45, no. 5 (October 1975): 744–55.

SCHWARTZ, MARY. "Sexism in the Social Work Curriculum." *Journal of Education for Social Work* 9 (Fall 1973):65–70.

SCHWARTZ, WILLIAM. "The Social Worker in the Group." *Social Welfare Forum,* 1961. New York: Columbia University Press, 1961, pp. 146–71.

SCHWARTZ, WILLIAM. "Social Group Work: The Interactionist Approach." In *The Encyclopedia of Social Work,* vol. 11, no. 16 (1971):1260–268.

SCHWARTZ, WILLIAM. "On the Use of Groups in Social Work Practice." In *The Practice of Group Work,* edited by William Schwartz and Serapio R. Zalba. New York: Columbia University Press, 1971, pp. 3–24.

SCHWARTZ, WILLIAM, and ZALBA, SERAPIO, editors. *The Practice of Group Work.* New York: Columbia University Press, 1971.

SEABURY, BRETT. "Arrangement of Physical Space in Social Work Settings." *Social Work* 16, no. 4 (October 1971):43–49.

SEABURY, BRETT A. "The Contract: Uses, Abuses, and Limitations." *Social Work* 21 (January 1976):16–23.

SEARLES, HAROLD F. *The Nonhuman Environment in Normal Development and Schizophrenia.* New York: International Universities Press, 1960.

SEIFER, NANCY. *Absent from the Majority: Working Class Women in America.* New York: National Project on Ethnic America of the American Jewish Committee, 1973.

SELBY, LOLA. "Supportive Treatment: The Development of a Concept and a Helping Method." *Social Service Review* 30, no. 4 (1956):400–14.

SELIGMAN, MARTIN. *Helplessness: On Depression, Development and Death.* San Francisco, California: Freeman, 1975.

SHAPIRO, JOAN. "Group Work with Urban Rejects in a Slum Hotel." In *The Practice of Group Work,* edited by William Schwartz and Serapio R. Zalba. New York: Columbia University Press, 1971, pp. 26–44.

———. *Communities of the Alone.* New York: Association Press, 1971.

SHAPIRO, STEPHEN, and RYGLEWICZ, HILARY. *Feeling Safe.* Englewood Cliffs, New Jersey: Prentice-Hall, 1976.

SHEEHY, GAIL. *Passages: Predictable Crises of Adult Life.* New York: Dutton, 1976.

SHERMAN, JULIA. "Social Values, Feminity, and the Development of Female Competence." *Journal of Social Issues* 32 (November 1976):181–195.

SILVERMAN, PHYLLIS R. *Mutual Help Groups: A Guide for Mental Health Workers.* Rockville, Maryland: National Institute of Mental Health, 1978.

SILVERMAN, PHYLLIS R.; MACKENZIE, DOROTHY; PETTIPAS, MARY; and WILSON, ELIZABETH, editors. *Helping Each Other in Widowhood.* New York: Health Services, 1974.

SIPORIN, MAX. "Situational Assessment and Intervention." *Social Casework* 53 (February 1972):91–109.

————. *Introduction to Social Work Practice.* New York: Macmillan, 1975.

SMALDINO, ANGELO. "The Importance of Hope in the Casework Relationship." *Social Casework* 56 (June 1975):328–33.

SMALLEY, RUTH ELIZABETH. *Theory for Social Work Practice.* New York: Columbia University Press, 1967.

SMITH, M. BREWSTER. "Competence and Socialization." In *Socialization and Society,* edited by John A. Clausen. Boston: Little, Brown, 1968, pp. 270–320.

SNOWDEN, LONNIE. "Toward Evaluation of Black Psychosocial Competence." In *Community Mental Health in a Pluralistic Society,* edited by S. Sue and T. Moore. New York: Human Sciences Press (in press).

SOMMER, ROBERT. "Small Group Ecology in Institutions for the Elderly." In *Spatial Behavior of Older People,* edited by Leon A. Pastalan and Daniel Carson. Ann Arbor: University of Michigan Press, 1970, pp. 25–39.

SPECK, ROSS, and ATTNEAVE, CAROLYN. *Family Networks.* New York: Vintage, 1973.

SPENCE, JANET; HELMREICH, ROBERT; and STAPP, JOY. "The Personal Attributes Questionnaire: A Measure of Sex Role Stereotypes and Masculinity-Femininity." *Journal Supplement-Abstract Service Catalog of Selected Documents in Psychology* 4 (1974):43.

SPIVACK, MAYER. "Archetypal Place." In *Environmental Design Research* vol. 1, edited by W.F. Preiser. Stroudsburg, Pa.: Dowden, Hutchinson and Ross, 1973, pp. 33–46.

STACK, CAROL. *All Our Kin.* New York: Harper and Row, 1974.

STEELE, FRED. *Physical Settings and Organizational Development.* Reading, Massachusetts: Addison-Wesley, 1973.

STEIN, HERMAN D. "The Concept of the Social Environment in Social Work Practice." In *Ego-Oriented Casework: Problems and Perspectives,* edited by Howard J. Parad & Roger R. Miller. New York: Family Service Association of America, 1963, pp. 65–88.

STEIN, IRMA L. "The Systems Model and Social Systems Theory: Their Application to Social Work." In *Social Casework: Theories in Action,* edited by Herbert S. Stream. Metuchen, New Jersey: The Scarecrow Press, 1971, pp. 123–95.

STERNE, MURIEL W., and PITTMAN, DAVID J. "The Concept of Motivation: A Source of Institutional and Professional Blockage in the Treatment of Alcoholics." *Quarterly Journal of Studies on Alcoholism* 26 (March 1965):41–57.

STONE, JOSEPH L., and CHURCH, JOSEPH. *Childhood and Adolescence.* New York: Random House, 1957.

STORMS, MICHAEL D., and MCCAUL, KEVIN, "Attribution Processes and Emotional Exacerbation of Dysfunctional Behavior." In *New Directions in Attribution Research,* vol. 1, edited by John Harvey. Hillsdale, New Jersey: Lawrence Erlbaum Associates, 1976, pp. 143–64.

STUDT, ELLIOT. "Social Work Theory and Implications for the Practice of Methods." *Social Work Education Reporter* 16 (June 1968):22–24 and 42–46.

SUNDBERG, NORMAN D.; SNOWDEN, LONNIE R.; and REYNOLDS, WILLIAM M. "Toward Assessment of Personal Competence and Incompetence in Life Situations." *Annual Review of Psychology* 29 (1978):179–211.

SWENSON, CAROL. "Social Networks, Mutual Aid, and the Life Model of Practice." In *Social Work Practice: People and Environments,* edited by Carel B. Germain. New York: Columbia University Press, 1979, pp. 213–38.

SZUREK, STANISLAUS. "Some Lessons from Efforts at Psychotherapy with Parents." *American Journal of Psychiatry* 109 (October 1952):296–302.

TOLSDORF, CHRISTOPHER. "Social Networks, Support, and Psychopathology: Concepts and Findings," Amherst, Massachusetts: University of Massachusetts, 1975 (mimeographed).

TRADER, HARRIET P. "Survival Strategies for Oppressed Minorities." *Social Work* 22 (January 1977):10–13.

TROLL, LILLIAN E. *Early and Middle Adulthood: The Best Is Yet to Be—Maybe.* Monterey, California: Brooks-Cole, 1975.

TUAN, YI-FU. "Geopiety: A Theme in Man's Attachment to Nature and to Place." In *Geographies of the Mind,* edited by David Lowenthal and Martyn J. Bowden. New York: Oxford University Press, 1976, pp. 11–39.

TURNER, FRANCIS J. "Psychosocial Therapy." In *Social Work Treatment: Interlocking Theoretical Approaches,* edited by Francis J. Turner. New York: The Free Press, 1974, pp. 84–111.

TYLER, LEONA E. *Individuality: Human Possibilities and Personal Choice in the Psychological Development of Men and Women.* San Francisco, California: Jossey-Bass, 1978.

VASSIL, THOMAS V. "Residential Family Camping: Altering Family Patterns." *Social Casework,* vol. 59, no. 10 (December 1978):605–13.

WEINER, B. *Theories of Motivation: From Mechanism to Cognition.* Chicago: Markham, 1972.

WEINER, HYMAN J. *Mental Health in the World of Work.* New York: Association Press, 1973.

WEISS, ROBERT S. "Transition States and Other Stressful Situations: Their Nature and Programs for their Management." In *Support Systems and Mutual Help: Multidisciplinary Explorations,* edited by Gerald Caplan and Marie Killilea. New York: Grune and Stratton, 1976, pp. 213–32.

WESTON, PETER, and MEDICK, MARTHA. "Race, Social Class, and the Motive to Avoid Success in Women." In *Readings in Child Development,* edited by J. Rosenblith; W. Allinsmith; and J. Williams. Boston: Allyn & Bacon, 1973.

WHITE, ROBERT W. "Strategies of Adaptation." In *Human Adaptation,* edited by Rudolf H. Moos. Lexington, Massachusetts: D.C. Heath and Co., 1976, pp. 17–32.

———. "Motivation Reconsidered: The Concept of Competence." *Psychological Review* 66 (September 1959):297–333.

———. "Competence and the Psychosexual Stages of Development." In *Nebraska Symposium on Motivation*, edited by Marshall Jones. Lincoln, Nebraska: University of Nebraska Press, 1960, pp. 97–141.

———. *Ego and Reality in Psychoanalytic Theory*. New York: International Universities Press, 1963.

———. *The Abnormal Personality*. New York: Ronald Press Company, 1964.

———. *The Enterprise of Living: Growth and Organization in Personality*. New York: Holt, Rinehart and Winston, 1972.

———. "Strategies of Adaptation: An Attempt at Systematic Description." In *Coping and Adaptation*, edited by George Coelho, David A. Hamburg, and John E. Adams. New York: Basic Books, 1974, pp. 47–68.

WHITTAKER, JAMES K. *Social Treatment: An Approach to Interpersonal Helping*. Chicago: Aldine Publishing Company, 1974.

———. "A Developmental-Educational Approach to Child Treatment." In *Changing Roles in Social Work Practice*, edited by Francine Sobey. Philadelphia: Temple University Press, 1977, pp. 176–96.

WOLOWITZ, HOWARD. "Hysterical Character and Feminine Identity." In *Readings on the Psychology of Women*, edited by Judith Bardwick. New York: Harper & Row, 1972.

WOLPE, JOSEPH, and LAZARUS, ARNOLD. *Behavior Therapy Techniques*. New York: Pergamon Press, 1966.

YARROW, MARIAN R.; CLAUSEN, JOHN A.; and ROBBINS, PAUL R. "The Social Meaning of Mental Illness." *Journal of Social Issues* 11 (March 1955):33–48.

Index